Foundations of public economics

CAMBRIDGE ECONOMIC HANDBOOKS

Editor:
Hugo Sonnenschein
Department of Economics, Princeton University

Previous editors:
J. M. Keynes (Lord Keynes)
D. H. Robertson (Sir Dennis Robertson)
C. W. Guillebaud
Milton Friedman
F. H. Hahn

Foundations of
public economics

DAVID A. STARRETT
Stanford University

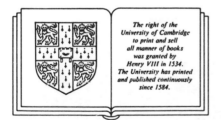

The right of the
University of Cambridge
to print and sell
all manner of books
was granted by
Henry VIII in 1534.
The University has printed
and published continuously
since 1584.

CAMBRIDGE UNIVERSITY PRESS

Cambridge
New York   Port Chester   Melbourne   Sydney

Published by the Press Syndicate of the University of Cambridge
The Pitt Building, Trumpington Street, Cambridge CB2 1RP
32 East 57th Street, New York, NY 10022, USA
10 Stamford Road, Oakleigh, Melbourne 3166, Australia

First published 1988
Reprinted 1989

Printed in the United States of America

Library of Congress Cataloging-in-Publication Data

Starrett, David A.
Foundations of public economics / David A. Starrett.
p. cm. – (Cambridge economic handbooks)
Bibliography: p.
Includes index.
1. Finance, Public.   2. Welfare economics.   I. Title.
II. Series.
HJ141.S66   1988   87–27892
336 – dc19

ISBN 0-521-34256-2 hard covers
ISBN 0-521-34801-3 paperback

British Library Cataloguing in Publication Data

Starrett, David A.
Foundations of public economics.
1. Finance, public
I. Title
336   HJ141

ISBN 0-521-34256-2 hard covers
ISBN 0-521-34801-3 paperback

To my father

Contents

Preface and acknowledgments

This book is an attempt to present a variety of important ideas from welfare economics and public finance in a coherent framework and to integrate my own recent research agenda into this framework. Although I hope the book will be suitable for use in graduate level courses, I have not tried to be either fully self-contained or completely comprehensive. Rather, I have tried to give a unified treatment of the main themes in applied welfare economics as I see them; further, I have assumed that the reader is familiar with material covered in a standard first-year microeconomics sequence (roughly at the level of Edmond Malinvaud's *Lectures on Microeconomic Theory* and Hal Varian's *Microeconomic Analysis*) and with the associated mathematical techniques of constrained optimization (as exposited in Michael Intriligator's *Mathematical Optimization and Economic Theory*). Although I have made no conscious effort to differentiate my product from other available sources, I think the reader will find more emphasis here on the expenditure side of public finance than in Anthony Atkinson and Joseph Stiglitz (*Lectures on Public Economics*) and more emphasis on local public issues than in Richard Tresch's *Public Finance: A Normative Theory*.

Many people have given me help in preparing this manuscript. In particular, Thomas Downes, Suzanne Scotchmer, David Wildasin, and several anonymous reviewers have read parts or all of it and provided useful comments. I should also thank classes of students who were subjected to early versions of the manuscript; I hope the final copy is improved as a result of their experience. There probably never would have been a manuscript at all were it not for the Center for Advanced Study in the Behavioral Sciences at Stanford, which provided me with exactly the kind of uninterrupted time necessary for such an endeavor. Further, the manuscript never would have been revised without the efforts of Michael Spence, whose software package *Technical Formatting Program* greatly facilitated the seemingly endless sequence of changes and corrections. Finally, I hope the reader will be able to see the influence of my mentor, Kenneth Arrow. It is no accident that his name is prominent in my reference list – his ideas lie behind many of the topics I discuss.

Notation

Most of the analysis of this book is conducted in a framework where the number of goods, households, clubs, and so on, is arbitrary. Consequently, it is very convenient to employ matrix notation and make full use of the associated vector calculus. Notation can be simplified further if we agree at the outset to certain conventions on vector orientations.

Prices (and "shadow" prices) will be assigned a natural orientation as row vectors, whereas quantities inherit a natural orientation as column vectors. On the rare occasions when we need to change the orientation, transposes will be indicated using curly brackets: { }. Thus, if P is a (row) vector of goods prices, $\{P\}$ is the corresponding column vector. These orientations will extend to functions as well. Thus, if $C(P)$ represents a demand system, it is thought of as a *column vector function*. Correspondingly, if $P(g)$ represents equilibrium prices as functions (say) of levels of public goods provided, it is to be thought of as a row vector function.

Variable subscripts always stand for a matrix index and whenever they are absent, we think of the variable as a vector (or matrix) over the associated index (or indices). Thus, P_i is the price of the ith good. Superscripts stand for matrix labels and will rarely, if ever, be treated as indices of some larger "supermatrix." For example, c^h represents the consumption vector of household h. We will use lowercase letters to represent consumption and production flow variables of *individual economic agents,* reserving the corresponding uppercase variables for economywide aggregates. Thus, C is aggregate consumption ($C = \sum_h c^h$). Individual stock variables will have capital letters; for example, B is consumer financial wealth.

When we need to refer to the number of elements in a vector, we do so using the symbol $|\cdot|$ (here, the centerdot is a universal variable). Thus, $|C|$ refers to the number of consumption goods.

We will use the gradient symbol (∇_x) to indicate partial derivatives with respect to a vector x. Again, we require some conventions with respect to orientation. Suppose we have a scalar function f of a vector x. Then the vector of partial derivatives will be denoted $\nabla_x f$. It will have the orientation of a column vector if x is a row vector and vice versa. For example, if $\Gamma(g)$ represents a cost function for producing a public-goods (column) vector g, then $\nabla_g \Gamma$ represents a *row* vector of marginal costs. (Note: frequently we suppress arguments of functions when the meaning is clear.)

Gradients of vector functions naturally form matrices, which will be oriented as follows. Suppose we have a column vector function $C(b)$, where b is a vector of *any* orientation. Then $\nabla_b C$ is the matrix

$$\nabla_b C = \begin{bmatrix} \partial C_1/\partial b_1 & \cdots & \partial C_1/\partial b_{|b|} \\ \partial C_2/\partial b_1 & \cdots & \partial C_2/\partial b_{|b|} \\ \vdots & & \vdots \\ \partial C_{|C|}/\partial b_1 & \cdots & \partial C_{|C|}/\partial b_{|b|} \end{bmatrix}.$$

Observe that orientation has been fixed so that each column corresponds to a partial derivative of the column vector with respect to one argument, and the number of columns equals the cardinality of b. Similarly, we orient the gradient of a row vector function so that each row corresponds to a partial derivative of the row vector.

Note that this last set of rules fails to specify an orientation for the gradient of a scalar function, so we still need the earlier rule specified for that case.

The conventions outlined so far are designed to simplify specific representations encountered in this book. However, they are generally consistent with common practice in a wider arena. Of course, we can apply these rules in series to construct matrices of second- (and higher) order partial derivatives. For example, the Hessian matrix for a scalar function $f(x)$ would be denoted: $\nabla^2_{x,x} f$ (and similarly for other matrices of second partials).

The inner product of matrices x and y will be written simply as xy. Naturally, the matrices must be compatible (x has the same number of columns as y has rows). Thus, if we want to express the inner product of price vector P with itself, we must write $P\{P\}$ (not PP). At a number of points that follow, we will encounter quadratic (and other bilinear) forms, and although all of these can be expressed in terms of the notation developed so far, it is convenient to introduce a separate notation. For example, suppose we encounter a quadratic form involving row vector t and compatible square matrix x; we could always write it as $tx\{t\}$, but instead we choose to express it as $\langle t, x, t \rangle$. More generally, $\langle s, x, t \rangle$ refers to a bilinear form where s has the orientation of a row vector (regardless of its natural orientation), t the orientation of a column vector, and x a matrix of compatible dimensions.

Extensive use will be made of Kuhn–Tucker–Lagrange methods for nonlinear programming. Except where otherwise stated, we will assume all functions are differentiable at least to second order and will work with first- and second-order conditions for optimality. Also, in the interests of notational economy, we will assume interior solutions whenever they seem natural; the reader is invited to replace equalities with the appropriate inequalities and complementary slackness conditions if boundary solutions are contemplated.

Because we want to use the simplest possible inner-product notation, names for variables and parameters must be single letters (otherwise, multiple letters have potentially ambiguous meaning). Even using all uppercase and lowercase Greek and Latin letters, this set of potential names is too small. Hence, we are forced to make two types of compromises.

First, a few letters will have dual meanings. The lists of symbols that follow give a dictionary of meanings with alternative meanings in parentheses. Note that most duplications involve the spatial model on the one hand and the temporal model with uncertainty on the other (these models will never be considered jointly). For example, the letter s is a time index in the latter model whereas it represents a location index in the former; similarly, r represents land rental rates in the spatial model and interest rates in the temporal model.

Second, a few names will be assigned using multiple (uppercase) letters. This will be done only when the associated variables rarely appear in algebraic expressions and have natural meanings as acronyms or words. Thus, for example, VAR and COV are the variance and covariance functions, and RP represents risk premium and TT terms-of-trade effect.

List of symbols: Latin letters

a	generic decision variable (Chapter 12, asset holdings)		A	firm debt
b	government private net inputs		B	bequests, household wealth
c	net individual consumption		C	aggregate net consumption
d	asset dividends		D	government debt
e	exponential symbol		E	expectations operator
f	production functions		F	generic function symbol
g	collective-goods levels		G	congestion levels
h	household index		H	household type
i	generic index		I	income compensation function
j	firm index		J	firm type
k	project capacity (local public finance, index of "active" community)		K	capital stock (size of common)
ℓ	land holdings		L	aggregate land (Lagrangian functions)
m	income levels		M	firm equity
n	population sizes		N	population aggregates (Chapter 7, government effective deficit)
o	status quo reference		O	international prices
p	market parameters		P	consumer prices
q	strategies in mechanisms		Q	producer prices
r	interest rates (land rental rates)		R	individual orderings (aggregate land rents)
s	time index (spatial location)		S	time horizon (Chapter 12, risk-sharing transfers)
t	tax rates		T	"direct" taxes
u	mechanism outcome function		U	direct utility functions
v	asset prices		V	indirect utility functions
w	gradient of welfare function		W	social welfare function
x	variable of integration (planning, social state)		X	Cartesian product (set of social states)
y	private net outputs		Y	aggregate net output
z	exogenous resources		Z	indirect welfare function

Notation

List of symbols: Greek letters

α	project parameter		
β	welfare weight		
γ	utility/cost parameters	Γ	costs and cost functions
δ	Taylor's series symbol	Δ	discrete increment
∂	partial derivative symbol		
ϵ	elasticities (regression residual)		
ξ	growth rates (Chapter 9, LM for quantity constraints)		
η	private activity levels		
ψ	pseudoprice of Arrow securities	Ψ	capital funds
κ	various constants		
λ	LM for income	Λ	tax distortion vector
μ	LM for government budget		
ϕ	transport cost	Φ	aggregate transport
ν	LM for profits		
π	firm profits	Π	aggregate profits
ρ	discount factors		
σ	town boundary	Σ	summation symbol
τ	tax function parameters		
χ	cost and type shares		
θ	compensating variation	Θ	naive consumer surplus
ω	state of the world	Ω	shadow values of collective goods
ζ	depreciation rates		

Note: Abbreviation LM means Lagrange multiplier.

PART I

Scope and limitations

CHAPTER 1

Introduction

We present here a synthesis of recent developments in normative welfare economics that have direct application in public finance. Within this rather broad subject, we will emphasize operational prescriptions for public policy in a "mixed" economy consisting of a public sector, a private-market sector, and some limited links and controls between them.

Since the book is mostly about normative economics, we start with a discussion of social objectives. Our approach is that of the "old welfare economics," and since the term "old" may connote "outdated" to some, we argue the point at some length. In the process, we air our views on the methodology of interpersonal comparisons and distributional equity. Having settled on a normative methodology, we use it to justify our conception of the mixed economy. Chapters 2 and 3 begin this development squarely in the tradition of competitive theory. We outline reasons why "direct" decision making is inadequate and summarize the case for market decentralization.

Staying in this tradition, we define collective goods by intrinsic characteristics that make them unmarketable. We develop a conceptual framework for studying such goods that is general enough to encompass many common examples such as natural monopolies, pure public goods [as defined by Samuelson (1954)], and "club" goods [as defined by Buchanan (1965)]. Although all these examples share an important common element, distinctions among them provide foundations for a normative theory of "fiscal federalism"; pure public goods are best allocated by a national entity, whereas club goods are best allocated by a more local entity. The ways in which these entities ought to do business and the relationships between them are explored in Chapters 5–7.

Initially, we search for planning mechanisms that simultaneously elicit necessary information and implement first-best decisions for collective-goods allocation much as the market system does for private goods. Although we can identify many well-known attempts along these lines, almost all of them suffer from incentive problems: Agents find that it is not in their interests to behave according to the specified rules. We end up rejecting planning mechanisms as first-best procedures in most cases but find some of the examples useful as building blocks for less ambitious

3

approaches to come later and in identifying biases that are likely to emerge when first-best planning is not possible.

Among the more controversial issues discussed here are the proposition [put forward by Tiebout (1956)] that less interference is required in the allocation of club goods (by local constituencies) than in the allocation of pure public goods and the view [argued by Bradford and Oates (1971)] that general revenue sharing (by the national government to the local governments) is irrelevant in the presence of a national tax system that correctly deals with equity considerations.

Part II also includes some general discussion of optimal public fund-raising. The question of tax versus debt finance is raised in Chapter 6, whereas issues involving optimal public pricing and indirect taxation are dealt with in Chapter 8. We explore and evaluate recent incarnations of the "Ricardian equivalence" doctrine, which dictates that the choice of tax versus debt finance is irrelevant. Although we do not accept strong versions of this doctrine, we do generally accept the view that issues involving the choice of debt can be reduced to issues involving the timing of taxation.

When discussing optimal taxation, we focus on the parallels between the rules of Ramsey public pricing and the rules of optimal-commodity taxation. We argue that these rules are useful and operational only if certain simple structural assumptions can be invoked; these assumptions seem reasonable in some applications of the Ramsey analysis but much less so for the optimal-commodity tax problem. Indeed, we suggest that most common interpretations of the optimal-commodity-tax rules are misleading at best.

Many people have argued that the "best" tax system we could have would be one that is broadly based in that most goods would be taxed at the same rate. We ask whether such claims could be justified on the basis of optimal-tax theory and discuss some of the practical considerations involved in constructing such a tax.

Beginning in Part III our general focus changes considerably. To that point, we have aimed at a comprehensive treatment of public issues; that is, we have sought institutional arrangements and planning procedures that can deal with the full range of public decision making simultaneously. However, from a pragmatic point of view, such aims turn out to be too ambitious, requiring, among other things, too much centralized information processing. At the very least, we require some political decentralization so that separate issues can be dealt with by semiautonomous agencies. *Benefit–cost analysis* provides a theoretical framework for implementing this decentralization. Projects (or programs) are evaluated one at a time, and various measures are developed to account for general equilibrium interactions.

Part III examines benefit–cost analysis as applied to projects or programs that are sufficiently small. The meaning of "small" here is roughly that implementation of the project will not change consumer marginal rates of substitution (a precise definition is given in the text). This restriction is quite useful in reducing information-gathering requirements, as we shall see. Although we couch the discussion in terms of evaluating small projects, the analysis can also be used to determine and evaluate first-order conditions for optimal allocations or to point the direction of large movements toward full optimality. However, some caution is required in adopting these interpretations. First, when projects are characterized by important elements of scale economies, the analysis of small versions may tell us very little about the desirability of large ones. For this reason, it is important to have a different methodology for evaluating large projects.

Second, even if all technologies are characterized by full convexity, it is still possible for first-order analysis to be a misleading guide to the optimal direction of movement. A germaine example has been provided by Diamond and Mirrlees (1973), who show that the optimal level of an external diseconomy can be higher than it would be in the absence of regulation (first-order analysis applied to an unregulated status quo would naturally dictate lower levels of the externality). This example and others like it depend heavily on the presence of strong income effects (as the inefficiency is removed, consumers are "better off," causing them to care much more about the good responsible for generating the externality). Generally, we think such examples are pathological since it is hard to believe that income effects are going to be so potent. It is partly for this reason that we place such a strong emphasis on first-order analysis in this book.

We identify two distinct, though related, methodologies associated with first-order benefit–cost analysis. The first of these values directs project inputs and outputs at market prices (when possible) and accounts for interactions between one project and the outside environment by adding (or subtracting) a sequence of correction terms. The other seeks to administer the corresponding corrections directly on valuations of the inputs and outputs.

The first method relates closely to the general theory of second best, since each correction term is associated with a particular second-best distortion present in the underlying mixed economy. For example, there will be a term associated with the presence of indirect taxation that can be evaluated using information about tax rates and tax base elasticities. Aside from the practical advantages of such decompositions, the approach provides a useful way to establish the optimality of market decentralization when there are no second-best distortions. We develop the relevant decompositions in Chapter 9 and use them to generate important operational rules for project analysis.

The second approach is identified with methods of *shadow pricing*. Namely, we seek to measure the marginal social benefit for particular project outputs and the marginal opportunity cost of project inputs and aggregate these to get a bottom line. Although the two approaches naturally must lead to the same bottom line, they involve quite different intermediate calculations and illustrate distinct theoretical principles. We develop the theory of shadow pricing in Chapter 10 and show how it can be used to illustrate and amplify on a number of theoretical propositions in the project analysis–development planning literature.

Chapters 11 and 12 apply the methodology of the previous two chapters to the study of problems involving spatial and temporal allocations. Applying the decomposition principles to problems in local community choice enables us to identify and measure the interactions between one community and the rest of the economy. These measures enable us to quantify the concept of *fiscal externality* and to identify several potential biases in local choice with respect to size and composition of local public-goods provision. We present a unified treatment that illustrates the relationships between various types of potential distortion.

Most discussions of project analysis in an intertemporal context focus attention on the social rate of discount. We apply the shadow-pricing theory of Chapter 10 to evaluate this rate in the mixed-economy environments of this book. Our analysis explains why there has been such a divergence of opinion concerning the correct size of the social discount rate, since the answer turns out to be quite sensitive to crucial elasticity assumptions.

When evaluating the impact of risk in social decision making, the decomposition approach again turns out to be most useful. We show how discount rates can be decomposed into a term reflecting pure impatience, a term associated with uninsurable risk, and a term associated with failure to allocate risk in an optimal way. We find that the second of these terms is closely related to risk measures found in the capital asset-pricing model, even though the latter is based on a much simpler structure. Moreover, we see that the third term can explain a number of examples of "pecuniary externality" that have appeared in the recent literature on incomplete markets.

Chapter 13 concludes Part III with a discussion of measurement techniques for identifying shadow prices. Since shadow pricing becomes problematic precisely when market prices misrepresent opportunity value, we must draw on methods outside of standard market econometrics. We focus on indirect methods such as using individual choice between life-threatening versus safe jobs to infer something about the shadow price of life or using land rent differentials to infer the shadow price of air pollution. We argue that procedures of this type have a common underlying theoretical structure (we label them *spanning methods*) and that the limitations of this structure are rather severe. The ensuing analysis is used to discuss and evaluate some commonly used hedonic methods.

First-order project analysis represents a relatively well developed methodology. And although it does present some measurement difficulties (as we discover in Chapter 13), this methodology constitutes a useful practical framework for analyzing and evaluating public programs. Unfortunately, however, a significant class of public projects cannot be considered small in the sense required by first-order analysis. These are projects that must be instituted (if at all) at a sufficiently large scale so as to change the relative valuation of commodities they use or produce. Part IV of this book looks at the state of the art in evaluating such projects.

Chapter 14 traces the development of exact methods for measuring net welfare of large projects. Although it is possible to construct such measures from sufficiently rich information about choices among sets of alternatives, we find that practical difficulties with implementation are far more formidable than was the case in Part II. Therefore, we devote the following chapter to a discussion of possible approximation methods.

Chapter 16 looks at ways of estimating the theoretical measures developed in the previous two chapters and asks how such estimates can be used to solve practical problems in benefit–cost analysis. Although we do not have much to say about actual econometric technique, we do comment briefly on the strengths and weaknesses of various methods. Finally, we analyze in Chapter 17 a class of problems that incorporates certain "large-project" features as well as a number of other characteristics that have appeared prominently in the book. Although hardly a neat summary of what went before, this chapter does serve to bring together a number of our major themes.

CHAPTER 2

Social objectives and direct decision making

Any book on normative economics ought to begin with some discussion of social objectives. Since the meat of this book involves practical methods for evaluating such objectives, and since the extant literature on social choice theory is voluminous, we choose not to spend a great deal of time on the subject here.[1] However, a short discussion of our basic philosophy is in order.

Fundamental to our approach is the implicit acceptance of "consumer sovereignty." Operationally, this principle means that only measures of individual preference affect social choice. We reject the paternalist view that government knows better than its citizens what is good for them. Having taken this position, it remains to decide how to measure individual preference and how to reconcile differences among these individual preferences.

We also accept the classical view of economic person as utility maximizer. If we think of preference as revealed by choice, the underlying choice functions must be consistent. Although violations of this principle of rationality can be found in the experimental literature, they seem to be exceptions rather than the rule, at least in a certainty context. Assumptions of rationality in an *uncertainty* context generate more serious objections, which we will comment on later. Unfortunately, we would not make much progress in this book if we tried to drop all principles of rationality unless we also dropped consumer sovereignty; the planner will have a hard time keeping hands off consumer preferences when they are inconsistent.

Operationally, we are going to represent individual preference on social alternatives by a utility function on these alternatives. We assume that these functions are at least twice continuously differentiable. Although such "smoothness" can be given an intuitively appealing justification, we adopt it here more for convenience than anything else; it enables us to conduct "first-order analysis" and to develop measures of welfare by integrating first-order measures. Without smoothness, first-order measures would always be approximations, and our analysis would be messy at best.

[1] See Sen (1970) or Mueller (1976) for an introduction to this literature.

So, we take smooth utility functions as the inputs into social decision making. Up to now, nothing we have done would be very controversial among economists, although we would certainly get some argument from other social scientists. However, when we specify a method of aggregation, the subject quickly becomes quite controversial. Disagreements arise as soon as we try to specify which properties of the utility functions can be used by the planner in the course of the aggregation. For example, can we use *cardinal* properties of these functions or must the derived social ordering be invariant to monotone transformations of individual utility functions? It has been argued that since only ordinal preference can be observed (at least in the certainty context), only ordinal information should be used. Unfortunately, it is difficult to formalize this restriction in a useful way. However, stronger restrictions in the same spirit can be formalized. For example, if we stipulate that social choice between any *pair* of alternatives depends only on individual ordinal rankings of these same two alternatives, we have Arrow's famous "independence from irrelevant alternatives" (IIA).[2] The added strength may be desirable per se since it guarantees that we will not be making any interpersonal comparisons of utility units in our social choice procedures.

But if we accept IIA, we will quickly find ourselves up against the bane of this literature: impossibility theorems. Indeed, Arrow showed that if we want a social welfare ordering that is universal (i.e., it can handle all potential individual preference configurations) and nondictatorial (i.e., it does not agree exactly with any particular individual preference) and satisfies the Pareto principle (to be discussed), it cannot satisfy IIA.[3] This is pretty unfortunate since we can think of quite a few other "reasonable" assumptions we would like to add before we would be completely satisfied with any resulting aggregation function. A voluminous literature now exists demonstrating that even if we are willing to drop IIA, we run into impossibilities as soon as a few other reasonable assumptions are added.[4]

The sad fact here is that we cannot have everything we want. Realizing this, there are several ways to go. We can forgo those desirable axioms on comparability, we can limit the set of issues to be resolved through a general social choice procedure, or we can impose some restrictions on the types of individual preference allowable as input to social choice. The first two approaches are associated with the labels "old welfare economics" and "new welfare economics," respectively. We compare and contrast these two first and take up the third later in the chapter.

[2] This condition is one of the axioms introduced in Arrow (1951).
[3] See Arrow (1950) for a proof.
[4] A number of these negative results are discussed in Sen (1970).

According to the new welfare economics, we are to restrict social decisions to those that can be made on the basis of the Pareto principle; that is, we should institute only those policies (or groups of policies) that make some people better off without making anyone else worse off. Stated in terms of utilities, the principle says we should never be satisfied with a vector of utilities that is interior to the set of attainable utility vectors; rather, we should always move toward the boundary in a direction of increasing (or at least nondecreasing) utilities for all. Clearly, as long as nothing more is said about the direction of movement, the rule is *ordinal* but does not fully resolve any existing conflict of interest.

Although the Pareto principle cannot be used to decide all issues, it does generate a well-defined decision procedure in the social contexts we shall consider. These are situations in which there is some status quo ante, and the government (or planner) is considering some change in it (call this a *project*). In the absence of specific transfers, such a project is likely to make some people (the *gainers*) better off but others (the *losers*) worse off. The Pareto principle becomes the "compensation principle with compensation"; a project is initiated if the gainers can (and *do*) compensate the losers in such a way that all of them are better off (or at least none of them are worse off).

Unfortunately, this principle has gained the reputation of being value free, meaning that it does not rely on any judgments about interpersonal comparisons. We argue that the reputation is richly *un*deserved. As soon as the principle is placed in a context where it has operational bite, value judgments are involved in its implementation. To see this, consider the status quo. If this is thought of as representing a position that is "infinitely bad" for everyone, the Pareto principle has no bite as applied to project analysis: Every project will look desirable. But as soon as a real status quo is envisioned, use of the compensation principle with compensation makes the implicit judgment that there is something good about the vector of utilities inherent in the status quo: Projects that improve on all components of *this* vector will be accepted, whereas alternative projects that lead to *other* Pareto-efficient utility vectors will be rejected.

We are not here to argue about whether there is justice in the status quo; there is a substantial "entitlements" literature extant that supports this view but also plenty of dissent.[5] Our point is simply that the compensation principle is not value free, at least not as usually applied. Given this, we prefer methods that bring the element of interpersonal comparison into the open rather than one that prejudges the distributional issue. However, we will find occasion in the sequel to compare and contrast

[5] The entitlements position is expounded by Nozick (1974); see Harsanyi (1955) and Rawls (1971) for some contrasting points of view.

our proposed methods to those involving the compensation principle both with and without compensation.

2.1 Interpersonal comparisons

How shall we make interpersonal comparisons given that we must? A natural answer (and the earliest one in the literature) is to postulate a welfare function that aggregates utility levels in the same way individual utilities aggregate individual consumption levels. Using such a function implies that in deciding between two different social states, we look only at individual utilities for those two states. Thus, this formulation is not simply a consequence of consumer sovereignty but requires in addition a "utility independence" assumption.

More generally, we could form a welfare measure that took utility *functionals* as arguments. Unfortunately, these mathematical objects are not easy to work with, and further, it is not clear what violations of utility independence we ought to introduce. So we will confine ourselves here to simple welfare functions.[6] What form should they take? Again, we could easily digress for several chapters discussing this question but instead will confine ourselves to a few remarks. An interesting framework for thinking about the question is the so-called original position. According to this view, the decision maker is someone with the universal traits of humanity but without personal identity; some like to think of this actor as "me before I know who I am."

Assuming that the decision maker is omniscient in the original position, he knows all the possible people he might be and their personal characteristics. The preferences he would exhibit in these circumstances become the social preferences. Thus, if we could agree on what "universal person" would do in these circumstances, we could agree on a social ordering. Unfortunately, the literature of the past 30 years has revealed that there is no agreement within the class of academics, let alone universal agreement.

Harsanyi (1955) and others looked at this problem as one of choice under uncertainty, with universal person having an equal chance of being each real person. Invoking standard axioms of choice under uncertainty, Harsanyi concluded that it was legitimate to treat individual utility functions as cardinal and further that "expected utility" should serve as the social welfare indicator. Assuming that the number of people is fixed, the derived formulation is equivalent to classical utilitarianism (summation of individual utilities).

---

[6] Utility independence is closely related to the axiom of "neutrality" in the social choice literature. See Sen (1970) for a discussion of this axiom and its shortcomings.

Rawls (1971), looking at things from the same point of reference, concluded that universal person ought to focus attention on the worst-off individual and do the best that was possible for him. Rawls's approach does not require cardinal utilities but does require that utility *levels* be comparable (so that in every situation we can say which of two individuals is worse off). His reasoning leads to the famous "Maximin" criterion.

These two formulations are quite different in their implications. Rawls's criterion is highly egalitarian, implying that substantial transfers ought to be made from "rich" to "poor." The Harsanyi criteria may involve some egalitarian tendencies but need not; indeed, its distributive implications depend on the properties of underlying cardinal utilities. If these functions exhibit strict concavity (diminishing marginal utility of income), certain kinds of egalitarian transfers (in particular those that involve no efficiency cost) will improve welfare, as we will see. However, should the utility functions happen to exhibit *increasing* marginal utility of income, some transfers that increase inequality will increase welfare; intuitively, utilitarian welfare must go up when we take money from the poor (who are assumed to be relatively inefficient at producing utility from income) and give it to the rich.

We see that it is not possible to evaluate the egalitarian properties of a particular welfare functional form without first specifying the underlying representation of individual utility. Thus, even if we adhere to the view that only ordinal properties of utility are observable, we must specify a particular numerical representation to use as input to the welfare function. Although we will not suggest any particular representation until Chapter 14, we will assume that the welfare function satisfies the following minimal egalitarian principle. Suppose we choose a representation of ordinal utility that exhibits concavity (though not necessarily strict concavity). Then, we assume that the welfare function applied to these inputs is quasi-concave (though, again, not necessarily strict).[7]

Quasi-concavity requires that society not exhibit a preference for inequality in utility levels (for any pair of utility vectors that lead to the same welfare level, the average utility vector must be at least as good). The particular formulations just discussed essentially constitute opposite ends of the spectrum of functions satisfying this property. All of our analytic formulations will be consistent with any such social welfare function on concave utilities. However, in our interpretations we sometimes will talk as though our function has more built-in egalitarianism than can be justified on the basis of these assumptions alone. Since the relevant underlying assumption involves marginal valuations, it is useful to change

---

[7] See Intriligator (1971) or Green–Heller (1982) for definitions and implications of various concepts of convexity and concavity.

the focus of the discussion somewhat. In the process we can introduce the framework for first-order analysis that will take center stage in Part III of this book.

Throughout much of the sequel we will consider "projects" that constitute changes away from some status quo. Such a project generates a welfare increment that we wish to measure. First-order analysis treats this increment roughly as though it were a differential. (We will be more precise with our definitions in Chapters 8 and 9.) Let V^h be the utility of individual h and W be welfare, so our utility function takes the mathematical form $W = W(V^1, \ldots, V^n)$. Let us examine the differential of this function:

$$dW = \sum_h \left[\frac{\partial W}{\partial V^h} \, dV^h \right].$$ (2.1)

Note that the welfare formulation enters (2.1) only through the partial derivatives with respect to each individual utility level.

It is desirable to modify this form for a variety of reasons, most of which we will not take up until later. However, one modification that makes sense even now involves the treatment of units. As it stands in the preceding, a change in individual utility units surely will change the differential unless some corresponding change is made in the welfare function. Thus, the indeterminacy discussed earlier manifests itself even in a first-order analysis. Since we do not want an arbitrary change in the measurement unit to affect social decisions, it is desirable to measure individual preference in a "unit-free" way. Suppose that we multiply and divide each utility differential by something (label it λ^h) also measured in utility units. Whenever there is a market sector (as there will be throughout most of this book), we will want λ^h to be the marginal utility of a numeraire unit to individual h. Next define $\beta^h = (\partial W/\partial V^h)\lambda^h$, and write the differential as

$$dW = \sum_h \beta^h \left[\frac{dV^h}{\lambda^h} \right].$$ (2.2)

Now, the term dV^h/λ^h is a pure number (independent of utility units). So it is natural to think of the β's as the fundamental marginal welfare units. In particular, if we want the welfare ordering to be invariant under changes in individual utility units, we do this by changing the welfare function in an offsetting way so that the β's remain constant. Note that this is all we have to do in order to achieve invariance to units so long as we restrict ourselves to a first-order analysis.

Partly for reasons just outlined, the β's have provided the focus for most discussions of distributional equity in the benefit–cost literature, where they are called *welfare weights*.[8] Although we are getting somewhat ahead of our story, it is useful to point out one implication for distribution policy. Suppose the government has the power to impose nondistortionary taxes and/or subsidies. Then, since β^h is the marginal welfare of a numeraire unit if given to individual h, a first-best distribution policy must involve equalization of the welfare weights (if two weights differ, welfare can be improved by the transfer of a unit from the individual with the lower weight to the one with the higher weight).[9]

Thus, in studying first-order policy problems, all that matters for distributional considerations is the systematic ways (if any) in which welfare weights differ from each other in the status quo. We will frequently espouse the "liberal" position that welfare weights are inversely related to income level. Since this position is controversial and certainly not implied by any assumptions made heretofore, we spend a little time talking about possible justifications.

Suppose we take the utilitarian view that once preferences are represented in the appropriate utility units, social welfare is a simple sum of utilities. With units so normalized, the partial derivatives of W are constant and equal. Then, all differences in the β's must derive from corresponding differences in the λ's. So we ask whether the marginal utility of income is declining in income level and suggest two possible reasons for believing that it is.

It is common practice in the theory of choice under uncertainty to make assumptions on how individuals will behave when faced with lotteries on income level. Although there certainly are situations where people show a preference for gambles, it seems reasonable to suppose that people show aversion to risk in most situations. That is, they prefer an amount of certain income to a lottery with the same expected value. Over ranges where people are risk averse, we know that their (von Neumann–Morgenstern) utility function must be strictly concave.[10] In particular, the marginal utility of income falls as income rises. Consequently, if we use von Neumann–Morgenstern utility functions as the inputs to utilitarian social welfare, the welfare weights will indeed vary inversely with income level.

Notice that broad use of this construction means we will use properties of utility that were derived in explicitly uncertain situations to make

---

8 For a discussion of these weights and some historical references, see Harberger (1978).

9 The reader might worry that such redistribution would have second-best welfare effects through impacts on prices. However, it can be shown that these effects are irrelevant in determining the optimal distribution. On the other hand, distribution policy will be more complicated when other second-best distortions are present, as we will see in Chapter 9.

10 See Pratt (1964) or Arrow (1965) for a discussion of the theory and measurement of risk aversion.

inferences about preferences over nonstochastic outcomes. Are these inferences valid? The argument for validity might run something as follows: People are averse to risk *because* "early" units of income are more valuable to them than the later ones so they will willingly give up the chance to get extra income as long as they can avoid the possibility of losing some early income. According to this view, the utility function has validity in a nonstochastic context, and we make use of the uncertainty apparatus only to reveal its shape.

Unfortunately, unless there is some other way of revealing this shape, we must consider the possibility that the shape is a consequence of uncertainty and not something more fundamental. Indeed, one might argue that risk aversion merely means that people do not like to be unsure of themselves, and the utility function is simply an abstract construction that helps us capture this fact; it has no validity outside the uncertainty context. Given this identification problem, the argument from risk aversion to diminishing marginal utility of income is tenuous.

An independent argument for the inverse relationship can be given on the basis of "diminishing returns to fixed factors," where leisure endowment plays the role of a fixed factor. Again, the argument must start from a determination of the "correct" cardinal representation of utility. We ask: What will happen to utility levels if we double *all* consumption levels? Thinking of utility as an aggregator, the answer almost has to be that it doubles, and the same ought to be true of all expansion factors. Accepting this, utility must be linear homogeneous in all arguments. Assuming that preferences are always quasi-concave and one argument (leisure) is upper bounded, we have an exact analogy with the theory of diminishing returns in production: Marginal utility of income will fall in income.

Of course, both these arguments rely on strong assumptions, and neither can be very persuasive unless we first accept the view that welfare should be neutral with respect to (or otherwise quasi-concave in) the vector of utilities. It seems clear that value judgments will remain crucial in any attempt to justify egalitarian tendencies.

2.2 Majority voting

Even if we agree on a welfare function, our job has just begun. How are we going to collect and coordinate information on individual preferences and/or the set of feasible social alternatives? Most of the rest of this book will be concerned with various indirect implementation procedures. Here we concentrate on direct methods involving voting. These methods simultaneously specify an aggregation of individual preferences and elicit the information necessary to implement it. Of course, in light

Table 2.1

	x^1	x^2	x^3
A	3	1	2
B	2	3	1
C	1	2	3

of the impossibility theorems discussed earlier, we do not expect to find a perfect decision-making procedure. However, we are able to find methods that work quite well if we are willing to accept certain restrictions on the domain of individual preferences.

Voting theory has a voluminous literature, only a small part of which we survey here.[11] We concentrate on methods of majority voting, partly because they are so prevalent in our social institutions and partly because they provide a good lead-in to our next topic, the theory of decentralization. Majority voting generates the following well-defined decision process whenever the number of voters is odd, the number of alternatives is finite, and abstentions are not allowed: (1) List the alternatives in some prespecified order, (2) run an election between the first two alternatives, (3) pair the majority winner against the next alternative, and (4) iterate the process until all alternatives have been considered.

Obviously, the number of necessary elections is 1 less than the number of alternatives, so we are going to have to worry about administrative cost when the set of alternatives is large. We ignore this problem for now and ask whether the outcome would be desirable from the point of view of social preference. Certainly, the outcome has some desirable properties: It is Pareto optimal, it treats people symmetrically, and it uses only ordinal information. However, it is flawed in general by a fundamental objection: The outcome frequently will depend on the prespecified ordering of alternatives. Thus, the method does not really resolve social choice issues but merely pushes them back to the choice of a prespecified ordering of alternatives.

Those readers familiar with the literature will recognize that our problem derives from the presence of "cyclic majorities." We illustrate it here with a rather concrete example. Suppose there are three voters (A, B, C) and society has six units of income to divide among them. Let us restrict attention for the moment to three alternatives (x^1, x^2, x^3) as specified in Table 2.1. Assuming that everyone has selfish preferences (and votes

[11] For more detailed discussions of voting models and the political process, see Black (1958), Sen (1970), and Kramer (1973).

truthfully in each election), it is clear that x^2 beats x^1, x^3 beats x^2, and x^1 beats x^3 in pairwise elections.

Consequently, if our prespecified order leads off with the pair (x^1, x^2), we will end up choosing x^3, whereas if we start with the pair (x^2, x^3), we end up with x^1. Clearly, the entire social choice problem has been passed back to the prior choice of an agenda for voting. And if we try to resolve the prior choice through majority voting, we enter an infinite regress.

One important implication of this deficiency is that control over the agenda can be a source of considerable power in some circumstances (readers who have served on committees probably already know this). Another implication is that "smart" voters may want to misrepresent their true preference on some of the votes. For example, suppose that the "agenda setter" has picked x^2 and x^3 for the first vote, and you are individual C. If you vote truthfully (and everyone else does), you can see that the outcome will be x^1, your worst alternative. But suppose you vote for x^2 in that first election. It wins and then beats x^1 in the subsequent election (assuming no one else cheats). Since you now get two units of income instead of one, the cheat has paid off. Such opportunities for strategic behavior make the normative properties of majority voting models all the more problematic.[12]

Of course, we knew that majority voting (or indeed any voting procedure) would exhibit shortcomings if we insisted on applying it to an unrestricted domain of preferences and alternatives. However, there is a well-known subclass of problems (involving restrictions on the preference domain) for which the most serious shortcomings disappear. This subclass involves decisions for which the relevant set of alternatives can be placed on a line in such a way that every voter has a quasi-concave (single-peaked) utility function. The "left–right" political spectrum is a classic example: Assuming that candidates can be placed on the spectrum in such a way that no one prefers candidates of both extremes to someone "in-between" them, the single-peaked assumption holds.

When preferences are single peaked, the outcome of majority voting is independent of the agenda and cannot be manipulated strategically to the advantage of any individual voter.[13] This outcome is the most moderate or central position possible: If we look at the preferred alternatives for each voter, it is the median of these on the spectrum. Clearly, this outcome must win in an election against any alternative: If the alternative is to the right of the median, the "median voter" and everyone to his

---

12 There is a deep connection between inadequacies of social choice procedures and incentives to misrepresent preferences. See Gibbard (1973).
13 This model and its implications are discussed in depth by Black (1958).

left (a majority coalition) vote against the alternative; the other case is symmetric.[14]

Consequently, whenever the median-preferred point comes up in an election (and it must sometime in any complete voting sequence), it is sure to win and will continue until the sequence terminates. We leave to the reader a demonstration that no voter can improve his final position by voting untruthfully at any stage of the voting.

Although one may object to the particular way in which majority voting aggregates preferences, the procedure clearly has more desirable (or at least more predictable) properties when our preference restriction condition holds than when it does not. Therefore, in designing a political system that utilizes majority voting, it is important to know how generally this restriction can be imposed on public-choice problems. We turn now to a model that seeks to organize political decision making in a way that takes full advantage of potential preference restrictions.

2.3   Bowen model

Analysis of voting on the political spectrum yields some worthwhile insights, but we are more interested here in applications to problems involving economic allocation. A most useful example is the Bowen model for allocating a pure public good.[15] Although we will not discuss the theory of public goods until Chapter 4, we get a little ahead of our story now in order to discuss this example.

Let us think of a partial equilibrium problem in which private-goods prices are fixed and a single pure public good (g) can be produced at private-goods cost: $\Gamma(g)$. Note that this formulation already assumes a version of the "mixed" economy where the government interacts with a private-market sector. Again, we defer systematic development of this

---

[14] The argument is best seen graphically. In the diagram, x^m is the preferred position of the median voter, whereas x^j is the preferred position of someone to his left. When x^m is paired against something further right (say, x^*), individual j must prefer x^m; otherwise, his preference has at least one "trough" and, therefore, at least two "peaks."

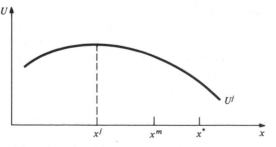

[15] The model was introduced by Bowen (1943).

model until later. Agent h is characterized by a utility function $U^h(g, c)$, where c is a "Hicksian" aggregate private-consumption good. The Bowen model assumes that lump-sum taxation is possible and reduces the allocation problem to a one-dimensional spectrum by prespecifying the tax-sharing rule. Bowen specified equal shares: $T^h = \Gamma(g)/N$, where N is the number sharing. Given this (or any other similar) rule, the allocation problem is reduced to the one-dimensional choice of g; agent h's preferences on this dimension are given by the indirect utility function

$$V^h(g) = U^h \left[g, m^h - \frac{\Gamma(g)}{N} \right], \tag{2.3}$$

where m^h is exogenous private income. As long as the consumer utility function is quasi-concave and the cost function is convex, it can be shown that the functions V^h are all single peaked.[16] So, majority voting generates a well-defined, strategy-proof outcome under those conditions.

Naturally, the Bowen model generates a Pareto-efficient outcome *within the class of possibilities it considers.* However, it actually does much better than this under one additional assumption. To see this, let us examine the first-order conditions determining the Bowen outcome. Letting superscript m refer to the median voter, this outcome (q^m) satisfies

$$\frac{\partial U^m/\partial g}{\partial U^m/\partial c} = \frac{\partial \Gamma(g^m)/\partial g}{N}. \tag{2.4}$$

On the left side of this expression we have the median voter's marginal rate of substitution (MRS) between public and private goods. Suppose that marginal rates of substitution are distributed in a symmetric way so that the *median* MRS equals the *mean* MRS. Then (2.4) implies

$$\sum_h \frac{\partial U^h/\partial g}{\partial U^h/\partial c} = \frac{\partial \Gamma(g^m)}{\partial g}. \tag{2.5}$$

But (2.5) is *precisely* the "Samuelson" condition for the optimal allocation of a public good.[17] When it holds, we know that even with *complete latitude* in the payment arrangements, we could not make a Pareto improvement in the allocation. Of course, the symmetry condition need not hold in all situations; indeed, there are classes of problems for which the Bowen method introduces a definite bias, as we shall see momentarily. However, symmetry does have some intuitive plausibility. Even if it holds only approximately, we will be close to the first-best allocation under reasonable regularity conditions.

---

16 The relevant general theorem is stated and proved in Berge (1963), chapter 8, section 8.
17 Although these conditions were known before Samuleson's day, he brought them into general circulation in the 1950s; see Samuelson (1954).

This success of the Bowen model has made it a centerpiece of normative political models in public finance.[18] However, when we attempt to broaden its range of applicability, we run into difficulties. In particular, note that the method will not be helpful in handling distributional conflicts; we explicitly assumed them away when we took the tax burden as fixed. Any attempt to reintroduce them will bring back the cyclic majorities of our previous example. (The necessary-preference restrictions never hold with respect to purely distributive issues.)

Some authors have suggested that cyclic majorities are unusual in the class of all orderings and therefore (presumably) unlikely to cause trouble.[19] But the earlier distribution example seems all too prototypical of economic allocation problems involving conflict of interest. Although these problems may be a small subset of the class of all possible problems, they still are ones we need to solve. So, in particular, we cannot expect methods of majority voting to be helpful in resolving distributional issues.

2.4   Political decentralization

Although the Bowen model cannot solve all our problems, we might hope to make efficient use of it in the following political decentralization: Each public good is assigned to an agency that uses Bowen procedures (presumably through some representative governing body) to choose the level of provision. A central authority handles general distributional issues and coordinates activities. This sort of decentralization is tremendously appealing for reasons quite apart from the properties of Bowen voting. Decentralization reduces significantly the amount of information that must be coordinated and processed by any one decision-making unit. Although costs of communication rarely are incorporated formally into economic models, it is clearly absurd to imagine a situation in which *all* the social alternatives are considered by a single decision-making unit; some "division of labor" is unavoidable.

Not only does decentralization reduce the information-processing burden on each unit, but it also reduces the total number of alternatives voted on. For example, if there are 10 different agencies each of which considers 10 different project levels, the number of votes taken is 90. However, the total number of social alternatives is 10^{10}, a *much* larger number! Reducing the number of votes in this way seems desirable, but then is there not some danger that we will miss the best combination? This

---

[18] See Bergstrom–Goodman (1973) for an early empirical implementation and Romer–Rosenthal (1983) for a recent discussion of the model's use and limitations.
[19] See, e.g., Davis–de Groot–Hinich (1972) and Kramer (1973).

Table 2.2.

	Social alternative			
	Park	Dam	Both	Neither
Type A (40%)	4	1	3	2
Type B (40%)	1	4	3	2
Type C (20%)	1	2	4	3

is exactly where the Bowen model looked promising before when we specified a tax-sharing rule yet achieved efficiency within a much larger set of alternatives. Can its success be extended to our decentralized context?

Unfortunately, there are important shortcomings to the Bowen model in this context. We explore these through a series of examples. In the first of these there are two "collective" goods: a dam (with hydroelectric project) and a park (with wildlife refuge). There are only two choices (yes or no) for each project, so there are four social alternatives altogether. Three different types of preferences are represented in society. A utility representation for these preferences is summarized in Table 2.2.

Note that this situation represents the simplest possible decentralized structure. To specify an outcome from decentralized voting, we must make some assumption about expectations. What do voters on the park think is going to happen to the dam project? Many answers are possible, and much print has been spent trying to sort them out. Here we will look only at outcomes that are "Nash equilibria." A Nash equilibrium in our example is a pair of outcomes of the two votes that, if expected at the outset, will be confirmed in the separate votes.

In particular, the outcome "neither" is a Nash equilibrium: When the park vote is taken (assuming no dam), it is seen as a vote between "park" and "neither." Since 60 percent of the voters prefer "neither," the park is voted down. The dam is voted down for similar reasons, so expectations are confirmed. Actually, the reader can check that "both" also constitutes a Nash equilibrium here, suggesting that initial expectations can be quite important in determining the outcome. Indeed, indeterminacy of outcome is a very common feature of Nash equilibrium; generally, we require a further theory of expectations before a unique outcome can be specified.

Since the status quo seems a plausible ex ante expectation, "neither" is plausible in our example. This outcome is undesirable since it is Pareto dominated by "both." Clearly, decentralized voting has cost us something

Table 2.3

	Project 1	Project 2	Project 3	Projects 2 and 3	All	None
Region 1	4	−1	−1	−2	2	0
Region 2	−1	4	−1	3	2	0
Region 3	−1	−1	4	3	2	0

here. By reducing the number of alternatives considered, we lost the best one (given status quo expectations, the option "both" is never considered). Note that there would have been no problem if we had engaged in pairwise voting on all four alternatives: "Both" wins against any of the others.

Decentralization fails here because of complementarities between the agencies. The preferences of group C (think of them as advocates of balanced development) on the park issue depend on whether the dam is constructed. We must coordinate the choices somehow to guarantee a desirable outcome. The necessary coordination may take place even in our decentralized context if, for example, vote trading is allowed. Then group A (the conservationists) may agree to vote for the dam in exchange for group B's votes on the park. Such "logrolling" arrangements begin to look like the market mechanism in politics and are roundly criticized in the popular press. But examples like the preceding suggest that the criticism is undeserved, at least in some circumstances. Indeed, we will argue in the next chapter that market mechanisms are the best way of coordinating decentralized operations in many contexts.

We will have more to say about logrolling in the following examples. Let us now look at one in which complementarities play no role. We have three projects, each of which benefits residents of a particular region but are to be paid for out of general tax revenue. Table 2.3 summarizes net benefits in numeraire units.

We construct the numbers so that the benefits from any collection of projects is simply the sum of individual project benefits, so there are no complementarities (only one pair of projects appears in the table; clearly, the others will be symmetric). Assuming that the regions are of equal size, the *only* Nash equilibrium with decentralized voting is "none." This follows from the observation that when a particular project comes up, voters in the other regions will want to vote against it *regardless* of what they expect to happen on other votes.

Table 2.4

	Project 1	Project 2	Both	Neither
Region 1	3	−2	1	0
Region 2	−2	3	1	0
Region 3	−2	−2	−4	0

Obviously, decentralized voting has failed again since "none" is Pareto dominated by "all." The problem here has less to do with decentralization than it does with properties of majority voting per se. Majority voting generates biases against projects that concentrate most of the benefits on a small group and spread the costs over a large group.

This bias can be illustrated in the Bowen model, where it derives from a violation of the symmetry assumption. Suppose we are allocating a public good g for which $\Gamma(g) = g^2$. There are three voters: Two have a marginal rate of substitution equal to unity (independent of project size) whereas one has a (constant) marginal rate of substitution equal to $1 + \gamma$, where γ is treated as a parameter. [Note that the magnitude of γ captures the degree to which the median MRS (unity) differs from the mean MRS $(1 + \frac{1}{3}\gamma)$.]

It is easy to check that $g = \frac{3}{2}$ in the Bowen equilibrium, whereas the Samuelson optimum requires $g = \frac{3}{2} + \frac{1}{2}\gamma$. The larger is γ, the more distorted is the Bowen equilibrium. Thus, we expect a bias against projects that concentrate benefits and spread cost (and by the same token, a bias in favor of projects that spread the benefits and concentrate the costs).

In the example of Table 2.3, three projects that concentrate benefits are voted down even though, taken together, everyone would benefit from them. Again, the reader will see that some form of vote trading (logrolling) would improve the situation since each region is more than willing to pay its share of the other project costs as long as the other regions reciprocate.

But before we get too enthusiastic about logrolling, let us look at one more situation. Here we modify the previous example by eliminating a project for region 3 and changing the other numbers as in Table 2.4. Note that we have rearranged the numbers so that the individual projects are undesirable on a simple cost–benefit basis. And it is still true that both projects fail under decentralized voting. However, if regions 1 and 2 logroll, they can assure passage of each other's project. Here, logrolling is allowing two groups with bad projects to collude so as to impose some of the costs on a "powerless" third party. The outcome is surely nonoptimal in a world where distributional transfers are possible since the joint project net benefits are negative; if region 3 had the power, it would willingly pay the other regions two "units" to drop their projects. In terms of voting theory, the collusion works because the two projects considered jointly spread benefits relatively broadly while allocating costs relatively narrowly (on region 3).

Thus, in judging the merits of logrolling, we need to ask what new allocations it makes reachable through voting. When we allow *anything* to be traded, there is a standard argument that trading will not stop until a Pareto-efficient outcome is reached (though equity need not be well served if those in weak bargaining positions are exploited).[20] However, if some trades are not allowed (as in the example where trading votes on projects is allowed although trading money is not), the outcome may be quite undesirable.

Before leaving the examples, we use them to illustrate one further difficulty with decentralized voting. The reader may have observed that there has been no discussion of cyclic majorities since the Bowen model was introduced. Indeed, we eliminated them on each issue considered separately by assuring that preferences be single peaked on each issue. That serves to resolve the indeterminacy on each separate vote (at least when there are no complementarities) but generally does *not* guarantee that there will be no cyclic majorities among the set of *all* alternatives. Such a cycle exists in the second example where the option all beats project 3, project 3 beats projects 2 and 3, and projects 2 and 3 beats all. Consequently, the ability to break our decision problem down into a sequence of "single peaked" issues is no real help if we ultimately are going to have to consider the set of all alternatives in finding a good outcome.

Given these and other shortcomings, we abandon the idea of a purely political solution to public-sector problems and begin to examine some more market-oriented methods. However, we will incorporate some aspects of our political decentralization when we analyze fiscal federalism in Chapters 6 and 11.

---

[20] This piece of folklore is commonly attributed to Coase (1960).

CHAPTER 3

Market decentralization

We found, in the previous chapter, that methods of political decision making are severely limited in their applicability. Tractability requires that the number of alternatives considered by any one political agency be relatively small. However, when we prune the set of alternatives either directly or through political decentralization, biases are likely to emerge in the resulting choices.

Of course, the market offers an alternative method of allocation and one that appears to require little in the way of administrative and/or coordination costs. Indeed, several of the troublesome examples in Chapter 2 appeared to yield to "market-type" solutions. Market decentralization through the "invisible hand" has at least as many information-conserving benefits as does political decentralization, but does it have any corresponding costs?

Much of the controversy in political economy during the past century has centered on whether we should allow the invisible hand to allocate resources. Many of the proponents of market decentralization have based their argument on the so-called two theorems of welfare economics, the one saying that a competitive equilibrium is Pareto efficient and the other saying that every Pareto-efficient allocation can be supported as a competitive equilibrium with an appropriate distribution of income. When the hypotheses of these theorems hold, market decentralization involves no costs.[1] The opposition has challenged both the assumptions underlying competitive behavior and the supposition that income distribution will be made "appropriate." Although some of their arguments are quite telling, this group has been noticeably on the defensive. That is, although they have been good critics, they have not advanced a coherent alternative of their own.[2]

We believe that this failure is rooted in some powerful *positive* arguments in favor of the price system involving its properties as a transmitter

---

[1] Mathematical demonstrations of these theorems were first given by Arrow (1951) and Debreu (1954). Staunch defenders of market mechanisms in practice include Friedman (1962) and Buchanan (1977).
[2] Among many voices in this chorus, prominent names include Galbraith (1967) and Kornai (1971).

of information. Everyone who studies modern economies comes to recognize the enormous amount of information that must be compiled and coordinated before a feasible (much less, optimal) allocation can be determined. The price system provides a cheap solution to these problems, one that seems difficult to match using nonprice methods. We already got some flavor of the inherent difficulties when we considered alternatives involving majority voting.

Furthermore, even if the necessary information is collected independently, modern programming methods used to determine a solution often tend to replicate what markets would have done anyway. It is almost as if we have no choice but to use markets for allocating a major part of the economy's resources. Indeed, it is suggestive in this regard that even in socialist economies where the market system is ideological anathema, pseudomarkets and/or black markets persistently emerge.

We sketch here an argument for the price system based on this position that it is the only game in town. We should be clear, however, at the outset that ours is not an argument for laissez-faire; many types of markets cannot be expected to work exactly as required for the ideal allocation method. Our position is more nearly a paraphrase of Winston Churchill on democracy: The price system may be the worst form of allocation – except when you consider the alternatives.

3.1   Command economy

Let us start with a model in which there is no individual preference; all decisions on what is to be produced are decided by an all-powerful central planner. (Note that there is no need for voting to reveal social preference here; the economic problem is simply one of coordination.) Suppose further that this planner specifies target net consumption levels by way of revealing his preferences. Of course, he recognizes a feasibility constraint, so he leaves one (without loss of generality, the first) net consumption level as a residual on which he will do the best he can.

He has available an exogenous set of production technologies. Each independent technology can be defined by an associated set of feasible net output vectors. We denote this set $\mathcal{Y}^j$ with typical element y^j for technology j. Independence means operationally that the social feasibility set is a vector sum over the sets $\mathcal{Y}^j$. Generally, we will assume "free disposal" (if one vector is possible, so is any other vector that is no larger in any component), although the assumption does not play a central role in our discussion. When, for example, production possibilities are defined by production functions (and free disposal holds), feasible net output vectors will be the set of points "underneath" the production function oriented in such a way that inputs are measured as negative and outputs as positive.[3]

A planning problem now is defined as follows: Let C_i be the target net consumption level for good i. To meet the target level, our planner must assign production choices $\langle y^j \rangle$ so as to satisfy the following inequalities:

$$C_i \leq \sum_j y_i^j, \quad \text{all } i. \tag{3.1}$$

(We can summarize these using the shorthand vector notation $C \leq \sum_j y^j$.) Now, assuming only that the planner believes more is better, he will seek to maximize the residual (C_1), leading to the planning problem

$$\max C_1 \tag{3.2}$$

subject to

$$C \leq \sum_j y^j, \tag{3.3}$$

$$y^j \in \mathcal{Y}^j, \quad \text{all } j. \tag{3.4}$$

To get some idea of the coordination logistics associated with this problem, consider a special case (known as activity analysis). Here, each production set consists of all nonnegative multiples of an activity vector a^j, that is, everything that can be obtained from the activity vector by applying the principle of "constant returns to scale." For example, the activity might involve combining one unit of labor, three units of seeds, one unit of land, and two units of water to produce one unit of corn; constant returns means we could operate this activity in any multiple or fractional amount we choose. In this case, the constraints in problem (3.2) can be replaced by

$$C \leq \sum_j x_j a^j, \quad x \geq 0, \tag{3.5}$$

where x_j is the scale at which we operate activity j. Note that the planner's problem has reduced to a standard linear program with activity levels x as variables, for which there are a myriad of solution methods.[4]

Nonetheless, logistic problems are formidable in any "real" application due to the mere size of the problem. The number of inequalities is equal to the number of distinct goods in the economy, and the number of variables is equal to the number of independent activities. Both are

---

[3] This description of production possibilities is introduced and motivated in greater detail by Koopmans (1957).

[4] The use of activity analysis to approximate general production opportunities is documented in Dorfman–Samuelson–Solow (1958). They also show how the power of linear programming can be brought to bear on economic problems involving activity analysis.

extremely large numbers in a modern economy, so large that simply finding a feasible solution to system (3.5) is a formidable task. Indeed, every
attempt to solve a system such as this one ends up solving a stylized system in which the "commodities" are already aggregate bundles consisting of many "similar" goods and the activities are statistical averages associated with producing average bundles from average bundles.[5]

Clearly, for such calculations to be useful, someone still is required to
make decisions about what happens "within bundles." We are led inexo-
rably to a hierarchical structure in which there are several levels of decision making with a system of communications linking them together.[6]
And we should expect from our discussions in the previous chapter that
considerable coordination will be required between agencies if the overall
outcome is to have any efficiency properties.

But perhaps we can solve (or at least *approximately* solve) our system
by a method other than brute force. Perhaps there are natural ways to
decompose the problem into manageable parts and then put it back together. Indeed, efficient computational methods frequently follow just
such an approach. Let us look at one of these now, the so-called dual, or
Lagrangian, method.[7] We return to problem (3.2) (although the method
naturally applies to our special case as well).

The solution method is constructive and proceeds in a number of iterative steps. First, we assign *multipliers* P_i to each of the material balance
constraints in (3.1). Then, we form a *Lagrangian* $L(y, P)$:

$$L(y, P) = \sum_j y_1^j + \sum_{i \neq 1} \sum_j P_i y_i^j. \tag{3.6}$$

(Note that by thinking of the first good as numeraire and setting $P_1 = 1$,
we can write this function in the vector form[8]: $L = P \sum_j y^j$.) The initial
values for the multipliers are arbitrary in principle, although judicious
choices frequently can improve the efficiency of the procedure.

Next y is chosen to maximize $L(y, P)$ subject *only* to the technological
constraints (3.4). Naturally, the resulting y's will not be expected to satisfy the material balance constraints (3.3) so an iterative adjustment is
performed. For a target that is not being reached in the current plan,
the multiplier is raised (putting more weight on that component in the

---

[5] The best known examples of these procedures are the so-called input–output studies associated with Leontief (1951). For a discussion of modified procedures appropriate for socialist and/or development planning, see Chenery–Clark (1959).

[6] Such multilevel procedures are discussed in Kornai (1967).

[7] This type of procedure has a long history in the literature. A good early exposition can
be found in Malinvaud (1967).

[8] Our conventions for representing inner products and other vector operations are spelled
out in the preface on notation.

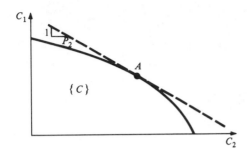

Figure 3.1

Lagrangian objective), whereas the multiplier is lowered for any targets exceeded (unless this multiplier is already zero, in which case it is left alone). We carry out maximization for the new multipliers and iterate the process until no more adjustments are called for. Observe that at this point all material balance conditions must hold.

Any rest point of the Lagrangian iterative procedure is known to provide a solution to the planner's original problem (3.2). Although we will not give a formal proof of this fact here,[9] there is a useful geometric intuition for it. Think of the production possibility set as a geometric object. This set is defined formally as

$$\left\{ C \mid C \le \sum_j y^j, y^j \in \mathcal{Y}^j, \text{ all } j \right\}. \tag{3.7}$$

The Lagrangian procedure maximizes a linear function (whose gradient is P) over this set. Thus, among other things, the procedure always picks out a point on the production possibilities frontier. The geometric picture for a two-dimensional slice (in the first two dimensions) is depicted in Figure 3.1. When the multiplier for good 2 takes the value P_2, the Lagrangian is maximized at point A.

Suppose that we are at a rest point of the iterative procedure. Could it still be possible to find another feasible production arrangement that would yield more net output of the first good yet still meet all targets? Any such point must have a smaller (or at least no larger) value of the Lagrangian linear function. Thus, net output must be lower for some good having a positive multiplier. But with a positive multiplier, the iterative procedure cannot stop until the target is exactly met, so no lower net output level can meet this target. The rest point must be optimal.

---

[9] A formal treatment of dual methods in linear and nonlinear programming can be found in Karlin (1959).

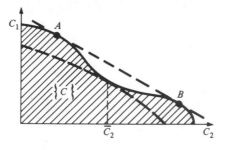

Figure 3.2

Note that we have not said anything yet about whether or not the Lagrangian method converges. In fact, there are cases where it definitely will not. For example, consider Figure 3.2. (Ignore the dotted curve in this diagram for now.) If $\bar{C}_2$ is chosen as the target, there is no linear function that will pick out the corresponding point on the production frontier; the Lagrangian procedure will cycle back and forth among points such as A and B. However, this type of difficulty will not arise if the production possibility set is *convex*. In that case, it is well known (and geometrically obvious) that each point on the production frontier will maximize a linear function over the feasible set for an appropriate choice of the gradient. Consequently, each choice of targets will correspond to a rest point of the Lagrangian procedure.

Of course, this still does not establish that convergence will occur for any initial choice of multipliers. Indeed, more is required here, and the theorems we do have that establish convergence are rather weak. Fortunately, however, convergence rarely seems to be a problem in practice. Although real iterative procedures rarely reach points of absolute rest, they tend to get quite close reasonably quickly.

Let us ask why this procedure is efficient computationally. Consider first the maximization step. Thinking of multipliers as "pseudoprices," the Lagrangian (3.6) can be interpreted as the sum over all technologies of "pseudoprofit." Maximization can be carried out through a sequence of independent smaller problems in which a production vector is chosen *separately for each technology* so as to maximize pseudoprofit. Thus, an efficient decentralization is achieved in which each decision-making unit (here they correspond to firms) need collect and coordinate information and make choices only with respect to a manageable subproblem of the grand design. The use of multipliers has enabled us to isolate the units. Without them, a firm surely needs to coordinate its plan with those who produce its inputs (and those who use its outputs). However, the multipliers effectively isolate firms from this interdependence; no firm needs to coordinate its plan with any other firm. The problems encountered in decentralized voting are thus circumvented. Unfortunately, the procedure does introduce some new difficulties involving incentives; we consider these shortly.

Of course, coordination problems do not simply disappear; they are dealt with in the adjustment process (which balances supply and demand). What can we say about the computational aspects of this process? At each stage the computations are quite easy: We simply check whether a particular argument satisfies a particular inequality. Of course, the computations may have to be done many times, but computers are especially good at doing that type of repetition. And although exact solutions rarely are obtained, small errors generally turn out to be unimportant.

Finally, there is one more advantage to the Lagrangian procedure: It provides extra information about the problem that would not be available had we used other methods. In particular, we learn something about the "opportunity cost" of the targets. We now know that the Lagrangian multipliers at a rest point represent the gradient of the production frontier at that point. Thus, P_i tells us (roughly) how much more of the first (residual) good we could have per (small) unit of the ith target we would sacrifice. More precisely, the maximizing value of C_1 defines the production frontier $C_1(C)$, and $P_i = -\partial C_1/\partial C_i$.[10] Knowing this sort of information, we can imagine that the planner might want to change some target, particularly if it were found to be especially costly.

3.2 General Lagrangian procedure and the envelope theorem

Our geometric justification of the Lagrangian procedure applies to all constrained problems, though the interpretation of particular components will differ from case to case. We can always form a "grand possibilities set" from vectors of values of the objective and constraining functions. Suppose we wish to solve a problem having the general form max $F_0(x, \bar{\gamma})$ subject to $F_i(x, \bar{\gamma}) \geq 0$, all i, where i indexes a set of independent constraints and $\bar{\gamma}$ is a set of fixed parameters. We seek a solution to this problem that will define appropriate choices x as a function of parameters γ. These choices define an optimal value of the objective for each set of parameter values. We represent this function as $Z(\gamma)$ and refer to it as the *indirect-objective function*.

The general possibilities set for our problem is formed by allowing the constraining functions and fixed parameters to take on arbitrary values.

---

[10] The minus sign appears because lowering the target involves lower values of the associated parameter.

Formally, we define this set as $\{F(x, \gamma), \gamma, \text{ some } x, \gamma\}$. Points on the frontier of such sets can be picked out either by setting constraint levels (0 for F_i, $i > 0$, and $\bar{\gamma}$ for γ) and maximizing the objective subject to these constraints or by maximizing a linear function of objective-cum-constraint functions. By varying the weights in the linear function as described in the preceding production example, any constrained optimum can be found, at least when the grand opportunity set is convex. And in any case, if the Lagrangian iterations converge, the resulting allocation must be optimal for the constrained problem.

In analyzing this class of problems, it is useful to define both a Lagrangian (L) and an extended Lagrangian $(\mathcal{L})$:

$$L(x, \lambda, \bar{\gamma}) = F_0(x, \bar{\gamma}) + \sum_{i>0} \lambda_i F_i(x, \bar{\gamma}), \tag{3.8}$$

$$\mathcal{L}(x, \gamma, \lambda, \mu) = F_0(x, \gamma) + \sum_{i>0} \lambda_i F_i(x, \gamma) + \sum_k \mu_k \gamma_k. \tag{3.9}$$

Whereas the function $\mathcal{L}(\cdot)$ is defined on the most flexible grand opportunity set, the more restricted function $L(\cdot)$ is all that we need to work with for the most part. To see why, note first that when γ is thought of as fixed and immutable at $\bar{\gamma}$, $L(\cdot)$ defines the appropriate linear function on the restricted opportunity set. Thus, as long as one is never interested in variations in underlying parameters, all the analysis can be carried out using $L(\cdot)$, as in our earlier example. However, use of $\mathcal{L}(\cdot)$ will reveal the shape of the opportunity set in the γ dimensions, and this information is exactly what we need to do comparative statics. Indeed, the previous geometric reasoning tells us that "equilibrium" values of μ reflect marginal valuations of parameters γ.

Optimization in the extended-opportunity set framework yields the following first-order conditions for the choice of x and γ:

$$\frac{\partial}{\partial x_j} \left[F_0(x, \gamma) + \sum_{i>0} \lambda_i F_i(x, \gamma) \right] = 0, \quad \text{all } j, \tag{3.10}$$

$$\frac{\partial}{\partial \gamma_k} \left[F_0(x, \gamma) + \sum_{i>0} \lambda_i F_i(x, \gamma) \right] = -\mu_k, \quad \text{all } k. \tag{3.11}$$

Thus, at a rest point of the extended-adjustment process,

$$-\mu_k = \left. \frac{\partial Z(\gamma)}{\partial \gamma_k} \right|_{\gamma = \bar{\gamma}} = \left. \frac{\partial L(x, \lambda, \gamma)}{\partial \gamma_k} \right|_{\gamma = \bar{\gamma}}, \quad \text{all } k. \tag{3.12}$$

This result is known as the *envelope theorem* in the economics literature and will be a useful tool of analysis for us in the sequel. Note that marginal valuation of parameters can be computed from the Lagrangian $L(\cdot)$ without any reference to the "extended" problem. Indeed, there is rarely any reason to work with the extended problem explicitly, since it is not helpful computationally either.[11] However, we will see an example in Chapter 5 where the extended problem has a natural economic interpretation and forms the basis of a planning mechanism.

Although the preceding discussion was carried out under assumptions of convexity, it turns out that conditions (3.10) and (3.11) are still *necessary conditions* for optimality whether or not those assumptions hold. The argument for this proposition can be seen intuitively by referring back to Figure 3.2. Suppose we replace the actual nonconvex opportunity set by the dotted convex subset having the same gradient at point $\bar{C}_2$. Given that we have reduced the available possibilities but the previous optimum is still available, it remains optimal in the modified problem. Since first-order conditions are the same for the two problems and characterize optimality in the modified problem, they must be necessary for optimality in the original problem.[12]

3.3   Market decentralization

Probably the reader has started to think of the pseudoprices as more than just "pseudo." The Lagrangian process described in Section 3.1 is isomorphic to the workings of competitive markets restricted to the production side: profit maximization (taking price as given) for firms and a *tâtonnement* adjustment process determining price so as to clear markets (with planners presumably owning all resources, including the firms, and specifying the final demands). Using real rather than pseudomarkets has tremendous further advantages in terms of informational efficiency. All of the information collection about supply and calculation of excess demand is done by the market institution.

Note in this regard that the problem of convergence of a market adjustment process is essentially equivalent to the corresponding convergence question for the Lagrangian method. Indeed, one can argue that real markets never actually clear just as iterative procedures never actually terminate. However, new considerations do arise when some real trades are made out of equilibrium. Much research has been conducted on the nature and implications of actual market adjustment, but that topic is beyond the scope of this book.[13] Generally, we will assume in the

---

[11] Extending the opportunity set is helpful computationally only when it serves to eliminate constraints from the maximization step. Thus, nothing is gained by freeing up parameter values *other than* constraint levels. See Arrow–Kurz (1970) or Varian (1978) for a discussion of the envelope theorem in economic contexts.

[12] See Intriligator (1971) for a rigorous demonstration of necessity.

[13] See Arrow and Hahn (1970), Chapter 13, for an overview of this topic.

sequel that private-sector market equilibria are actually reached. However, we will discuss briefly a class of "quantity-constrained" models in Chapters 9 and 10.

Of course, with the current incomplete institutional structure, there is likely to be a problem with incentives. Unless managers of firms are thoroughly altruistic, why should they go to any effort to maximize profit? If the decentralization is to be really effective, no one else is going to know whether they do or do not, and the profits accrue to the planners, not the managers. This difficulty (and variants of it) is the bane of the theory of market socialism.[14] It tends to persist as long as ownership of resources is in public rather than private hands. Unfortunately, though, even if we are willing to add private ownership, there are further incentive problems associated with competitive behavior (e.g., why should a large firm take price as given?). We return to a discussion of general incentive problems in Chapter 5.

Suppose now that we push our decentralization further so as to accommodate consumer sovereignty in the determination of demand. That is, we assume that individual households do the consuming, that they have preferences that can be represented by a quasi-concave utility function $U^h(c^h)$ for household h, and that the planner cares only about the vector of utility levels achieved. Rather than specify a welfare function, we suppose that the planner is now concerned only with achieving Pareto efficiency.[15] That is, the focus shifts from production efficiency to "utility efficiency." To parallel previous developments, we formulate the relevant problem by setting utility targets (U^h) for all but the first individual, who is treated as the residual. Then by varying these targets, we could trace out the entire Pareto-efficient set. Ultimately, of course, some further criteria will be required to choose a particular point on that frontier, but we do try to resolve this distributional issue here. Our new planning problem becomes

$$\max U^1(c^1) \tag{3.13}$$

subject to

$$U^h \le U^h(c^h), \quad \text{all } h, \tag{3.14}$$

$$\sum_h c^h \le \sum_j y^j, \tag{3.15}$$

$$y^j \in \mathcal{Y}^j, \quad \text{all } j. \tag{3.16}$$

---

[14] Market socialism is an attempt to design the economic system so as to get the major benefits of the price system without private ownership. See Lange (1936) for an exposition.

[15] Since we have yet to introduce a status quo, the Pareto criterion is still value free at this point.

(Note that we are measuring the consumption variables as *net consumption*: gross consumption minus exogenous resources; thus, in the "labor time" dimension, c represents minus net labor supply whereas gross consumption equals leisure time. Clearly, utility can be thought of as a function of either type of variable, and the net consumption convention turns out to be convenient for us in much of the sequel.)

As an example of standard constrained optimization, this problem can be solved using the Lagrangian method, and we should expect a decentralization to emerge naturally. We can proceed either by assigning some additional multipliers to the new constraints (3.14) or by retaining these constraints as side conditions. For expositional purposes, we take the second option and write the Lagrangian in the following form:

$$L(c, y, P, w) = U^1(c^1) + \sum_j Py^j - \sum_h Pc^h. \tag{3.17}$$

Having fixed P, the Lagrangian is to be maximized subject to the remaining side constraints at each iteration. Observe that for each firm this problem reduces to pseudoprofit maximization as before. For households (other than the first), choice of c^h generates the subproblem

$$\min Pc^h \tag{3.18}$$

subject to

$$U^h \le U^h(c^h), \tag{3.19}$$

that is, each household is to minimize the pseudocost of achieving a fixed utility level. Except in pathological cases, this cost minimization problem is the exact dual of utility maximization subject to a budget constraint.[16] Thus, the optimal plan can be decentralized if the planner assigns appropriate lump-sum income levels m^h and allows (competitive) consumers to maximize utility subject to a budget constraint.[17] The correct levels must be chosen to make the utility targets just attainable by associated households.

Consequently, if all agents will behave as stipulated, the planner need only adjust pseudoprices *and* income levels so as to clear markets and achieve utility targets at any rest point, thereby reaching a socially efficient outcome. Of course, in the full market decentralization, prices adjust

[16] See Varian (1978) for a detailed discussion of duality in consumer theory. Cases where duality fails to hold in this context were discovered by Arrow (1951) and are discussed in Arrow–Hahn (1970).

[17] Of course, convexity of preference is required here. Also, the first consumer must be treated slightly differently. He must be given all the leftover income; his optimization subject to a budget constraint will maximize a weighted difference between utility and cost as required by the social objective.

on real markets, and the planner is left with only one task: the choice of income (thence utility) distribution. Note that ideal decentralization is going to require that households take both prices *and* incomes as exogenous; in particular, the procedure will not work unless the planner is able to institute *lump-sum* taxes and transfers.

To this point it might seem that, apart from incentive problems, there would be no reason to interfere with private-market allocations and little need for a book on *public* economics! However, our formulation has implicitly made a number of assumptions that are especially conducive to the market solutions. The efficient breakdown of optimization into small subparts requires that technologies be separable and further that each choice variable affect only one agent directly. Thus, it is important to ask how reasonable those assumptions are and whether market decentralizations can be extended to situations where they fail. We take up these issues in Chapter 4. Furthermore, we assumed that markets naturally exist for all the commodities to be allocated. This assumption seems reasonable if we visualize the model in a static framework (although even there we can think of exceptions such as air pollution). However, the assumption is more problematic when we pass to an intertemporal context. Let us see whether the model of previous sections can be extended to cover such contexts.

3.4   Extensions to an intertemporal context with uncertainty

Up to now, little has been said about the nature of the commodity vector, although the natural presumption would be that we are talking about a static certainty model where consumption means the known vector of consumption goods today. However, this vector is (mathematically) of arbitrary length, so we are free in principle to give other interpretations. In fact, at the "cost" of making these vectors quite long, we can incorporate most features of an intertemporal model with uncertainty.

A   *Time without uncertainty*

Although time and uncertainty are inextricably linked in reality, it is useful to begin by considering the first without the second. Our model becomes intertemporal if we think of all commodity vectors as indexed *both* by type of good and by time (and similarly for associated multipliers or market prices). Thus, for example, decentralized market prices will be represented by a grand vector of the form $P = (P_1, P_2, ..., P_S)$, where P_s is a vector of prices at date s. Of course, this formulation does require that we think of time as discrete and the planning horizon (S) as finite, but even these restrictions can be dispensed with in principle (we will discuss such considerations in Chapter 6). As always, we are free to pick a price normalization by choosing a numeraire, and the usual choice is dollars in date 1. Then, all prices can be thought of as quoted in terms of numeraire units; in particular, P_{sk} represents the price of good k at date s in terms of dollars in date 1. We call such prices *present-value* prices.

Let us review our earlier discussions with the new interpretation in mind. When we assign multipliers to material balance constraints of the future, we know they will represent pseudovalues of present-value prices. Firms that engage in investment (meaning they produce net outputs in several periods) will be expected to maximize their present value: $Py^j = \sum_s P_s y_s^j$ in the Lagrangian decentralization. The corresponding household budget constraint also is now stated in present-value terms.

Thus, the model of Section 3.3 can be interpreted as intertemporal, and as far as the planning aspect goes, there is little more to say. However, when we invoke the market decentralization, we must face the fact that many of the required markets do not exist in the real world. We must be able to trade *today* each good in the future; that is, we require a complete set of *futures* markets. Although these markets do exist for a few standardized goods such as grains and metals, they are absent for things like labor, machinery, and most consumer goods.

Fortunately, most of these markets turn out to be redundant in our present certainty context. Indeed, suppose that *spot* markets exist at each date (markets for trading goods at that moment of time). Then, all we really require is the capacity to trade a *single* good across time; each potential futures trade decomposes into one intertemporal trade and two spot trades. Now, the institutions to support this market structure certainly do exist. The obvious intertemporal market is one for trading the numeraire, that is, a bond market; it is sufficient that one bond exist for each potential maturity date in the future.[18]

Since it is natural to think in terms of this revised market structure, it is useful to change the price variables in a way that corresponds to it. Consequently, in the sequel we will let P_s be *spot* prices at date s; each such price vector naturally is normalized in terms of the numeraire at that date. Then, the price of a one-period bond becomes the market discount factor (the value today of one dollar tomorrow). Alternatively, we can convert to interest rates. Suppose that the one-period interest rate is r_s so that each dollar invested today must be worth $1 + r_s$ dollars tomorrow; then, the value of a dollar tomorrow is $1/(1 + r_s)$.

---

[18] The "sufficiency" of bond markets in an intertemporal context has been well understood for some time. An excellent early discussion was given by Hicks (1939a).

Note carefully that every other asset will be redundant in our certainty context, assuming (as we must) that all agents are free to trade on either side of the bond markets. The rate of return for any asset (such as a futures contract) can be computed in terms of the numeraire (through use of spot market prices). Given free-trade opportunities, the law of one price must hold: Each of these assets must earn the same rate of return. They become perfect substitutes, and we need have only one.

The same type of arbitrage argument shows that the return on a two-period bond must be the product of the returns on successive one-period bonds. Generalizing, we see that the S-period discount factor takes the form

$$\frac{1}{\prod\limits_{s=1}^{S} (1+r_s)}. \tag{3.20}$$

Present values are computed by summing discounted spot values using these discount factors. The entire story of Section 3.3 can be retold in these terms. We will have more to say about this story, particularly with reference to the associated budget constraints, in Chapters 6 and 7.

B   Uncertainty

Of course, all assets are not perfect substitutes in reality because different assets have different risk structure. That is, there is a richness in securities that presumably is there to help us deal with uncertainty. The question naturally arises: Is the set of assets rich enough to decentralize uncertainty in the same way that bond markets serve to decentralize time?

Well, let us try to identify the necessary assets. We can best make use of the previous formalization by adopting a "state-of-the-world" approach to uncertainty. The concept of state of the world involves complete resolution of uncertainty. To know the state is to know what the weather is going to be, which people will have accidents and what kind, what physical principles will be discovered and when, and anything else in the exogenous world about which we are presently uncertain. Once a state is specified, the world looks like the certainty version just discussed.

Consequently, the reader should see how we can incorporate uncertainty into the framework of Section 3.1. We let ω index state of the world and append this index to all commodity vectors. Of course, to stay in vector space format, we must assume a finite collection of states (just as we implicitly assumed a discrete set of dates earlier). Although this assumption is by no means natural here, we stick with it for the moment.

Having thus reduced to the previous case, we can deduce the corresponding decentralization. It requires "contingent futures" markets; that is, it must be possible to trade (today) each dated commodity in each state of the world. Now, obviously, these markets are even scarcer than simple futures markets (and those were scarce enough). However, as before, many of these are redundant, and we can economize on them much as we did before.

Suppose, as before, that we have a complete set of spot markets together with a set of assets for trading the numeraire in each "dated state." Then, every contingent contract can be constructed using a sequence of trades on these markets, so any additional assets will turn up redundant. These assets frequently are referred to in the literature as *Arrow securities*.[19] It follows that a market structure consisting of spot markets at each date together with a security for each dated state would be sufficient to decentralize the first-best allocation under appropriate behavioral assumptions.

There are at least two practical shortcomings to this story. First, the behavioral assumptions are somewhat more severe than in the static model. Agents must correctly anticipate market conditions in each state of the world. Of course, these conditions must be knowable *in principle* since the state resolves all uncertainty; but it is quite another matter to assume that everybody knows. Second, the number of states is astronomically large (if indeed it is finite at all). Consequently, the likelihood of any particular state is so small that no one would devote any resources to running or participating in the associated contingent security market.[20] Consequently, we should expect that the best decentralization with uncertainty will involve incomplete markets. We will develop a model with appropriately incomplete market structure in Chapter 6 and explore its implications for public decision making in Chapter 12.

---

[19] Arrow (1953, 1970a) was first to formalize these ideas.
[20] There are other reasons to expect incompleteness deriving from the problems of adverse selection and moral hazard. However, we will not treat these problems in any detail in this book. See Radner (1982) for some further discussion.

CHAPTER 4

Theory of collective goods

Given the informational advantages of decentralization (which we discussed in the previous chapter), we will classify decisions as *collective* only if they cannot be executed efficiently through market decentralization, that is, by operating a sufficiently large collection of private markets. Note that a decision may be collective (by our definition) yet still admit a *non*market decentralization; indeed, there is a large literature on mechanism design that aims at finding these decentralizations. We will discuss this literature in Chapter 5.

To see what decisions cannot be handled through the market, it is useful to look at how a market might naturally emerge in an example. Let us consider the allocation of garbage. In the absence of any institutions for handling it, people will get rid of their own as best they can, presumably by dumping on one another. Let a_g^{hi} be the amount of garbage dumped by h on i. Then the consumption of garbage by agent h is $\sum_i a_g^{ih}$. We assume that each agent cares only about his final allocation of garbage and not at all about the allocation to others. Thus, agent h's utility may be represented by a function defined on net consumption[1]:

$$U^h = U^h \left(\sum_i a_g^{ih} - z_g^h, c^h \right), \tag{4.1}$$

where z_g^h represents his fixed endowment of garbage and c^h is net consumption of a single (or composite) private good. Each maximizes subject to the condition that he must allocate his garbage somewhere: $\sum_i a_g^{hi} = z_g^h$.

In defining a decentralized equilibrium here and later, we will assume Nash (1950) behavior on the part of agents; that is, we assume that each agent decides on his own garbage allocation taking as given the decisions of others.[2] Equilibrium occurs when everybody's expectations are real-

---

[1] As discussed in the previous chapter, the use of net consumption is for notational convenience only. As long as resource availability is exogenous, this choice of unit simply amounts to a translation of the origin.

[2] Of course, it is possible that response behavior will be more sophisticated than this in some situations. However, when there are large numbers of agents interacting (as will be the case throughout most of this book), it is not clear that response calculations are worth anybody's effort so the Nash (1950) assumption seems reasonable.

ized. Here, the situation is particularly simple since the decision to dump elsewhere is best for each agent regardless of what others are doing (in the parlance of game theory, dumping is a dominant strategy for each agent).

Except by chance, the decentralized equilibrium will not be efficient. We should expect this since the private decisions of one agent enter directly into the preferences of another, generating a classic case of externality. Actually, the equilibrium is indeterminate in this case since people are indifferent as to where they dump. However, we can imagine a symmetric equilibrium in which everyone will wind up with equal amounts of garbage. Then, as long as people have different tolerances for garbage, we expect to find a pair of agents (h, i) for which

$$\text{MRS}^h_{ac} \equiv -\frac{\partial U^h/\partial a}{\partial U^h/\partial c} > -\frac{\partial U^i/\partial a}{\partial U^i/\partial c} \equiv \text{MRS}^i_{ac}. \tag{4.2}$$

(Here, agent h has a lower tolerance for garbage than agent i.) Clearly, the outcome is inefficient since agent i can give some amounts of both consumption and garbage to agent h in such a way as to make them both better off.

Given this and other opportunities for barter, there is a natural process by which a market will emerge. The person with the highest tolerance for garbage has an incentive to offer collection services to others at a price in terms of consumption goods. Indeed, if agent i is able to set terms of an arrangement with agent h, he will collect the first unit of garbage for a fee equal to MRS^h_{ac} and enjoy the full surplus $\text{MRS}^h_{ac} - \text{MRS}^i_{ac}$. Of course, other agents have similar incentives, and assuming that there is enough competition to generate a single exchange rate, garbage has been effectively incorporated into the market system. Letting P_g be this exchange rate, agent h will choose its net consumption of garbage (c^h_g) so as to

$$\max U^h(c^h_g, c^h) \tag{4.3}$$

subject to

$$c^h + P_g c^h_g = 0.$$

Stated in this form, the price of garbage will be negative, but otherwise we find ourselves in a classical Arrow–Debreu framework where, of course, competitive equilibrium is Pareto efficient. The price of garbage (assuming that it is not manipulable) effectively insulates each agent from the actions of others and assures that everyone will exhibit the same trade-off rate at equilibrium.

4.1   Typology of collective goods

Our example suggests that the market is a natural decentralizing mechanism, one that is likely to arise spontaneously to correct for situations in which allocations are otherwise inefficient. Thus, in characterizing collective goods, it suffices to concentrate on features of commodities that make them "unmarketable" (or at least not efficiently marketable). Further, all significant externalities must have these same defining characteristics; otherwise (as in the garbage example), we can introduce a (possibly artificial) private good so as to generate the relevant efficiency in allocation.

So we ask: What was required to make the market work in our example? First, it was implicitly assumed that a property right could be defined and enforced. Without this provision, there would be nothing to prevent the garbage collector from redumping garbage after he had already accepted money for collecting it, and consequently no reason why anyone would pay him in the first place.

Second, it had to be true that once the property right was established and trades started to take place, a competitive (hence efficient) price would emerge from the trading process. Failure of the first precondition for markets leads to a discussion of the *nonexcludable* goods, whereas failure of the second leads to considerations of natural monopolies and the *nonrivalrous* or *nondepletable* goods. Many authors have noted similarities in the nature of naturally monopolized goods and nonrivalrous goods, and we propose to formalize these connections here. Therefore, we will begin our discussion of the nature of collective goods with a two-way classification.[3]

But before characterizing collective goods, it is worthwhile indicating the contrasting concept of a *private* good. Such a good must be one for which individual use can be identified and costlessly monitored. Further, this good must be fully rivalrous in that total use is the sum of individual uses. (Actually, full rivalry requires a careful interpretation of the previous sentence; we will give a more formal statement momentarily.) Note that we assumed in Chapter 3 that all commodities had these properties; consequently, our discussion of market decentralization was restricted to the allocation of private goods.

A   *Excludability*

To establish a workable property right, we must be able to assign ownership of the good to a single individual in a meaningful way and monitor

[3] The distinction between nonexcludability and nonrivalrousness was first spelled out in detail by Head (1962). The general collective goods framework is due largely to Musgrave (1959). Our discussion follows most closely the treatment in Baumol and Oates (1975).

the transfer of it among individuals in a (relatively) costless way. A meaningful assignation of ownership requires that the holder be able to withhold the benefits (or costs) associated with the commodity from others – thus, the idea of excludability. Among the familiar examples of nonexcludable goods are fish in a certain segment of the ocean, oil under a certain acre of land, air and water pollution over certain sections of real estate, and use of a particular section of unfenced land. Notice that the last example is different in that exclusion is possible, though costly. Actually, exclusion is possible in principle in some of the other examples: We could erect barriers in air or water that prevent the interchange across boundaries, though the cost would be prohibitive.

Thus, we can rank commodities according to the cost of setting up and enforcing a private property right. All commodities involve some cost in this regard, if only the costs of enforcing contracts and preventing stealing. Whether the costs are worth bearing for a particular good is an inherently nonconvex problem (since the choice is effectively a binary one). In classical studies of private goods, it is implicitly assumed that these costs are worth bearing, whereas they clearly are not worth bearing in the prohibitively costly cases (such as air and water pollution). For some intermediate cases the answer may depend on context. Land enclosures provide the best example. In sparsely settled areas, the costs of building fences to partition land may outweigh the benefits to be achieved through efficient land allocation, but as population density increases, the balance is likely to tip the other way, and enclosure becomes desirable.

We will have more to say about the nonconvex exclusion issue later. However, for now, we will think of all goods as being classified as either excludable or nonexcludable. Nonexcludable goods are a subset of collective goods, since they cannot be allocated through the private market.

B   Nonrivalrousness

Assuming that it is possible to exclude, the question remains whether it is *desirable* to exclude and more particularly whether it is desirable to exclude using the market. We can think of cases where it is undesirable to exclude at all, even though we could. The best known example would be "radio broadcasts," where my access to it does not in any way diminish your capacity to benefit from it. We call such a good nonrivalrous. Stated in slightly different terms, a good is nonrivalrous when the opportunity cost of the marginal user is zero. Clearly, the market cannot be used to allocate these goods efficiently: Competitive pricing must lead to a price equal to marginal opportunity cost so revenues (which would be zero for these goods) cannot cover full costs.

Of course, rivalrousness is a matter of degree, the degree being defined by the size of the marginal opportunity cost. The classic examples of radio broadcasts and information lie at one extreme (and even information involves some degree of rivalry to the extent that dissemination costs are nonzero). It turns out to be natural to define the other extreme on this scale by the condition that marginal opportunity cost is at least as large as average provision cost. We will see why formally a little later, but informally the idea is that these goods are the ones that can be allocated efficiently through the market. We will refer to such goods as *fully rivalrous*.

Obviously, the property of full rivalry may depend on the level of provision; we will explore this dependence in our discussion of the theory of clubs in what follows. We define *pure private goods* to be those that are both excludable and fully rivalrous regardless of the level of use; they must have the property that the marginal opportunity cost is always at least as large as the average provision cost. These are the excludable goods for which total use (defined as the sum of individual use) is produced using a convex technology. Referring back to Chapter 3, we see that this is precisely the class of goods studied there; this class admitted a market decentralization regardless of the level of demand (assuming competitive behavior).

Opportunity cost of the marginal user may be measured in goods required (as, e.g., the costs of maintaining a highway or bridge) or utility foregone (as, e.g., the congestion costs associated with extra use of a park or museum). Consequently, we could further subdivide the *partially rivalrous* category: natural monopolies for the first case and congestible public goods for the second. The formal analysis of these two subtypes is very similar, as we should expect. We will highlight these similarities in the sequel.

4.2   Efficient allocation of a collective consumption good

We consider now allocation rules for collective goods and/or externalities in a simple partial equilibrium context where there is one composite private good and one collective consumption item. We allow this item to involve both nonexcludable and (partially) nonrivalrous elements. In formulating the model, we invoke the following two principles: (1) Variables representing nonexcludable items (or characteristics) must enter all agents preferences symmetrically – everyone must get anything that anyone gets. (2) Rivalry through congestion enters as a nonexcludable item; users cannot be insulated from the effects of crowding. Further, we assume for now that rivalry is impersonal; that is, it can be effectively measured by total use irrespective of the division of use.[4] We relax this assumption in Section 4.4.

With these principles in mind, we employ the following representation of preferences (assumed convex) for agent h:

$$U^h\left[g, \eta^h, \sum_i \eta^i, c^h\right], \tag{4.4}$$

where g represents the nonexcludable element of the collective good under study, η^h represents individual use of any excludable element, and $\sum_i \eta^i$ represents congestion rivalry.

The supply side is represented by a cost function (in terms of the private good) of the form

$$\Gamma = \Gamma\left[g, \sum_i \eta^i\right]. \tag{4.5}$$

Costs will depend both on the type of facility and total use as long as there is some degree of "service rivalry." Note that the argument representing service rivalry is the same as that representing congestion; one enters the utility function, whereas the other enters the cost function. Frequently, we will label this argument G. We make no assumptions on the shape (and hence convexity) of $\Gamma(\cdot)$, although some restrictions will be imposed later.

We claim that most collective consumption goods will fit reasonably well as special cases of this formulation. For example, thinking of national defense as nonexcludable with no element of observable choice in its use, only g enters, and we have the Samuelson formulation of a pure public good. Or, take the case of television programming (assume that everyone has a television and that scrambling devices are costlessly effective). Here, a particular program represents an excludable good that is perfectly nonrivalrous. Hence, U^h will depend on the type of program (g) and time spent watching it (η^h) whereas Γ depends only on g. This example shares many of the features of the Samuelson pure public good and, indeed, will submit to an identical analysis in the case where everyone wants as much as they can have. The difference is that now we can (and should) allow people to turn off their sets.

As a third example, consider electricity, an excludable commodity with service rivalry. Here, U^h depends only on η^h (and c^h) whereas Γ depends only on $\sum_i \eta^i$. The public problem in this case will be purely one of increasing returns to scale.

---

[4] See Hochman (1982) for a more detailed discussion of congestion effects in clubs and some suggestions for more general formulations.

For an example in which all elements appear simultaneously, consider a museum. Assuming that all are going to share a single museum (or we are restricting attention to those who will), the type of museum is not excludable, so it is represented by the variable g. Then η^h represents individual use (visits), and $\sum_i \eta^i$ represents congestion due to crowding. On the cost side, g and $\sum_i \eta^i$ represent capital and maintenance costs, respectively.

In situations where a single good is to be shared by all (for whatever reason), we are thus led to a welfare formulation of the form

$$\max W\left[U^1\left(g, \eta^1, \sum_i \eta^i, c^1\right), \ldots, U^N\left(g, \eta^N, \sum_i \eta^i, c^N\right)\right] \qquad (4.6)$$

subject to

$$\sum_h c^h + \Gamma\left[g, \sum_i \eta^i\right] \le 0.$$

Note that in formulating the social constraint, we treat c as an excludable, fully rivalrous good. This is in keeping with our supposition that it represents a private good. Also, we retain the convention that c represents *net* consumption (consumption minus exogenous resources).

We analyze this problem using the Lagrangian method outlined in the previous chapter. Letting μ stand for the Lagrangian multiplier on our social resource constraint, the first-order conditions for maximizing our Lagrangian are

$$\frac{\partial W}{\partial U^h} \frac{\partial U^h}{\partial c} = \mu, \quad \text{all } h,$$

$$\sum_h \frac{\partial W}{\partial U^h} \frac{\partial U^h}{\partial g} = \mu \frac{\partial \Gamma}{\partial g},$$

$$\frac{\partial W}{\partial U^h} \frac{\partial U^h}{\partial \eta} + \sum_i \frac{\partial W}{\partial U^i} \frac{\partial U^i}{\partial G} = \mu \frac{\partial \Gamma}{\partial G}, \quad \text{all } h.$$

Although we do not know the "market-clearing" value of μ, we can identify properties that an optimal solution must possess by using the first of these equations to eliminate μ from the remaining two. This procedure yields the following necessary conditions for optimality[5]:

$$\sum_h \frac{\partial U^h/\partial g}{\partial U^h/\partial c} = \frac{\partial \Gamma}{\partial g}, \qquad (4.7)$$

$$\frac{\partial U^h/\partial \eta}{\partial U^h/\partial c} = \frac{\partial \Gamma}{\partial G} - \sum_i \frac{\partial U^i/\partial G}{\partial U^i/\partial c}. \qquad (4.8)$$

[5] For a demonstration that these conditions are indeed necessary even in the absence of convexity assumptions, refer back to Chapter 3 or see Intriligator (1971).

The first of these conditions is the Samuelson rule for allocating a pure public good. It always applies to the allocation of any nonexcludable element in the social problem. The second condition pertains to the allocation of the excludable, partially rivalrous element. For the case of only service rivalry it is the familiar rule of marginal-cost pseudopricing. (If the good is perfectly nonrivalrous, the pseudoprice ought to be zero; we should allow free access.) When both types of rivalry are present, our rule says that the pseudoprice of η should equal full marginal opportunity cost, which will be the sum of its service and congestion components (the congestion terms are negative as long as congestion is undesirable). Of course, our necessary conditions need not be sufficient to characterize optimal choices in the absence of convexity assumptions. We will return to this issue at various points in the sequel.

4.3   Classical theory of clubs[6]

There is little more to say at this level of generality about the allocation of nonexcludable goods. However, for excludable goods, we need to consider the possibility that different groups get different things. Indeed, the choice of such groups ought to be part of the social problem. Consideration of this issue links our current discussion to the theory of clubs. We begin our discourse with the case in which all members of a club are to be alike. This is a useful starting point for several reasons. First, it was the starting point for the theory of clubs, historically. Second, it enables us to isolate the issue of club size as distinct from club composition. Third, if there are enough people of each type and no complementarities among types, we may expect to see segregation, with each type picking a club best suited to its particular taste. We ask whether segregation will be an "equilibrium" outcome in the next chapter.

What is the best we could hope for in constructing clubs for a homogeneous population? In considering this issue we assume that social preference treats all homogeneous members symmetrically. Thus, a welfare indifference curve between any two individual utilities will be symmetric around the 45 degree line. Then, the egalitarian assumptions we made in Chapter 2 imply that we will want to give equal utilities to all members of the club in the present circumstances. The argument goes as follows. For a given club membership and common level of g and G, the set of feasible private allocations is convex in our formulation (even though there may be increasing returns to membership size and common provision level). Therefore, given identical members and a concave representation

6 The first formalization of this model was given by Buchanan (1965). See Wooders (1978) or Wildasin (1986), chapter 2, for less "partial equilibrium" versions of the story than given here.

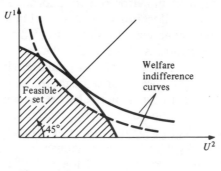

Figure 4.1

of utility, the utility possibility set is symmetric and convex. But when we maximize a symmetric quasi-concave function over a symmetric convex set, the outcome must lie on the generalized 45 degree line of equal utilities (see Figure 4.1). Indeed, we see from this reasoning that not only will we want to give all members of the club equal utility, but, in fact, we will choose to give them identical allocations as well. (Note, however, that these conclusions need not follow if the underlying feasible set is nonconvex, and indeed we will see examples where "unequal treatment" is optimal later.)

Knowing these features of an optimal plan, suppose that we choose a club size (and allocation) to maximize the utility of a representative member. Call this the *utility-maximizing* club. Since everyone in the club is to get the same allocation, we certainly cannot do better than this. Can we do as well? Clearly not if (e.g.) the total population is less than the derived efficient club size. Indeed, it seems that we can never quite succeed unless the population happens to be an exact multiple of the efficient club size. The issue here has a better known analogue in the theory of production, where the corresponding question would be: Is an industry's average cost ever exactly equal to the "minimal" average cost of a representative component firm? Indeed, we will see that the choice of an efficient firm size within an industry can be thought of as an "optimal club" problem.

Although exact "success" (as defined in the preceding) is always unlikely when the optimal club size is unique, it becomes more likely as soon as there is any latitude in this size. Presumably welfare in utility-maximizing clubs will be insensitive to the addition or subtraction of a few marginal members; specifically, suppose that any number of members between $\underline{n}$ and $\bar{n}$ will suffice for this purpose. Geometrically, we are saying that "indirect" utility as a function of n is flat between these bounds (see Figure 4.2).

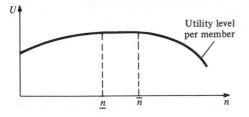

Figure 4.2

This flexibility "multiplies" as soon as we expand to several clubs (we can make the clubs all "small" or all "large" or use some intermediate sizes). Indeed, x clubs can optimally accommodate any number of members between $\underline{n}x$ and $\bar{n}x$. For small x's, these intervals will be disjoint (and we would not be able to accommodate populations in the "holes"). However, for x sufficiently large, the interval for x clubs overlaps the interval for $x+1$ clubs; this happens when x satisfies the condition $(x+1)\underline{n} < x\bar{n}$, that is, when $x > \underline{n}/(\bar{n}-\underline{n})$.

Further, we can be sure that we want at least x clubs whenever $N > x\bar{n}$. (In fact, we will want more since N will exceed the largest number of members that can be put into x utility-maximizing clubs.) Thus, a sufficient condition for "successful" allocation is

$$\frac{N}{\bar{n}} > x > \frac{\underline{n}}{\bar{n}-\underline{n}}, \quad \text{some integer } x, \quad \text{or} \quad \frac{N}{\bar{n}} \geq \frac{\underline{n}}{\bar{n}-\underline{n}} + 1 = \frac{\bar{n}}{\bar{n}-\underline{n}}. \quad (4.9)$$

We can facilitate interpretation by taking inverses to obtain

$$\frac{\bar{n}-\underline{n}}{\bar{n}} \geq \frac{\bar{n}}{N}. \quad (4.10)$$

Successful allocation can be achieved as long as the percentage of tolerance in utility-maximizing club size is at least as large as club size relative to total population. For example, if $\bar{n} = 1{,}000$ and N is on the order of 100,000, we expect to find approximately 100 clubs, and we can fill them successfully as long as efficient club size will allow plus or minus five members.[7]

Obviously, efficient club sizes will not always be small enough to satisfy (4.10). Nonetheless, the utility-maximizing club makes a useful benchmark for comparison, especially since it is quite difficult to fully characterize efficient allocations when the tolerances fail.

---

[7] Wooders (1978, 1980) gives a more mathematical discussion of admissible tolerances. She also discusses "approximately" optimal allocations in situations where there are no tolerances.

Thus motivated, we analyze the following problem:

$$\max_{g,\,\eta,\,n,\,c}\ U(g,\eta,n\eta,c) \tag{4.11}$$

subject to

$$nc+\Gamma(g,n\eta)=0,$$

where n is the number of members of the representative club. Of course, n is a discrete variable, so strictly speaking, we ought to state necessary conditions in terms of upward and downward first differences. However, since the current context implicitly assumes that utility is locally linear in n at the optimum, there is no approximation involved in doing analysis on that variable.

Proceeding as in the previous section, we derive the following necessary conditions for a utility-maximizing club:

$$n\frac{\partial U/\partial g}{\partial U/\partial c}=\frac{\partial\Gamma}{\partial g}, \tag{4.12}$$

$$\frac{\partial U/\partial\eta}{\partial U/\partial c}=\frac{\partial\Gamma}{\partial G}-n\frac{\partial U/\partial G}{\partial U/\partial c}, \tag{4.13}$$

and

$$-nG\frac{\partial U/\partial G}{\partial U/\partial c}=\Gamma-G\frac{\partial\Gamma}{\partial G}. \tag{4.14}$$

The first of these tells us how to choose the nonexcludable element. Recall that this element refers to the size and/or type of the facility when we are thinking of local public goods, whereas it might refer to the quality (or other characteristics) of a good being produced under conditions of increasing returns to scale. Examining (4.12), we see that as long as clubs are to be mutually exclusive (no spillovers) each should choose these characteristics in accordance with the Samuelson conditions (sum of marginal benefits equals marginal cost).

The remaining conditions are most conveniently discussed in special cases that isolate the two types of rivalry. (The reader is invited to combine the two cases as an exercise.)

A   *Pure service rivalry*

When the rivalry term G enters only through the cost function, (4.13) and (4.14) reduce to

$$\frac{\partial U/\partial\eta}{\partial U/\partial c}=\frac{\partial\Gamma}{\partial G} \tag{4.15}$$

and

$$\Gamma = G \frac{\partial \Gamma}{\partial G}. \tag{4.16}$$

These conditions are best interpreted in terms of a pseudodecentralization (in fact, we will make the decentralization explicit in the next chapter). Thus, we think of the marginal rate of substitution between η and c as a pseudoprice. Then, (4.15) tells us that the pseudoprice of services should equal marginal cost, whereas (4.16) tells us that pseudorevenue (pseudoprice times amount provided) exactly covers cost. Dividing by G, this second condition may be reinterpreted as saying that marginal opportunity cost equals average cost. We see that optimal club size is characterized by the condition that the collective good be fully rivalrous when shared by such a group. We can conclude further that, in the present case, optimal behavior can be decentralized through a competitive market since marginal cost pricing will cover costs. All we require is that the optimal number of clubs (here number of firms) be large (which naturally is a condition we need anyway if we expect them to behave competitively).

When will the optimal number of firms be large? Clearly, when the scale of a firm operating at the point where average cost equals marginal cost (the point of minimum average cost if the average cost function is U-shaped) is small relative to the size of the market. This is precisely the condition for viability of competition stated in many standard texts. Indeed, the reader should realize that this case merely replicates, analytically, a very standard graphical analysis of an industry.

B *Pure congestion rivalry*

Here, the efficiency condition (4.13) becomes

$$\frac{\partial U/\partial \eta}{\partial U/\partial c} = -n \frac{\partial U/\partial G}{\partial U/\partial c}. \tag{4.17}$$

Note that this takes the form of a Samuelson allocation condition with congestion playing the role of a nonexcludable public "bad." The corresponding decentralization will involve a Pigovian tax rule in which the pseudoprice (tax) should be set equal to the sum of marginal congestion damage generated on other members of the club.[8]

The "group size" condition (4.14) now reduces to

$$-Gn \frac{\partial U/\partial G}{\partial U/\partial c} = \Gamma. \tag{4.18}$$

---

[8] Such tax schemes were elucidated by Pigou (1947). We will examine general versions of these schemes in the next chapter.

We see that pseudopricing at marginal opportunity cost (here, marginal congestion cost) would yield shadow revenue that exactly covers total costs. Again, efficient club size is characterized by the condition that the collective good be fully rivalrous at the margin. The reader should see that by combining the analyses of cases 1 and 2, we can derive a generalized rule with this same interpretation. Thus, it provides a quite universal characterization of utility-maximizing club size. This result has a strong intuitive appeal: Given that members are going to be treated symmetrically, a "new" member can be expected to contribute the average cost of the collective good. If this contribution exceeds the marginal opportunity cost to the group, he should be included; otherwise, he should not. An efficient club must involve equality of the marginal and average cost.

4.4   Heterogeneous clubs

So far, our analysis has been couched entirely in terms of homogeneous clubs; that is, all members of any particular club consist of individuals who are identical in all relevant respects. However, this feature will not always be present in optimal sharing arrangements when there is heterogeneity in the population at large. For one thing, if there are not enough people of each distinct "type" to fill out the efficient club size, we may want to lump types in order to take advantage of economies of scale. But suppose this factor is not present (so, whereas there may be several types of households, each type is represented by many people). Will optimal allocation involve types separating themselves out into segregated clubs or mixing together in heterogeneous clubs? Let us explore this question in the context of our model.

First, we can show that under our maintained assumption of impersonal rivalry (the degree of rivalry depends only on total use and not the composition of use), full separation is optimal. We demonstrate this proposition for the case of two types $(1, 2)$ and leave the generalization as an exercise. We allow people of separate types possibly to differ in tastes, private good endowments, and skills. Here $U^i(\cdot)$ represents the utility function of type i, $i = 1, 2$.[9]

Let (g^i, G^i, η^i, c^i) be the utility-maximizing arguments for each type $(i = 1, 2)$ in a segregated club generating utility levels u^1 and u^2. Suppose we try to do better for both types in a club with n^{i*} members of type i consuming c^{i*} and η^{i*}, respectively, and providing g^* collectively. Since we assume rivalry is impersonal, $G^* = n^{1*}\eta^{1*} + n^{2*}\eta^{2*}$. Thus, if both types

---

[9] Note that differences in private-good endowment alone would generate differences in these functions given that we measure consumption net of endowment.

prefer the new situation, revealed preference tells us that the configuration $(g^*, G^*, \eta^{i*}, c^{i*})$ is not available to type i in a segregated club. Therefore, if type i individuals attempted to form such a club by inviting in G^*/η^{i*} members, they would be unable to pay the necessary costs; that is,

$$c^{i*}G^*/\eta^{i*} + \Gamma(g^*, G^*) > 0, \quad i = 1, 2. \tag{4.19}$$

But if we multiply these inequalities by $n^{i*}\eta^{i*}/G^*$ and sum them, we see that

$$n^{1*}c^{1*} + n^{2*}c^{2*} + \Gamma(g^*, G^*) > 0, \tag{4.20}$$

so the proposed mixed club is not viable. Segregation must be optimal in our model with anonymous rivalry and large numbers of each type.[10]

Thus, we see that mixing of types always involves some "cost" (as the incumbent types are forced to compromise on collective choices) that we want to avoid unless there are some corresponding "benefits." However, there might be some such benefits in the form of complementarities among types. These could take a number of forms. It might be that some types (e.g., males and females) enjoy each other's company and consequently generate less rivalry across types than within type. We may expect to see some mixed clubs (singles bars, dance clubs) form for these reasons.[11] Alternatively, there may be complementarity on the cost (production) side. If club members are involved in producing something that requires a variety of skills (as in a factory town), diversity may be required for production efficiency.[12]

Let us see how the analysis of optimal sharing changes when cost (production) complementarity is present. We continue to assume that there are only two types of individuals $(1, 2)$ and introduce complementarity by allowing the cost function to depend on the fraction (χ) of type 1 people in the club. How can we tell whether it is desirable to have "mixed" clubs in this situation?

Suppose we decide to maintain segregated clubs. Then (assuming there are many agents of each type) each would choose club size and allocation as previously indicated. This procedure would lead to potential utility levels for the two types $(\bar{u}^1, \bar{u}^2)$. With this hypothetical solution in mind, society might ask whether there are any mixed arrangements that do better for both types. We can find out by setting up the following Pareto efficiency problem (for convenience, we ignore congestion rivalry here):

---

[10] Segregated outcomes were suggested by Tiebout (1956) and explored in McGuire (1974).
[11] This motivation for mixed clubs is analyzed in Berglas (1976), Berglas–Pines (1981), and Scotchmer–Wooders (1986).
[12] Early examples of mixed clubs motivated in this way were given by Berglas (1976).

$$\max_{g,\,\eta,\,c,\,\chi,\,n} U^1(g, \eta^1, c^1) \tag{4.21}$$

subject to

$$U^2(g, \eta^2, c^2) \geq \bar{u}^2,$$

and

$$n(\chi c^1 + (1-\chi)c^2) + \Gamma(g, n(\chi\eta^1 + (1-\chi)\eta^2), \chi) = 0.$$

Think of the fraction χ as chosen last in (4.21) so that we can define a best plan for each such fraction. This plan defines an indirect utility function for type 1: $V^1(\chi)$. Now if there is a χ for which $V^1(\chi) > \bar{u}^1$, some configuration involving mixed clubs is desirable.

Whether or not we want mixed clubs naturally depends on the degree of complementarity present. Indeed, if χ does not enter the cost function at all, we already know that mixing is undesirable. At the other extreme, if both types are essential to the production of the public service that in turn is essential in consumption, no segregated club will be viable, and all clubs will be mixed.

Suppose that complementarities are strong enough so that some mixing is desirable. What can we say about the optimal sharing arrangements? Well, for one thing they are likely to depend on the relative numbers of the two types. Let us restrict attention to plans that always give equal utility to any pair of agents of the same type and also assume that all clubs that do form must be self-sufficient. We seek a characterization of the Pareto-efficient frontier in type utility for this situation. Intuitively, it will be determined as follows: Compute the fraction that is optimal for problem (4.21). If this fraction is larger than the ratio present in the population (so that type 1 is "relatively scarce"), the best arrangement will be to fill up clubs using the fraction χ^1 until all type 1's are exhausted and then put remaining type 2's in segregated clubs. Similarly, if type 2's are relatively scarce, a (probably different) ratio χ^2 is determined, and some type 1's are in segregated clubs. When neither type is relatively scarce, then generally, all clubs will be identical microcosms of the economy as a whole. The "within-club" private-goods allocation then can be varied to determine a Pareto frontier (see Figure 4.3).[13]

Although the optimal composition of clubs is indeterminate without knowing something about relative scarcity, the conditions characterizing efficient size are invariant as long as there are many people of each type. This is best seen by observing that the first-order condition for choice of

---

[13] See Scotchmer–Wooders (1986) for a more general discussion of heterogeneous clubs from a game theory perspective and references to other relevant literature.

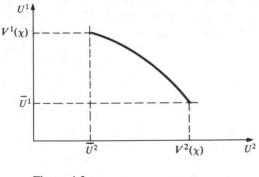

Figure 4.3

n in problem (4.21) is the same as before; club size is correct when the average and marginal provision costs are equal.

We conclude that whenever partially rivalrous goods can be shared by groups of utility-maximizing size, they should be shared in such a way as to take on many of the characteristics of a private good. In fact, full market decentralization generally is possible. We will develop this proposition at length in Chapter 5 when we discuss Tiebout-type mechanisms for allocating local public goods.

4.5   Persistent scale economies in club size

Our analysis of utility-maximizing clubs provides a benchmark against which other situations can be analyzed and compared. For example, suppose that increasing returns prevail throughout in the sense that marginal opportunity cost always remains below average cost. Then, clearly, it will be best to have a single club that encompasses the entire group. Referring back to the discussion and analysis of our general rule (4.8), we can guess that efficient decentralization will require a "two-part tariff" consisting of a use charge (which serves to cover marginal costs) plus a fixed charge to cover the difference between average and marginal cost.[14] We will discuss the mechanics of assessing this fixed charge in Chapter 5. Note that when the club is too small in the sense just described above, a new member will confer benefits on the group (and a leaver will impose costs). These benefits and costs constitute the "fiscal externalities," which we will analyze in Chapters 5 and 11.

[14] Such pricing rules have a long history. They play a central role in the literature on "peak-load" pricing. See, e.g., Nelson (1964) and Dreze (1964).

The situation just discussed (natural monopoly, uncongestible public good) had a long history well before anyone thought about the theory of clubs. Naturally, the issue of number of clubs does not arise as long as a single club is always too small. However, some interesting questions do arise when the efficient club size is neither so large as to dictate a single club nor so small as to admit utility-maximizing clubs. In particular, we may find situations where the best clubs we can have are too large (as compared to the most efficient club size). A prototype for this situation is the case where there are enough people for one club but not for two. Let us look at a problem in which there is to be only one club but where we can exclude some members of the population from it so that club size is still a decision variable. (Implicit in our formulation is the assumption that we cannot do better with two or more clubs.) For convenience, we treat a homogeneous population that experiences only pure congestion rivalry.[15]

Let the number of club members be denoted n and the number excluded be $N-n$, where N is the total population. Due to our symmetry and convexity assumptions, the principle of "equal treatment" guarantees that all members of the club will get the same allocation $(g, \eta, n\eta, c^1)$. Similarly, all nonmembers get the same allocation $(0, 0, 0, c^2)$. Naturally, we expect the private-goods allocations to differ, the expectation being that we will want to compensate nonmembers to some degree. Hence, our welfare problem takes the form

$$\max W[\underbrace{U(g, \eta, n\eta, c^1), \ldots}_{\text{repeated } n \text{ times}}, \underbrace{U(0, 0, 0, c^2), \ldots}_{\text{repeated } N-n \text{ times}}] \qquad (4.22)$$

subject to

$$nc^1 + (N-n)c^2 + \Gamma(g) = 0.$$

Given that the planners can freely distribute the private good in our formulation, the reader might think that the outcome will involve equal utility for all. But this conclusion would be quite wrong even if we assume that the welfare function is *strictly* concave, since club membership is a discrete (and thus nonconvex) choice. When the feasible set is sufficiently nonconvex, the optimum no longer involves equal treatment, as can be seen in Figure 4.4.

Here, we may expect club members to be better off than others at the optimum; although outsiders can be compensated with private goods, it is costly to push the compensation very far if private goods are comple-

---

[15] The following analysis is a synthesis of several different models developed in the 1970s. These were summarized in a survey article by Sandler–Tschirhart (1980).

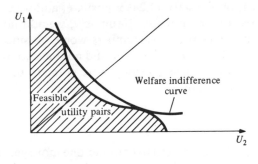

Figure 4.4

mentary with public goods (so that club members will have better uses for these goods than nonmembers). We will run across similar "unequal treatment of equals" at several points in the sequel.[16]

Focusing now on allocation rules, the reader will see that rules for allocating g and η within the club are the same as they were before; they involve Samuelson conditions in which marginal rates of substitution are summed over members of the single club. We see here a general principle: The rules for choosing a within-club allocation should not depend on the structure of clubs as long as outsiders are fully excluded from the club collective good and the structure can be chosen independently.

We ignore the discreteness element in n as before and derive the following first-order condition for efficient club size:

$$-G\frac{\partial U^1/\partial G}{\partial U^1/\partial c} = \frac{\Gamma}{n} + \frac{N}{n}c^2 + \left[\frac{U^1}{\partial U^1/\partial c} - \frac{U^2}{\partial U^2/\partial c}\right]. \qquad (4.23)$$

Examining this condition we see that the club size here generally will be larger than the efficient club size derived earlier. In particular, the marginal opportunity cost of the extra member exceeds the average provision cost by the amount

$$\frac{N}{n}c^2 + \left[\frac{U^1}{\partial U^1/\partial c} - \frac{U^2}{\partial U^2/\partial c}\right]. \qquad (4.24)$$

Belonging to the club cannot involve a utility penalty or we would simply do away with the club entirely. Thus, as long as nonmembers get some

16 An early treatment of this issue is found in Mirrlees (1972b). Of course, we could generate equal treatment here in an ex ante sense if we conducted a fair lottery to determine club membership. However, we are restricting ourselves to a world of certainty for the present.

compensation in the allocation $(c^2 > 0)$, (4.24) is positive, and we are in a region of diminishing returns to club size. Intuitively, we add households to the club even if it makes previous members worse off since we thereby raise the utility level of some outsiders. We did not have to worry about this consideration before because outsiders were going to become members of their own first-best clubs.

4.6   Spatial clubs

Before leaving the theory of clubs, we need to consider one more generalization. Club theory frequently is applied in local public finance where a club is identified with a local community. Clearly, there is a spatial element in these situations that has not been captured heretofore. Indeed, the fact of spatial separation introduces an element of "club rivalry" that is independent from the rivalries we have been discussing. When agents occupy space, one person's use of space near the collective good precludes another's use of the same space (and may force the first person to a less desirable position). This consideration generates an efficient club size even if the collective good is perfectly nonrivalrous in the sense described earlier.

We begin with a "bare-bones" model that illustrates most clearly the element of spatial rivalry; later in this section, we will generalize considerably. A nonrivalrous collective good is to be shared by a homogeneous group of people living around it. Each person occupies one unit of land (fixed for now so there is no choice of residential density).[17] To enjoy the collective good, one must visit it, and the cost of visiting (in terms of the private-good numeraire) per unit distance traveled is ϕ. People care about location only to the extent that it affects this cost. Thus, there is a clear social incentive to keep people as close as possible to the "center" so we suppose that the club is organized in a circular disk with the collective good at the center. Letting σ be the radius of this disk and n the number sharing, we must have $\sigma = (n/\pi)^{1/2}$ (the collective good takes up no space). Note that we are again treating the population as if it were a continuous variable.[18]

---

[17] Although the shape of a land parcel obviously matters to consumers, we ignore this factor by assuming that preferences depend only on area. See Berliant (1985) for an attempt to deal more realistically with land consumption.

[18] As in the previous section, we interpret continuity as approximating an underlying discrete variable rather than as an actual "continuum" of people. Although the continuum assumption is common in the spatial literature (see, e.g., Beckmann, 1969), that interpretation leads to many problems concerning the interpretation of an "individual." Some of these are discussed in Berliant (1985).

The total transport cost Φ that must be incurred in this configuration is[19]

$$\Phi = \int_{x=0}^{\sigma} 2\pi x(\phi x)\, dx = 2\pi\phi\, \frac{\sigma^3}{3}. \tag{4.25}$$

Now, we can see why there must be a cost associated with larger sizes. When extra members are added to the club, they will have to travel further than others so the average transport cost must rise. Under our special assumptions, we can quantify this effect. Using the relationship between σ and n, we can think of total transport cost as a function of n. This cost per person is measured as

$$\frac{\Phi(n)}{n} = \frac{2}{3}\phi\left[\frac{n}{\pi}\right]^{1/2}, \tag{4.26}$$

and its rate of increase in n is

$$\frac{d}{dn}\left[\frac{\Phi(n)}{n}\right] = \frac{1}{3}\phi(n\pi)^{-1/2} > 0. \tag{4.27}$$

Thus, the choice of a club must trade off the benefits of public good cost spreading against this increased per-person transport cost. We now analyze this trade-off for a utility-maximizing club.[20] Recall that this formulation requires that the efficient club size be small relative to the total population. Our problem becomes

$$\max U(g, c) \tag{4.28}$$

subject to

$$nc + \frac{2}{3}\pi\phi\left[\frac{n}{\pi}\right]^{3/2} + \Gamma(g) = 0.$$

Here, the transport term plays the role of "rivalry cost." (We have dropped the other rivalry terms from utility and cost functions; the reader is invited to combine all three types of rivalry.) Transportation has no value to the members per se but must be incurred if they want to share the collective good. Note that this cost goes up at a rate faster than n so that adding members necessarily raises the associated cost per member.

Using (by now) standard procedures, we derive the following necessary conditions for the optimal club:

---

[19] The number of people in an annulus of width dx at distance x is $2\pi x\, dx$, and each of these incurs transport costs of ϕx. Total transport is obtained by integrating over all occupied distances.

[20] This trade-off was first studied by Mirrlees (1972b) and Starrett (1974). See also Arnott (1979).

$$n \frac{\partial U/\partial g}{\partial U/\partial c} = \frac{d\Gamma}{dg}, \tag{4.29}$$

$$\frac{1}{3}\phi \left[\frac{n}{\pi}\right]^{1/2} = \frac{\Gamma(g)}{n}. \tag{4.30}$$

The first of these is the familiar Samuelson condition. Referring to (4.27), the second may be interpreted as saying that the increase in transport cost imposed on the group by a marginal member should equal the average cost of the collective good; again, the marginal rivalry cost should equal the average provision cost.

Since this principle is quite general, the reader should be able to guess what will happen if we combine various elements of rivalry in a single model: Efficient size will require that average provision cost equal the *sum* of the various marginal rivalry costs.

Before leaving the bare-bones model, it is worth pointing out one further relationship that sheds light on the orders of magnitude involved. Using the formula for Φ, (4.30) may be written as

$$\tfrac{1}{2}\Phi = \Gamma(g). \tag{4.31}$$

The cost of the collective good should be equal to exactly one-half the transport costs in the utility-maximizing spatial club. This relationship is somewhat special to our symmetric two-dimensional specification, but it is approximately correct in more general contexts.[21]

Now we turn to a model that drops the requirement of radial symmetry and allows for choice on number of trips and amount of land occupied. To formulate the optimal club problem in this context, we need to address the equal-treatment-of-equals issue again. Once the amount of land occupied is subject to choice, there is reason to believe that first best will dictate unequal treatment. The argument goes like this: People close in impose externalities on everyone further out. Therefore, we may want those closest in to have especially small plots. But then, if land is complementary with other consumption goods, we may want these people to have relatively low utilities as well.[22]

Despite this argument, we present a formulation that treats equals equally. There are several reasons for this choice. First, political considerations probably will force this constraint on us in any democratic society. Second, maximizing the utility of a representative member allows for easy comparison with previous results. And finally, when we turn to

---

[21] See Starrett (1974) for a discussion of generalizations that allow for general configurations of land and many types of people.

[22] The underlying nonconvexity here involves discreteness in location choice.

decentralization schemes in the next chapter, there would be no hope of decentralizing unequal treatment.[23]

The spatial dimension now will be modeled as follows: Land is divided into a set of zones (indexed by s). Land within a zone is treated as homogeneous and perfectly divisible; let $L(s)$ be the amount of land in zone s. Each household must be assigned to a single zone, and given that "within-zone" allocations will satisfy standard convexity conditions, everyone assigned to a particular zone will get the same allocation. Consequently, the relevant choice variables for our club planner are collective-goods characteristics g, number sharing n, and for each zone, use level $\eta[s]$, numeraire consumption $c[s]$, and number of residents $n[s]$.

These variables are chosen to

$$\max U \qquad (4.32)$$

subject to

$$U\left(g, \eta[s], c[s], \frac{L[s]}{n[s]}, s\right) \geq U, \quad \text{each } s, \qquad (4.33)$$

$$\sum_x n[x] = n, \qquad (4.34)$$

$$\sum_x n[x]c[x] + \sum_x n[x]\phi[x]\eta[x] + \Gamma(g) = 0, \qquad (4.35)$$

where $\phi[s]$ is the transport cost (from s) per unit use of the public facility. Note that we allow place of residence to enter preferences directly and that we suppress a separate land use variable $\ell[s]$ by taking account of the fact that sharing will be equal (within zone).

Here, it proves useful to retain specific reference to the Lagrangian multipliers; we assign $\beta[s]$, ν, and μ, respectively, to the three constraints in problem (4.32). Using first-order conditions for the numeraire to "normalize" as before, we derive the following necessary conditions for optimality:

$$\frac{\partial U[s]/\partial \eta}{\partial U[s]/\partial c} = \phi[s], \quad \text{each } s, \qquad (4.36)$$

$$\sum_x n[x]\left[\frac{\partial U[x]/\partial g}{\partial U[x]/\partial c}\right] = \frac{\partial \Gamma}{\partial g}, \qquad (4.37)$$

$$\left[\frac{\partial U[s]/\partial \ell}{\partial U[s]/\partial c}\right]\frac{L[s]}{n[s]} + c[s] + \phi[s]\eta[s] + \frac{\nu}{\mu} = 0, \quad \text{each } s, \qquad (4.38)$$

$$\nu = 0. \qquad (4.39)$$

---

[23] Actually, many of the characterizations presented in the text are still valid in a regime of unequal treatment. See Kanemoto (1980).

The first of these conditions tells us that we should allocate η just as we would any private good, whereas the second tells us we should allocate g just like any nonexcludable item. The remaining two conditions relate to the allocation of people. They must jointly imply an efficient club size condition analogous to (4.18) and (4.30) as well as rules for division of the land. We focus for the moment on the club size condition.

Since we worked with averages or aggregates in the past, we find the corresponding condition here by aggregating (4.38) over the population. Multiplying each of these equations by the appropriate $n[s]$, summing, and substituting from the material balance condition (4.35) yields

$$\Gamma(g) - \sum_x \left[\frac{\partial U[x]/\partial \ell}{\partial U[x]/\partial c} \right] L[x] = n \frac{\nu}{\mu}. \tag{4.40}$$

Now ν/μ is the marginal value of an extra club member (normalized in numeraire units). Further, we know that $\Gamma(g)/n$ should be thought of as the associated marginal benefit. Consequently, marginal rivalry cost is measured by the average pseudo-land-rent. Optimization on n ($\nu = 0$) then leads to the so-called Henry George theorem: Cost of the public good should equal the pseudo-land-rent in the optimal spatial club. Of course, we would add to these rents a congestion and/or maintenance charge if other elements of rivalry are present. The Henry George theorem seems remarkable when first encountered, but it has a simple intuitive explanation. Since rivalry involves pure spatial separation here, the marginal cost of rivalry ought to be reflected in the marginal premia on space.[24] In our bare-bones model, this premia could be measured in terms of transport costs. But differential land rent turns out to be the right measure in broader contexts.

Finally, return briefly to the rules for allocating land within the club. They are characterized by combining (4.38) and (4.39), which yields

$$\left[\frac{\partial U[s]/\partial \ell}{\partial U[s]/\partial c} \right] \frac{L[s]}{n[s]} + c[s] + \phi[s]\eta[s] = 0, \quad \text{each } s. \tag{4.41}$$

Although these conditions can be given a pseudomarket interpretation, their import is much clearer when we turn to an actual decentralization in the next chapter.

---

[24] There are many versions of this theorem in the literature. For example, see Starrett (1974), Arnott–Stiglitz (1979), and Hartwick (1980). The theorem is named after Henry George, not because he discovered it but because he was an early and vociferous advocate of the land tax; see George (1955).

PART II

Decision making in a mixed economy

CHAPTER 5

Planning mechanisms

We made a case for market decentralization in Chapter 3, arguing that it was informationally cheap (in fact, costless) in terms of information needed by the planner and that under some circumstances it could be used to generate desired outcomes. However, we began to see some limitations to its use in Chapter 4, where we developed a whole class of goods that could not be allocated through standard private markets. So now we ask whether there are more general allocation procedures that will work for more general economic environments.

Of course, planning problems would be relatively simple if the planner could costlessly obtain all the relevant information; he would then be in a position to compute and administer directly the optimal allocation. However, such informational requirements are far too stringent. The planner cannot possibly obtain and verify the accuracy of all necessary information. Consequently, any reasonable planning mechanism is going to involve some decentralized elements; the planner is going to have to rely on economic agents to provide some information (and perhaps make some decisions) that cannot be monitored (or verified). Clearly, once planning procedures have this feature, incentive issues are sure to arise as well.

Toward the end of this chapter, we will discuss planning mechanisms in the abstract, making precise the nature of decentralization requirements and associated incentive problems. However, we lead into the subject first with a discussion of some examples that are close in spirit to the market mechanism. The reader will not only get a feel for what a mechanism is but will also be introduced to the Lindahl method for allocating pure public goods and the Tiebout method for allocating local public goods. These discussions will illustrate the place and importance of incentive compatibility in planning. The chapter concludes with a discussion of the art of the possible (and impossible) in general mechanism design.

5.1 Extended market procedures for nonexcludable goods

We restrict attention in this section to an allocation problem where there is a collection of nonexcludable goods produced by firms that affect consumer welfare. Examples would include national defense and air pollution, so there is no presumption that the nonexcludable items are desirable (or even that people agree on whether they are desirable).

Let y_g^j be firm j's net output of nonexcludable goods. Nonexcludability means that the total net output of those goods by firms appears as consumption to each household. Thus, if we tried to decentralize using the procedures of Chapter 3, we would fail since purchases of one household would enter directly into the preferences of other households. Indeed, it seems clear that if we allow the allocation of such goods to be determined in private markets, the outcome would almost surely be nonoptimal. The reason is that any individual who contracts for such a good automatically confers net benefits on others (who cannot be excluded) so the private benefit from the purchase will differ from the social benefit; unless the contractor is appropriately altruistic, the contracted level will be incorrect from a social point of view. We seek a planning procedure that corrects for this distortion yet is still informationally decentralized.

One way to neutralize the externality while retaining a market-type framework is to have each consumer contract separately for the *entire* amount of nonexcludable goods. We can derive a planning mechanism along these lines by introducing independent variables for household consumption of the nonexcludable goods (c_g^h) and then imposing the additional constraints

$$\sum_j y_g^j = c_g^h, \quad \text{all } h. \tag{5.1}$$

These constraints will naturally generate pseudoprices when we use a Lagrangian procedure to solve the social planning problem, prices that may vary from consumer to consumer. Such prices sometimes are referred to as *personalized*, or *Lindahl*, prices in the literature and can be used to define a decentralized planning procedure involving associated personalized markets.

Using the same welfare framework and notation for private goods as before, we state the planning problem as

$$\max W(U^1(c_g^1, c^1), \ldots, U^N(c_g^N, c^N)) \tag{5.2}$$

subject to

$$(y_g^j, y^j) \in \mathcal{Y}^j, \quad \text{all } j,$$

$$\sum_h c^h \leq \sum_j y^j,$$

and

$$\sum_j y_g^j = c_g^h, \quad \text{all } h.$$

Proceeding as in Chapter 3, we assign Lagrange multipliers P to the material balance conditions for private goods and P_g^h to the consumption constraints for household h and write the Lagrangian using the natural decentralization groupings:

$$L = \sum_h \left[\frac{\partial W}{\partial U^h} U^h(c_g^h, c^h) - Pc^h - P_g^h c_g^h \right] + \sum_j \left[Py^j + \left(\sum_h P_g^h \right) y_g^j \right]. \quad (5.3)$$

Recall that (given enough convexity), an optimal allocation can be achieved through an iterative procedure that (1) sets pseudoprices and individual incomes arbitrarily, (2) maximizes L subject to technological constraints, (3) adjusts pseudoprices to correct for resulting supply–demand imbalances, (4) adjusts incomes to achieve distributional aims, and (5) iterates until no further adjustments are required. Note that, here, the price must be adjusted on each personalized market separately, and the net price to producers for nonexcludable goods is the sum of personalized prices.

Glancing back at the form of our Lagrangian, we see that this iterative procedure will decentralize as long as each agent can be made to treat all relevant prices as parametric. Under this stipulation, the Lagrangian will be maximized (for any given P's) if each firm maximizes profit over its technologically feasible set and each household maximizes utility subject to a budget constraint where public goods are contracted for at personalized prices. By introducing new consumption variables, we have succeeded in decoupling the interdependence among agents, although we need some new adjustment processes to balance the new demands with supplies.

The Lindahl allocation method is essentially a specialization of the preceding procedure to the case of a single public good.[1] Similar constructions can be used to decentralize virtually any type of interdependence among agents.[2] (As an exercise, the reader might work out the necessary "personalized markets" for decentralizing consumer jealousies.) All that one need do is index all variables by the agent to which they "belong" and define artificial markets to enforce equality wherever my personalized variables are linked to yours through some type of interdependence.

Are we to conclude that all economic conflicts can be solved by these methods? Hardly. Even the reader who has never heard of the Lindahl method is probably already suspicious of the personalized markets. First, each of these markets has exactly one individual on the buying side, a situation that characterizes monopsony and is rarely if ever conducive to

[1] The method is named after Lindahl, who developed it in a bargaining context. See Lindahl (1967) or a later exposition by Foley (1967).
[2] Arrow (1970b) was the first to demonstrate this principle formally.

price-taking behavior. Second, even if we have only one collective good, there are an awful lot of these markets – one for every man, woman, and child in the country. Surely, our neglect of transactions costs is hard to justify here.

The theory of mechanism design has been very responsive to the first of these objections by imposing conditions like *incentive compatibility* on allocation procedures, as we shall see. Unfortunately, it has been much less responsive to the second, as we shall also see.

Let us think a little bit more about the nature of the Lindahl markets. It is useful in this regard to ask a question that has generated considerable controversy in the literature: In an externality situation where one group imposes a nonexcludable externality on another, should the losers be compensated for costs imposed?[3] According to the Lindahl method just discussed, the answer would be yes; the "polluter" would pay a compensating (personalized) price to each affected party. But it is also true that this payment is unnecessary in that it is lump sum in character. Indeed, it is *essential* that any payments be lump sum, and this is where the confusion arises. To see this, let us add a little further structure to the economic problem under discussion.

Suppose that air pollution is the relevant externality and that consumers can take some action (such as installing filters or air conditioning) that will affect the level of pollution they incur. In particular, we suppose that there is an activity that determines consumer air quality (η^h) as a function of ambient air quality faced (c_g^h) and private-goods inputs (a^h). Hence, the underlying utility function $\hat{U}^h$ has the form

$$\hat{U}^h = \hat{U}^h[\eta^h(c_g^h, a^h), c^h - a^h]. \tag{5.4}$$

The variables a^h should be thought of as intermediate goods used in consumer activities. Thus, the utility function we used earlier will be the indirect utility function obtained by maximizing $\hat{U}^h$ over choices of a^h. The relevant maximization leads to first-order conditions:

$$\nabla_\eta \hat{U}^h \nabla_a \eta^h - \nabla_c \hat{U}^h = 0, \tag{5.5}$$

where we have suppressed the arguments for convenience. These conditions tell us that the marginal opportunity cost of private goods in consumption should be equated to the marginal benefit they could generate in cleanup (note that both terms in the marginal benefit are expected to be negative).

---

[3] This controversy stems from the work of Coase (1960), who suggested that the assignment of property rights (and thus the nature of compensation) would be irrelevant. For a systematic, modern discussion of the issues, see Baumol–Oates (1975).

Now return to the question of compensation. Suppose we decided to pay this compensation according to air quality actually incurred. We do this by charging $\hat{P}_\eta^h \eta^h$ (since the personalized price is negative, the charge turns up as a net payment). Such a charge cannot be optimal and therefore must be inconsistent with the correct Lindahl scheme. To see this, look at the choice of a^h in the new decentralization. First-order conditions for this choice are

$$\nabla_\eta \hat{U}^h \nabla_a \eta^h - \nabla_c \hat{U}^h = \lambda^h \hat{P}_\eta^h \nabla_a \eta^h > 0. \tag{5.6}$$

Therefore, at the equilibrium, the marginal private (and social) benefit from added cleanup effort is positive; more cleanup should be done. It is not done because the recipient sees that his compensation for pollution goes down whenever he engages in cleanup. Clearly, compensation should not be a function of his cleanup effort.

The same line of argument just given can be generalized to show that payments for nonexcludable externalities should not be sensitive to any of the recipient's private decisions; that is, given the level of public decision variables, households should not have any influence over the size of their payments. Of course, Lindahl compensation $P_g^h c_g^h$ has this property *as long as* personalized prices are taken as given. The household chooses c_g^h so as to reveal his marginal benefit:

$$P_g^h = \nabla_\eta \hat{U}^h \nabla_c \eta^h. \tag{5.7}$$

And since adjustments are made until c_g^h equals the amount supplied, the payments are fully lump sum in character *as long as* the consumer never perceives that he can influence price.

Consequently, it is true that the compensating payments are inessential as far as correct resource allocation is concerned. The only essential contribution of the Lindahl markets is to reveal the consumer's marginal benefit from nonexcludable goods (or externalities). Unfortunately, we have reason to believe that the markets cannot deliver, even on this limited objective. Consumer "monopsonists" have every incentive not to reveal correctly. If we try to make them pay, they will understate their demand in an attempt to "free ride," whereas if we dispense with actual payments, they will overstate demand so as to get something for nothing.

Due to these and other difficulties, we abandon the Lindahl process as a practical planning mechanism. However, in light of the lump-sum nature of Lindahl payments, we need not abandon the entire approach if we can find some other way of learning the consumer marginal benefits for nonexcludable goods. These could then be used to construct "efficient" prices (taxes) on producers. We defer until Chapter 13 a discussion of techniques for learning marginal benefits and discuss briefly how a tax scheme will work when they are known. (We will refer to such schemes as *Pigovian tax systems.*)[4]

Rather than return to a full formal treatment, we sketch the workings of a Pigovian tax system, leaving the details to the reader as an exercise. The procedure iterates on private-goods *prices*, individual incomes, *levels* of nonexcludable goods, and *marginal rates of substitution* for consumers between the nonexcludable goods and the numeraire. The iterative planning step proceeds as follows. First, tax rates t_g are computed as the sum of the marginal rates of substitution:

$$t_g = \sum_h \left[\frac{\nabla_{c_g} U^h}{\lambda^h} \right]. \tag{5.8}$$

Firms then maximize profits using these taxes as the prices for nonexcludable goods. From this maximization we get levels of the nonexcludable goods for the next iteration and net supplies of the private goods.

Meanwhile, consumers optimize subject to a budget constraint involving only the private goods, taking as given the levels of the nonexcludable goods. They thus determine marginal rates of substitution for the next iteration and net demands for the private goods. Then, a *tâtonnement* process determines private-goods prices.

Finally, the planners must determine an income policy for the next iteration. Since they have collected tax revenue from firms, this money must be returned as part of the policy. The reader should see that if and when the iterations stop, all *necessary* conditions for an optimum will be satisfied. It follows that *if* a solution to the necessary conditions is unique, the Lindahl scheme and the Pigovian scheme yield identical outcomes; the one pays compensation directly in Lindahl markets, whereas the other pays it indirectly as a lump-sum return of the Pigovian tax revenue.

However, there are important differences in the properties of the two schemes when nonconvexities serve to generate multiple solutions to the necessary conditions. Referring back to the analysis of the Lindahl scheme (and recalling relevant passages in Chapter 3), we see that any rest point of the Lindahl mechanism must be optimal. But the same cannot be said for the Pigovian scheme. The distinctions are best illustrated in Figure 5.1, which depicts a pollution problem in stylized graphical form.

In order to retain the standard orientation of commodities as "goods," we measure pollution from right to left in the diagram. The curve MB refers to the marginal benefits from cleanup and is computed as the sum of the marginal rates of substitution between clean air and the numeraire. We have drawn it so as to increase in some region, a property that reflects

---

[4] The general method here is associated with Pigou, as first outlined in his book (1947).

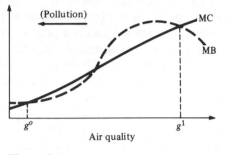

Figure 5.1

a saturation effect; generally, there is a maximum amount of damage pollution can do, and as this level is approached, marginal damages (and the marginal benefit of cleanup) must fall. Thus, in this range, MB increases with air quality (decreases with pollution). A rising marginal-benefit schedule reflects some element of nonconvexity, and the reader should see that such a nonconvexity is inherent in problems involving external diseconomies.[5]

The curve MC reflects producer's marginal costs of reducing pollution; we draw it in conventional form, implying that the underlying production technologies are nice and convex. As drawn, there are three intersections of the two curves, and we argue that any of these can be supported as a rest point of the Pigovian tax scheme. At each of these points, if the corresponding level of pollution is expected and consumers correctly report MB, firms wish to stay at this level (remember that necessary conditions are sufficient for the firm's optimization under our current assumptions). Although the middle point can be eliminated on the grounds that it is unstable against small perturbations of the iterative process, the other two are both locally stable.

Although we would have to get ahead of ourselves to make rigorous statements about the welfare ranking of these two points, it should be clear that g^1 is better than g^0; as we clean up pollution moving from g^0 to g^1, marginal benefits generally exceed marginal costs. Thus, reliance on a Pigovian scheme can get us stuck in a nonoptimal position. Intuitively, we are so saturated with pollution at g^0 that the benefits of a small change are insufficient to justify the costs even though a large change would be desirable. So the Pigovian scheme guarantees efficiency *only* with respect to small (marginal) changes.

---

[5] This point was first discussed systematically by Starrett (1972). A more technical justification may be found in Otani–Sicilian (1977).

The only possible rest point for the Lindahl scheme is g^1 (the second-order conditions for consumer optimization are violated at g^o). However, with nonconvexities present, there may be no rest points to the Lindahl scheme (just as there may not be any competitive equilibria in the classical model in the absence of full convexity). Indeed, g^1 is not a rest point here if no a priori upper bound can be imposed on the level of pollution. This is so because at price P_g consumers will see that there is no upper bound to the amount of money they can make by selling pollution rights (taking price as given, as they must), whereas by assumption, there is a finite amount of damage that can be done to them. Clearly, in this type of situation we are going to need information on the desirability of large changes in order to design a good mechanism. Some relevant techniques in this regard are discussed in Part IV.

Before leaving the world of Lindahl and Pigou, we use the current framework to discuss "second best" for the first time, a topic that will occupy center stage most of the time in the sequel. Suppose we find it impossible to collect useful information on the marginal costs of pollution. How should we proceed with the allocation of other resources? Should we regulate pollution at all? If so, how should we allocate pollution among firms? As we shall see, the answers to all these questions depend on context. In particular, they depend on the extent and nature of controls available to the planner. We look here at an example where the answers are neat and clean. The reader is advised to enjoy this one, as the answers will hardly ever be this nice again!

Suppose that the planner will be able to specify a level of total pollution, although the optimal level is unknown. The planner should reason as follows: Whatever choice of level I make, I should arrange things so as to optimize conditional on that level. If this optimization can be decentralized in such a way that the total level is unaffected, the outcome will be second-best optimal (for that total level).

We can analyze the second best simply by substituting a fixed level g for c_g^h wherever the latter appears in our first-best welfare problem. Having done this, our Lagrangian takes the form

$$L = \sum_h \left[\frac{\partial W}{\partial U^h} U^h(g, c^h) - Pc^h \right] + \sum_j [Py^j + P_g y_g^j]. \qquad (5.9)$$

Observe that the appropriate decentralizations look the same as before except that consumers take pollution level as given and are not compensated. Only the adjustment process is slightly different. Now the price of pollution (P_g) must be adjusted so as to equate the aggregate profit-maximizing levels of pollution (y_g^j) to the target level g; the price is raised if the target is exceeded and vice versa. The net effect of this procedure is to assure that whatever target is chosen, it is achieved at least social cost.

Several institutional arrangements have been proposed for administering the preceding decentralization. The most straightforward is one where the planner sells rights to pollute, the total number of rights offered being equal to the preassigned target. Note that successful administration requires that the proceeds be returned to consumers in a distributively optimal way and that pollution levels can be monitored but does not require any information to the planner concerning the marginal benefits or costs of pollution. An alternative method involves issuing "pollution tickets" to firms in some prespecified way (which serves to define the property right), allowing a free market in tickets, and checking tickets against effluent by way of enforcement.[6]

5.2   Problem of the common

One of the oldest externalities discussed in the economics literature involves sheep (or, e.g., cattle) grazing on unfenced ("common") land. It was recognized early on that such land would generally be overutilized relative to the first best. Later, it became clear that this situation could serve as a prototype for many similar economic problems. Indeed, the role of the common can be played equally well by a fishing ground, an oil reserve, a highway, or a park.

Naturally, common property constitutes a special case of our class of collective goods. The meaning of a common resource requires us to think of it as nonexcludable, so we can apply what we know about the allocation of such items. (In particular, it should not surprise us to be told that the private market will not allocate such items appropriately.) However, the problem of the common has some additional structure that enables a more detailed analysis and generates a more satisfactory decentralized planning mechanism.

The added structure derives from thinking of the common as a factor of production. To illustrate, land is an input into the production of wool, and oil reserves is a factor in the production of gasoline; further, if we take an activity approach to consumer behavior, highways can be thought of as an input to leisure travel or museums as an input to cultural understanding. We assume there is a production function of the form $\eta = \eta(a, K)$, where a is a vector of private-goods inputs and K is the size of the common.

---

[6] Baumol–Oates (1975) go into more detail on the mechanics of such schemes.

The presence or absence of rivalry in the use of the common now helps to determine the shape of η. If K is completely nonrivalrous in use, doubling the amount of variable input used with a fixed amount of K effectively doubles all inputs; for example, if K represents information, the same piece of information can be used with each extra unit of variable input. Thus, if there are no essential indivisibilities, it is natural to assume constant returns to the *fixed* nonrivalrous input, and we see that the presence of such inputs introduces an element of increasing returns overall.[7]

On the other hand, if K is fully rivalrous, we expect to see constant returns to scale as all inputs are varied. This situation fits the case of oil reserves closely; it also fits land and highway lanes if we are careful to think of these items as time indexed (two parties are well advised not to occupy the same highway lane space at the same time!). When these conditions apply, the collective nature of the common derives entirely from the element of nonexclusion that is clearly present in the case of a fishing ground, highway lane, or oil reserve.

Let us isolate the "problem of the common" as follows. We assume that, aside from η, there is one other private good that is both consumed and used as an input in producing η. For the moment, we treat supply of both this good and the common (Y and K, respectively) as exogenous. Under these assumptions, we can write the social planning problem as

$$\max W[U^1(c^1, \eta^1), \ldots, U^N(c^N, \eta^N)] \tag{5.10}$$

subject to

$$\sum_i c^i + a = Y,$$

$$\sum_i \eta^i = \eta(a, K).$$

With K fixed, this problem has the same structure as those studied in Chapter 3 and admits to a market decentralization. Thus, there would be no "essential" social problem here as long as the common were fixed in size (so that the relevant aggregate technology is convex) and was allocated by a single agent who could be made to behave competitively.

But suppose there are many independent producers on the common. Then, unless we modify the competitive mechanism, each user will impose congestion externalities on the others, and the outcome will be inefficient. To get some insight into the appropriate mechanism design, it is useful to examine the nature of this inefficiency. When access to the

---

[7] There are a number of interesting relationships between public inputs and aggregate returns to scale. See Starrett (1977) for details.

common is unrestricted, the outcome will depend on what proportion of output accrues to each of the individual users. As long as all users are in symmetric positions, the answer must be that the percentage of total output for each user is equal to his percentage of total variable input. This implies that users can expect to reap the average product for an additional unit input rather than the marginal product. We can see this formally as follows: A competitive user j will choose his input a^j to maximize

$$P_\eta \frac{a^j}{a} \eta(a, K) - P_c a^j. \tag{5.11}$$

Assuming that our user acts under the assumption that other users will not react systematically to his choices (so that $a - a^j$ is treated as exogenous), the optimal choice of a^j must satisfy

$$P_c = P_\eta \left[\frac{a(\eta + a^j \partial\eta/\partial a) - a^j \eta}{a^2} \right]$$

$$= P_\eta \left[\frac{a^j}{a} \frac{\partial\eta}{\partial a} + \left[\frac{a - a^j}{a} \right] \frac{\eta}{a} \right]. \tag{5.12}$$

We see that if the user is very small relative to the whole (so that a^j/a is negligible), he will equate the price of the input with the value of its average product; and in any case he will equate price with some weighted average of the marginal and average product. The implications for efficiency of allocation now are seen to depend on the degree of rivalry present on the common.

Suppose, first, that there is no rivalry. In this case, we saw that there would be constant returns to the fixed common; additional users impose no "crowding-out" externality on other users. Consequently, the marginal and average product will be identical, and "free access" generates an optimal allocation of a fixed common. Of course, allocation problems will reemerge as soon as the size of the common becomes subject to economic choice – efficiency in use dictates no charge for access, yet supply will not be forthcoming unless producers are compensated. Optimal supply will require the payment of nonmarket subsidies much as in the case of collectively consumed goods. We will look again at a slightly modified version of this problem in Chapter 17.

Let us return to the case of a fully rivalrous common. Now, there are diminishing returns to the fixed common; the marginal product will fall in a and consequently be less than the average product. Hence, the incremental user will always push the total use of input to a point where the input price exceeds the value of the marginal product. Thus, in a

Nash equilibrium, the common will be overutilized relative to the first best.[8]

The market failure here derives from the fact that we do not efficiently ration the scarce resource (common). And since exclusion from pieces of the common is assumed to be prohibitively expensive, we cannot ration its use directly through the market. But exclusion from the common as a whole generally *is* possible, so we can employ a Pigovian-tax-type solution instead. We tax sheep at the rate at which external costs are imposed on others. Since the extra sheep reaps the average product to its owner but only the marginal product to society, the difference must represent lost product to others and forms the basis for a corrective tax. Note that the special symmetry of this problem implies an equal (and easily computed) tax rate for all users; all that is required for implementation is knowledge of the aggregate production function. (The reader may want to derive the correct tax formula and show that its use serves to decentralize the first best.) Of course, as with any Pigou-type tax scheme, we must worry about possible multiple solutions to the necessary conditions. However, it turns out that solutions are unique here as long as the production function $\eta(\cdot)$ is concave.

Moreover, if the tax revenue is not returned to the "losers," it can be used to provide correct incentives for potential producers of the common resource. To see this, we make use of Euler's equation for functions homogeneous of degree 1.[9] As applied to the production function $\eta(\cdot)$, we have

$$\eta = K \frac{\partial \eta}{\partial K} + a \frac{\partial \eta}{\partial a}. \tag{5.13}$$

Thus, the difference between the average and marginal product of a relates directly to the marginal contribution of additional common. Consequently, tax revenue T must satisfy

$$T = aP_\eta \left[\frac{\eta}{a} - \frac{\partial \eta}{\partial a} \right] = KP_\eta \frac{\partial \eta}{\partial K}. \tag{5.14}$$

Thus, if the tax revenue per unit of common is used as a subsidy rate to suppliers of the common, the latter will be induced to supply up to the point where the marginal provision cost is equal to the value of the marginal product. We will pursue this intuition more systematically when we imbed the present model in an intertemporal context (Chapter 17). Of

---

[8] As mentioned in Chapter 1, this type of conclusion can be violated if income effects are sufficiently strong relative to substitution effects. However, the conclusion stands here, since there are no income effects in production.

[9] See Varian (1978), mathematical appendix, for a derivation of this equation.

course, there may be some difficulty in constructing a planning adjustment process such that the supplier(s) will take price as given. We defer to Section 5.5 further discussion of such incentive issues.

Many other issues involving common property can be analyzed as variations on our basic model. For example, if there are several different pieces of common property, one may ask about their relative utilization. Although the average piece of (rivalrous) property still will be overutilized with free access, it is possible for less valuable parcels to be underutilized. This occurs when the fact of average overutilization raises the price of the private input sufficiently. We will not deal further here with such general equilibrium issues.[10]

5.3 Tiebout-type models of club decentralization

Charles Tiebout suggested many years ago that local public goods could be decentralized in a way that was immune to the free-rider incentive problem.[11] However, he did not propose a precise mechanism, and much controversy has ensued over whether such a mechanism could be found. We will try to argue here that such a mechanism exists only under the rather severe assumptions of the utility-maximizing club model (cf. Chapter 4). Recall the central requirement of that model: There must be enough households of each type to populate many clubs of utility-maximizing size. When these conditions hold, we found that the club good should be shared in such a way as to have many of the characteristics of a private good. Therefore, it is not so surprising that we could find a market-type decentralization.

Let us return to the Model of Section 4.3. Recall that this model assumed no complementarities among types so that segregated clubs are desirable. Suppose that club planners compete for subscribers by offering packages consisting of provision level g, club size n, and so on. For expositional purposes (and to illustrate the importance of efficient club size), we start by supposing that club sizes and use levels are predetermined in an arbitrary way. We label these levels $\bar{n}$ and $\bar{\eta}$. With these restrictions, a package consists simply of collective-goods levels g and a uniformly distributed tax to pay the costs of provision: $T = \Gamma(g, \bar{G})/\bar{n}$. Assuming that all such feasible packages are offered, each household sees itself as free to choose any club in the spectrum. (The associated choice frequently is referred to as "voting with one's feet" in the literature.) Thus, household h sees itself as facing the problem

---

10 See Weitzman (1974) and de Meza–Gould (1985) for further discussion of these issues.
11 The seminal paper here was Tiebout (1956). For a summary of developments since then, see Stiglitz (1983).

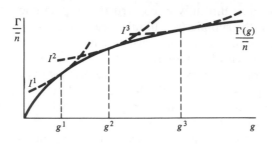

Figure 5.2

$$\max_{g,c} U^h(g, \bar{\eta}, \bar{G}, c) \qquad (5.15)$$

subject to

$$c + \Gamma(g, \bar{G})/\bar{n} = 0.$$

Comparing (5.15) with similar choice problems from Chapter 4, we see that h will choose the level of collective goods that is best for sharing among $\bar{n}$ agents with preferences U^h. Remembering that there are many of these agents, we will find a whole series of such clubs filling up with subscribers. We see right away the importance of large numbers: If there are not enough households to fill up a club, its promoter will end up promising something that cannot be delivered.

Let us think a little about how the free-rider problem has been avoided here. Households see the subscription spectrum as a nonlinear price for the collective good. As long as no one believes his behavior will influence this price function, each person's choice correctly reveals his preference (marginal rate of substitution between the public and private good). Obviously, it is important that a full range of choice be available exogenously, so that the household can operationally compare the benefits of incremental collective goods with the associated additional costs.

It is difficult to imagine this exogenous spectrum in a real institutional setting unless there is likely to be some clientele for the various points on it. Thus, diversity of preference (for public and private goods) becomes an important ingredient in the Tiebout story. Clearly, different types will segregate themselves by choosing different preferred packages (see Figure 5.2) so sufficient diversity will serve to fill out the spectrum.

Suppose that there are enough people of each type so that everyone can be fitted into a club of his choice. Does this "solve" the congestible public-goods problem? Obviously, not completely, since we have ignored the club size issue. And unless $\bar{n}$ happens to have been chosen correctly, the outcome will not even be stable against further competition among clubs. To see this, let $V^h(n, \eta)$ be the indirect utility function (after choice of club) for agents of type h; that is, V^h is the maximizing value of utility in problem (5.15) as a function of the fixed parameters. Recalling the discussion in Chapter 3, we use the Lagrangian function to evaluate derivatives of V^h with respect to these parameters. The value of an added member is computed as

$$\frac{\partial V^h}{\partial n} = \eta \frac{\partial U^h}{\partial G} - \lambda^h \eta \frac{\partial \Gamma}{\partial G} + \lambda^h \frac{\Gamma}{n^2}. \tag{5.16}$$

To facilitate interpretation, it is useful to multiply through by n, divide by λ^h (the marginal utility of c), and rearrange slightly:

$$n \frac{\partial V^h / \partial n}{\partial V^h / \partial c} = \frac{\Gamma(g)}{n} + G \frac{\partial U^h / \partial G}{\partial U^h / \partial c} - G \frac{\partial \Gamma}{\partial G}. \tag{5.17}$$

The left side of (5.17) measures the benefits to the existing club of adding a new member and will be positive if average provision cost Γ / n exceeds marginal rivalry cost (note that we are allowing for both types of rivalry) at the current level of n and vice versa. These benefits constitute a "fiscal surplus" and will play a central role in our discussion of local public policy in nonoptimal settings (see Chapter 11).[12] When the fiscal surplus is positive, optimizing clubs obviously will have an incentive to compete with each other for members.

We can imagine such incentives generating an iterative process, and we will comment on the performance of such processes momentarily. However, we can refine the Tiebout choice process so as to determine the optimal sizes in the first stage; further as a by-product, we generate the correct use levels η that have been ignored heretofore. Suppose club planners offer a spectrum of opportunities characterized as follows. Households get to choose (g, G) directly and face a price of services equal to $\Gamma(g, G)/G$. Thus, the household choice problem may be stated as

$$\max_{g, G, \eta} U^h(g, \eta, G, c) \tag{5.18}$$

subject to

$$\frac{\Gamma(g, G)}{G} \eta + c = 0.$$

Households do not choose the number sharing directly. This number is left to the discretion of the club planner who will choose $n = G/\eta$ so as to

---

[12] Such measures of fiscal surplus were derived first by Buchanan–Goetz (1972). Also see Flatters–Henderson–Meiszkowski (1974) and Starrett (1980a).

deliver the desired level of G.[13] Note that this choice also guarantees that the planner will cover his costs from the sale of services since each member will pay $(\Gamma/G)\eta = \Gamma/n$.

Now it is easy to see that this mechanism replicates the utility-maximizing club solution. Given the planner's rule, each household could think of itself as choosing n rather than G with the knowledge that $G = n\eta$. But if this change of variable is made, the choice problem (5.18) is equivalent to the utility-maximizing formulation (4.11). Thus, we achieve the first best through decentralization.[14]

Not only have we accomplished more here, but our decentralization looks more standard. The Tiebout tax is no longer seen as lump sum in character; rather, it is realized as the price of a purely private good (η). We get away with this here precisely because the properly allocated collective good has the fundamental characteristics of a private good: A charge at marginal cost is correct for covering full cost. We seem to have found a rigorous justification of the Tiebout intuition. Furthermore, our method can be generalized to deal with situations in which heterogeneous clubs are optimal, *assuming* that the service price can be made different for different types of people.

Unfortunately, though, the qualifying assumptions for our story are quite severe even in the homogeneous case. If there are many different types of people, it is hard to imagine that there will be sufficiently many people of *each separate* type to facilitate the utility-maximizing subdivisions. On the other hand, if there are only a few types, it is hard to see where the a priori spectrum will come from (observe that the spectrum now includes not just collective-goods levels but associated congestion levels as well).

It would be desirable if we could relax the assumption that a full spectrum was initially available. Let us try to modify our story by specifying an iterative process whereby (1) initially households choose among a fixed set of limited options, (2) club planners search for welfare-improving packages, (3) households reorganize themselves in light of new opportunities, and so on.

Whether such mechanisms work (achieve the first best) depends in subtle ways on details of the specification. One particularly important requirement involves the behavior of club managers; they cannot simply optimize

---

[13] As in the previous chapter, there is an "integer" problem here if the utility-maximizing club size is unique. In that case, we would have to be satisfied with "approximate" equilibria in the sense of Wooders (1980). Note that we cannot avoid this problem by assuming a continuum of people and appealing to Aumann (1966); the club nonconvexity is too large to be covered by his theorem.

[14] The basic idea behind this story can be traced back to Pauly (1970) and McGuire (1974). It has been recently articulated by Berglas (1982).

Table 5.1. *Household characteristics*

Type	Preferences	Endowment
A	$(2g_1+g_2)/n$	1
B	$(g_1+2g_2)/n$	1
C	$(2g_3+g_4)/n$	1
D	$(g_3+2g_4)/n$	1

with respect to current members but must actively search for packages that will attract other members. A simple example illustrates why: Suppose that, initially, all clubs happen to offer the same package. Then all different types are indifferent as to where they go and (suppose) all clubs end up with the average composition of types. Subsequently, each club manager optimizes conditional on having the average composition, and the process ends. This outcome generally is not optimal since club diversity is desirable when tastes for the collective goods differ (at least in the absence of complementarities).

The reader might hope that this example is pathological. If we had just started off with some diversity, surely we would have come out all right. But unfortunately, starting with "some diversity" is not enough. To be sure of reaching the first best, we must start with enough diversity to generate the optimal club composition at the outset. The point here is sufficiently important that we illustrate it with a second example (due to Truman Bewley).[15]

There are four collective goods (g_i, $i = 1, ..., 4$), one (composite) private good, and four different types of households (indexed A–D). To illustrate that our difficulty has nothing to do with the nature of collective goods, we will model them as if they were private in character. In particular, they are to be fully rivalrous; if a public service level g is to be shared by n members, the effective consumption level per household is g/n. (Note that this implies an indeterminate efficient club size.) Household characteristics are summarized in Table 5.1.

All "public services" are produced according to the same constant-returns-to-scale technology: Two units of any public service can be produced for each unit of private-good input. Initially, four different club configurations are offered. All of these offer club sizes of $n = 2$. The first two tax all private endowment and provide public-service vectors $g^1 = (2, 0, 2, 0)$ and $g^2 = (0, 2, 0, 2)$. The other two tax one-half of private endowment and provide $g^3 = (1, 0, 1, 0)$ and $g^4 = (0, 1, 0, 1)$.

---

15 We have modified the example in Bewley (1981) slightly for expositional purposes.

Clearly, given the nature of preferences, no one will want to join the latter two clubs. Types A and C want to join the first club whereas types B and D want to join the second. Everyone expects to get a utility level of 2. Suppose that types A and C pair up (and similarly for types B and D). Then, *given this composition,* there is nothing club managers can do to improve the situation even though a change in composition to full segregation makes everyone better off ($U = 4$). The full optimum will not be reached unless the initial selection is rich enough to generate full segregation right from the start.

The phenomenon just discussed illustrates a nonconvexity that is fundamental to problems involving local public goods. Think of the following highly stylized version of our welfare problem. Society must choose membership lists for clubs (let the complete vector of these be denoted n^*) and collective-goods vectors within clubs (let the corresponding vector be denoted g^*). Social welfare can be thought of as a function of these: $W = W(n^*, g^*)$. Now think of an institutional arrangement whereby club managers take n^* as given and optimize with respect to g^* whereas households take g^* as given and optimize with respect to n^*. This procedure is well known to reach the overall optimum whenever W is jointly concave in all arguments. But this is *exactly* the procedure that fails in our examples.

Where are the associated nonconvexities? Of course, there is the indivisibility associated with households. But this element turns out to be inessential; our difficulties will persist even if we pass to a model with a continuum of people. The real culprit is the "shared-good" element. Functions such as g/n or gn are not jointly concave in both arguments, and therefore, we cannot expect to generate an independent decentralization of the components g and n.[16]

But once we accept the view that club managers must actively search, free-rider incentive problems are sure to emerge. Such managers must be able to determine things about consumer preferences they cannot learn from consumer choice among the initial set of alternatives. Some writers have attempted to finesse this difficulty by assuming "utility-taking" behavior on the part of club entrepreneurs; that is, the entrepreneurs believe that they can attract a resident through any policy that keeps his utility constant.[17] However, even if this assumption is reasonable (a question we will address in Chapter 11), entrepreneurs must "know" potential constituent preferences in order to act rationally. Clearly, we no longer have a complete solution to the preference revelation problem.

[16] These nonconvexities were first noted by Dreze (1974). They also play a role in the "incomplete-markets" literature, as we will see later. The need for entrepreneurial club managers has been discussed recently by Henderson (1985).

[17] See, e.g., Wilson (1986) or Scotchmer (1985b).

Even more difficulties emerge when we try to decentralize situations where there are not enough people of a given type to populate many clubs. For example, suppose (as in Section 4.5) that there are enough people to populate one optimal club but not two. Recall that the best thing to do then is to have one club of larger-than-optimal size. But given that configuration, how are we to prevent an entrepreneur from trying to split off a smaller (optimal) group, leaving the rest "out in the cold"? Also, who is to enforce the required transfers to the outside group? We are back to needing a central government in this situation.[18]

5.4   Decentralizing spatial clubs: Henry George theorem

While recognizing the preceding difficulties, it is instructive to work out a decentralization for spatial clubs that parallels our mechanism for congestible clubs. We return to the model of Section 4.6, in which space generated the only element of rivalry. Thus, recalling equation (4.40), it seems clear that land is the appropriate private good for club managers to rent out and that total rent collections ought to pay for the appropriate levels of the public good. Consequently, we expect households contemplating membership in a club offering public facility g to face a problem of the form

$$\max_{\eta, c, \ell, s} U(g, \eta, c, \ell, s) \tag{5.19}$$

subject to

$$c + r(g, s)\ell + \eta\phi(s) = 0$$

for some rent function to be specified.

We must assume that these potential members have rational expectations in the following sense: They know that the rent gradient will adjust so that each will be indifferent concerning location (for those locations that are occupied). Note that when this expectation is realized, the equal-treatment conditions (4.33) surely will be satisfied; clearly, any decentralization that utilizes competitive determination of land rent must result in equal treatment. Further, potential members know that whatever rent structure they see, total rents will be used to pay for the public goods. Hence, the dependence of r on g must satisfy

$$\sum_x r(g, x)L(x) = \Gamma(g). \tag{5.20}$$

Given that potential members recognize this relationship, they will correctly see land rent as a "price" for public provision.

---

[18] A number of authors have studied equilibrium allocations allowing for "full information" on the part of club managers. See, e.g., Richter (1978), Epple–Filimon–Romer (1983), and Greenberg (1983).

Now, suppose there exists an exogenous spectrum of collective facilities g satisfying these conditions. We argue that household choice will generate optimal spatial clubs. As usual, the number of members in a club is determined as a residual; people determine which zones are desirable by bidding for the land, and undesirable zones will remain unoccupied even at zero rent. We show that household choice of the remaining variables replicates the characterizing conditions of utility-maximizing clubs. First, observe that choice of η replicates conditions (4.36). Next, examine the conditions for choice of ℓ and g:

$$\frac{\partial U[s]/\partial \ell}{\partial U[s]/\partial c} = r(g,s), \quad \text{each } s, \tag{5.21}$$

$$\frac{\partial U[s]/\partial g}{\partial U[s]/\partial c} = \frac{\partial r(g,s)}{\partial g}\ell[s], \quad \text{each } s. \tag{5.22}$$

The first of these, substituted into the household budget constraint, replicates (4.41). Indeed, from this perspective, it is clear that (4.41) dictates that land should be allocated within the club as it would be in a competitive market.

Aggregating (5.22) over all residents yields

$$\sum_x n[x] \frac{\partial U[x]/\partial g}{\partial U[x]/\partial c} = \sum_x \left[\frac{\partial r(g,x)}{\partial g} \right] L[x], \tag{5.23}$$

which, in light of (5.20), replicates the Samuelson condition (4.37). Finally, "Henry George supposition" (5.20) in conjunction with aggregated private budget constraints guarantees the material balance condition (4.35). Hence, all necessary conditions of the optimal spatial club are satisfied in the Henry George decentralization.[19]

Thus, a local government that owned the land (or could tax all land rent) would need no other sources of revenue to finance optimal levels of local public expenditure. Of course, this conclusion does rely on the assumption that spatial separation constitutes the only source of rivalry. If we reintroduce congestion or service rivalry, the constituency would require additional revenue. However, these funds would be obtained through the sale of services so again there would be no need for any additional taxes. Other kinds of taxes are required only when club membership is small relative to the utility-maximizing size. But we should emphasize one more time that none of these solutions can be decentralized in an incentive-compatible way without the type of restrictive assumptions discussed in the previous section.

---

[19] Among the many authors who have proposed this sort of decentralization, the best developed implementation is that of Berglas (1982). We ignore the possibility that necessary conditions might not characterize the optimum.

5.5   General mechanism design

We now explore the possibility of designing general mechanisms that are self-policing in that they eliminate the incentive problems we have been encountering. The class of mechanisms to be studied is characterized as follows: Let $\mathfrak{X}$ denote the set of social states. At present, we put no restrictions on what sorts of things might belong in a description of the social state. We assume that agent h has a preference ordering R^h over social states. The action taken by agent h in the course of planning is denoted q^h. (In the interpretation of mechanisms as "game forms," actions are referred to as strategies.) A planning mechanism is defined by a function from strategies to social states: $x = u(q^1, ..., q^N)$.

To specify a particular mechanism, we must choose strategy spaces for agents and pick an outcome function. For example, in the iterative Lindahl mechanism, strategies consist of demand functions relating desired levels of the collective goods to personalized prices, and x is the level that results from iterative adjustment when these functions are utilized. Any monitoring ability the planner has will be incorporated in the size and shape of the strategy spaces. For example, if the planner had full information and monitoring ability, he could specify a behavior for the agents so the strategy sets would be singletons. Clearly, this case would involve no problems of incentive compatibility, problems that arise precisely because the planner has severely limited scope for monitoring.

When monitoring is restricted, the set of admissible strategies ($\mathfrak{Q}$) must be big enough to contain all the choices that are "consistent" with a particular agent, and the agent must be free to choose among these. Thus, if, for example, strategies are "demand functions," we might be able to restrict them to those that satisfy the weak axiom of revealed preference (on the grounds that everyone should exhibit at least this degree of rationality), but we could not put restrictions on the size of a particular elasticity since we have no way of identifying the agent's true utility function. Thus, we see that the concept of a mechanism is necessarily somewhat decentralized (at least in the interesting cases), with the degree of decentralization determined by the planner's monitoring capacity.

To determine an outcome that is consistent with "free choice," we need to say what each agent knows and/or believes about the behavior of other agents. We may expect agents to choose differently if they think their choices will influence the behavior of others than otherwise. Since expectations are difficult to identify at best, we will be on safest ground if we can design our mechanisms so that the best strategy for each agent is *independent* of the strategies chosen by others; then everyone will ignore feedbacks, since they are "payoff irrelevant." These considerations lead to the concept of dominant-strategy mechanisms, which we now formalize.

Given two strategy configurations q and $\hat{q}$, we define a new strategy configuration $q \,|\, \hat{q}^h$ to be the situation where everyone plays his q strategy except agent h, who plays $\hat{q}$. Then q^{*h} is a *dominant strategy* for h if

$$u(q \,|\, q^{*h}) \, R^h \, u(q), \quad \text{all } q \in \mathcal{Q}. \tag{5.24}$$

(Here, q and Q are to be thought of as configurations of strategies and strategy sets; when q^h is a finite dimensional vector, q is a matrix.)

We then say that a planning mechanism $u(\cdot)$ is a *dominant-strategy mechanism* if there exists a dominant strategy for each agent. Letting q^* denote the configuration of dominant strategies, the outcome is $u(q^*)$. One desirable objective of planning is to design dominant-strategy mechanisms. Of course, this is not the only objective; if it were, we would simply make the outcome independent of strategy choice (rendering all strategies dominant). However, we want the outcome to have some additional normative properties such as, for example, Pareto optimality. Formally, we have in mind that the outcome should be some well-defined function of the underlying characteristics of the economic environment. Letting γ denote the configuration of such characteristics, we could represent the desired *choice function* by a correspondence $Z(\gamma)$. In the sorts of economic allocation problems we have been studying, γ refers to parameters of the utility and production functions and Z represents the choices that our social welfare function would dictate given those parameters. We think of γ's as parameters that are unobservable to the planner so that he must have a plan that will work for all possible values that the parameters might take (a set denoted Γ).

We now ask: What choice functions can be implemented by dominant-strategy mechanisms? Since the latitude in choice of strategy spaces seems enormous, one might hope to implement almost any choice function using a sufficiently complicated strategy space. However, it turns out that very few choice functions can be implemented in this way. Part of the explanation derives from the fact that much of the apparent latitude in choosing strategy spaces is spurious due to the so-called revelation principle. As applied to dominant-strategy mechanisms, it tells us that we can restrict attention to game forms in which each agent's strategy amounts to an "announcement" of his own unobservable characteristics.

Although a rigorous justification requires some care, the basic idea behind this principle is quite simple. Let γ^h be the "characteristics" of agent h (and γ for the corresponding configuration of characteristics). Now, we need to think of R^h and q^{*h} as functions of γ^h. Suppose we rewrite the dominance condition (5.24) taking account of these functional relationships:

$$u[q^*(\hat{\gamma}) \,|\, q^{*h}(\gamma^h)] \, R^h(\gamma^h) \, u[q^*(\hat{\gamma})], \quad \text{all } \hat{\gamma} \in \Gamma. \tag{5.25}$$

Note that the requirements in (5.25) actually look weaker than those in (5.24); now the other agents are restricted to playing strategies consistent with possible private characteristics whereas they might not have been before. However, assuming that the planner can compute strategy as a function of characteristics, these extra restrictions could have been imposed from the outset (on Q), and the apparent weakening is spurious. And assuming that characteristics contain *all* the private information, planners *must* be able to compute these functions.

Now, suppose we look at the following "direct-revelation" mechanism. Agents announce (reveal) their private characteristics, and the outcome is $Z(\gamma) = u[q^*(\gamma)]$. That is, planners compute the dominant strategies for announced γ's and determine the outcome from the existing dominant-strategy mechanism. Our dominance condition for $u(\cdot)$ translates directly into the following statement about $Z(\cdot)$:

$$Z(\hat{\gamma} \mid \gamma^h) \, R^h(\gamma^h) \, Z(\hat{\gamma}), \quad \text{all } \hat{\gamma} \in \Gamma. \tag{5.26}$$

Verbally, $Z(\cdot)$ is a dominant-strategy mechanism, and "truth telling" is the dominant strategy.[20] We will call direct-revelation mechanisms with this property *straightforward*. Of course, the revelation principle does not mean that we have to use a straightforward mechanism (we may be able to find something less cumbersome); however, it does imply that if we can find any dominant-strategy mechanism at all, we can find one that is straightforward. Taking account of the revelation principle, we see that our design problem essentially reduces to finding a social choice procedure that is "strategy proof." Consequently, the reader should begin to anticipate negative results in light of our discussion in Chapter 2.

The main characterization result in this area relates the existence of straightforward mechanisms to certain monotonicity properties of the underlying choice functions. The characterizing condition is roughly as follows: Suppose that for one set of characteristics (γ) the choice function picks out alternative a; let $aR^i(\gamma)b$ for some agent i and an alternative b. Then it is not possible for alternative b to be selected when characteristics of i (and only i) are changed (label the new characteristics γ') unless $bR^i(\gamma')a$. When this condition holds for all agents and alternatives, we say the choice function is *individually person-by-person monotonic* (abbreviated IPM).

It is easy to see why IPM is required for straightforward implementation. If a is strictly preferred to b when characteristics are γ' in the situation described, type i will want to lie and say his characteristics are γ in

---

20 Actually, it is possible that the direct-revelation mechanism could have other (nontruthful) dominant strategies, in which case our substitution is certain to work only if agents always choose to be truthful whenever the truth is a dominant strategy. See Dasgupta et al. (1979) for further discussion of this point.

order to get a; hence, truth will not be a dominant strategy for him. Unfortunately, IPM is a strong condition. Since it is stated on pairs of alternatives, it implies Arrow's condition of independence from irrelevant alternatives and consequently serves to rule out interpersonal comparisons of utility. Thus, at the very least, we must give up on one of Arrow's other axioms if we are to achieve straightforward implementation. Since we would be hard pressed to justify giving up Pareto optimality or nondictatorship, our only real hope is to allow restrictions on the domain of characteristics.

Even allowing for such restrictions, most of the results in the literature are negative in character. For example, it is not enough to know that the social state involves an allocation of private goods and that consumers have selfish quasi-concave preferences; various authors have shown that only dictatorial choice functions admit straightforward implementation in this situation as long as the number of agents is finite.[21] Indeed, as long as some agent has an influence on price (no matter how small), the incentive problem seems to be intractable. Only if we are willing to make even stronger restrictions on preferences can we hope to find incentive-compatible mechanisms. The single-peakedness condition is one restriction that is strong enough, as we saw in Chapter 2. And we will look (in Chapter 16) at another success that results from a different type of restriction on the form of preferences.

Of course, there is still the possibility of implementing "more" preference configurations by relaxing the requirement of dominant strategies. For example, we might hope to do a lot better by accepting outcomes that are only Nash equilibria in strategy space (meaning that each agent's strategy is optimal *given* that others are playing their equilibrium strategies). However, this avenue of escape has proved to be pretty much a dead end as well. Although the conditions for Nash implementation generally are weaker than for straightforward implementation, they are not much weaker; indeed, unless the characteristics domain is restricted in fairly significant ways, Nash implementability will actually imply straightforward implementability [see Roberts (1970), Maskin (1979), and Dasgupta et al. (1979) for precise statements].

Furthermore, Nash implementation (when possible) generally seems to require an even larger strategy space than under direct revelation; each agent must report not only his own characteristics but also (his beliefs about) those of everyone else.[22] Such a space seems to be too unwieldy to be of any practical use.

---

[21] This result was first proved by Hurwicz (1972); it was strengthened by Dasgupta et al. (1979).

[22] See Maskin (1983) for a description of such a mechanism.

Thus, it seems that except in some quite restrictive economic environments, we will not be able to design planning schemes that resolve all incentive problems. Consequently, the lofty aims we have espoused for public economics to this point must be scaled down.

CHAPTER 6

Models of a mixed economy

To this point we have espoused a rather ambitious view concerning the objectives of government planning. We sought "first-best" solutions and placed no a priori restrictions on the scope of government activity. Unfortunately, we were forced to conclude in Chapter 5 that there was little hope of finding incentive-compatible mechanisms that were both workable and comprehensive in coverage. Therefore, we will limit our objectives in most of the sequel.

The nature of our limitations involves leaving a large segment of the economy in an uncontrolled market sector and using a variety of indirect methods to allocate remaining goods in a public sector. This view of the scope of public activity is most easily justified on positive grounds: The U.S. economy has evolved into one having this mixed structure, so we want to know how well it can be expected to work. However, there is some reason to believe that the mixed economy can be given a normative justification as well. That is, such a division of responsibility in allocation may be the second-best optimal organizational form when all informational and incentive costs are accounted for correctly.

Although we cannot prove the second-best optimality of a mixed-economy structure, we can draw on material from earlier chapters to give an informal argument. We saw in Chapter 3 that market decentralization involves a considerable saving in information collection and transmission as compared to other potential allocation methods; further, such decentralization achieves a first-best allocation for the class of private goods if agents can be made to behave competitively. Now, even if agents cannot be induced to behave exactly as competitors, it seems likely that the efficiency loss from such deviations might be outweighed by the informational costs of direct intervention. On the other hand, we saw that the distortions caused by private-market allocation are much more serious for the class of collective goods so that intervention is correspondingly more desirable.[1]

---

[1] Variants of these arguments have been advanced implicitly or explicitly as justification for study of the mixed economy and "benefit–cost" analysis ever since economists began to take a normative view of the purpose of government activity. Pigou (1947) was among the first to explicitly adopt this philosophy. The view that public intervention ought to be linked to market failure was advanced formally by Bator (1958).

Assuming we have justified a limited scope for public activity, there remains the question of how it should be organized. We could attempt to use direct mechanisms of the type discussed in Chapter 5, in which the planner simultaneously elicits relevant information and generates decisions. Or, we could collect information as best we can in one operation and make decisions separately. Our experience with planning mechanisms suggests that the good ones are too cumbersome to use even in quite limited contexts, leading us again to the view that indirect methods are second (or perhaps third) best.

Although we think that a focus on indirect planning mechanisms as distinct from direct ones is useful and appropriate, there is a countervailing argument. If we assume that all agents are perfectly rational, every indirect mechanism becomes a direct one: People know how the information collected is going to be used in the future and take this knowledge into account in determining their behavior. Our view of the mixed economy in the sequel implicitly assumes that these feedback links are broken; that is, we assume that the information collected does not depend on how it is going to be used. Again, whereas there are no theorems that justify this view of limited rationality, we think it is reasonable.

With no further justification, we accept the mixed economy as the object for study in most of the rest of this book. The remainder of this chapter is devoted to laying out the basic features of the associated model when the public-sector planner is thought of as a single agent. The following chapter discusses the structure of planning within the public sector.

6.1 Static model

A "canonical" version of the appropriate static model is well established in the literature, and we will adopt it with virtually no modification.[2] However, we want to discuss some hidden underlying assumptions and allow for a number of generalizations. Dynamic versions with or without uncertainty are less well established, and indeed, there are some important controversies having their roots in the nature of the dynamic formulation. We discuss these at some length toward the end of the chapter.

Our mixed economy will consist of a market sector in which some subset of commodities is allocated on private markets and a "public" sector in which all other economic decisions are made. Except as noted, the division of responsibility between these two sectors will be treated as predetermined. The economic actors consist of households, private producers, and the government.

---

[2] Most features of the formal model are attributable to Diamond and Mirrlees (1971).

A   *Households*

We will assume throughout that households have convex preferences and behave competitively on the private markets; thus, consumer prices appear as parameters in their decision problems. Also appearing as parameters will be all public decision variables. These will include tax rates and schedules, levels of collective goods, income transfers, and any other decision variables of the public sector. (Note that this formulation does implicitly assume that households do not take into account any influence their activity on private markets might have on public decisions.) Although we can think of situations where some of these assumptions will be violated, they seem generally reasonable.

At times we will find it important to have a separate notation for sales and purchases of private goods. One can avoid this necessity if one is willing to divide the commodity space into goods that consumers only buy and those that they only sell. However, we reject this approach since it cannot handle commodities such as land. Thus, let c^{h-} be the purchase vector of household h and c^{h+} the sales vector. Both vectors have the dimension of the private-goods space, so we must think of them as incorporating zeros in (say) the sales vector for goods that are purchased (but not sold). Consequently, the net purchase vector may be written as $c^h = c^{h-} - c^{h+}$, and the gross consumption vector is net purchases plus exogenous holdings (z^h). When the distinctions are immaterial, we will utilize the notational simplicity that can be achieved through the use of the "net consumption" concept.

The form of consumer budgets is going to depend on the nature of government tax and/or transfer programs. We want to allow for linear and nonlinear taxes on sales and/or purchases and possible lump-sum taxes or transfers. For now all we need say is that the tax system can be summarized by specifying a finite collection of parameters (such as graduated tax rates). These together with the public provision levels will constitute the public parameters.

Consumer choice is constrained, then, by the requirement that purchases net of taxes cost less than the value of sales (also net of taxes) plus any exogenous components of income (transfers, profits, etc.). Consumer choices are determined through a standard constrained optimization of individual utility functions U^h yielding demands and supplies as functions of the public- and private-sector parameters. Price vectors to consumers will not always be defined independent of transactions levels (as, e.g., when we have a nonlinear commodity tax), but when they are, let P^- be the purchase price vector and P^+ the sales price vector.

B   *Private producers*

We want to make minimal assumptions on the behavior of firms. In particular, we want to allow for noncompetitive behavior of various sorts. Note that once such behavior is allowed, use of the market is second best quite apart from our success in allocating collective goods. And we might want to attack this second-best aspect directly through government regulation of industry. However, since this topic is more commonly discussed in the context of theories of industrial organization, we will not deal with it here.

The sales and purchase vectors of firm j will be denoted by y^{j+} and y^{j-}, respectively. Again it will be useful to define a net output vector y^j, as the difference between these two. Firm behavior is assumed to determine these vectors as functions of the public and private parameters. If (but *only* if) behavior is competitive, these will be producer supply and demand functions. In other cases (e.g., when producers are monopolists), these functions will depend on all parameters of the households that go into determining demand elasticities. Since such functions can be quite complex, it is fortunate that much of what follows does not depend on their form.

Since we will not be interested in studying nonlinear commodity taxes on firms (for reasons to be discussed later), producer prices always are well defined. We let Q^- and Q^+ be the purchase and sales price vectors, respectively. Profits of firm j will be denoted π^j. In our static model, we assume that profits are shared among consumers in exogenously fixed proportions. Note that under these assumptions, transactions costs for consumers may be thought of as functions of producer price and tax parameters.

C   *Public planning*

The government decides on the levels of all public decision variables (we defer for the moment the question of how these decisions are to be made). For the most part, we will think of the output of the public sector as consisting of collective-good provision levels and net transfers of a market "numeraire." This restriction to goods and services is not without content. It leaves out completely the lawmaking and enforcement activities of government as well as paternalistic activities such as the setting of a social conscience or the evolution of a social philosophy. One may argue that some of these activities are not appropriate for government, but surely some of them are. However, it seems reasonable to think of economics as restricted to the study of allocating commodities (and services), leaving other social decisions to other social sciences.

We assume that collective goods g are produced directly in the public sector using private goods b that are purchased in the market. We could also allow such goods to be directly contracted for from private producers if we were willing to complicate the notation somewhat; however, the added generality does not seem to be worth that cost. The government acts as a competitor on private markets and uses the tax system to pay for its net purchases and implement distributional objectives.

Now we come to an important hidden assumption, namely, that private-sector market equilibrium exists smoothly as a function of public decisions. That is, for any particular status quo choices by the government, forces of supply and demand act to determine all private-sector prices, and further that these equilibrium prices will vary in a differentiable way as functions of government choice. Although this is hardly the place for a technical discussion of equilibrium theory, a few comments seem appropriate. First, our framework contains a number of features that are known to cause trouble with "existence." Both the possibility of monopolistic competition and the presence of commodity taxes fall in this category.[3] Indeed, with no possibility of lump-sum taxation, there are finite upper limits to the amount of revenue the government could collect; if our status quo specification asked for more than this, clearly there could be no equilibrium. So we cannot ask that equilibrium exist for every conceivable status quo. Rather, we will ask that equilibrium exist for some status quo and for all variations in a "neighborhood" of it. Even to get this much, we will have to assume that elements of monopoly power in the private sector are not sufficiently strong to generate discontinuities in supply.

Second, *uniqueness* of equilibrium generally is required before we can hope to achieve smoothness. (When equilibrium is nonunique, we may be forced to jump discontinuously among a discrete set of equilibrium points.[4]) This is bad since sufficient conditions for uniqueness are excessively strong, especially in the presence of commodity taxes.[5] However, there is hope if we are willing to relax our requirements a little. Under some assumptions regarding smoothness of underlying utility and

[3] Nonexistence problems stemming from a monopoly element are discussed by Roberts–Sonnenschein (1977); Shoven (1974) takes up corresponding issues involving indirect taxation.

[4] Some equilibria may disappear when small changes are made in underlying parameters. See Balasko (1978) for an exposition of this subject.

[5] See Arrow–Hahn (1970), chapter 9, for a general discussion of uniqueness requirements and Foster–Sonnenschein (1970) for specific reference to problems involving commodity taxes.

production functions (which we surely must make), "most" status quo equilibria possess a smooth extension to the surrounding neighborhood (even though there may be other equilibria outside the neighborhood).[6]

Existence and smooth extensions in a neighborhood is all that is required for the analysis of Part III of this book. Our approach there can be summarized as follows. We will think of the economy as starting from some relatively arbitrary status quo equilibrium. Then we analyze the welfare effect of various small changes the planners might make in public choices. The assumption of "smooth extensions" is used to justify treating the underlying equilibrium as a locally smooth function of these choices. However, in Part IV large changes in public variables will be contemplated and stronger assumptions will be required. Such requirements will be noted and discussed as they arise.

6.2   Intertemporal considerations

As discussed in Chapter 3, there is no technical difficulty in extending static models of competitive decentralization to a dynamic context, and we can use such an extension to generalize the static mixed economy. In so doing, we will depart slightly from convention in order to save on notation. When we introduce a time index on goods and interpret the new decentralization, prices of goods tomorrow will be stated in terms of some normalization (typically today's numeraire). Thus, these prices are to be interpreted as present-value prices, prices that would prevail on appropriate futures markets. Now, although these markets rarely exist, we saw in Chapter 3 that the same market outcomes can be achieved by a combination of (1) spot markets at all dates and (2) a one-period asset for transferring (numeraire) wealth from period to period.

Since this combination generally does exist, we want to work in that framework. Thus, we need notation for spot prices and an interest rate for the one-period asset. We will use the *same* notation (with an *s* subscript) for spot prices (at date *s*) as was used in the static model and will reserve *r* for interest rates.

Our extension naturally treats time as a discrete variable (so that *s* just becomes another index on commodity vectors). However, time is a continuum, and some would argue that any choice of period is arbitrary. We do not take the associated debate very seriously since either a discrete or a continuous representation would have to be thought of as an abstraction as applied to market institutions. We want to choose the one that is

---

[6] Precise statements and proofs of these results are found in Debreu (1976). For a discussion of the relevant background mathematics and some extensions to other problems in economics, see Balasko (1978) and Dierker (1982).

most useful for analyzing a relevant class of problems. Unfortunately, there are conflicting criteria in this regard. The continuous representation allows use of very powerful mathematical techniques, but they only prove helpful when we make some quite restrictive assumptions concerning additive separability over time. Consequently, we will carry along both representations in much of what follows.

A   *Households*

Intertemporal structure raises several important questions concerning the nature of budget constraints. These questions arise with respect to both individual and governmental budgets, when the relevant time horizon is unbounded. We discuss individual budgets here and take up the relevant issues for the government in the next chapter, on government budgeting.

As we know, complete markets in the intertemporal context requires spot and asset markets at each date, on all of which individuals must be able to trade freely. For the asset markets, this means that agents must be able to borrow and lend as much as they like at the going interest rate (subject only to being able to discharge their obligations eventually). This assumption of "perfect capital markets" is less palatable than the corresponding assumption of completeness in the static model, but we will stick with it for a while. As argued informally in Chapter 3, the presence of these markets implies that the sequence of period-by-period consumer budget constraints collapses in effect to a single constraint on the present value of transactions. However, our reasoning there was implicitly restricted to the case of *finite-time* horizons, so it is worth delineating the precise relationships more carefully.

At date s, a representative consumer will enter with a net asset balance, which we denote B_s (this may be positive or negative). He will earn (or pay) interest during the period at the rate r_s on these balances. In addition, he may receive some exogenous income (m_s) and will make net purchases on spot markets that will cost $P_s c_s$. (We think for the moment of all taxes being lump sum and so appearing in the m terms rather than affecting transactions prices.) Thus, the budget constraint at date s takes the form

$$B_{s+1} = (1+r_s)B_s + m_s - P_s c_s. \tag{6.1}$$

Should we choose to work in continuous time, it is easy to see that this constraint would take the alternate form:

$$\dot{B}_s = r_s B_s + m_s - P_s c_s, \tag{6.2}$$

where a dot over a variable indicates time derivative. Now, assuming that the B variables are not subject to any constraints aside from (6.1) or

(6.2), we can substitute these equations recursively (alternatively, integrate) to obtain corresponding present-value constraints:

$$\sum_{s=0}^{S} \frac{P_s c_s - m_s}{\prod_{x=0}^{s}(1+r_x)} = B_0 - \frac{B_S}{\prod_{x=0}^{S}(1+r_x)} \tag{6.3}$$

$$\int_{s=0}^{S}\left[(P_s c_s - m_s)\exp\left(-\int_{0}^{s}r_x\,dx\right)\right]ds = B_0 - B_S \exp\left(-\int_{0}^{S}r_x\,dx\right), \tag{6.4}$$

where date 0 is taken to be the present and date S is some terminal date in the future, to be discussed.

Suppose that our representative household is born in date 0 and lives a nonstochastic fixed lifetime of length S. Then, the effective budget constraint on such a household is properly represented by (6.3) or (6.4), with B_0 interpreted as bequests from parents (or other sources) and B_S as bequests to children or other sources. When individuals constitute the family unit, our model will consist of a large collection of households with lifetimes overlapping in time. Under that view, it is reasonable to impose the constraints that all bequests be nonnegative (one cannot expect to die with outstanding debts). Indeed, the reader should see that these nonnegativity requirements constitute the *only* effective constraint on household behavior. We refer to the model just outlined as the *overlapping-generations* model.

Alternatively, it has been suggested that the appropriate family unit is an "extended family" consisting of an individual *together* with all his descendants. This approach is appropriate if one believes that the family as a whole acts as a single optimizing unit utilizing a utility function that already aggregates the preferences of all members. (Note that intermarriage of families cannot be handled easily by this view, a fact to which we will return later.) Now B_S refers to an internal saving decision for the family and could perfectly well be negative. Consequently, given our remarks in the previous paragraph, a question arises as to what effectively constrains family behavior. Of course, if there is a finite-time horizon for the family as a whole, a nonnegative final bequest will provide this constraint. But since no armageddon is entirely convincing, we would like to be able to treat the horizon as unbounded.

The puzzle and its solution can best be seen by considering the possibility of a so-called Ponzi game. Suppose each parent borrows money, committing the children to paying it back; but when the debt comes due, a child simply borrows more under the same type of arrangement. Assuming that they can keep this up indefinitely, there is no effective constraint on the resources available to the family at the outset. But note that, in order to keep it going, the family debt must grow at least as fast as the rate of interest (interest plus principle must be borrowed at each successive stage). Assuming that we can put *any* finite uniform bound on the size of family debt, the scheme falls apart. Indeed, suppose we impose such a bound (which seems quite reasonable) and take limits on both sides of (6.3) as S goes to infinity. Given that B_S is uniformly bounded, the last term on the right side is forced to zero, assuming only that interest rates are uniformly bounded away from zero. Thus, we arrive at the effective constraint

$$\sum_{s=0}^{\infty} \frac{P_s c_s - m_s}{\prod_{x=0}^{s} (1+r_x)} = B_0. \tag{6.5}$$

The model in which a finite number of extended families coexist, each subject to a constraint of the form (6.5), will be referred to as the *dynasty* model. Clearly, there is room for a whole range of models "between" the pure overlapping-generations model and the pure dynasty model; we can have some intergenerational altruism without having fully consistent intergenerational preferences (such models would be natural for dealing with interfamily marriage). As we shall see, a number of controversies in the theory of public finance turn on which among these alternative views is correct.

B   *Firms*

When we discussed the decentralization of production in Chapter 3, little was said about financial arrangements. In the static model, the firm simply paid out its profit in fixed proportions to an exogenously specified set of owners. In the dynamic complete-markets model the firm used bond and/or Arrow security markets to convert its present value to similar once-and-for-all payments. However, this story is really unsatisfactory since we would like to allow ownership of firms to change over time. Also, we want to be able to address some issues in corporate tax policy that depend critically on the financial structure of the firm.

Therefore, we outline a model of the firm here that emphasizes the connections between real decisions and financial structure. We will argue that in the absence of differential tax treatment of the firm's financial instruments, the financial structure of the firm ought to be irrelevant to real decisions, so that the story told in Chapter 3 still applies. The analysis will be carried out here for a certainty world and extended to a general incomplete-markets framework in Chapter 12.

To simplify somewhat, we will focus on firms with a finite "lifetime" and assume that the interest rate on bonds is constant through time. Firms can finance through equity and/or debt. Let M_s^j and A_s^j be shares and debt of firm j at date s. The following discussion focuses on a particular firm and drops the superscript j. Shares sell at price v_s and pay a flow dividend (in numeraire units) at rate d_s per share. Since all assets must be perfect substitutes for one another, equity must pay the same instantaneous rate of return (in continuous time) as bonds; that is,

$$\frac{\dot{v}_s}{v_s} + \frac{d_s}{v_s} = r, \quad \text{all } s. \tag{6.6}$$

Financial decisions consist of net share and debt issue and a dividend rate. Thus, the cash flow constraint of the firm takes the form

$$v_s \dot{M}_s + \dot{A}_s + Q_s y_s = r A_s + d_s M_s. \tag{6.7}$$

Define the value of the firm to be $\pi_s = v_s M_s + A_s$ (we will see that this definition is consistent with earlier usage momentarily). Then, without saying anything about the behavior of the firm, we can obtain the following differential equation for π by substituting (6.6) into (6.7) and rearranging:

$$\dot{\pi}_s - r \pi_s = -Q_s y_s. \tag{6.8}$$

Assuming that all financial choice variables are unconstrained in sign, we can integrate this equation to determine the value of the firm just as we integrated the consumer cash flow constraint to determine wealth. Letting S represent the lifetime of the firm, we find

$$\pi_t = \int_{s=t}^{S} Q_s y_s e^{-r(s-t)} ds + \pi_S e^{-r(S-t)}. \tag{6.9}$$

Since the firm liquidates by date S, $\pi_S = 0$, and its value in date t must be simply its discounted *real* present value. Further, given that everyone knows the equity will pay rate of return r, current owners care only about the current value of equity (v_t). Therefore, if the firm is acting in the interest of its shareholders, it will choose its production plan to maximize discounted present value (thus maximizing $v_t M_t + A_t$); and it seems that owners are completely indifferent as to the financial structure of the firm (financial structure has no effect on share price given the real production decisions).

We can gain further insight into "financial irrelevance" by examining dividend policy specifically. Some have argued that the firm must pay dividends (at least eventually) if its equity is to have any value.[7] The argument for this position can best be appreciated by returning to the asset-pricing equation (6.6). Since it has the same form as (6.8), it integrates in

---

[7] See King (1977, 1983) for detailed versions of this argument.

the same way to determine a relationship between share prices and dividend streams:

$$v_t = \int_{s=t}^{S} d_s e^{-r(s-t)} \, ds + v_S e^{-r(S-t)}. \tag{6.10}$$

Now if the shares become valueless at liquidation, it appears that share price must indeed equal the discounted value of dividends. However, this position is incorrect as long as the firm can repurchase its shares (so that there is no sign constraint on $\dot{M}$). As long as all shares are ultimately repurchased, the terminal asset price will be the final transaction price and need not be zero. The firm can choose to pay out its value through any combination of dividends and share repurchase. And we have seen that the effect on current share value will be the same no matter how this is done as long as the firm maximizes real present value and fully liquidates in the end.

Of course, if the firm is legally restricted from share repurchase, it cannot avoid payment of dividends completely, although it could still wait until the end and make a once-and-for-all liquidation payment.[8] Another important requirement for irrelevance is that owners not care whether they receive the value of the firm through dividends or through capital gains when they sell their shares back. Obviously, owners will no longer be indifferent if they are taxed differently on these two types of income; once differential taxation is allowed, financial policy takes on new interest.

6.3   Uncertainty and missing markets

Too much of economics, and especially public finance, is discussed in a context of "certainty." We say this because it is obvious that almost every real economic decision involves some important unknown consequences. Perhaps one can argue that the static certainty model is useful as a building block of analysis, but it is hard to imagine a useful dynamic model that ignores uncertainty. For example, think about the budget constraint (6.5). Recall that it corresponds to an institutional setting in which there are spot markets and loan markets at each date. Further, it is an operational constraint *only* if spot prices (and interest rates) for *future* dates are known for certain *today*, a situation that seems hard to imagine in reality.

We take the state-of-the-world approach to modeling uncertainty. We assume that the state space can be represented as a subset of the continuum.

---

[8] Although the Internal Revenue Service does have rules against a regular continuing policy of share repurchase, it does not seem to have been very effective in preventing this method of payout.

At times, we may want to think of the subset as "proper," as for example, in the Arrow–Debreu model, where the number of states is treated as finite. Let ω be the state of the world; thus, once ω is revealed, all uncertainty is fully resolved. Outcomes are represented as *random variables*: functions from ω to relevant consequences.

Of course, we saw in Chapter 3 that it is possible in principle to extend our market decentralization so as to deal with uncertainty. However, the required market structure would need to include at the very least a separate asset market for each state of the world. And since any particular state of the world is quite unlikely to occur, no one would be willing to devote any resources to running (or participating in) such a contingent security market. Generally, economists tend to ignore the costs of running markets on the implicit assumption that these would be worth incurring to get the associated allocation benefits. But this position seems absurd here, so any reasonable model of the mixed economy under uncertainty must incorporate an "incomplete" market structure.

Once we accept the inherent incompleteness of markets, several new modeling issues need to be addressed. For one thing, we need to think again about the sequencing of decisions. When markets are complete, we argued that all market decisions are effectively made at the outset: Since all contingencies can be planned for at that time, there is no need for recontracting at later dates. However, once the market structure is incomplete, recontracting is likely to be desirable, and we must consider a *sequential* market structure. For example, suppose that today's trading opportunities include some futures markets but no *contingent* futures markets. A farmer is likely to want to sell some of his crop on these markets even though he does not yet know the extent of the harvest (state of the world). But, when the state is revealed, he will want a new (spot) market to open so that he can sell more or buy up a shortfall depending on his ex post circumstance.

Consequently, we want to deal with a market structure that consists of spot markets at each date together with a limited set of assets for trading across states and dates. Real examples of these are futures markets, insurance contracts, bonds, and equity. Ideally, we would like to have the existing set of assets endogenous to the model. That is, we would have assets created when (and only when) some "market maker" found it profitable to do so. Unfortunately, however, such models are virtually intractable (due largely to the nonconvexity inherent in setup costs), and we are forced to treat the set of existing assets as exogenous in the sequel.

Following previous procedures, we want to take as given the market equilibrium on these markets as a function of public-choice parameters. Thus, we summarize briefly what is known about the existence of such equilibria. One might hope that our sequential model would have similar equilibrium properties to the complete model. Since sequential markets allow trade within some subspace of the "contingent commodity" space, as long as we stay inside a given subspace, the model must behave like our static prototype.

Unfortunately, however, the spanned subspace depends on what prices happen to prevail. Suppose, for example, that there are two states and two goods, and the market structure consists of spot and futures markets only. As long as the second-period spot prices differ from one another in the two states of the world, the futures markets can be used to construct a pair of "Arrow securities," each of which pays a dollar in one of the two states of the world and nothing in the other. (To construct an Arrow security for state 1, buy forward the good that will be relatively more valuable in state 1 and sell just enough of the other good forward to come out even in state 2.) Clearly, in this case, markets are effectively complete and we span the whole space. However, should it happen that the spot prices are *identical* in the two states, futures markets are useless for trading across states, and a much smaller subspace is spanned.

Problems arise for existence (and efficiency properties) of equilibria when economic forces push us toward prices for which the spanned subspace collapses discontinuously (leading to discontinuities in supply and/or demand functions).[9] How serious are these problems for us? Well, fortunately not really any more serious than some of the difficulties we have already disposed of. "Unpleasant" examples involve a "knife-edge" feature. It just happens that equilibrium in the large space involves exactly the wrong prices for sustainability using the proposed assets. Such an event seems unlikely in an economy drawn at "random" from the set of all possible economies. Fortunately, this line of reasoning can be made precise; well behaved equilibria are "generic" here in the same sense that local smoothness of equilibria is generic in the static model.[10]

Consequently, study of changes in private-sector equilibrium as functions of public decisions generally will be valid in the sequence economy. Unfortunately, however, the required scope of public decision making may become quite large in that context, as we will see in Chapters 12 and 16.

Incompleteness in the market structure forces us to address one further issue concerning the nature of expectations and the welfare aggregation. When markets are complete, the nature of expectation formation is unimportant since each contingency can be planned for independently, and

---

[9] Detailed examples are given by Hart (1975). Similar examples are presented for situations involving differential information by Kreps (1977).

[10] A general discussion of these types of results together with further references can be found in Radner (1982) and Duffie (1986).

the relative price of contingent securities reveals all an agent needs to know about the relative likelihood of events. However, without such information, it will matter a great deal how individuals aggregate their preferences across the set of possible states. For the most part, we assume that individuals have identical probabilistic beliefs and are expected-utility maximizers. In particular, there is a mutually agreed-upon probability distribution on ω, and each individual evaluates ex ante well-being by first evaluating utility of a certain outcome conditional on being in state ω and then computing expected utility using this distribution.[11] We will allow ex post utilities to be state dependent.

Social preference now takes as inputs *expected* utilities and makes interpersonal comparisons to generate a social welfare function:

$$W = W(E_\omega V^1, \ldots, E_\omega V^N). \tag{6.11}$$

Although we do not want to spend space on a detailed justification of our formulation here, we mention briefly some possible alternatives. For example, the planner might aggregate ex post preferences and *then* take expectations. We reject this approach on the grounds that there is no point in trying to make interpersonal comparisons ex post given that individual well-being must be considered ex ante. Indeed, a reasonable extension of the concept of consumer sovereignty would have it that any two situations involving equal ex ante utilities for all agents ought to be considered socially indifferent. But this stipulation leads directly to the formulation (6.11).

Of course, we would feel uneasy accepting ex ante utilities if some individuals had incorrect expectations and we knew it. In that case there would be a strong temptation to introduce some element of paternalism. It is partly for this reason that we assumed identical expectations (otherwise, someone has to be wrong). Although not essential, we probably want to think of these beliefs as being correct.

There is a deeper question of whether individuals have probabilistic beliefs at all. If they do not, we lose all of the structure inherent in probability spaces and must fall back on the so-called state preference approach; individuals form ex ante utility by aggregating across consumption vectors in various states of the world, just as they would aggregate across different types of consumption in the static model. (Note that these functions can be well defined without any reference to probabilities.) Some of the results discussed in later chapters have analogs in the more general state preference model, and we will point these out as we go along.

---

[11] Canonical versions of the expected utility theory may be found in Savage (1954), Raiffa–Schlaifer (1961), and Fishburn (1970). Those who have recently questioned the empirical validity of the expected-utility hypothesis include Kahneman–Tversky (1979) and Machina (1983).

CHAPTER 7

Government budgeting and fiscal decentralization

To this point, our conception of the mixed economy has treated the public sector as monolithic. However, we observe a considerable degree of government decentralization in practice, and indeed, we would expect to find some such structures in a second-best organizational design for much the same reasons we argued for market decentralization of private goods earlier. Here, we will develop a model of government structure that is roughly consistent with the actual organization of the U.S. public sector. We will emphasize normative properties of this structure, drawing on earlier discussions of political decentralization and mechanism design.

One possible approach to public-sector design would be to mimic closely the structure of market decentralization. That is, we could divide up responsibilities into a large collection of fully autonomous agencies, each of which would be responsible for the allocation of a narrow range of collective goods. Autonomy would be achieved by having each individual agency elicit information on preferences and assess separate taxes and/or user charges. To the extent that "true" information is learned, it can be used to organize finance according to the so-called *benefits principle* – household payments for the collective goods and services would be directly related to benefits received.

This mode of organization has many desirable features. First and foremost, it eliminates entirely the need for centralized information gathering and the associated cost of bureaucracy needed to administer and coordinate activities. Further, to the extent that the finance tax can be made a charge for services rendered, it will act like a price that will induce the relevant clientele to reveal their preferences. Thus, we see that full decentralization is particularly appropriate for the class of goods that we analyzed in the club models of Chapters 4 and 5.

However, there are strong arguments against extending this degree of autonomy to cover all activities of the government. These involve both distributional and efficiency considerations. First, it is clear that finance on the benefits principle involves adherence to the Pareto improvement rule and therefore fails to achieve any redistributional aims. Unless we feel comfortable with the status quo distribution, some "meta-agency" is going to be required for organizing appropriate redistributions. Second, separate finance arrangements lose much of their appeal when we turn to the class of pure public goods. For one thing, it is no longer desirable to use the taxes as an allocation price, as we saw earlier. And within the class of nonexcludable goods at least, there will be substantial duplication of effort on the finance side since each agency will be collecting from roughly the same group of households. It seems obvious that there would be some (perhaps substantial) administrative cost saving from centralizing financing operations in a single agency. The "redistribution" agency seems to be a natural for this purpose.

Let us consider for the moment the opposite extreme in this regard: a single agency handling all financing and redistributive payments. Assuming this operation is successful, each agency could proceed with project selection taking as given the methods of finance and the extent of redistribution. We would, however, require a new "budget" bureau to parcel out net revenue among the various agencies. This bureau will need to engage in substantial coordination and communication with agencies and their constituencies in order to know the correct priorities. The institutional arrangements just outlined conform in a stylized way to the structure of the U.S. federal government, although neither the revenue bureau (IRS) nor the budget bureau (OMB) have quite the monopoly power described. (Congress and the Treasury play major roles in both arenas.) Further, we engage in some fiscal decentralization of both functions below the federal level, where it may be argued that the advantages of autonomy are more compelling.

We take up general issues involving government budgeting in the remainder of this chapter. For pedagogical convenience, we conduct the discussion in a context where lump-sum (nondistortionary) tax instruments are available, deferring issues of optimal "indirect" finance to the next chapter.

7.1 Unified government budget

Let us think for the moment of the revenue department as monolithic in that all public activities are to be financed out of the same general revenue fund. Then we can talk about a unified government budget that defines the overall constraints on government spending. We begin to discuss the nature of these constraints by looking at the issue of tax versus debt finance. Since our concern for the moment is with macroconstraints, we will discuss the budget in terms of numeraire aggregates.

How should the revenue agency choose the mix between tax and debt finance, and how will its choices affect the options available to the budget agency? Since the government can be thought of as a comprehensive dynasty, we can draw on our discussion of the dynasty model in the last chapter to answer these questions. The government "cash flow" constraint at a particular instant (in continuous time) takes the form

$$\dot{D}_s = r_s D_s + \Gamma_s - T_s, \tag{7.1}$$

where D is aggregate level of government debt, Γ is aggregate net cost of government purchases, and T is aggregate net tax receipts. Since D is a free-choice variable to the government, we can integrate just as we did the corresponding constraint for the household in the previous chapter to obtain an aggregate present-value constraint on the profile of government expenditure over time:

$$\int_{s=t}^{S} \left[(T_s - \Gamma_s) \exp\left(-\int_t^s r_x \, dx \right) \right] ds = D_t - D_S \exp\left(-\int_t^S r_x \, dx \right). \tag{7.2}$$

There is a useful interpretation of this relationship in terms of the concept of "unfunded liability." Suppose the government has projected tax and spending programs forward $S - t$ periods into the future (from date t). If receipts are going to fall short of proposed expenditures, the difference can be thought of as an implicit (or unfunded) liability of the system. And if the government actually follows through on the plan, this liability will show up as outstanding government debt as of date S. Thus, we can interpret the government budget constraint as requiring that any unfunded liability must be backed up by debt "when the time comes."

We now ask whether and how the government should use debt policy in financing its operations. Let us ask first whether the cost of government can be effectively lowered through the use of debt. Can the government effectively reduce the taxes it needs to collect through the substitution of debt? If so, we are clearly all better off since the act of lending is a voluntary one that cannot worsen individual welfare, whereas the corresponding taxation clearly does.

The simplest way in which the government can substitute debt for taxes is to (1) tax less now, (2) borrow to make up the difference, and (3) tax more later to pay off the debt when it comes due. This procedure changes the structure of tax payments but does not change the net present value of tax collections since the discounted present value of necessary future tax payments must exactly match the initial tax savings. The operation may still have real effects on the economy, as we will see later. But for now we are after bigger game: Can debt be used to reduce the discounted present value of tax collections?

Suppose the government "rolls over" the debt when it comes due and thereafter always borrows to pay off any maturing debt plus interest. Can the government play a successful Ponzi game along these lines? As we saw in the previous chapter, the size of the debt must grow at the rate of interest for such a scheme to work. But although such indefinite growth seems inconceivable for a household, it is not so absurd for the government; after all, the public debt is only a collective obligation to pay ourselves individually so there is no obvious reason why it ought to be limited in size. The real issue now becomes one of feasibility. Is it possible for the government to maintain an appropriately growing debt forever?

There is one important situation where the scheme may well be feasible, namely, when the prevailing interest rates are less on balance than the prevailing growth rates. In this case, the outstanding debt from our Ponzi scheme becomes smaller (or at least no larger) relative to the size of the economy as time passes, so the necessary borrowing may well be possible without upsetting the underlying equilibrium. When it does work, the scheme actually does get us "something for nothing." We get the same government spending with a lower net tax obligation; the debt itself has no effect on welfare since all activity on the loan market is voluntary.

The reader may well be suspicious at this point, particularly if he has been taught about the impossibility of a free lunch. Indeed, just where is this free lunch coming from? To answer, we must review what we know about dynamic inefficiency. Any inefficiency can generate a free lunch if only it can be corrected at no administrative cost (indeed, politicians promise us this palliative every day!). Here, the relevant inefficiency involves overinvestment; when interest rates are consistently below growth rates, we can "eat" some of our capital and still produce at least as much per person in perpetuity.[1] Our Ponzi game performs this operation in effect: Assuming that interest rates do not change (and private saving is less than perfectly elastic), the initial borrowing must displace private investment and subsequent borrowing guarantees that the displacement is permanent. We do not have to "pay" anything for this displacement in the dynamically inefficient world, so it clearly is desirable. The government should play more and bigger Ponzi games as long as the economy remains dynamically inefficient.[2]

Of course, there must be some limit to the size of the Ponzi game since there is a limit to the size of the associated dynamic inefficiency. As the government attempts to borrow larger and larger amounts, eventually we will observe upward pressure on the interest rates. And should they come to exceed the growth rate, the Ponzi scheme suddenly becomes nonviable.

---

[1] This argument is best known in the context of the Solow (1956) and Diamond (1965) one-sector model. However, the principle is known to hold quite generally. See Starrett (1970), Cass (1972), and Mitra (1979).
[2] Of course, private agents could play the same role if they were infinitely lived and similarly unconstrained in borrowing. See Burbridge (1983) for an example of this sort.

To see this, suppose we start in a situation where interest rates generally exceed the growth rate. Now any Ponzi debt growing at the rate of interest must become arbitrarily large relative to the size of the rest of the economy; at some point it will be impossible to get the public to hold this debt at any finite interest rate, and the economy breaks down. Since this will be anticipated (in our present world of certainty), the government will not be able to borrow anything without an implicit agreement to retire the debt through use of taxes at some time in the future.[3]

This line of reasoning can be formalized as follows: Let ξ_s be the instantaneous growth rate at date s. Then we propose as a minimal constraint on the government a *uniform* bound (through time) on the size of the public debt relative to the size of the economy. If A is the size of the economy at date t, its size at date S is $A \exp(\int_t^S \xi_s \, ds)$. Therefore, our new constraint may be stated as

$$\limsup_{S \to \infty} D_S \exp\left(-\int_t^S \xi_s \, ds\right) < \infty. \tag{7.3}$$

Assuming (as we are now) that the interest rates are uniformly bounded above the growth rates, (7.3) implies

$$\limsup_{S \to \infty} D_S \exp\left(-\int_t^S r_s \, ds\right) = 0. \tag{7.4}$$

But returning attention to (7.2), we see that (7.4) will serve to effectively constrain government spending. Indeed, if S increases without bound, the last term on the right side of (7.2) must vanish, leading to the present-value constraint

$$\int_{s=t}^{\infty} \left[(T_s - \Gamma_s) \exp\left(-\int_t^s r_x \, dx\right) \right] ds = D_t. \tag{7.5}$$

Note carefully what has happened. Aside from the initial level of debt, all reference to debt policy has disappeared completely from the effective constraint. The present value of future tax collections must exactly cover the present value of planned expenditures *together* with any outstanding obligations. Or, stated another way, it is impossible for the government to maintain an unfunded liability into the indefinite future.

We see that in the dynamically efficient world, the government has *no* chance of replacing tax finance with debt finance. Debt can be used to create differences in the pattern of taxes versus expenditures, but that is all. Thus, our unified budget department is effectively constrained on the

---

[3] The preceding arguments have been reasonably well understood for the dynamically efficient case for some time. See, e.g., Ferguson (1964) or Barro (1974). See Tirole (1985) for a concise recent treatment of both cases.

present value of its expenditures. The upper bound on these is the present value of all tax collections, and the revenue department will engage in debt finance only to facilitate desired discrepancies in the two time profiles.

7.2 Impact of intergenerational (and other) governmental transfers

We will assume in most of the sequel that our world is dynamically efficient. We cannot assess the empirical evidence for this assumption until we incorporate uncertainty and risk premiums into our story. But from a purely theoretical point of view, there is not much point to further discussion of the dynamically inefficient case: A free lunch is available, and the government ought to provide it – end of story.

We argued in the previous section that even in the dynamically efficient case, there is still a role for debt finance in changing the time profile of payments. But some would argue that this role too is irrelevant.[4] To adjudicate this issue, let us examine the sense in which use of debt alters the "true incidence" of government cost.

When our government budget constraint takes the form (7.5), the public debt D_t appears to impose a burden on the future; taxes must be collected from future generations to retire this debt *in addition* to any taxes that pay for their public services. Thus, at least in a statutory sense, some of the cost of government is being transferred to the future. But that still does not guarantee that some of the real economic cost is so transferred, and it is here that the distinction between the overlapping-generations and dynasty models becomes crucial.

Suppose (as a point of reference) that the government had no debt at date zero and ask what difference the debt level at date t will make on who pays. Consider the dynasty model in which a typical family is alive at both dates. Recall that (in that model) a "sufficient statistic" for family tax liability is the present value of taxes paid; such a family does not care whether it pays taxes now or later as long as the present value nets out the same. Thus, government debt policy is irrelevant: There is no need for the family to change the size or timing of desired consumption; if the government chooses to defer the tax liability ($D_t > 0$), our family will simply "undo" the effects by saving an equal amount to pay off the future tax liability.

---

[4] The basic argument for irrelevance goes back to David Ricardo (and is sometimes referred to as "Ricardian equivalence"). It was popularized and extended by Barro (1974); see Bernheim–Bagwell (1986) for further extensions and criticism.

Similarly, the government cannot transfer any of the burden of future spending to the present as long as families are free to borrow against the future. Of course, the argument does require perfect capital markets and (in the latter case) possibly the ability to leave debts to one's heirs. Whenever the government has more effective access to capital markets than the private sector, we should expect government debt to have real effects.

Even if capital markets are perfect, government debt can transfer the effective burden of government spending to future generations in the overlapping-generations model. As soon as the household bequest is "untied" from future family tax liabilities, transferring taxes to future generations also transfers the effective burden. Now a switch from tax to debt finance makes the present group of households strictly better off (they pay less and do not care about the fact that later generations will have to pay more) and may well have real economic implications for such things as the degree of capital formation or the level of economic activity, depending on specific characteristics of the economic environment.

The reader should see that similar reasoning and conclusions will hold with respect to any government transfer policy. Whenever the agents involved are part of a single optimizing unit with access to the same transfer trade-offs as the government, public transfer policy will be neutral. So, for example, we can conclude that "pay-as-you-go" social security will have no effect on private saving in the dynasty model. Taxing the young will cause that group to save less, but the old will always compensate by leaving larger bequests (saving more). Of course, when the bequest link is absent (as in the pure overlapping-generations model), we instead expect to find that pay-as-you-go social security would lower private saving.

An important question arises concerning the redistributive properties of transfers in models where links exist between the relevant agents (through bequests, gifts, donations to a common charity, and the like) even though we do not observe full interpersonal optimization. Complete analysis of such a model would take us outside the framework of this book, so we confine ourselves to a brief informal discussion. As long as families are linked through donations, gifts, or any other direct transfers that are freely variable at the margin, our previous arguments will guarantee that the set of consumption patterns achievable to the group depend only on the present value of their aggregate tax obligation. Consequently, government debt (or other transfer) policy will not change the set of consumption plans available to the group.

Now, suppose that agents care about the transfers they make only as these affect the consumption levels within the group (bequests are valued *only* for the future consumption they enable). Then, even if agents have different preferences on the pattern of consumptions they would like to see, the Nash equilibrium outcome under one transfer policy remains an equilibrium under any alternative transfer policy: If each person expects others to make the appropriate compensating transfer payments, he will see his opportunity set (defined on consumption vectors for the group) unchanged and will choose the same consumption as before by leaving his own appropriate transfers.[5] To see this point, think, about the following example: The government seeks to transfer income from Mr. Smith to Ms. Jones, both of whom make positive contributions to a common charity. Suppose that (after the transfer is made) Smith decides to lower his charitable contribution by the same amount as the lost income (leaving him with the same private consumption as before). Then Jones will see that her opportunity set, defined on own private consumption and the "size" of the public charity, is exactly the same as it was before the transfer (she has more but the charity has correspondingly less). Thus, if these levels are what she cares about, she will achieve her previous optimal mix by giving the extra income to charity. But if this policy for Jones is anticipated by Smith, similar reasoning will lead him in fact to contribute less. These policies are therefore self-confirming in the Nash sense, and the transfer policy is ineffective.

Of course, these "neutrality" conclusions will change if the transfer links are broken. If members of the current generation are not planning to give positive bequests to their children (and are prevented from giving negative ones), debt policy will transfer the real cost of government to future taxpayers.[6] In the previous example, if Smith never planned to contribute to charity anyway, he will not be in a position to contribute less when his income falls so that his net position will have to worsen and the transfer has a real effect. The same conclusion may hold when the links are present if people care about the transfers per se rather than simply for the consumption they facilitate. To see why, think about the example in this circumstance. If Smith cares about the size of his own contribution rather than the size of the overall charity, he will not want to lower his contribution by the full amount of his lost income even if he expects Jones to contribute that amount more. Indeed, we expect the income transfer policy to have a negative impact on the utility level of Smith.

We conclude that public debt and other government transfer policies have a redistributive role only to the extent that the relevant group of

---

5 These arguments are formalized by Bernheim–Bagwell (1986), who argue further that *all* lump-sum transfer programs of the government will be rendered impotent when linkages are active. They suggest as a consequence that models with too many active linkages are not very realistic.
6 See Bergstrom–Blume–Varian (1986) for some results when constraints on linked variables are binding.

agents are not actively linked as described in the preceding discussion. The nature and efficacy of such links clearly becomes quite important in determining public policy. However, regardless of how one comes out on these issues, we will see momentarily that public debt is a very valuable government instrument for quite different reasons.

7.3   Capital account for government

There is at least one further reason why the level of government debt may give a misleading picture of effective burden. Suppose accumulated debt had been used to finance public investment, the payoff from which is going to accrue to households of the future; surely we would want to say that there is less of a burden than if the debt had been used to finance a potlatch in the past. Indeed, the effective burden ought to involve canceling discounted future benefits from public investments against the outstanding debt. Of course, to make this concept operational, we would need a capital account for the government.

Partly for reasons just outlined, economists have been calling for a separate capital account in the government budget. We outline here a very aggregated version of these accounts and comment on the associated "effective deficit." The version is aggregated in that we assume the flow of services from government capital can be measured in the same numeraire units as other government consumption. Then, it seems natural to define *net public liability* (call it N) as the outstanding financial debt minus the present value of future public benefits from investment.

Assuming that we can measure the flow of services from public investment (admittedly a tall order in some cases), we can set up an accounting system that incorporates the effective deficit. The differential equation governing current account is unchanged except that we must divide government expenditures between consumption C^g and investment I^g:

$$\dot{D} = rD + C^g + I^g - T. \tag{7.6}$$

(We will sometimes suppress the time index in flow equations for notational convenience.) Although the government capital stock may be difficult to measure directly, there is a natural way to define it given that we can quantify the flow of services from investment (C^{kg}); namely, we define K^g to be the amount by which the discounted future flow of services exceeds the discounted future investment expenditures. Thus,

$$K_t^g = \int_{s=t}^{\infty} (C_s^{kg} - I_s^g) \exp\left(-\int_t^s r_x \, dx\right) ds. \tag{7.7}$$

Differentiating (7.7) with respect to time yields the following flow equation for capital account:

$$\dot{K}^g = rK^g + I^g - C^{kg}. \tag{7.8}$$

Finally, we can merge the two accounts to obtain the following flow and stock-accounting equations for the net public liability $(N = D - K)$:

$$\dot{N} = rN + C^g + C^{kg} - T, \tag{7.9}$$

$$N_t = \int_{s=t}^{\infty} [T_s - C_s^g - C_s^{kg}] \exp\left(-\int_t^s r_x \, dx\right) ds. \tag{7.10}$$

Comparing (7.9) with (7.6), we see that the effective deficit will equal the current-account deficit only if the government is investing at exactly the same rate as it is consuming capital services. By contrast, if we are not investing at all (and using the current-account deficit to finance a potlatch), the effective deficit is correspondingly larger. On the other hand, the effective deficit could be much smaller if the government is using deficit finance to build up capital. Clearly, the effective burden on the future (to the extent that there is one) cannot be determined in the absence of a systematic capital account. While admitting that there are formidable problems involved in correct measurement of capital services, we believe that some effort should be made to provide such an accounting.

7.4   Problems in budget coordination

Once we centralize the revenue functions, the budget bureau must play a key role as intermediary between the project-producing agencies and the revenue bureau. This bureau will face many of the information-processing problems we identified with centralization in Chapters 2 and 3. Agencies will be submitting a myriad of projects for consideration, and an enormous amount of information is required in order to assess their relative merits.

   Indeed, even if the bureau does not attempt to optimize, it will face formidable feasibility problems. Most programs involve ongoing spending in order to be effective (think of defense contracts or the space program). Hence, in any given year many of these expenditures involve precommitments from the past. Further, a large fraction of activities are best set up in terms of schedules rather than fixed-payment totals. For example, the income tax, unemployment compensation, social security payments, and medicare benefits all involve graduated schedules. Consequently, actual payments from these programs in a given year are "uncontrollable"; they will depend on factors such as the state of the economy, fluctuations in health costs, retirements, and the like.[7]

We conclude that there are pragmatic reasons why the budget bureau should take a long-term approach to the budget. Not only is balancing the budget at each date unnecessary, but it is virtually impossible. Debt is the only instrument flexible enough to smooth out the year-to-year variations in program requirements. We believe that even the most dogmatic advocates of balanced budgets should recognize this role for public debt. Indeed, our view of responsible debt management would be this: The government must maintain confidence that it is ready, willing, and able to raise future taxes to pay off the public debt eventually; that is, it should guarantee that the projected schedules of receipts and expenditures do not imply unfunded liabilities into the indefinite future. To break this public trust has very serious consequences. Usually, these manifest themselves in the form of hyperinflation as people, realizing that interest rates are going through the roof, refuse to hold (non-interest-bearing) money.

Of course, we want more than just feasibility. An ideal budgeting process must make the proper choice of priorities among subagencies. Although it is possible to imagine how we might build some "economic" incentives into this activity, they appear impractical (and we know from our discussion of planning mechanisms that there are serious impediments even in theory to designing workable schemes). Consequently, we may as well accept the fact that the process will be inherently political. How well should we expect the political process to do in this regard? In particular, can we identify any likely biases in resulting decisions?

We can get some insight into these questions by referring back to our discussions of voting procedures in Chapter 2. There, it was noted that decentralized voting would lead to biases when (1) separate projects were complementary in nature or (2) benefits were more (or less) concentrated than costs. Since congressional budget decisions are made largely through a sequence of decentralized votes, we can expect some of these biases to turn up there.[8]

Although some problems undoubtedly arise from failure to account properly for complementarities, these are minimized through the grouping of related projects in a common agency. However, problems attributable to concentration are particularly likely to arise in the present context: Many projects (such as water resource development or shipbuilding

---

[7] The issue of controllability in the federal budget is discussed and analyzed by Wildavsky (1979).

[8] Of course, other distortions may arise to the extent that the government is unresponsive to the wishes of its constituency. Although some economists (notably James Buchanan) place a lot of emphasis on these distortions, we will not attempt to study them systematically.

contracts) are quite local in benefits, so if they are to be paid for out of general revenue, benefits are concentrated relative to costs for each considered separately. Consequently, in the absence of logrolling, we expect to see such projects fail when they ought to succeed. Alternatively, when there is effective logrolling, we may find a group of these projects (which collectively concentrate costs on the outsiders) pass when they ought to fail.

What can we do about this class of problems? We may want to rely on more regional decision making. And it may be possible to do so without forgoing efficient revenue collection through the use of "revenue sharing." We look next at possibilities along these lines.[9]

7.5   Fiscal federalism

The preceding discussion has brought into focus the conflicting objectives raised earlier. If we attempt to organize decision making in such a way that neither costs nor benefits are concentrated, we are driven back in the direction of local autonomy and apparently away from revenue integration. It seems that the ideal degree of centralization of public functions must be decided by weighing the relative importance of these factors on a case-by-case basis. Since most countries do operate with several "layers" of government, the topic is worth discussing for positive as well as normative reasons.

Congestible public goods seem the most likely candidates for local autonomy since it is possible and desirable to exclude and set up mutually exclusive constituencies. Let us recall briefly some principles from our discussion of such goods. We argued in Chapter 4 that each type of congestible collective good has a "natural" constituency determined by the optimal number of households in a sharing group. Thus, if the principle of autonomy were universally applied, we would find each household belonging to a number of overlapping constituencies, potentially one for each collective good. Naturally, this arrangement would be extremely cumbersome if carried out literally so we expect the number of constituency layers to be rather limited.[10] Once this compromise is made, we are going to find that some goods must be allocated by political groups that are too small and others by groups that are too large. Naturally, these mismatches will have implications for resource allocation.

There are three (sometimes four) recognizable layers in the United States: town, (county), state, and federal. Although this number may

---

9 This role for revenue sharing was developed by McLure (1971).
10 The "layer cake" model of fiscal decentralization is discussed in detail by Oates (1972).

well be about right, we should be cautious about claiming any optimality here. Many state boundaries are wrong for the purposes at hand; for example, many argue that California should be split into two common-interest groups, whereas New York City probably would be better linked with the state of New Jersey than with upstate New York. Furthermore, urban areas surely suffer from not having a metropolitan constituency, as anyone who has lived in the Massachusetts or San Francisco bay areas can attest.

A   *Spillovers and matching grants*

Whenever we choose a political unit that is smaller than the optimal constituency, it is desirable (and sometimes necessary) to allow spillovers. For example, it is efficient to allow the roads in a given state to be used by out-of-staters. Consequently, road-building decisions confer externalities (called *spillovers* in the literature on regional economics) on households outside the political unit. This fact will lead to underprovision when the externalities are positive unless we correct for externality.

We know from our discussions in Chapter 5 that externalities can be treated through the use of Pigovian taxes. Here, these taxes take the form of *matching grants*.[11] Take the example of the interstate highway system. Suppose (for expository purposes) that half the benefits of a typical state's construction accrue to outsiders and that we want to leave decision making in state hands. Then the federal government ought to match each dollar of state spending with a dollar from general revenue. Clearly, this arrangement will lead to correct state incentives, and the method will generalize to any desired sharing ratio.

Another (poorly understood) example of matching grants is the "general revenue-sharing" program of the Nixon era. Sharing was general in that no particular spending programs were encouraged, but the program was still "matching" in that payments to a state or locality were proportional to the local revenue collection. Thus, payments constituted a subsidy rate on local public spending. Of course, such a program is appropriate from an efficiency point of view only if localities tend to underprovide local public goods when left alone. We will look at the arguments for and against this position in Chapter 11.

Although matching grants can be used in principle to handle all situations with "undersized" constituencies, there are severe limitations to their usefulness in practice due to information requirements and associated

[11] Wilde (1971) discusses allocation effects of matching grants (and other forms of revenue sharing) in more detail than we consider here.

bargaining problems. For example, consider the problem of deciding on a bridge access route. The access route can go through any of three communities; each community wants the bridge but also wants access through one of the other communities. We can imagine the state setting up a system of compensatory payments that could generate the correct decisions, but unfortunately communities are likely to recognize that they have some monopoly power over the "prices" (the true externality costs are not easily identified by the state). If so, the process will reduce to a bargaining problem that may or may not lead to an efficient outcome. Any effective solution here probably is tantamount to having a metropolitan authority coordinate the information directly.

B   *Unconditional revenue sharing*

The other type of fiscal mismatch occurs when the optimal constituency is small relative to the decision-making unit. This is the natural situation when the decision-making unit is large to accommodate revenue integration yet many of the decisions are local in scope. Of course, we could always make a single decision at the national level and impose it on each subgroup, but this would vitiate the potential benefits of local autonomy: We want to allow diversity in local tastes to be translated into diversity in local public expenditures. So we have another mismatch problem: When a sequence of local proposals is considered in a national forum, we will face the issues of bias discussed earlier; also, it is costly to have representatives of one region become informed about all issues in other regions.

Could we possibly have the best of both worlds? Could we collect the money at the national level and transfer part of it to local authorities for disbursement? Since we are trying to encourage local autonomy in decisions, we want the transfers to be "unconditional," so we are suggesting unconditional revenue sharing. We examine briefly the potential scope for such programs.

One school of thought in the literature would have it that unconditional revenue sharing is irrelevant, and although we are denying one crucial assumption of that argument, it still serves to restrict the class of outcomes we can hope to achieve.[12] The irrelevance proposition applies in a world of rational agents who can make costless lump-sum transfers. In this circumstance, it is argued that anything the federal government can do through transferring (unconditional) money to local jurisdictions, it could do equally well by transferring the same amount of money *directly* to the local residents. After all, one cannot force localities to spend more

12 A careful analytic version of this argument was given by Bradford and Oates (1971).

than they want to; if we put too much money in the local treasury, local residents can simply lower local taxes by the excess amount. But lowering taxes by the excess amount is exactly the same outcome we get if the federal government returns some federal tax receipts to local residents. Thus, "irrelevance," and the federal government need engage in a transfer policy *only* with respect to individual households, *not* with respect to localities.

The reasoning here is identical to that involved in the neutrality results of the previous section. As long as (1) there are effective lump-sum transfer links within the local jurisdiction and (2) members of the jurisdiction care only about the level of their public and private goods, the federal government cannot expect to affect the mix of these goods through unconditional revenue sharing.

There is a contrasting opinion that revenue sharing is effective as a method of finance for local public expenditure. It is suggested that money put in the public budget will tend to be spent on local public goods, whereas money given to individuals will be spent predominantly on private goods; that is, there is a so-called *flypaper effect* – money tends to "stick where it hits." Clearly, if there is such a flypaper effect, some of the assumptions behind the neutrality model must be violated. We can predict the scope and nature of such nonneutralities in revenue sharing by identifying these violations.

Suppose we find that it is costly and time consuming to change internal transfer arrangements. Then, we would naturally expect to see a flypaper effect in the short run. However, this consideration would not generate any permanent effects (unless behavior exhibits some form of "irrational" inertia) since the jurisdiction would eventually be updating its transfer laws as a matter of course. On the other hand, long-run effects may result if local taxation is administratively (or otherwise) more costly than federal taxation. (Recall that this is the situation we had in mind when we argued for revenue integration.[13])

Although we defer most issues concerning the relative costs of various types of taxation to the next chapter, we jump ahead a little to discuss implications for revenue sharing. In practice, virtually all sources of taxation are shiftable to some degree (and are consequently not lump sum). And the degree of shiftability is particularly severe for most sources of local taxes. Local sales and income taxes may be very costly to a region if they induce business to go elsewhere. Further, the property tax is unshiftable only on the comparatively narrow base of land value, since capital improvements are quite mobile in the long run. Now, if localities reach

[13] See Courant–Gramlich–Rubenfeld (1979) and Hamilton (1983) for a more detailed discussion of arguments behind the flypaper effect.

the point where they exhaust their relatively "safe" tax base before they reach the first-best level of local public consumption, they will spend revenue-sharing funds on local public goods even though they would not be willing to raise the corresponding money through local taxes.

Thus, unconditional revenue sharing can have long-run effects to the extent that it is effective in lowering the marginal local "tax costs." However, we argue that the allocative role for such transfers is still pretty limited. For one thing, it is hard to imagine that revenue sharing could fully supplant local sources without also eliminating effective local choice. Indeed, political reality suggests that if the sharing is really to be unconditional, it will have to be based on simple and fair rules of division; any real diversity in local spending patterns will have to be financed from local sources.[14] The only role left for unconditional revenue sharing is to provide a common base level of public spending that enables local constituencies to finance marginal spending out of the least costly local sources.[15] We will reexamine these issues from the perspective of the local community in Chapter 11.

---

[14] A good example to illustrate the limited potential of revenue sharing is provided by the California experience with Proposition 13. That proposition limited the potential local revenue so severely that state revenue sharing to localities was required to pay for public schools. One consequence was that a state decision on levels was imposed uniformly on localities (except to the extent that the latter could and did find ways of setting up parallel funding sources).

[15] However, Feldstein (1975) suggests a way in which matching government grants could be used to facilitate local choice while assuring a certain degree of "fairness."

CHAPTER 8

Public pricing and optimal-commodity taxation

We complete our analysis of the general budgeting problem in the mixed economy with a discussion of "optimal" finance. We focus on a particular constituency (which we assume must be self-sufficient) and ask how it should best collect money to finance its operations. In principle, the issues here involve both optimal pricing of publicly provided excludable goods and optimal taxation to pay for unfunded costs of providing nonexcludable goods. Although the first of these problems is not of major importance in the U.S. economy, it is worth our attention for several reasons. First, it does play an important role in budgeting for some of the European socialist democracies. Second, the "public-pricing" and "optimal-taxation" problems have strikingly similar structure so that each provides insight into the nature of the other. Finally, the public-pricing problem provides a useful transition from "optimal-planning" problems of the type discussed in Chapters 3 and 5 to the type of second-best analysis for the mixed economy that will occupy us in much of the sequel.

8.1   Optimal public pricing

We start with the budgeting problem for a very simple government, one that provides only excludable goods and has no taxing powers. "Public" activity involves producing some subset of excludable goods and selling them in such a way as to cover all costs (a constraint that follows from the lack of taxation power). Alternatively, the following model can be applied to the analysis of a government enterprise required by law to balance its budget. Although the second interpretation is more realistic, the first is useful in making comparisons with the "optimal-tax" model to follow.

The reader should realize from our earlier discussions that the problem just posed has effectively already been solved for cases where the technology is convex; in that case the first-best policy of pricing at marginal costs will result in nonnegative profits, and the new constraint would be irrelevant. Thus, the problem is significant for us only when the public-sector technology exhibits increasing returns to scale in the relevant range so that we will be forced to charge prices in excess of marginal costs; of course, this is also the principal situation in which we expect to see the government marketing excludable goods to begin with.

Rather than jump directly into a full general equilibrium setting, we retain some partial equilibrium features by assuming the existence of a Hicksian aggregate private good, which we take to be the numeraire. As in the past, we represent the public-cost function in terms of this numeraire as $\Gamma(\cdot)$. We anticipate the general vector notation to follow by representing aggregate net consumption as a vector $C = (C_0, C_\#)$, where subscript 0 indexes the numeraire and # indexes the vector of publicly provided goods. Since there will be no initial endowments of the publicly provided goods, gross consumption will equal net consumption here, except for the numeraire. Public outputs are sold at prices $P_\#$ so the public-enterprise budget constraint may be written as

$$\pi = P_\# C_\# - \Gamma(C_\#) \geq 0. \tag{8.1}$$

We make two further concessions to partial equilibrium simplicity. First, we assume a single (representative) consumer. As will be seen, the operational significance of this assumption is that we ignore distributional considerations. Second, we ignore the private-production sector just as we did in Chapters 4 and 5. Should the public enterprise happen to make a profit, we assume it can (and is) returned to the consumer in a lump-sum way. Consequently, the competitive consumer choice problem takes the form

$$\max_C U(C) \tag{8.2}$$

subject to

$$PC = \pi,$$

where $P = (1, P_\#)$. Optimal behavior determines demand functions $C(P, \pi)$ and defines an indirect utility function on prices and income: $V(P, \pi)$.[1]

Our government now plays the role of a benevolent monopolist, taking the demand functions faced as given and choosing a pricing policy to maximize the consumer's indirect utility. Formally, the public-pricing problem is stated as

$$\max_{P, \pi} V(P, \pi) \tag{8.3}$$

subject to

---

[1] The use of *net* consumption, though notationally convenient, can be confusing at first. Here, our consumer will be using his endowment of the numeraire together with any profit generated to purchase the government outputs; consequently, we expect C_0 to be negative. If, instead, we distinguished between gross consumption (C') and exogenous resources (Z), the budget constraint could be written as $PC' = Z_0 + \pi$.

$$P_\# C_\#(P, \pi) - \Gamma[C_\#(P, \pi)] = \pi, \quad \pi \ge 0.$$

Although this problem and the similar optimal-tax problems to follow generally do not satisfy standard convexity assumptions, we continue our practice from previous chapters of analyzing Lagrangian necessary conditions for optimality. However, we will take into account the possibility of multiple solutions to the necessary conditions in the next section.

Hence, we assign multipliers μ and ν to the two constraints and form the Lagrangian

$$L(\cdot) = V(P, \pi) + \mu[P_\# C_\#(P, \pi) - \Gamma[C_\#(P, \pi)] - \pi] + \nu\pi. \tag{8.4}$$

Optimizing with respect to the ith price yields

$$\frac{\partial V}{\partial P_i} + \mu C_i + \mu \sum_j P_j \frac{\partial C_j}{\partial P_i} - \mu \sum_j \frac{\partial \Gamma}{\partial C_j} \frac{\partial C_j}{\partial P_i} = 0. \tag{8.5}$$

Equation (8.5) constitutes a system of equations (one for each i) that, together with an additional equation for π, characterize optimal pricing. Since we will be working with such systems frequently in the sequel, it is useful to represent them in a shorthand vector notation. Using the orientation conventions discussed in the preface, we represent the preceding system by the single-vector equation

$$\nabla_P V + \mu C_\# + \mu\{[P_\# - \nabla_C \Gamma] \nabla_P C\} = 0, \tag{8.6}$$

where we have omitted the symbol # from the argument of gradients for convenience.[2]

Observe that (8.6) involves information revealed by demand and cost functions as well as a gradient of the indirect utility function. Consequently, "duality" relations between indirect utility and market demand are valuable tools of analysis here (and in similar situations later). These relations can be derived from the envelope theorem discussed in Chapter 3; in particular, $\nabla_P V = -\lambda C_\#$, where $\lambda = \partial V/\partial \pi$, the "marginal utility of income."[3] Substitution into (8.6) yields

$$(\mu - \lambda)C_\# + \mu\{[P_\# - \nabla_C \Gamma] \nabla_P C_\#\} = 0. \tag{8.7}$$

---

[2] Note the use of { } (denoting transposes) in this expression. Since C has the orientation of a column vector, we want to think of (8.6) as a column vector equation. But $P \nabla_P C$ has the natural orientation of a row vector so we use the transpose in order to generate consistency. These conventions are set forth systematically in the preface on notation.

[3] Although we assume the reader is familiar with these ideas, it is useful to keep in mind the basic intuition behind them. Assuming that the consumer makes no adjustment in demand, an increase in price by one unit will cost an extra C in numeraire, that is, an extra λC in utility. And though the consumer probably will want to adjust consumption, such adjustment has no first-order effect on utility given optimizing behavior before the price change. See Diewert (1981) for an exposition of this subject.

Finally, the choice of π generates one more necessary condition:

$$\lambda - \mu + \mu [P_\# - \nabla_C \Gamma] \nabla_\pi C_\# + \nu = 0. \tag{8.8}$$

Before deriving the rules of optimal pricing, we focus on a related issue that will be important in broader contexts: Should the government treat dollars in its budget in the same way as it treats dollars in the consumer's pocket? Here, the marginal value of the first kind of dollars is represented by μ, whereas the marginal value of the second kind is represented by λ, so we are asking whether $\mu = \lambda$. Examining the system (8.6), we see that $\mu = \lambda$ if and only if

$$[P_\# - \nabla_C \Gamma] \nabla_P C_\# = 0. \tag{8.9}$$

Consequently, as long as the Jacobian of the demand system is nonsingular, $\mu = \lambda$ if and only if marginal-cost pricing is optimal. But, examining (8.8), we see that these two conditions can hold simultaneously only if the nonnegative profit constraint is not binding ($\nu = 0$).

Thus, $\mu \neq \lambda$ unless the problem reduces trivially to the first best. What relationship should we expect between μ and λ? The following argument looks compelling: Multiplier μ should exceed λ since an extra dollar in the government budget would allow planners to bring prices a little closer to marginal costs and reduce the second-best distortion. We will see that this reasoning is almost always correct and forms the basis for the concept of *excess burden* to be discussed at length in Chapter 10.

Although we can say some useful things about the optimal-pricing rules at this level of generality, it is more instructive to start with an even simpler model in which there are no cross-price effects in demand among the collection of publicly provided goods (more general pricing rules will be discussed in the next section). Then the ith equation in (8.7) involves only the ith demand function; multiplying and dividing this equation by $P_i / \mu C_i$ then yields

$$\frac{\mu - \lambda}{\mu} = -\frac{P_i - \partial \Gamma / \partial P_i}{P_i} \frac{\partial C_i}{\partial P_i} \frac{P_i}{C_i} = -\frac{P_i - \partial \Gamma / \partial C_i}{P_i} \epsilon_i, \tag{8.10}$$

where ϵ_i is the own-price elasticity of the ith public output in demand.

These equations define the so-called Ramsey pricing rules.[4] Verbally, they tell us that the relative markups of price over marginal cost should be inversely proportional to the own-price elasticities for each good. The proportionality factor will be determined by the condition that profits equal zero. Here, we can see that $\mu - \lambda$ must be positive under normal conditions. As long as all own-price elasticities are negative, all markups

---

[4] The rules are named after Frank Ramsey, who first derived them in 1927.

must be of the same sign [from (8.10)]. And if all markups were negative, surely profits would be negative; consequently, all markups are positive, and $\mu > \lambda$.

There is a useful intuition for these rules, although it requires that we anticipate some formal developments that come later. Suppose we restrict output below the competitive level on market i. There is a welfare cost to doing this since consumers then put a higher value on the product than the marginal cost of producing it. It seems reasonable that this welfare cost is proportional to the gap between price and marginal cost (we will demonstrate this rigorously in Chapter 9). Now, as output falls, profit goes up at the rate

$$\frac{d\pi}{dC_i} = -\frac{P_i}{\epsilon_i} - \left[P_i - \frac{\partial\Gamma}{\partial C_i}\right]. \tag{8.11}$$

Consequently, if we divide (8.11) by the markup, we get a measure of the efficiency with which market i generates profit per unit welfare cost (label this measure EEF_i). We find

$$\text{EFF}_i = -\frac{1}{\epsilon_i}\frac{P_i}{P_i - \partial\Gamma/\partial C_i} - 1. \tag{8.12}$$

Thus, we see that, given the rate of markup, markets with inelastic demand are more efficient than those with elastic demand at generating profits; indeed, we should allow a greater degree of price distortion in those markets, and the optimal rules simply involve equating efficiencies across all markets.

8.2   Diamond–Mirrlees optimal-commodity-tax framework

We pass now to a general model of the mixed economy and ask the corresponding questions concerning optimal finance. In particular, we reintroduce nonexcludable goods and deal with a world of many consumers. The nature of government "controls" changes considerably from those of the previous section. Most collective-good outputs are not sold, so planners no longer have direct control over prices. Therefore, revenue must be raised through various types of taxes, and the associated tax rates constitute a new set of controls.

Of course, levels and types of spending also constitute new controls, but we will take these as given in this chapter and ask for the best possible finance of those given levels. In later chapters we will discuss project analysis and the interdependence of project choice with methods of finance.

We discussed earlier the choice between tax and debt finance. The choice turned out to be either irrelevant (if one believes in the dynasty model of the family) or reduced to the problem of choosing the timing of taxation in the appropriate intertemporal context (if one believes in the overlapping-generations view of the family). Therefore, we will limit ourselves to a discussion of optimal taxation here. Although time will not appear explicitly, the model can be interpreted as intertemporal subject to the caveats discussed in Chapter 6. However, most specific discussion of intertemporal issues in optimal taxation will be deferred to Chapter 12. Further, we will be restricted to a certainty situation until the section on broadly based taxes.

We learned in Chapter 3 that lump-sum taxation always is optimal in a competitive world as long as it can be instituted in an unconstrained way. There was a strong suggestion that lump-sum taxes would be optimal in the mixed economy unless other second-best considerations are important. Thus, the question of optimal taxation generally is interesting only when there are some restrictions on the possibilities of instituting lump-sum taxes. Of course, the most satisfactory way to model optimal taxation would be to think of the set of tax instruments as endogenous; the government would choose the most effective set possible subject to some reasonable incentive and participation constraints on the part of taxpayers. We will motivate the sorts of limitations imposed here from this point of view later in the chapter.

However, for now we simply assume that there are no sources of lump-sum income except profits of firms and that these profits constitute the only feasible lump-sum tax base (τ is the uniform tax rate). Furthermore, among the class of all possible indirect tax schemes, we focus on linear commodity taxes, that is, fixed charges per unit of a good bought or sold. Although some progress has been made in studying optimal nonlinear taxes, the analysis involves fairly sophisticated mathematics and is beyond the scope of this book. Note, however, that we will discuss general types of taxation in a nonoptimal context later in the book.

To treat commodity taxes in a general way, we would need to adopt the notation that explicitly distinguishes sales from purchases. However, it is simpler to start with a version in which cancellations occur naturally, and we only have to keep track of net sales.[5] One important case that can be treated in this way is when households and firms always participate on the same side of each market on which they do business with one another and all commodity taxation takes place on that set of transactions. Such a situation can represent sales taxation in a world where neither intermediate goods in production nor resource transactions among households are taxed. Although these restrictions limit the planner's options, they

---

[5] This model and most of the analysis in Section 8.2 was developed by Diamond–Mirrlees (1971) and Diamond (1975). See Mirrlees (1987) for a recent overview of this subject.

provide us with a simple starting point. Furthermore, they are restrictions we may actually want to impose under certain circumstances, as we will see later.

Under these assumptions, commodity taxation can be represented as follows: Let P be the net price vector faced by competitive households. This vector is the same for all households since we are assuming that there is no differential taxation among households and all households are on the same side of each market. Similarly, let Q be the corresponding vector of prices to firms. Then, $t = P - Q$ is a vector of net tax rates.[6] Of course, if commodity i is a resource sold from households to firms, a positive t_i reflects a net subsidy rather than a tax. However, accepting this somewhat unorthodox sign convention allows us considerable notational convenience.

For now, we assume that all private agents behave competitively. Thus, a typical firm (j) will choose net output to[7]

$$\max Qy^j \tag{8.13}$$

subject to

$$y^j \in \mathcal{Y}^j,$$

where the technologies may depend on a collective-goods provision but are assumed not to involve any externalities. This choice defines a supply function and an indirect profit function $\pi^j(Q, g)$; and given enough smoothness, we know from duality that $\nabla_Q \pi^j(\cdot) = y^j(\cdot)$.

A typical consumer choice problem takes the form

$$\max U^h(g, c^h) \tag{8.14}$$

subject to

$$Pc^h \leq (1 - \tau)\pi_h,$$

where π_h is the household's share of before-tax profits. Optimal choice defines demand functions and an indirect utility function $V^h(g, P, \pi_h, \tau)$.

We assume that when the government does trade on private markets (making net purchases b), it acts as a competitor. Thus, control over prices is exercised only through choice of tax parameters. There is an ambiguity in this and similar models as to whether the government trades

---

[6] Note that these taxes are being quoted in rates per unit *good* rather than per unit *value*. There is no difficulty in restating the analysis for the case of ad valorem taxes, but we will not do so here.

[7] Of course, the firm only gets $(1 - \tau)Qy^j$, where τ is the rate of tax on profit. However, the choices that maximize after-tax profit also maximize before-tax profit (the pure profit tax is nondistortionary). After-tax profit will be $(1 - \tau)\pi(\cdot)$.

at consumer or producer prices. This ambiguity is naturally unimportant since the true cost of goods to the government will be the same whether it pays consumer prices and collects the tax from itself or pays producer prices to begin with. Whichever view (or mixture of views) is taken, the government budget constraint takes the form

$$tC + \tau \Pi \geq Qb, \tag{8.15}$$

where, as usual, economywide aggregates are represented by the appropriate uppercase letters.

We should make it clear that our profits tax is not the same as a corporate income tax (although they would be indistinguishable in the static context). The tax here is on revenue net of all costs, *including capital costs* in the intertemporal context. Thus, it is a tax on pure profit and (important for us) is therefore lump sum in nature. On the other hand, the corporate income tax has a statutory incidence on capital to some degree. It is imposed on revenue net of *variable* costs, with some allowances for depreciation and investment credits. If the depreciation allowances are sufficiently generous to allow "expensing" (writing off all capital costs as they occur), the corporate income tax will look just like our profit tax, but otherwise it covers more than pure profit and is not lump sum in nature.

Our optimization will involve fixing b (and g) and choosing the vector t to maximize welfare subject to this budget constraint. *When all profits are taxed,* the choice can be normalized without loss of generality due to the fact that the "scale" of the tax vector is irrelevant. To see this, suppose that we are using tax vector t and decide to use instead $t + \kappa P$, where κ is a scalar multiple. We argue that there will be a new equilibrium in which producer's prices do not change whereas consumer's prices "inflate" by the factor κ: Since relative prices do not change to any private agent, no one's behavior changes. (It is important for this conclusion that consumers have no sources of lump-sum or profit income so that their opportunity sets are unchanged.) With everyone making the same decisions, the government must wind up extracting the same resources from the system as before. As a check that they do, compute the new tax revenue: $tC + \kappa PC$. Revenue from the "extra" tax is zero since individual budgets imply $PC = 0$; therefore, since C does not change, tax revenue does not change.

Since the choice of κ is irrelevant, it is useful to choose it in order to make some tax rate zero (so one good is untaxed without loss of generality). Incidentally, the preceding argument also shows that it is futile to try to raise revenue by taxing all expenditures at the same rate (at least when there are no elements of lump-sum income that can be "reached" by this ploy). The problem is that a uniform linear rate requires that sales be subsidized and the value of sales for each household equals the value of purchases.

Even when profits are not taxed, it is necessary to pick some tax normalization just to guarantee that the optimal-tax problem is well defined. The reason is that, without a normalizing constraint, the government will want to exercise the ploy just mentioned so as to effectively tax profits. By inflating all consumer prices relative to producer prices, the real value of profits can be driven to zero, allowing the government to tax profits through the back door. (We will look at a formal version of this argument in Section 8.5.) Consequently, we may as well always assume that some good is untaxed.

In order to evaluate the effect of a tax choice on welfare, we need to know what happens to the private-sector equilibrium as the tax vector is varied. Although this is a lot to know, suppose for the moment that we do. That is, we know functions, $P(g, b, t)$, that tell us the vector of consumer prices as functions of the government choices. It is conceptually useful to think of obtaining these functions by solving the material balance equations ($C = Y - b$) for prices as functions of parameters; of course, due to zero-order homogeneity, we are only able to solve for relative prices, so again we will normalize by treating the untaxed good as numeraire. As discussed in Chapter 6, equilibria generally will not exist for all such choices so we must implicitly assume that consistent choices are made.

8.3   Full-commodity-tax discretion

Let us start with the situation in which pure profit can be (and is) taxed fully (or, equivalently, we are in a socialist economy, where the government owns the firms) and the government is completely free to differentially set commodity taxes (subsidies) subject only to the normalization.

Now our optimal-tax problem may be stated as

$$\max_t W[V^1(g, P(g, b, t)), \dots, V^N(g, P(g, b, t))] \qquad (8.16)$$

subject to

$$tC[g, P(g, b, t)] + \Pi[P(g, b, t) - t] \geq [P(g, b, t) - t]b.$$

We retain (for convenience of notation) the convention that t, Q, ... have the dimension of the full-commodity space; thus, the price vectors have 1's appended in the numeraire position, whereas the tax vector has a zero there. When we need to refer to the truncated vectors (omitting the numeraire), we will indicate them using a subscript #, just as in the previous section.

The reader may wonder why the government budget still appears as a constraint in this problem. After all, the material balance conditions (which have been "substituted out") subsume individual budget constraints, and by Walras's law, whenever all those hold with equality, the government budget must balance. However, recall that we were only able to determine *relative* prices using the material balance conditions; thus, one such condition was redundant in that calculation and must be added back now. Of course, the particular condition to add back is irrelevant, so we choose the one (government budget) that turns out to be simplest to work with.

Here and in the sequel we assume that optimal solutions exist to problems of this type and that the Lagrangian conditions are necessary for this optimum. Although violations of these assumptions are not always pathological, they involve technicalities outside the scope of this book.[8] However, it is definitely *not* reasonable to assume that the Lagrangian conditions are *sufficient* for optimality; we have no reason to expect the price equations to be concave and therefore cannot expect problem (8.16) to be concave in t. Consequently, we need to account for the possibility of multiple solutions to the necessary conditions in what follows.

With that caveat in mind, let us assign a multiplier μ to the government budget constraint and examine the first-order conditions for choice of t. In computing these, we represent first-order welfare change using the "welfare weights" (cf. Chapter 2) and make use of duality relationships (as in the previous section) to evaluate derivatives of the indirect utility and competitive profit functions. Thereby, we obtain, from the chain rule,

$$\nabla_t P_\# \left[-\sum_h \beta^h c_\#^h + \mu Y_\# - \mu b_\# + \mu\{ t_\# \nabla_P C_\# \} \right] + \mu [C_\# - Y_\# + b_\#] = 0. \quad (8.17)$$

Observe that there are two ways in which changes in tax rates affect welfare: through changes in budget requirements and through induced changes in consumer prices. Further, we see from material balance conditions that effects through the budget exactly cancel. Raising taxes (with P fixed) generates more revenue from the transactions tax but loses an equal amount from the profits tax (as Q falls). Thus, *all* the welfare effects of tax changes work themselves out through consumer prices; the first-order conditions simplify to

$$\nabla_t P_\# \left[-\sum_h \beta^h c_\#^h + \mu C_\# + \mu\{ t_\# \nabla_P C_\# \} \right] = 0. \quad (8.18)$$

Observe that the necessary conditions will be satisfied if the vector in square brackets is made to be identically zero [we label this term $\Lambda(\mu)$ for

---

[8] When differential taxation of profits is allowed, optima generally would not exist. See Mirrlees (1972a).

future reference]. However, if there should be multiple solutions to the necessary conditions, can we be sure that $\Lambda(\mu) = 0$ in them all? We can here, under the additional assumption that the matrix $\nabla_t P_{\#}$ has full rank; then *every* solution to the necessary conditions satisfies

$$\Lambda(\mu) \equiv - \sum_h \beta^h c_{\#}^h + \mu C_{\#} + \mu\{t_{\#} \nabla_P C_{\#}\} = 0. \tag{8.19}$$

These formulas define optimal-tax rules in the current context. Although they are difficult to interpret usefully without making additional simplifying assumptions, some general characteristics are noteworthy.

First, note that computation will involve knowing demand derivatives and welfare weights but no further information about equilibrium relationships. Thus, although we assumed full information about price functions in equilibrium, it turns out to be unnecessary in doing computations. How did we get away with this? To see how, return to (8.18). Each component on the left side represents the marginal welfare impact from increasing the associated tax, and all these welfare impacts work through changes in consumer prices. If we needed all the information contained in *these* formulas, we would need the price equilibrium functions. But as long as control over the tax vector can be translated into full control over the price vector (here is where the rank condition plays a role), the planner can pretend to control consumer prices directly in determining the optimal-tax rules.

Note particularly that the optimal rules imply that there will be no marginal welfare effects from price changes (i.e., no "pecuniary externalities"). This absence of pecuniary externalities is the general rule in first-best welfare economics (where a price change affects buyer and seller welfare in equal and opposite ways) but unfortunately rarely applies outside that context. Much of the elegance of optimal-tax theory derives from this important price control feature, as we shall see. To see how fragile this feature is, think about what will happen when households own the private firms and there is no profits tax. Then, individual welfare will be affected by producer prices (through profit income) as well as consumer prices, and the single set of tax rates will be insufficient to control both.

But, at least for now, the tax rules are determined by optimizing welfare over choices of consumer prices (with appropriate adjustments in producer prices); the first term in (8.19) reflects the direct cost in consumer welfare from raising prices, whereas the other two terms give the welfare equivalent of the increased government revenue that can be raised thereby. The reader will notice a strong similarity between the form of these rules and the corresponding form (8.7) in the previous section. Aside from the presence of welfare weights here, they are identical, with t playing the role of markups over marginal cost. Once we recognize that the optimal-tax problem reduces to choosing consumer prices (subject to the budget constraint), this analogy should be expected, and we can exploit it in elucidating the optimal rules.

In particular, if we reintroduce assumptions of the first section (no distributional considerations and no cross-price effects in demand except in connection with the numeraire good), the associated Ramsey pricing rules will translate directly into optimal-tax rules. Therefore, further discussion focuses on the reasonableness of these assumptions and the consequences of relaxing them.

Let us discuss first the issue of cross-price effects. To isolate the relevant considerations, we temporarily ignore distributional considerations by setting all welfare weights equal to a common value ($\bar{\beta}$). Having done this, the characterizing equations for optimal-tax rules may be written as

$$\sum_{k>0} \frac{t_k}{C_i} \frac{\partial C_k}{\partial P_i} \equiv \sum_{k>0} \frac{t_k C_k}{P_i C_i} \frac{P_i \partial C_k}{C_k \partial P_i} = \frac{\bar{\beta} - \mu}{\mu}, \quad \text{all } i > 0. \qquad (8.20)$$

Observe that we now have a system of equations involving own- and cross-price elasticities that could be solved to determine the relative tax rates. The taxes can be thought of as determining a set of weights to associate with each elasticity, and the tax rates are optimal when the weighted sum of own- and cross-price elasticities is constant across all goods. Clearly, these equations will imply the "inverse-elasticity" rules of Section 8.1 if there are no cross-price effects.

However, the inverse-elasticity rules are misleading in this context even if the required assumptions do hold. The reason is that when we assume away so many cross-price effects, we automatically put restrictions on the relative magnitude of own-price elasticities. This is best seen if we look at what happens when there are no cross-price effects with *any* goods, including the numeraire. Then, the own-price elasticity of any good can be determined by differentiating the (aggregated) consumer budget identity ($PC = m$) with respect to the ith price and dropping all cross-price terms:

$$C_i + P_i \frac{\partial C_i}{\partial P_i} = 0, \quad \text{all } i. \qquad (8.21)$$

Dividing through by C_i, we see that all own-price elasticities must be minus one. Consequently, the inverse-elasticity rule turns out to be a uniform tax rule in this case!

The only way we could get an inverse-elasticity rule that entailed differential tax rates would be if the only cross-price effects involved the untaxed good. Then, own-price elasticities will differ to the extent that these cross-price elasticities differ. Indeed, differentiating the budget identity again and allowing for these effects yields

$$\epsilon_i = -1 - \frac{1}{C_i} \frac{\partial C_0}{\partial P_i}. \tag{8.22}$$

This situation may fit fairly well in the Ramsey pricing problem where the numeraire denotes a broad market aggregate, but it seems inappropriate in the optimal-tax context; it would be most surprising if *all* cross-price effects worked themselves out through the *single* untaxed good.

Thus, if we want to analyze optimal-commodity taxation at a reasonable level of generality, we must allow for general cross-price effects. Although clean interpretations of tax rules are hard to come by in this context, there is one qualitative feature that is worthy of note. Namely, it is still true (in the absence of distributional considerations) that all discrepancies in optimal tax rates must be related to cross-price effects with the untaxed good. To see why, differentiate the budget identity again, retaining all potential effects and separating off the untaxed good (index 0):

$$\sum_{k>0} \frac{P_k}{C_i} \frac{\partial C_k}{\partial P_i} = -\frac{\partial C_0}{C_i \partial P_i} - 1 = -\frac{C_0}{P_i C_i} \frac{P_i}{C_0} \frac{\partial C_0}{\partial P_i} - 1, \quad \text{each } i > 0. \tag{8.23}$$

Now compare (8.23) to the optimal-tax equations (8.20). Should the right sides in (8.23) happen to be independent of i, if we set $t_i = \kappa P_i$ for some appropriate constant κ, we obtain a solution to (8.20). Thus, if all taxed goods exhibit similar cross-price effects with the untaxed good, a uniform tax rate is optimal. We will examine the case for uniform taxation further in Section 8.5. In any case, we see that all of the action in determining differential rates must derive from differences in cross-price effects with the untaxed good.

Of course, the preceding discussion was predicated on equal welfare weights. What additional complications should we expect from distributional factors? First, observe that it makes no sense to ignore them a priori in the present context (as we have done): This context takes as given the *necessity* of using commodity taxes and therefore implicitly admits the impossibility of lump-sum transfers; therefore, it is hard to see how we can expect to optimize separately on the income distribution. We expect the optimal-tax choices to trade off efficiency and equity concerns.

Although equity considerations are not easy to quantify, we can argue at least intuitively that they will tend to have opposite implications for relative tax rates from what we found on the basis of efficiency considerations only. Let us examine the optimal-tax rules when there are no cross-price effects among taxed goods (so that the efficiency rules are easy to recognize) but welfare weights are unequal. By adding and subtracting $\bar{\beta} C_{\#}$ to the optimal-tax equations (8.19), we can express the optimal tax rates as

$$\frac{t_i}{P_i} = -\frac{1}{\epsilon_i} \left[\frac{\mu - \bar{\beta}}{\mu} - \sum_h \left[\frac{\beta^h - \bar{\beta}}{\mu} \right] \frac{c_i^h}{C_i} \right], \quad \text{all } i. \tag{8.24}$$

We see that tax rates will be lower than implied by the inverse-elasticity rules for goods consumed relatively more by the "deserving" groups (for whom $\beta^h > \bar{\beta}$) and vice versa. But these goods are likely to be the "necessities" for which demand elasticity is relatively low. Thus, equity considerations tend to lower optimal tax rates that would otherwise have been relatively high (on the basis of efficiency considerations only) and vice versa. In this situation, we see that there is indeed a direct conflict between the objectives of efficiency and equity, so the bottom line for relative tax rates is ambiguous.

8.4 Limitations on tax discretion

Up to now, we have made some strong assumptions concerning the planner's range of second-best controls. What happens if profits are privately owned and cannot be taxed or the number of potential commodity tax rates is somehow limited? Well, the best that can be said is that things get messy. We will pursue the subject far enough to expose the relevant mess but will not work out all the gory details since practical tax policy is unlikely to hinge on them anytime soon.

A   *Untaxed profits*[9]

Suppose, now, that we revert to a "private-ownership" economy in which profits are untaxed. As earlier, π_h is profits accruing to household h. We continue to assume that firms behave competitively[10] so the gradient of π_h with respect to Q may be thought of as the net output vector "owned" by household h. We label this vector y_h for convenience.

Retaining for the moment the view that the government has complete discretionary control over commodity tax rates, our optimal-tax problem becomes[11]

$$\max_t W[V^1(g, Q(g, b, t) + t, \pi_1(Q(g, b, t))), \dots,$$

$$V^N(g, Q(g, b, t) + t, \pi_N(Q(g, b, t)))] \tag{8.25}$$

---

[9] This section is based largely on the work of Dasgupta and Stiglitz (1972).

[10] When firms do not behave competitively, government tax policy will have some additional second-best welfare effects to the extent it alters firm behavior. These could be incorporated in our analysis at the cost of one further layer of complexity.

[11] It is more convenient in this section to work directly with producer price functions and define consumer prices as $Q + t$.

subject to

$$t \sum_h c^h[g, Q(g, b, t) + t, \pi_h(Q(g, b, t))] \geq Q(g, b, t)b.$$

Proceeding as before, the first-order conditions may be reduced to

$$\nabla_t P_\# \left[-\sum_h \beta^h c_\#^h + \mu C_\# + \mu \{ t_\# \, \nabla_P C_\# \} \right]$$

$$= \nabla_t Q_\# \left[-\sum_h \beta^h y_{h\#} + \mu Y_\# - \mu \sum_h (t_\# \, \nabla_\pi c_\#^h) y_{h\#} \right]. \qquad (8.26)$$

We see immediately that if producer prices should turn out to be invariant to tax increases (i.e., the full incidence of commodity taxation is on consumers), the optimal-tax rules reduce to the previous case. But otherwise, they must be modified to take account of the independent effects producer prices have on welfare. Clearly, in this general situation, it is not possible to state the correct rules without incorporating directly the market equilibrium (incidence) relationships relating taxes and prices.

There seems to be little point in pursuing detailed analysis of the new tax rules. Indeed, for practical purposes, our best hope would be that they pretty much reduce to the previous case anyway. This will be true if we can argue (empirically) that the circuitous path from taxes to producer prices to profits to extra consumption is so tenuous that terms on the right side of (8.26) are insignificant compared to those on the left.

B   *Limited commodity tax discretion*

Suppose now that only a restricted subset of goods can be taxed.[12] We divide the commodity vector into two parts: $x = (x_I, x_{II})$, where index set I runs over those goods that can be taxed (or subsidized) and index set II runs over those that cannot.[13] It is convenient to treat the numeraire as a member of class II. We will deal only with the "socialist" economy, although the analysis of this and the previous section could be combined with no theoretical difficulty. Our new planning problem takes the form

$$\max_t W[V^1(g, Q_I(g, b, t) + t, Q_{II}(g, b, t)), \ldots,$$

$$V^N(g, Q_I(g, b, t) + t, Q_{II}(g, b, t))] \quad (8.27)$$

subject to

---

[12] This section generalizes Stiglitz–Dasgupta (1971).

[13] Some additional generality could be achieved by allowing some goods in class II to be taxed at rates not subject to discretionary choice. The reader is invited to provide an analysis of this case.

$$tC_I[g, Q_I(g, b, t) + t, Q_{II}(g, b, t)] + \Pi[Q(g, b, t)] \geq Q(g, b, t)b.$$

Following well-worn procedures, we obtain the necessary conditions:

$$\nabla_t P_I\left[-\sum_h \beta^h c_I^h + \mu C_I + \mu\{t\nabla_{P_I} C_I\}\right] = -\nabla_t P_{II}\left[-\sum_h \beta^h c_{II}^h + \mu C_{II}\right]. \quad (8.28)$$

Again the tax rules will reduce to the previous case *if* a certain separability condition holds, namely, if changes in the tax rates have no marginal effects on the prices of untaxed goods. Otherwise, we need to worry about the pecuniary externalities through the uncontrolled prices of these goods.

The considerations here parallel those encountered with untaxed profits. To institute the general rules will be very demanding on data and computation, but since the effects through cross-price impacts are likely to be small, we may be able to argue for the rules of Section 8.1 as a good approximation.

8.5 Broadly based taxes

From the discussion of the previous section, the reader probably will agree that aside from the "ideal" case of full control, no cross-price effects among taxed goods, and no distributional effects, optimal taxes will be impossible to compute. Furthermore, even in the ideal case, we need to have different tax rates (in general) on each good; this arrangement is likely to be administratively quite costly, a consideration we have ignored heretofore.

The question naturally arises: Could we find a simple tax structure that gets reasonably close in welfare terms to the optimum? If so, it seems likely that the simple tax actually would dominate once administrative costs were properly accounted for. The so-called broadly based taxes are supposed to fill this bill. There are two separate arguments for broadly based taxes. The first suggests that we can make the tax so broadly based that it is lump sum in net effect and therefore nondistortionary. Naturally, given what we have learned already in this chapter, the base will have to be broader than what can be achieved from taxing only net transactions. The second argument (which we take up later) suggests that a uniform transactions tax on all but one good is "almost" second-best optimal. Unfortunately, neither of these arguments correctly accounts for distributional considerations, as we will see.

To motivate the construction of a broadly based tax, let us examine the general intertemporal budget constraint of Chapter 6 (considerations involving uncertainty will be added later). We take the discrete, overlapping-generations version (6.3) and rewrite it so that all net consumption terms appear on the left and all income terms on the right:

$$\sum_{s=0}^{S} \frac{P_s c_s}{\prod_{x=0}^{s}(1+r_x)} + \frac{B_S}{\prod_{x=0}^{S}(1+r_x)} = B_0 + \sum_{s=0}^{S} \frac{m_s}{\prod_{x=0}^{s}(1+r_x)}. \qquad (8.29)$$

Now suppose we tax all net consumption including bequests at the same ad valorem rate (t). That is, for every dollar's worth of net purchases, the buyer must pay t dollars in tax. The corresponding after-tax budget constraint is

$$\sum_{s=0}^{S} \frac{(1+t)P_s c}{\prod_{x=0}^{s}(1+r_x)} + \frac{(1+t)B_S}{\prod_{x=0}^{S}(1+r_x)} = B_0 + \sum_{s=0}^{S} \frac{m_s}{\prod_{x=0}^{s}(1+r_x)}. \qquad (8.30)$$

The reader will see immediately that (8.30) is equivalent in terms of available opportunities to the constraint

$$\sum_{s=0}^{S} \frac{P_s c_s}{\prod_{x=0}^{s}(1+r_x)} + \frac{B_S}{\prod_{x=0}^{S}(1+r_x)} = \frac{1}{1+t}\left[B_0 + \sum_{s=0}^{S} \frac{m_s}{\prod_{x=0}^{s}(1+r_x)}\right]. \qquad (8.31)$$

Consequently, a uniform ad valorem tax on net consumption is equivalent to a tax at rate $1-(1/1+t)$ on all components of lump-sum income. Here, we have a rigorous argument for the claim made earlier that a uniform transactions tax could be used to "reach" all components of lump-sum income. And, of course, the resulting tax is fully lump sum in nature.[14] Unfortunately for us, though, the amount of "tax base" that is available from these income sources is too small to be of much practical use.

How could we add to this base? Well, if we were in a position to tax *gross* rather than *net* consumption, we would reach all of household wealth. Think of gross consumption (c') as net consumption plus exogenous resources $(c+z)$ and write our budget constraint in the form

$$\sum_{s=0}^{S} \frac{P_s c_s'}{\prod_{x=0}^{s}(1+r_x)} + \frac{B_S}{\prod_{x=0}^{S}(1+r_x)} = B_0 + \sum_{s=0}^{S} \frac{m_s + P_s z_s}{\prod_{x=0}^{s}(1+r_x)}. \qquad (8.32)$$

Clearly, if we were able to tax all of *gross* consumption at a uniform ad valorem rate, we would reach (as tax base) everything on the right side

---

[14] Dixit (1970) was among the first to use this type of argument as justification for a uniform tax. Sandmo (1974) pointed out the limitation that derives from limited sources of lump-sum income.

of (8.32). The sum of all components on the right side constitutes the present value of all resources available to our household and is usefully thought of as household wealth. So we can think of a uniform tax on gross consumption as equivalent to a wealth tax. And observe that wealth, as so defined, is exogenous for the household so that such a tax would be lump sum in character.

Can we approximate a wealth tax in practice? Obviously, we need to channel all economic activity through the market and distinguish between sales and purchases so that we can tax "all sales" or "all purchases." There are two approaches available depending on which side we try to tax. Pure-*accrual* taxation attempts to tax components of wealth directly, whereas pure-*realization* taxation attempts to tax components of gross consumption. We begin to discuss some of the mechanics of these methods here, although some important details must wait until we reintroduce uncertainty later.[15]

The pure-accrual method taxes each component of income as it is *first* earned. Thus, bequests and other forms of lump-sum transfers are taxed when first received, whereas resources are taxed when they first come available. The accrual tax is *not* an income tax primarily because it does not tax income earned from "secondary" assets. That is, when a household uses some income to purchase an asset, any fully anticipated return on the asset is considered secondary and is exempt from taxation under the accrual method.

Note that were it to be taxed, some components of wealth (those initially saved) would be taxed twice, and we would not have a uniform tax rate. Indeed, a tax on saving translates directly into a differential tax on future (compared to current) consumption. Since this distortion plays a major role later (in Chapter 12), we illustrate it here in a two-period situation with a single-consumption aggregate in each period. Assuming that all income (including that from interest payments) is taxed in both periods at the common rate τ, we have the two budget constraints

$$c_1' + \chi = z^1(1 - \tau), \tag{8.33}$$

$$c_2' = (z_2 + r\chi)(1 - \tau) + \chi = z_2(1 - \tau) + \chi[1 + r(1 - \tau)], \tag{8.34}$$

where χ is net saving. Eliminating this free-choice variable from these equations, we obtain the consumer's present-value constraint:

$$c_1' + \frac{c_2'}{1 + r(1 - \tau)} = \left[z_1 + \frac{z_2}{1 + r(1 - \tau)}\right](1 - \tau). \tag{8.35}$$

We see that the effective consumer interest rate is $r(1 - \tau)$, and our tax is no longer fully lump sum in character since there is now a gap between

15 For a more detailed discussion of accounting procedures, see Goode (1976).

second-period consumer and producer prices. The associated current-value tax (using producer goods as the current-value numeraire) is given by

$$t_2 \equiv \frac{1+r}{1+r(1-\tau)} - 1 = \frac{r\tau}{1+r(1-\tau)}. \tag{8.36}$$

Consequently, a perfect broadly based tax must avoid taxing intermediate items (such as interest income).

The pure-realization method seeks to achieve the same goal by taxing all final spending but no intermediate spending. Thus, when assets are bought and held for later "realization," they are not taxed, but when goods are bought for final consumption, they are taxed. Note that our approach so far requires that bequests be treated as realization. If bequests are treated instead as secondary assets, the considerations are somewhat different, as we will see. There are some complications with the realization method concerning the treatment of durable goods, particularly those having a second-hand market. We postpone temporarily a discussion of these and some similar problems concerning the treatment of capital gains in the accrual method.

Assuming that such technical details can be handled, how well will these methods do at approximating a wealth tax? Since the methods are constructed to guarantee that components are taxed at most once, shortcomings will be due to failure to tax some components at all. The accrual method will miss resources that are never sold (or otherwise appropriately identified), whereas the realization method misses consumption goods that are never bought. In the absence of an underground (barter) sector, resources that are not sold must be consumed yet not bought, so both methods are likely to miss the same things. This parallelism remains true in value terms even when there is barter, since the value of the resources offered will be commensurate with the value of the consumption received.

We see that both of these methods will be successful at achieving a sufficiently broad base only to the extent that they can force all resources into the market (or otherwise identify and tax unmarketed resources). Unfortunately (but not by now surprisingly), we bump against incentive problems in this regard. If the government could costlessly identify all household resources, it could construct the required tax. However, to find out about nonmarketed goods requires obtaining information that households have incentives to conceal. Think about the case of leisure, a large consumption item that is not bought on the market. One might think that the value of leisure is easy to measure since leisure time plus labor time is observable. But households can conceal the correct value by taking leisure "on the job" and simultaneously accepting a lower wage rate (making the value of time appear lower). Perhaps even more difficult to identify correctly are barter activities and in-kind transfers among the self-employed. Such incentive difficulties lead to the view that the government is forced to restrict itself to observable market transactions in choosing the operational tax base. Indeed, this argument can be pushed further to suggest that tax rates must be linear; unless the government can monitor and collect taxes on *total* household transactions a household can defeat the purpose of a progressive schedule by engaging in a sequence of small transactions.[16]

We now see the "metaeconomic" rationale behind the second-best tax framework studied earlier in this chapter. No matter how comprehensive we try to make an accrual tax, some nonmarketed items will escape the net. Further, as long as leisure is one of the things that escapes, the resulting tax is not very broadly based at all since labor income is the largest component in total income and leisure time is a large part of labor time. Consequently, any justification of such a tax as approximately first best would have to fall back on a claim of inelasticity in labor supply. Otherwise, failure to tax leisure is distortionary, and we expect people to work less than would be first-best optimal. The magnitude of this effect is much studied and quite controversial. Generally, it seems that there is not much supply elasticity with respect to the "head of household," but there may be much more with respect to other members.[17]

Even if a broadly based tax is necessarily distortionary, we might still be able to argue that a second-best tax system would involve a uniform rate of taxation on the available tax base. To see why this might be so, we need to relate back to the analysis of Section 8.3. Assuming there is no "underground" economy, a broadly based realization tax fits (roughly) the framework of commodity taxation with labor time as the untaxed good and uniform ad valorem rates on all other consumption goods. As we saw, this arrangement is second-best optimal (in the absence of distributional considerations) if all cross-price effects with leisure (as the untaxed good) are appropriately similar in magnitude. These conditions can be related to separability properties of the underlying utility function [see Atkinson and Stiglitz (1972), Sandmo (1974), Sadka (1977), and Deaton (1981)]. Although the necessary restrictions probably are not exactly met, uniform taxation might still be "third-best" optimal once we take into account the added administrative costs of differential taxation.[18]

However, we must introduce an important caveat at this point. All of the preceding arguments for a broadly based tax are based on pure

---

[16] Similarly, a regressive schedule can be defeated as long as households can engage in resale from large purchases.

[17] See Pencavel (1987) for a survey of empirical estimates in this area.

[18] For a related discussion of welfare comparisons among alternatve broadly based taxes, see Helpman–Sadka (1982).

efficiency considerations. Indeed, there is *no* presumption that a comprehensive linear (flat) wealth tax would have any desirable distributional characteristics. To the extent that the tax is comprehensive, it will have no effect on the after-tax wealth distribution. This is good if we believe that the initial distribution is optimal but not otherwise. Thus, for those who believe that the free-enterprise system tends to be inequitable in the absence of an active redistribution policy, broadly based tax systems will be desirable only if they can be made nonlinear. We consider some of the possibilities in the last section.

8.6   Practical problems with uniform tax systems

Let us assume now that we have agreed to institute a uniform tax of the type discussed in the previous section and address some practical problems associated with identifying "intermediate" transactions.

A   *Durable goods and human capital*

Durable consumer goods and human capital present similar problems for realization and accrual taxation, respectively. The purchase of a durable good is intermediate since actual consumption of services comes later; hence, a pure-realization tax would wait and tax the value of consumption services. However, this is impractical for obvious reasons. But, fortunately, there is no danger of double taxation from taxing the initial purchase as long as we *never* tax the consumption services. We would, though, need to provide tax credits for sale of such durables on second-hand markets.

A similar problem arises when we tax labor income in the pure-accrual tax once investment in human capital has taken place; labor time becomes intermediate, being the "return" on an acquired asset. Again, there is no danger of double taxation as long as resources devoted to investment in human capital are not taxed. However, some tax base may be missed to the extent that there are nonmonetary services generated from human capital.

B   *Uncertainty: insurance and capital gains*

To the extent that private insurance and asset markets provide full risk-sharing opportunities, the principles developed in the preceding imply that uniform ex ante taxation should exempt all insurance and asset instruments. This point is most easily seen in the context of the Arrow security model introduced in Chapter 3. Think about the budget constraint in state ω, which takes the form

$$P(\omega)c'(\omega) = P(\omega)z(\omega) + S(\omega). \tag{8.37}$$

[Here $P(\omega)$ denotes spot prices in state ω and $S(\omega)$ holdings of the Arrow security for state ω.] Letting $v(\omega)$ be security prices and assuming that everyone can trade freely at these prices, these constraints collapse as before to a single ex ante wealth constraint:

$$\int_\omega v(\omega)P(\omega)c'(\omega)\,d\omega = \int_\omega v(\omega)P(\omega)z(\omega)\,d\omega. \tag{8.38}$$

We see that all components of ex ante wealth again are reached by a uniform ex post tax on consumption (or resources) with no tax or subsidy on asset holdings. And it is easy to see that this same conclusion would hold for any other set of assets that spanned the entire Arrow security space. Thus, for example, there would be no taxation of capital gains since these are anticipated payoffs in particular states for the associated assets; further, there would be no deductions for losses due to accident, since these could be insured against if desired.

However, as soon as we leave the world of complete markets, the meaning of uniform taxation is not even clear, and the treatment of uncertainty is more problematic. Once markets are incomplete, the sequence of budget constraints does not collapse as earlier, so no single concept of ex ante wealth is compelling. Although it is difficult to say much about optimal taxation in this framework, we can imagine that the government may want to use the tax system as a way of improving the allocation of risk.

C   Bequests and dynasty model

Let us return briefly to the treatment of bequests. Our analysis heretofore has implicitly assumed the overlapping-generations framework. In that model it seems reasonable to treat bequests as realizations and to include them in the tax base. However, this would be inappropriate (at least from the standpoint of efficiency) in the dynasty model. There, bequests constitute saving within the extended family, and to tax them would be to double-tax components of wealth earned by one family member but consumed by a later family member. Consequently, those believing in the dynasty model argue that bequests ought to be exempted from a broadly based tax.

8.7   Distributional concerns

As mentioned earlier, it is difficult to justify a single broadly based linear tax (even if all the measurement mechanics can be handled) unless one believes that distributional considerations are of second-order importance. Assuming we do believe that a fairly comprehensive tax base is more or less necessary from an administrative standpoint, there are still a number of ways we might modify the structure outlined previously to better serve equity concerns. First we might incorporate some limited variation in tax rates. For example, even if we believe that taxing bequests distorts intra-family savings incentives, we might still choose to tax them as a means to improving (over time) an inequitable ex ante wealth distribution. We might even choose to tax bequests at a *higher* rate than other consumption if, for example, we thought that the principle of "equal opportunity" was sufficiently important (and ought to apply to each generation separately). Further, if we are sufficiently egalitarian, we might push this compromise further and tax all saving as a way of transferring wealth from the rich (who save more) to the poor (who save less).

Of course, everyone would prefer to find nondistortionary ways of achieving egalitarian aims. For example, we might try to make the wealth tax nonlinear and generate progressivity by making the marginal tax rate an increasing function of wealth. But how is this to be done? What we observe each period is household *income* that may or may not be a good proxy for wealth. And without knowing wealth, we do not know the appropriate bracket to apply. We can institute "income-averaging" schemes to circumvent this difficulty, but they are complicated and nullify the biggest advantage of the broadly based tax, simplicity. Indeed, a constant marginal tax rate seems very desirable precisely because we can determine the correct tax today without knowing anything about yesterday or tomorrow.

Some degree of nonlinearity can be introduced without interfering much with the constancy of the marginal rate. One possibility involves instituting an exemption level each period: No tax is paid on the first X dollars of income with a constant marginal rate applying thereafter. This scheme introduces progressivity into the tax structure and is nondistortionary as long as income always exceeds the exemption level (otherwise, an individual has a distorting incentive to transfer income from good to bad periods). A related but "more progressive" plan is the so-called negative-wealth tax. Here, everyone is effectively given an income "guarantee" at the outset and then pays a constant marginal tax rate on all earned income. Although there is no guarantee that such schemes are best in the class of all feasible nonlinear tax schemes, they do have strong theoretical appeal.

PART III

First-order project analysis

CHAPTER 9

Decompositions and general theory of second best

In most of the rest of the book, we will focus on project analysis. The framework (as developed in Chapters 6 and 7) is one in which decentralized government agencies make independent decisions on collective-goods provision in a mixed economy. The underlying status quo can be any configuration of publicly determined variables that is consistent with private-sector equilibrium. In particular, there will be no presumption of optimality in any of these choices. Any proposed change in this status quo can be thought of as defining a *project*. Hence, our concept of a project covers such diverse activities as a weather satellite, a pollution cleanup campaign, and a tax reform proposal. Naturally, the agencies cannot act completely independently since they are linked through the budget constraint. Further, we want agencies to take into account all relevant interdependencies. The principal aim of project analysis is to find ways of measuring project net benefits that correctly account for general equilibrium relationships and other interdependencies in this economic setting.

Throughout Part III we restrict attention to first-order welfare measures. We will give a precise operational meaning to "first order" in what follows, but informally, our approach amounts to introducing projects in such a way that their size is well defined and finding the best linear approximation to welfare contribution as a function of size. We develop the methodology first in a certainty model with a single jurisdiction allocating uncongestible goods for a closed economy. The analysis is extended to cover multiple jurisdictions allocating the full range of collective goods in Chapter 11 and to incorporate uncertainty with incomplete markets in Chapter 12. Our ultimate aim here is to find measures that can be implemented with observable data. However, we will fall short at many points on the "observability" criterion. We defer issues of identification and estimation to Chapters 13 and 16.

We distinguish two different approaches to first-order project analysis. The first (to be discussed in this chapter) breaks measures up into additive component parts. As we shall see, there are a variety of ways in which such decompositions can be executed, each associated with a different categorization of economic problems. Initially, we will develop one that yields terms for first best and a separate term for each distinct element of second best. This particular decomposition we associate with the general theory of second best as developed by Harberger and Lipsey–Lancaster.[1]

A second approach focuses on each commodity separately and aggregates all relevant considerations into a single term for each commodity involved in the project; this term naturally has the interpretation of a shadow price, or social valuation per unit of associated commodity. We take up the theory of shadow pricing in the next chapter.

9.1   Diamond–Mirrlees framework

We begin with the Diamond–Mirrlees framework, in which taxation is assumed to entail some combination of lump-sum and linear commodity taxes, and the latter type are imposed only on net transactions between households and firms. These assumptions will be relaxed in the following two sections. Concerning status quo tax choices, we assume only that they are made in a consistent way; that is, the government invokes some rule for setting tax rates in such a way as to satisfy the budget constraint. Therefore, in market equilibrium, t, T, and P must be determined jointly as functions of g and b so as to satisfy the functional relationship

$$Q(g,b)b = t(g,b)C(\cdot) + T(g,b) + \tau(g,b)\Pi(\cdot), \qquad (9.1)$$

where $C(\cdot)$ and $\Pi(\cdot)$ are the corresponding reduced-form functions of g and b. Assuming that these functional relationships are known, we could express welfare as a function of g and b alone. Letting $Z(g,b)$ be this function, we have

$$Z(g,b) = W[V^1(g, P(g,b), T^1(g,b), \pi_1(g,b)), \ldots,$$
$$V^N(g, P(g,b), T^N(g,b), \pi_N(g,b))]. \qquad (9.2)$$

We are looking for a practical way to measure Z.

Part III looks at such measures for small projects. We formalize the "size" of a project as follows: Think of potential projects as a one-dimensional family parameterized by a scalar variable α, with $\alpha = 0$ corresponding to no project; that is, $g = g(\alpha)$, $b = b(\alpha)$, and $[g(0), b(0)] = [g^o, b^o]$ (the status quo). For example, if our project produces increments of a single output (say, Δx) in some prespecified way, we could set $\alpha = \Delta x$. We assume that this can be done in such a way that g and b are smooth functions of α; this requires naturally that we be able to talk about small project changes (in particular, there can be no significant indivisibilities).

---

[1] Early discussions of second best were given by Lipsey and Lancaster (1957) and Harberger (1971). Decompositions of the sort discussed here can be found in Lesourne (1975) and Starrett (1979b).

In fact, as we shall see, the procedures of Part III are of quite limited usefulness when there are any types of large nonconvexities in the choice of government project. We take up these and related problems in Part IV.

Our welfare measure now can be thought of as a function of α, and by "first order" we shall mean the best linear approximation to Z around the status quo, that is, $(dZ/d\alpha)\,d\alpha$. Since the total derivative is cumbersome to write out in complicated equations, we will abuse the notation somewhat by writing total derivatives with respect to α using the gradient symbol ∇_α.[2] Differentiating and using duality theory as in Chapter 8, we write

$$\nabla_\alpha Z = \sum_h \frac{\partial W}{\partial V^h} \lambda_h \left[\frac{\nabla_\alpha V^h}{\lambda^h} \right]$$
$$\equiv \sum_h \beta^h [\Omega^h \nabla_\alpha g - \nabla_\alpha P c^h - \nabla_\alpha T^h + \nabla_\alpha \pi_h], \qquad (9.3)$$

where Ω^h is a vector of marginal rates of substitution between collective goods and the numeraire and β_h is a welfare weight, as defined earlier. The reader should note that these welfare weights represent the only remaining place where interpersonal comparisons impact on the analysis given our restriction to first-order measures. Furthermore, as long as we think of the welfare weights as being invariant to the choice of individual utility units (the right assumption to make, we think), our first-order measures will be strictly ordinal.[3]

A Second-best distributional terms

Although welfare weights have been with us for some time, some writers have argued that they are not very useful in practice.[4] For one thing, evaluations are complicated by the fact that price changes cannot be canceled out once the gainers and losers have potentially different welfare weights. Given this difficulty, the best way to evaluate $\nabla_\alpha Z$ is to first substitute from the consumer budget constraints; since these constraints hold as a function of α,

$$-\nabla_\alpha P c^h - \nabla_\alpha T^h + \nabla_\alpha \pi_h = P \nabla_\alpha c^h, \qquad (9.4)$$

and we have

$$\nabla_\alpha Z = \sum_h \beta^h [\Omega^h \nabla_\alpha g + P \nabla_\alpha c^h]. \qquad (9.5)$$

---

[2] The parameter α never enters any function independently so there is no danger of confusing total and partial derivatives with respect to it.

[3] The reader may want to refer back to Chapter 2, where we discussed these considerations in more detail.

[4] See, e.g., Harberger (1978).

The cost of the project now is expressed as "opportunity cost" or value of the foregone alternative (presumably, $\nabla_\alpha c^h$ is negative for most goods). Note that this formulation is independent of the nature of taxation or the behavior of firms, so the use of opportunity cost is valid for a broad class of environments.

However, this formulation still requires for its implementation that we have *full disaggregated* information on demands in *all* markets, a tall order in most cases. But suppose we rearrange terms in a different way; we can split the welfare measure into two parts, one that can be aggregated and simplified and another that we may be able to analyze by other methods.

Analytically, we perform the split by choosing a number κ (to be discussed in what follows) and writing

$$\nabla_\alpha Z = \kappa \sum_h \left[\frac{\nabla_\alpha V^h}{\lambda^h} \right] + \sum_h (\beta^h - \kappa) \left[\frac{\nabla_\alpha V^h}{\lambda^h} \right]. \tag{9.6}$$

We can further motivate our decomposition from the point of view of isolating costs of second-best distortions. If κ is chosen to be the average of the β_h's (call this average $\bar\beta$), the second term represents a pure-distribution effect; it will be zero if all welfare weights are the same or if all the project net benefits are equally distributed. In particular, the second term will vanish if the income distribution satisfies conditions of first-best optimality (so that the marginal social welfare of a dollar is the same wherever applied). Thus, the distribution term may be interpreted as the contribution to welfare change due to our failure to distribute income optimally. We will see how to isolate costs of other second-best distortions similarly in what follows.

After substitution and aggregation across individuals in the first term, we have

$$\nabla_\alpha Z = \bar\beta[\Omega \nabla_\alpha g + P \nabla_\alpha C] + \sum_h (\beta^h - \bar\beta) \left[\frac{\nabla_\alpha V^h}{\lambda^h} \right], \tag{9.7}$$

where $\Omega = \sum_h \Omega^h$ is a "Samuelson pseudoprice" vector for g. Here $\nabla_\alpha Z \, d\alpha$ measures the welfare benefits of a sufficiently small project $(d\alpha)$. It is useful to compare this measure to a commonly used first-order indicator, namely, the change in national product. The two measures would agree only if there were no distribution term and national product correctly incorporated collective goods.[5]

---

[5] These statements hold even in a dynamic context since the value of competitive investment (which will appear in national product) must equal the value of future consumption in enables [which appears in a time-dated version of (9.7)].

Clearly, the distribution term will be difficult to evaluate precisely since it still involves disaggregated information. However, it may be possible to find good approximations in practice. For example, suppose that we can predict the *distribution* of net benefits and the correlation between the welfare weights and these net benefits. This latter coefficient (call it σ) might be thought of as the estimated regression coefficient in an econometric equation of the form

$$\beta^h - \bar{\beta} = \sigma \left[\frac{\nabla_\alpha V^h}{\lambda^h} \right] + \epsilon_h. \tag{9.8}$$

Then, the distribution term can be computed as

$$\sum_h (\beta^h - \bar{\beta}) \left[\frac{\nabla_\alpha V^h}{\lambda^h} \right] = \sigma \sum_h \left[\frac{\nabla_\alpha V^h}{\lambda^h} \right]^2. \tag{9.9}$$

Thus, computation requires only the correlation parameter and the second moment of the net benefits distribution. Note in particular that if the net project benefits are uncorrelated with the welfare weights, the distribution term vanishes. Thus, the possibility of no correlation adds a little more generality to the situations when it is legitimate to measure welfare using simple numeraire aggregates.

When there is a nonzero correlation, σ is a parameter that reflects both the degree of correlation and the relative importance of equity considerations, so the size of this parameter reflects a value judgment that must be made before any valid welfare inferences can be drawn.

B   *Second-best measures for market distortions*

Many authors have discussed the second-best impacts of commodity taxation and monopoly power in isolation.[6] We can show that such second-best impacts can be separated out here, although *only* with respect to the pure efficiency part of the measure. That is, we show that each element of market distortion generates its own second-best term in a way that is additive with respect to the second-best term for distribution already discussed.

Using the price identities ($P = Q + t$) and material balance constraints that hold as functions of α [$C(\alpha) = Y(\alpha) - b(\alpha)$], we can decompose opportunity cost into the market cost of the project plus two other terms:

$$P \nabla_\alpha C = (Q + t) \nabla_\alpha C = -Q \nabla_\alpha b + Q \nabla_\alpha Y + t \nabla_\alpha C. \tag{9.10}$$

[6] See, e.g., Lerner (1944) and Harberger (1971).

The last of these other terms is attributable to indirect taxation, since it will be zero when all the tax rates are zero. It is computed as the change in tax revenue given *fixed* tax rates. Thus, we have rigorously justified the intuitive argument used in the previous chapter: Induced extra units of a taxed good generate a second-best surplus because consumers value them more highly than it costs to produce them at the margin.

The remaining term measures the change in profit at fixed producer prices and captures two factors: the change due to net benefits from collective goods and a change attributable to noncompetitive behavior. To see this, we separate out effects attributable to collective goods:

$$Q \nabla_\alpha Y = Q \nabla_g Y \nabla_\alpha g + Q \nabla_\alpha Y \mid_{g=g^o}. \tag{9.11}$$

The first term on the right side of (9.11) represents the change in profits attributable to new collective goods. The second will be zero for firms that behave as competitors. The reason is that the vector $\nabla_\alpha Y \mid_{g=g^o}$ was a feasible direction of movement for the firms at status quo prices and provision levels, so if firms are competitive maximizers, neither a positive nor a negative move in this direction can improve profits at fixed prices.[7]

When private firms do not take price as given and/or maximize profits, the associated term is not zero and represents the welfare impact of the project on the second-best nature of production. We compute it by calculating the change in profit with provision levels fixed computed at *fixed* producer prices. (Elsewhere, the "monopoly" distortion generally is expressed in a different form involving markups. We comment on the connection between these two measures in the sequel.)

Note carefully that it would *not* be correct to measure benefits by "first-order change in tax revenue" or "first-order change in profits" since these terms would include quantities generated by changes in tax rates or producer prices. Such changes never generate real welfare effects (except as they influence the distributional term); when tax rates or prices change, one side of the market gains whereas the other loses an equal amount. Outside the distributional term, these units are counted equally and therefore cancel. Of course, we do not see any pure transfer items (such as lump-sum taxes) in our measures for the same reason.

Reuniting the pieces of our puzzle, we obtain the decomposition

$$\frac{\nabla_\alpha Z}{\bar{\beta}} = [\Omega + Q \nabla_g Y] \nabla_\alpha g - Q \nabla_\alpha b + \sum_h \frac{\beta^h - \bar{\beta}}{\bar{\beta}} \left[\frac{\nabla_\alpha V^h}{\lambda^h} \right]$$
$$+ Q \nabla_\alpha Y \mid_{g=g^o} + t \nabla_\alpha C. \tag{9.12}$$

---

[7] This argument does rely on smoothness in the technology. Although we are maintaining such assumptions for convenience, the basic story here will carry over to more general situations.

Thus, our measure of marginal welfare change consists of the standard first-best benefit–cost calculus together with three additive terms representing the three elements of second best.

Observe that there is no presumption concerning the sign of these terms. In particular, they do not represent "deadweight loss" as it is usually defined. If a project increases the demand for a taxed good (ceteris paribus), it generates a second-best benefit. The idea behind deadweight loss stems from the view that we must lose something in passing from first best to second best. This is true in the neighborhood of the first best, as we will see in Chapter 15, when we look at second-order approximations; but once we are away from the first best, actions we take may serve to better or worsen our (status quo) second-best position.

Finally, note that it is almost surely not optimal to follow the first-best rules of benefit–cost analysis in deciding on project levels. Such a rule would involve equating marginal benefit Ω to marginal market cost $Q \nabla_g b$ and would only be optimal if the marginal project had no equity effects and did not affect the production of "monopolized" goods or consumption of taxed goods; the latter condition would require that the demand for taxed goods be additively separable from the demands for project inputs and outputs. Thus, our formulation gives us a way of stating precisely the conditions of separability required in order that distortions in one sector of the economy not affect the first-best optimality conditions in other sectors.[8]

9.2   Intermediate-goods taxation and quantity constraints

We generalize the model now to incorporate a wider class of tax structures and quantity constraints. These two topics are best treated together since they both require that we distinguish between sales and purchases. Rather than develop an explicit representation of technological relationships we have not needed up to now and would not use in the sequel, we will restrict attention to quantity constraints on households. Also, for convenience, we will assume in the remainder of this chapter that the collective goods do not affect firms.

We start with the most general *linear* tax system and then take up nonlinear tax schedules. All transactions vectors will be broken up into two parts: sales and purchases; a plus superscript will denote sales, and a minus superscript will denote purchases. Thus, for example, y^{j+} denotes the sales vector of firm j and c^{h-} is the purchase vector of household h.

---

[8] The separability issue was first raised by Davis–Whinston (1962). A more systematic discussion can be found in Negishi (1972).

Similarly, Q^- is the purchase price vector for firms, and so forth. (Refer back to Chapter 6 for further discussion of this framework.)

The government will generate differences in the four price vectors by imposing linear commodity taxes as follows: (1) $P^- - Q^+$ represents the tax vector on sales by firms to households, (2) $P^+ - Q^-$ represents the tax vector on sales by households to firms, and (3) $Q^- - Q^+$ represents the tax vector on sales by firms to firms. Notice that once these taxes have been set, $P^+ - P^-$ must be determined so there cannot be any independent choice of tax rates on transactions among households. This restriction must be adhered to as long as the "law of one price" is to hold; that is, as long as the government cannot impose different transaction prices on an agent depending on the identity of the other transacting party.

Of course, the government might face further restrictions on what it can do. Perhaps it cannot tell whether a household or firm is selling (or buying), in which case we will get a uniform tax structure where $Q^+ = P^+$ and $Q^- = P^-$. Then, $P^- - P^+$ can be interpreted as a "transactions tax vector." Furthermore, the optimal-tax framework discussed earlier is another special case, where $Q^+ = Q^- \equiv Q$ and $P^+ = P^- \equiv P$. Note that to enforce this structure, the government must be able to avoid taxing intermediate goods (such as hardware) even when they are to be taxed as final consumption; we have implicitly assumed this was possible heretofore.

Employing our new notation, the profits of firm j become

$$\pi^j = Q^+ y^{j+} - Q^- y^{j-}, \tag{9.13}$$

whereas the budget constraint of household h takes the form

$$P^- c^{h-} - P^+ c^{h+} = m^h. \tag{9.14}$$

Observe that there is nothing in our formulation to prevent firms or households from buying and selling the same good simultaneously, although optimizing agents clearly will not do so as long as the associated tax rate is positive. Of course, by the same token, there is an incentive problem with subsidies. The government will have trouble controlling a subsidy program unless it can effectively prevent simultaneous buying and selling. We will not concern ourselves further with this problem here. However, we do need to impose nonnegativity constraints on sales and purchases explicitly, since some of them are sure to be binding in the present context.

We introduce constrained transactions by imposing upper bounds on sales and purchases by households. Although we do not attempt to explicitly model the origins of these constraints, we must assume that there is a consistent equilibrium system that determines the active bounds as part of the overall status quo equilibrium.[9] Thus, the new optimization problem for household h is stated as

$$\max_{c's} U^h(g^h, c^{h-} - c^{h+}) \tag{9.15}$$

subject to

$$P^- c^{h-} - P^+ c^{h+} = \pi_h - T^h,$$

$$0 \le c^{h-} \le \bar{c}^{h-},$$

$$0 \le c^{h+} \le \bar{c}^{h+}.$$

Let ξ^{h+} and ξ^{h-} denote the Lagrange multipliers associated with the new quantity constraints. Constraint levels naturally will appear as new parameters in consumer indirect utility functions, and we want to think of these transaction upper bounds as variable (e.g., the project may generate new employment possibilities). To the extent that the project does affect such variables, it generates some new second-best welfare effects that we want to measure. The best known contributions of this sort in the literature are the so-called multiplier effects of macro-public-finance. We will develop the connections with this literature momentarily.

The analysis, though more complex, follows the same general steps as before. (The reader is invited to fill in these steps as a test of understanding.) Using the envelope theorem and substituting from the individual budget identity, we can write

$$\frac{\nabla_\alpha V^h}{\lambda^h} = \Omega^h \nabla_\alpha g + P^- \nabla_\alpha c^{h-} - P^+ \nabla_\alpha c^{h+} + \frac{\xi^{h-}}{\lambda^h} \nabla_\alpha \bar{c}^{h+} + \frac{\xi^{h-}}{\lambda^h} \nabla_\alpha \bar{c}^{hi}. \tag{9.16}$$

The opportunity cost of the project has been modified in two ways. First, the foregone alternative is weighted differently depending on how it was foregone. If more sales are made (as, e.g., with labor), they are weighted at the selling price, whereas lost purchases are weighted at the purchase price. Second, new terms appear representing the added benefit from relaxing binding constraints. We can perform some further decomposition on each of these terms.

Since there is nothing new to say about the form of the distribution term, we will concentrate on the "pure-efficiency" part of welfare change.

[9] Models of this character have been constructed by Barro–Grossman (1976), Benassy (1977), and Malinvaud (1977), among others. See Dixit (1976) for further discussion of public finance issues in this context.

After aggregation and substitutions using material balance conditions, the market component of opportunity cost may be expressed as

$$P^- \nabla_\alpha C^- - P^+ \nabla_\alpha C^+ = Q^+ \nabla_\alpha b^+ - Q^- \nabla_\alpha b^-$$
$$+ Q^+ \nabla_\alpha Y^+ - Q^- \nabla_\alpha Y^- + (P^- - Q^+) \nabla_\alpha C^- + (Q^- - P^+) \nabla_\alpha C^+$$
$$+ (Q^- - Q^+)[\nabla_\alpha Y^- + \nabla_\alpha b^- - \nabla_\alpha C^+]. \tag{9.17}$$

Note the similarities of the measures obtained here with those of the previous section. Terms on the first line constitute the first-best cost, with government market transactions evaluated at producer's prices. The next two terms reflect change in profit at fixed producer prices and will be zero if firms behave competitively (since we are ignoring the potential impact of collective goods here). The remaining terms reflect second-best contributions due to indirect taxation.

Having distinguished between sales and purchases, we can reinterpret the second line in terms of "markups" when the private firms behave like monopolists. Suppose we focus on a particular firm that produces a single output (y^+), faces parametric prices for its inputs, and minimizes the cost of whatever output is produced (such behavior is characteristic of a monopolist, though not of a "satisficer"). Formally, the firm solves a subproblem

$$\min Q^- y^- \tag{9.18}$$

subject to

$$(-y^-, y^+) \in \mathcal{Y}$$

defining derived demands for factors $y^-(y^+, Q^-)$ and a cost function

$$\Gamma(y^+, Q^-) = Q^- y^-(y^+, Q^-). \tag{9.19}$$

Now we can see that our second-best term involving firm purchases can be expressed in terms of partial derivatives of this cost function[10]:

$$Q^- \nabla_\alpha y^- = Q^- \nabla_y y^- \nabla_\alpha y^+ = \frac{\partial \Gamma}{\partial y^+} \nabla_\alpha y^+. \tag{9.20}$$

Consequently,

$$Q^+ \nabla_\alpha y^+ - Q^- \nabla_\alpha y^- = \left[Q^+ - \frac{\partial \Gamma}{\partial y^+} \right] \nabla_\alpha y^+. \tag{9.21}$$

In words, our second-best term is measured by the markup over marginal cost times the increase in the amounts produced. Although this measure

[10] In this derivation, we have dropped a term of the form $Q^- \nabla_Q y^-$. It must be zero for a cost minimizer for the same reason that $Q \nabla_Q y$ was zero for a profit maximizer in the previous section.

has the advantage of being easy to compute, we reiterate that it will not apply to firms of the type described by March and Simon (1963) or Baumol (1967) that do not maximize profits. We must revert to our more general measure to correctly account for such firms.

The second-best contribution due to indirect taxation now contains three terms. This particular form is appropriate for interpretation in the plausible situation where there are no transactions between households. Then, the first term represents the sum over commodities of the tax on sales from firms to households times the change in that tax base; the second has the same interpretation for sales from households to firms. Finally, since $Y^- + b^- - C^+$ is the excess of purchases by firms and the government over what households bought, it must represent the vector of purchases by firms from other firms. Thus, the third term represents the intermediate-goods taxes times the change in the amounts of intermediate-goods transactions. As an exercise, the reader might verify that when the tax structure is "uniform," our second-best contribution reduces to transactions tax rates times the change in transactions base. Thus, the principle tax rate times change in tax base appears to be quite general for measuring second-best contributions from linear indirect taxation. (However, the reader is cautioned that this result does not always hold for other kinds of taxes; we will give an example in the next section.)

Returning to the general expression (9.16), we analyze the new terms associated with quantity constraints. Aggregating, substituting from first-order conditions for consumer optimization, and making use of the fact that nonnegativity constraints and quantity constraints never bind simultaneously, these terms may be reexpressed as

$$
\sum_h \left[\frac{\xi^{h+}}{\lambda^h} \nabla_\alpha \bar{c}^{h+} + \frac{\xi^{h-}}{\lambda^h} \nabla_\alpha \bar{c}^{h-} \right]
$$

$$
= \sum_h \left[\frac{\nabla_c U^h}{\lambda^h} - P^- \right] \nabla_\alpha \bar{c}^{h-} + \sum_h \left[P^+ - \frac{\nabla_c U^h}{\lambda^h} \right] \nabla_\alpha \bar{c}^{h+}. \tag{9.22}
$$

For each consumer, changes in the ration levels induced by the project are multiplied by the gap between that consumer's pseudovalue (reservation price) and the market value of the rationed good.

Note the similarity of interpretation with other second-best terms; quantity constraints play the role of tax base, whereas the gap between reservation price and market price plays the role of tax rate. These types of net benefits appear most frequently in the literature with respect to employment in Keynesian public finance. A commonly accepted procedure amounts to applying the preceding theory (when only labor supply is constrained) under the assumption that $\nabla_c U^h = 0$ for all effectively rationed individuals, so that the second-best contribution becomes simply labor income generated by the project $(P^+ \nabla_\alpha \bar{c}^{h+})$. Thus, this approach is only valid when labor supply functions are totally inelastic (so that there is no labor leisure margin) and each individual is either employed or unemployed. Perhaps this assumption is reasonable for some people (such as heads of household with only one type of usable skill), but it clearly is not valid generally. Indeed, most individuals have second-best jobs they could hold when rationed in their first-best activity. Regardless of whether they choose to work in these jobs, the associated wage constitutes a lower bound on their associated value of leisure.

To make correct operational use of the new terms requires information on reservation prices and quantity constraints. The difficulties in measuring reservation prices are quite similar to those involved in measuring Ω, and we will review the relevant state of the art in Chapter 13. Assuming we are able to accurately measure reservation prices, the other problem (identifying quantity constraints) disappears. Intuitively, we will be able to tell whether there is a quantity constraint simply by observing whether there is a gap between market versus reservation prices; and if there is, any increase in market activity must entail a relaxation in the constraint.

We can justify this argument more formally as follows: Since the associated multipliers are positive only when quantity constraints bind, the expression $\xi^{h+}(\alpha)[\bar{c}^{h+}(\alpha) - c^{h+}(\alpha)]$ must be identically zero in α. Differentiating, we can write

$$\xi^{h+}[\nabla_\alpha \bar{c}^{h+} - \nabla_\alpha c^{h+}] + \nabla_\alpha \xi^{h+}[\bar{c}^{h+} - c^{h+}] = 0. \qquad (9.23)$$

But any gap between c and $\bar{c}$ requires that the Lagrange multiplier be zero in a neighborhood of $\alpha = 0$ (relaxing the constraint is valueless) so the second term in (9.23) is zero. Consequently, it is legitimate to replace $\nabla_\alpha \bar{c}$ by $\nabla_\alpha c$ in our second-best measures.[11]

9.3   Nonlinear taxes

Finally, we extend our discussion to cover nonlinear tax structures such as the U.S. income tax. Since it is difficult to identify the defining characteristics of a firm, there are problems associated with imposing nonlinear taxes on firms. For example, if the tax rate increases with size, a large firm will want to split into two parts for tax purposes. Although these incentive problems are not necessarily insurmountable (indeed, the corporate income tax is somewhat nonlinear), we will restrict taxation on firms to the linear type already discussed. Thus, Q^- and Q^+ will continue

---

[11] For a more rigorous justification of this argument in the context of general envelope theorems, see Arrow–Enthoven (1961).

to represent the buying and selling prices to firms (and these are independent of the amounts transacted).

Consumer prices are no longer defined independent of the level of transactions. Households will be thought of as paying the base (producer) prices plus a tax that may depend on the amounts transacted. Let the function $T^h(c^{h+}, c^{h-}, Q^+, Q^-, m^h, \tau)$ denote the total commodity tax bill paid by h, where τ is a vector of tax schedule parameters. Note that this formulation is general enough to include virtually all types of tax in the U.S. system. For example, a graduated resource tax would be represented by a function with the single argument $Q^{h-}c^{h+} + m^h$. Further, a tax on interest income can be incorporated as well since accumulated savings balances are functions of previous sales and purchases.

We drop reference to quantity constraints in the analysis to follow. As an exercise, the reader might want to carry these along and show that the corresponding second-best measures will be unchanged from what we previously derived.

Household h now faces a problem of the form

$$\max U^h(g, c^{h-} - c^{h+}) \tag{9.24}$$

subject to

$$Q^+ c^{h-} - Q^- c^{h+} + T^h(c^{h+}, c^{h-}, Q^+, Q^-, m^h, \tau) = m^h.$$

As always, $V^h(\cdot)$ denotes the associated indirect utility function. Using duality and budget substitutions as before, we obtain the following opportunity cost form for individual welfare measure:

$$\frac{\nabla_\alpha V^h}{\lambda^h} = \Omega^h \nabla_\alpha g + [Q^+ + \nabla_{c-} T^h] \nabla_\alpha c^{h-} - [Q^- - \nabla_{c+} T^h] \nabla_\alpha c^{h+}. \tag{9.25}$$

Notice that this form is essentially as before, except that "consumer prices" may differ from household to household. These effective prices are measured as transactions price net of marginal tax cost per unit purchased (sold).

Aggregation and further substitution from material balance conditions yield the welfare decomposition

$$\frac{\nabla_\alpha Z}{\bar{\beta}} = \sum_h \frac{\beta^h - \bar{\beta}}{\bar{\beta}} \left[\frac{\nabla_\alpha V^h}{\lambda^h} \right] + \Omega \nabla_\alpha g + Q^+ \nabla_\alpha b^+ - Q^- \nabla_\alpha b^-$$

$$+ Q^+ \nabla_\alpha Y^+ - Q^- \nabla_\alpha Y^-$$

$$+ \sum_h [\nabla_{c-} T^h] \nabla_\alpha c^{h-} + \sum_h [\nabla_{c+} T^h] \nabla_\alpha c^{h+}$$

$$+ [Q^- - Q^+][\nabla_\alpha Y^- + \nabla_\alpha b^- - \nabla_\alpha C^+]. \tag{9.26}$$

Observe that this expression has exactly the same form as before, except that we evaluate change in tax revenue at fixed *marginal* tax rates.

It is instructive to interpret our general measure in the special case of a graduated resource tax. We find, in this case, that the tax term in (9.26) takes the form $\sum_h (dT^h/dm)Q^{h-}\nabla_\alpha c^{h+}$. Clearly, it is no longer true that this measure entails the marginal tax rate times the change in the tax base. Changes in the income base associated with price movements or exogenous components do not contribute to the associated second-best welfare term. Thus, we must be careful in using that principle when the tax base is a composite (such as income).

9.4   Practical rules and pitfalls of benefit–cost analysis

Although we have yet to address some difficult problems involving uncertainty and large projects, our analysis already suggests a set of useful guidelines for benefit–cost analysis. Since there is a tendency in actual studies to count too many things, some of these guidelines are better stated in terms of do not's rather than do's. As will be seen, most of these guidelines are based on the assumption that distributional benefits are absent or accounted for separately.

Perhaps the single most important and useful guideline tells us to ignore all activity on secondary competitive markets. This guideline is best elucidated with the help of an example. Suppose we are considering an irrigation project, one of whose impacts will be to stimulate the demand for tractors. Should we count extra tractor sales or profits as part of project benefits? As long as tractors are not taxed, extra sales generate canceling benefits and costs, since the buyer's marginal gain is equal to the seller's marginal loss. And as long as the tractor industry is competitive, the seller's marginal loss (price) will equal marginal social opportunity cost; profit reflects a normal return to capital and adds nothing "extra" to social benefit. Only if one could argue from a distributional perspective that one side of the market is more deserving than the other would there be a net welfare impact.

The fact that we can ignore indirect effects in most competitive markets is quite important in that it reduces substantially the amount of information that needs to be collected and processed for benefit–cost studies. We will see just how helpful this "conservative" feature is when we turn to a context where it is absent, namely, benefit–cost analysis in a quantity-constrained world. Of course, some effects on third markets should be counted. At the very least, any direct effects of the public project on production possibilities in such a market should be counted. These will be reflected in increased profits (at fixed producer prices). Further, any second-best distortions present in such markets generate secondary welfare contributions, as we have seen.

Such secondary benefits sometimes crop up in unexpected ways. For example, consider the case of employment benefits. Assuming, for the moment, that labor markets are competitive (no quantity constraints) and that labor supply is not taxed, the preceding discussion would suggest that there are no legitimate "employment benefits." However, this view ignores the welfare system, which acts in some ways like a subsidy to unemployment (tax on employment). To the extent that extra employment reduces welfare payments, the project induces a second-best benefit in the employment market just as it does when it increases the "base" in any taxed market. Assuming that the marginal compensation schedules remain unchanged, this benefit will be measured by induced reduction in welfare payments.

Another important do not: Ignore all direct transfers. This injunction applies to all lump-sum payments by the government as well as many induced regional transfers. Of course, such transfers may have some distributional impact, but otherwise their net welfare impacts cancel out exactly. As an illustration of this principle, suppose the employment generated in the previous example occurred at the expense of lost employment in other regions (so that net aggregate employment was unchanged). Then, employment benefits in the "project" region are just canceled by employment costs elsewhere. The same argument tells us to ignore profits earned by firms that move into the project area, assuming these profits were foregone elsewhere. Only "supernormal" profits directly attributable to the project can be counted. Note carefully that this principle implicitly takes the point of view of society as a whole. Indeed, our discussion suggests that there will be differences between regional and national objectives when resources are mobile among regions. We will attempt to measure these differences in Chapter 11.

When quantity constraints are generally present, some of the preceding simplicity is lost from benefit–cost rules. In particular, all indirect impacts on quantity-constrained commodities will generate welfare effects. And relaxation of one quantity constraint generally induces relaxation in many others through "multiplier" and "trickle-down" effects. Multiplier benefits occur, for example, when extra employment today generates extra income (and saving) that calls forth the demand necessary to relax any employment constraint in place for tomorrow and all later dates in the future. Benefits trickle down when resources drawn away from one use open up new opportunities for other, quantity-constrained resources. For example, employment at a high-skill level may draw "overqualified" people away from lower-skilled occupations, relaxing the associated constraints there. All of these effects on welfare need to be counted in judging a project.

Thus, although general equilibrium propagation through the price system generally washes out in the welfare calculus, the corresponding propagation through quantity constraints does not and must be correctly accounted for.[12] Further, the practitioner's problems are compounded by the fact that *what* to count depends on the unobservable opportunity costs. Unforgivable sins are committed when one counts, for example, employment benefits for workers who merely switched from equally attractive alternative jobs.

[12] Actually, one might argue that similar considerations apply with respect to second-best tax effects since changes in the tax base may occur for many different taxed goods in many different periods. However, price-induced substitutions seem to "die out" quickly compared to multiplier effects.

CHAPTER 10

Principles of shadow pricing

Much of applied welfare economics as it has developed over the past several decades involves the study and use of shadow prices. Since (as we will argue) shadow pricing means different things to different people, we start with a rather broad definition and spend some time talking about various alternative meanings of the term. *Shadow pricing* will refer to the study and use of first-order welfare impacts associated with changes in the levels of particular goods or groups of goods.

This definition accords with the common view of what a shadow price stands for. Suppose we are talking about some input to a government project. Then the shadow price ought to be opportunity cost per unit of increasing this input, and the correct way to measure this opportunity cost is by the marginal welfare foregone. Ambiguity in the definition arises over the ceteris paribus assumptions. When an input level is changed, what other things are allowed to change with it? Obviously, something must change in equilibrium or else an infeasibility develops. And it would be silly to ignore this infeasibility here since the shadow price would be zero if we do.

On the other hand, issues of feasibility frequently are ignored when economists discuss shadow pricing of *outputs*. We ask, for example, what would an extra unit of public good be worth if we had it? (And never mind how would we get it?) Here, shadow price becomes a hypothetical construction. Having obtained such a price, we proceed by comparing it with the least cost way of actually getting an extra unit.

Clearly, it is useful to think differently about the ceteris paribus assumption in different contexts. But to avoid confusion, it is important to be precise about the assumptions in each context. We can achieve precision by specifying which variables are to be treated as independent in each instance. We may choose these so that there are feasibility constraints linking the independent variables, in which case the associated shadow prices will be hypothetical. Having chosen the independent variables, the model must be specified in such a way that equilibrium determines all remaining (dependent) variables as functions of the independent ones.

We will look at several different ways of making these specifications momentarily. However, before doing so, we contrast the general approach of shadow pricing from that of decomposition and point out some potential pitfalls in the interpretation of shadow prices. Let us refer back to the fundamental decomposition equation (for simplicity, we assume in this chapter that collective goods do not affect firms):

$$\frac{\nabla_\alpha Z}{\bar{\beta}} = \Omega\,\nabla_\alpha g - Q\,\nabla_\alpha b + \sum_h \frac{\beta^h - \bar{\beta}}{\bar{\beta}}\left[\frac{\nabla_\alpha V^h}{\lambda^h}\right] + Q\,\nabla_\alpha Y + t\,\nabla_\alpha C. \tag{10.1}$$

Since the change in government inputs is weighted by producer prices in this expression, one might be tempted to say that the shadow prices of such government inputs should be producer prices. But that statement would not have any operational meaning here; there is no consistent specification of independent and dependent variables under which b is independent with Q as its shadow price vector. For those statements to be true, the variables C and Y would have to be independent, whereas (9.11) was derived under the assumption that C, Y, and b were linked through market equilibrium conditions.

We can see that Q has no operational significance as a shadow price another way. Using market identities, we can write

$$t\,\nabla_\alpha C = t\,\nabla_\alpha Y - t\,\nabla_\alpha b. \tag{10.2}$$

Substituting (10.2) into (10.1) and recombining terms, we have the alternative decomposition

$$\frac{\nabla_\alpha Z}{\bar{\beta}} = \Omega\,\nabla_\alpha g - P\,\nabla_\alpha b + \sum_h \frac{\beta^h - \bar{\beta}}{\bar{\beta}}\left[\frac{\nabla_\alpha V^h}{\lambda^h}\right] + Q\,\nabla_\alpha Y + t\,\nabla_\alpha Y. \tag{10.3}$$

Now, the government inputs are weighted by consumer prices. Should we conclude that they now serve as shadow prices? Obviously not unless we envisage a context in which b changes whereas none of the other terms in the decomposition will. Again, it is clear that there is no such consistent context.

None of this is meant to denigrate the decomposition approach. Indeed, it may be particularly helpful when we are concerned with practical measures (we have reasonable information on changes in tax revenue and profits). Also, it serves the purpose of breaking complex expressions into simple component parts each of which has a natural interpretation. And as we shall see momentarily, legitimate shadow prices frequently can be expressed in terms of such component parts.

10.1   Categories of shadow prices

Let us distinguish several potentially useful contexts for shadow pricing. First, think of the "most hypothetical" situation already mentioned: We ask what the extra unit would be worth if we had it, *and nothing else in the system changed*. Call this the *detached* context. As examples, the detached shadow price of g will be Ω, that for b will be 0, and that for agent h's leisure (in a quantity-constrained situation) will be $\partial U^h/\partial L$. At the other extreme, suppose we think of a planning problem in which all relevant constraints have been built in. The parameters of such a problem are the independent variables, and arguments chosen by the planner are the dependent variables. Call this the *programming* context. Each parameter has a programming shadow price equal to the rate at which the objective will go up per extra unit of that parameter. When the programming problem appears in the form

$$\max_{x} F_0(x) \tag{10.4}$$

subject to

$$F_i(x) \leq \gamma_i, \quad i = 1, \ldots, k,$$

where the γ's denote exogenous parameters, the interpretation of a programming shadow price should be very familiar. For a particular γ_i it will be the Lagrange multiplier associated with the ith constraint. More generally, programming shadow prices can be computed from the envelope theorem, as indicated in Chapter 3.

It is worth noting that the welfare measures of the previous chapter can be interpreted as programming shadow prices. The context is one in which project scale α is thought of as the only parameter. Assuming that we could set up a programming problem that determined outcomes as a function of scale, $\nabla_\alpha Z$ would be the programming shadow price of α.

Among the many other possible consistent frameworks for defining shadow prices, there is one that occupies an important place in public economics.[1] It treats project variables (g, b) as independent with all other variables dependent on them through equilibrium conditions. Note carefully the hypothetical element present here. With g and b thought of as independent, the equilibrium must be definable as functions of *all* combinations, not just those that are technologically possible. The shadow price of g_i denotes the social worth of an extra unit of g_i assuming that it could be had without changing b or any of the other g's.

Since welfare now is to be thought of as a function of both b and g, the new context (call it the *project* context) is that of (9.2):

---

[1] This framework is implicit in Diamond–Mirrlees (1971) and recurs in Little–Mirrlees (1974) and Dasgupta–Marglin–Sen (1972).

$$Z(g, b) = W[V^1(g, P(g, b), T^1(g, b), \pi_1(g, b)), \ldots,$$

$$V^N(g, P(g, b), T^N(g, b), \pi_N(g, b))]. \quad (10.5)$$

Consequently, the project shadow price vector for g is $\nabla_g Z$, whereas that for b is $-\nabla_b Z$.[2] The following discussion will concentrate primarily on finding formulas for evaluating project shadow prices.

10.2   Formulas based on second-best decomposition

How can we evaluate partial derivatives of Z in (10.5)? Fortunately, most of the constructions of the previous chapter are still available to us. To see this, recall our procedure there. We defined g and b as functions of α and totally differentiated with respect to α. Now we simply want to differentiate with respect to g and b separately. And since all budget and material balance conditions are assumed to hold as functions of g and b separately, all substitutions that we made using these conditions before can still be made here. In this process, all demands and supplies are interpreted as reduced-form functions of g and b. We indicate these functions with an asterisk. Thus, $c^{h*}(g, b) = c^h[g, P(g, b), T^h(g, b), \pi_h(g, b)]$, and similarly for all other behavioral functions. Formulas must look the same as before except that terms like $\nabla_g b$ disappear since g and b are chosen independently. Thus, we have immediately the following two analogs of (9.12), which decompose shadow prices in much the same way as we decomposed the project before:

$$\frac{\nabla_g Z}{\bar{\beta}} = \Omega + \sum_h \frac{\beta^h - \bar{\beta}}{\bar{\beta}} \left[\frac{\nabla_q V^{*h}}{\lambda^h} \right] + Q \nabla_g Y^* + t \nabla_g C^*, \quad (10.6)$$

$$-\frac{\nabla_b Z}{\bar{\beta}} = Q - \sum_h \frac{\beta^h - \bar{\beta}}{\bar{\beta}} \left[\frac{\nabla_b V^{*h}}{\lambda^h} \right] - Q \nabla_b Y^* - t \nabla_b C^*. \quad (10.7)$$

These two expressions give us the relevant shadow prices normalized so that they are measured in numeraire units ($\bar{\beta}$ is the average marginal welfare of a dollar). Such a normalization is obviously appropriate if we want to compare shadow prices with market prices (as we do). Given this desired choice of units, the notation can be simplified somewhat by transforming the welfare function so that the average marginal welfare of a dollar is unity ($\bar{\beta} = 1$) at the status quo.[3] Then, the welfare shadow prices will be automatically normalized.

---

[2] Since shadow prices of economic "goods" generally are thought of as positive whether they refer to inputs or outputs, we change sign when referring to inputs.

[3] Of course, the welfare representation must be changed whenever we change the status quo, but this will not cause us problems as long as we remain in the context of first-order analysis.

Here, we will discuss primarily the shadow price equation for b, leaving the other case to the reader as an exercise. Obviously, there will not be much to say beyond the general sorts of remarks found in Chapter 9 unless we find some simplifying principles, look at special cases, or both. Let us start with some interesting special cases.

Suppose that all changes in exogenous elements of income must be uniform across people. This condition naturally holds if there are no such elements (no lump-sum taxes and no profit income) but could hold more generally (as, e.g., if we have a negative income tax with uniform guarantee). Actually, what we require is slightly weaker, namely, that changes in exogenous income do not correlate with the welfare weights. Such lack of correlation allows us to simplify distributive terms considerably.

To see this, let us write individual utility change in the following additive form:

$$\frac{\nabla_b V^{*h}}{\lambda^h} = -\{\nabla_b Pc^h\} - \nabla_b T^h + \nabla_b \pi_h. \tag{10.8}$$

Given our assumptions, the last two terms in this expansion do not depend on h. Therefore, since a covariance is additive in either term and takes the value zero whenever one of its arguments is constant, the distributive term in (10.7) reduces to

$$\sum_h (\beta^h - 1) \left[\frac{\nabla_b V^{*h}}{\lambda^h} \right] = -\sum_h [(\beta^h - 1)\{\nabla_b Pc^h\}]. \tag{10.9}$$

Thus, the distributive term is measured by the correlation between welfare weights and individual consumptions of a particular "market basket" of goods; the weights used in making up the market basket are to be determined by the relative price changes induced by increased demand for b.

Let us suppose further that firms behave competitively so that we can ignore the "monopoly profit" term. (The reader is invited to generalize the following discussion so as to include this term.) Then the shadow price vector for b takes the form[4]:

$$-\nabla_b Z = Q + \sum_h [(\beta^h - 1)\{\nabla_b Pc^h\}] - t \nabla_b C^*. \tag{10.10}$$

We are left with two relatively simple "gaps" between shadow price and market price (Q). Both of these have been discussed in the literature though usually only under even more restrictive assumptions. Verbally, the two gaps are characterized as follows: An increase in the government demand for good j will result (through equilibrium adjustments) in a

---

[4] This formulation is roughly consistent with that used in Feldstein (1972).

change in the cost of consuming c equal to $\nabla_{b_j} Pc$. The shadow price for j should be below the market price to the extent that (cereris paribus) changes in consumer cost correlate negatively with the welfare weights and vice versa. Thus, we attach a relatively low shadow cost to inputs whose use drives up the cost of necessities less than it drives up the cost of luxuries.

In addition, shadow price should be below market price to the extent that (ceteris paribus) the induced changes in private consumption increase tax revenue at fixed (ex ante) tax rates and vice versa.[5] The reasons here are much as in the previous chapter: Expanding a commodity tax base is welfare improving (to a first order), and we want to encourage use of an input that generates such an "externality." Of course, to separate out these shadow price influences commodity by commodity, we would need detailed information on how the incidence of demand for one good affects equilibrium prices (and demands).

It is tempting to simplify further by making some assumptions concerning the nature of these equilibrium relationships. For example, suppose that increases in the demand for good j led to changes in the price(s) *only* of good j. Then, in evaluating the gaps, we need look only at private net demands for good j. Unfortunately, such "separability" assumptions are always strong in the present context and are frequently inconsistent. Indeed, if good j is untaxed, increased demand for it by the planner requires that some tax rate (and associated consumer and/or producer price) change elsewhere in the system.

One fairly common interpretation of the second gap involves these inconsistent assumptions. When only one good is taxed (say i), this interpretation would have it that the shadow price of good j should fall short of its market price whenever good j substitutes for the taxed good in consumption. But will substitutability necessarily imply $t_i \, \partial C_i^* / \partial b_j > 0$? Not necessarily. Recall that $C^*(\cdot)$ is a reduced-form demand function that depends on b through *all* induced price effects. Now, extra public demand for j probably will increase P_j, and this would cause an increase in C_i *if nothing else happened;* but the requirements for new tax revenue will also force an increase in t so P_i is likely to rise as well. Since the second consideration will tend to lower demand for i, the net effect is indeterminate.

The likelihood that prices of taxed goods will go up *regardless* of what else happens (when the government expands marginally) suggests that we should observe a general tendency for project shadow prices to exceed market prices. Indeed, we gave an intuitive argument for this position

---

[5] This factor is emphasized by Baumol–Bradford (1970) and Negishi (1972).

earlier in the context of optimal taxation. We will attempt to quantify this bias in Section 10.4.

10.3   Case of tradeable goods

Given our discussion at the outset of the chapter, the reader should realize that when new choice variables are "added" to a problem, resultant shadow prices are likely to change. An important example that illustrates this point is provided by the case of tradeable goods. Suppose the planners are always free to export and/or import tradeable goods at fixed world prices (label these O). Then, regardless of the remaining specification, we can argue that the relative shadow prices of two tradeables must equal their relative world prices.[6] And the argument will illustrate a useful way to reason about shadow prices.

Assume that goods 1 and 2 are tradeable and that the planner is thinking about substituting good 2 for good 1 as public input. He can take one unit of good 1 (that he had been planning to use), export it, and use the proceeds to import some of good 2. At the given world prices, he will be able to import O_1/O_2 units of good 2. Note carefully that these transactions can be done *without* changing any of the dependent variables (such as domestic prices) of the system. Therefore, the *only* effect of these transactions on Z will occur through the direct changes in b. Consequently, he will want to make the substitution unless

$$\frac{\partial Z}{\partial b_1} \geq \frac{O_1}{O_2} \frac{\partial Z}{\partial b_2}. \tag{10.11}$$

However, he will want to substitute in the opposite direction unless this inequality is reversed, so we must have

$$\frac{\partial Z/\partial b_1}{\partial Z/\partial b_2} = \frac{O_1}{O_2}. \tag{10.12}$$

That is, relative shadow prices do equal relative world prices. Note that this conclusion requires virtually no assumptions about the nature of distortions in the domestic economy. *All* that is required is the capacity to make independent choices in the trade dimensions.

Of course, as to *absolute* shadow prices, all we could assert is

$$-\nabla_b Z = \kappa O, \quad \text{some constant } \kappa, \tag{10.13}$$

for the vector of tradeable goods. And the determination of κ requires information about the rest of the system, as we will see.

---

6 This point is emphasized in Dasgupta–Stiglitz (1974) and amplified by Warr (1977).

10.4   Formulas based on optimal taxation

A justifiably famous result from the work of Diamond and Mirrlees (1971) tells us that when commodity taxation is optimal, firms behave competitively, and all profits are taxed, the relative valuation of private goods by planners should be the same as that by private firms. This result sometimes is interpreted as saying that planners should use Q for shadow prices, although this interpretation is not correct given our definition of shadow price.

We derive the Diamond–Mirrlees result by using the structure of the optimal-tax framework to simplify the shadow-pricing formula (10.7). To that end, we will utilize one degree of freedom in this (and other) equations, which was noted in Chapter 9 but has been suppressed since. Our initial decomposition was formed by adding and subtracting an arbitrary constant times the sum of the normalized marginal utility changes. Subsequently, we set this constant equal to the average welfare weight in order that the "distribution" term be zero when the welfare weights happen to be equal. However, now that we no longer care about the structural decomposition, there is no reason to stick to this choice. Therefore, we revert to the more general form of (10.7):

$$-\nabla_b z = \kappa Q - \sum_h (\beta^h - \kappa) \left[\frac{\nabla_b V^{*h}}{\lambda^h} \right] - \kappa Q \nabla_b Y^* - \kappa t \, \nabla_b C^*, \qquad (10.14)$$

where κ is the arbitrary constant.

With no profit income accruing to consumers, b affects private-consumption levels only through its effect on consumer prices. Consequently,

$$\nabla_b C^* = \nabla_P C \{ \nabla_b P \}. \qquad (10.15)$$

Further, our current assumptions imply that the next to the last term in (10.14) and the last two terms in (10.8) are zero. Substituting (10.8) and (10.15) into (10.14), our shadow-pricing formula becomes

$$-\nabla_b Z = \kappa Q + \left\{ \nabla_b P \left[\sum_h \beta^h c^h - \kappa C - \kappa \{ t \, \nabla_P C \} \right] \right\}. \qquad (10.16)$$

The last term in our new expression represents a pecuniary externality involving welfare effects through price changes. Since it looks pretty complicated, we have not made much progress yet. But now, we use the fact that κ is a free choice and that tax rates are set optimally. The term in brackets is quite familiar from Chapter 8. Recall that optimal taxation can be characterized by the condition that the ratio

$$\mu^k = \frac{\sum_h (\beta^h c_k^h)}{C_k + \sum_j t_j (\partial C_j / \partial P_k)} \qquad (10.17)$$

is independent of k for all taxed goods. Thus, if we set κ equal to the common ratio (μ in the notation of Chapter 8), the vector in brackets vanishes identically except in the untaxed numeraire component. Since prices never change in that component, the inner product vanishes, yielding

$$-\nabla_b Z = \mu Q. \tag{10.18}$$

We have derived the fundamental result of Diamond and Mirrlees. The *relative* shadow prices of any pair of government inputs are equal to their relative producer prices. There is a useful characterization of this result in terms of production efficiency: The government should act to ensure that the marginal rate of technical substitution between all pairs of private goods is the same "inside" the government as it is elsewhere, consequently achieving aggregate production efficiency.

Among important propositions in economics, this is one of the most elegant but least intuitive. Indeed, there is a plausible intuitive argument against it deriving from the general theory of second best (cf. Chapter 9). When second-best distortions exist, we expect to observe trade-offs among efficiency criteria; therefore, should we not give up a little production efficiency in order to lessen the distortion from indirect taxation? The general rule is yes, but the answer here (as we just proved) is no. The key to this puzzle is an element of independence. With the power to set separate tax rates on each good, the government exerts control over consumer prices *independent* of the levels of producer prices. Therefore, it is free to pursue first-best efficiency in production without paying any price elsewhere. There is a close analogy with the pollution tickets scheme of Chapter 5 where control over the aggregate pollution level justified a first-best distribution of pollution rights *whether or not* the aggregate level was chosen correctly.

When shadow values for the collective goods are computed similarly, we again find that all indirect effects through price changes are eliminated so that

$$\nabla_g Z = \sum_h \beta^h \Omega^h + \mu t \, \nabla_g C. \tag{10.19}$$

Here, there is an extra correction to the pseudoprice reflecting the *direct* influence of collective goods on the consumption tax base.[7]

Sometimes the "production efficiency" result is taken to mean that the government shadow prices for private goods should be *equal* to producer prices. However, this is going too far. The *absolute* shadow price vector is not Q but a constant multiple of Q. We should ask: What does this

---

[7] If we reintroduce a direct influence of collective goods on firms, a further term would enter to measure the impact of this influence.

constant represent, and how should it influence decision making? We can
get an illuminating interpretation of it by seeing where it comes from and
what it means in the analysis of Chapter 8.

Refer back to the original-tax problem (8.14). Since g and b were treated
as parameters, this problem defines an indirect welfare function: $Z(g, b)$.
And the derivatives of Z with respect to b are precisely the shadow prices
we have been discussing. (For comparison purposes, we assume a normalization such that $\bar{\beta} = 1$.) Thus, we can use the envelope theorem to
provide an independent derivation of the shadow price formula. Differentiating the Lagrangian for problem (8.14), we find

$$-\nabla_b Z = \mu Q + \left\{ \nabla_b P \left[\sum_h \beta^h c^h - \mu C - \mu \{ t \nabla_P C \} \right] \right\}. \tag{10.20}$$

Observe that this formula has exactly the same form as (10.16). The term
in square brackets vanishes due to optimal-tax rules (8.17), and μ (since it
represents the Lagrange multiplier for the government budget constraint)
can be interpreted as the value of a numeraire unit in the government
budget relative to the value of a lump-sum unit (which has been normalized to 1). Naturally, if the government raised its money through lump-
sum methods, this number would be unity. However, we suggested earlier that money in the government budget may be more costly because
the alternative way of raising it involves second-best taxation.

Indeed, the early literature took this result for granted and argued that
the government always should hold itself to a higher standard than private firms because government spending imposes an added deadweight
loss (which is frequently referred to as *excess burden* in the literature).[8]
Although this conclusion may be generally true empirically, it cannot be
proved theoretically. The difficulty is a common one in problems involving second best (indeed, one that we have encountered before). Starting
from a position that is already second best, a new project may have a positive or negative effect on marginal deadweight loss; only if the effect is
positive will the previous argument be correct.[9]

How can we evaluate the magnitude of μ? Well, we can actually calculate it using formulas (10.17), where the commodity k could be chosen
arbitrarily. But for both computational and expositional reasons, it is
best to multiply each equation in (10.17) by the associated tax rate on
that good, sum them, and then solve for μ[10]:

$$\mu = \frac{\sum_h (\beta^h t c^h)}{t C + \langle t, \nabla_P C, t \rangle}, \tag{10.21}$$

---

[8] See especially Pigou (1947).
[9] This critique was first raised by Dasgupta–Stiglitz (1972).
[10] Obviously, the weights used in such a procedure are irrelevant if taxation is optimal.

where we have used our notation for a bilinear form in the denominator (see preface for details). This expression for the excess-burden markup agrees with measures of marginal deadweight loss derived in the optimal-tax literature, except that most authors confined themselves to the case of identical consumers so that the welfare weights were absent.[11] Some went on to generate further decomposition using Slutsky conditions, a procedure that is not particularly instructive here since aggregate demand generally fails to satisfy Slutsky conditions.

Suppose, for the moment, that welfare weights do not correlate with consumption so that the numerator in (10.21) becomes tax revenue. Since tax revenue better be positive, μ must then exceed unity if the quadratic form (in the denominator) were negative definite. Several plausible arguments can be given for the required negativity. For example, it is sufficient that all own-price effects are negative and "dominate" cross-price effects. Also, it is enough that substitution effects tend to dominate income effects (the Slutsky substitution matrix is always negative definite).

However, it is theoretically possible to find exceptions. Suppose that the optimal-tax structure is dominated by a tax on labor, the aggregate supply of which is backward bending (due to a strong income effect). Then the own-price contribution of labor to the quadratic form is positive (consumption of leisure goes up as the wage rises). Further, if all extra potential wage income is consumed as leisure, there will be no cross-price effects, and μ can be positive.

Increased taxation actually *improves* the cost of second best in this example since more labor is supplied (getting us closer to first-best supply) as the tax rate is raised (and the after-tax wage falls). This observation explains why the government would rather raise marginal revenue through the indirect tax system than through lump-sum methods in the example. Actually, our example still is not completely convincing, since the optimal-tax structure cannot be totally dominated by a wage tax unless labor is in perfectly inelastic supply (in which case it is not backward bending). Rather than try to construct a convincing general equilibrium example, it is more instructive to generalize our approach to cover nonoptimal taxation where examples such as the preceding are valid.

However, before leaving the optimal-tax framework, we comment briefly on distributional considerations. When welfare weights correlate with net tax revenues, marginal excess burden must be adjusted accordingly. The correlation will be negative whenever (1) *absolute* tax collections correlate positively with income and (2) income levels correlate negatively with welfare weights. The first condition holds even for quite regressive tax structures (and certainly for all progressive ones); only if we

---

[11] See, e.g., Atkinson–Stern (1974) and Auerbach (1982).

collect more from the poor than the rich, does it fail. The second condition obviously involves a value judgment (cf. our discussion in Chapter 2), but one that is commonly held. When the conditions do hold, the correct marginal excess burden to apply will be lower than what we would get if we ignore distributional considerations.

The appropriate intuition for this factor is as follows: When costs are measured in numeraire aggregates, they tend to overstate welfare costs, since a bigger than average share of these costs is borne by households with lower than average welfare weights. Of course, a similar statement can be made about marginal benefits measured in numeraire aggregates. We will return to these issues again in the next section.

10.5   General expressions for marginal cost of government spending

We showed in the previous section that when commodity taxation was optimal, the departures of government shadow prices from producer prices (on private goods) could be captured by a single number: μ. This observation suggests a different decomposition for evaluating shadow prices in general; it will involve a "markup" number (analogous to μ) that is common to all projects, and a correlation due to the nonoptimal nature of taxation that will differ depending on particular characteristics of the project. To see how this decomposition can be obtained, return to (10.16) (note that we retain the normalization $\bar{\beta} = 1$):

$$-\nabla_b Z = \kappa Q + \left\{ \nabla_b P \left[\sum_h \beta^h c^h - \kappa C - \kappa t \, \nabla_P C \right] \right\}. \tag{10.22}$$

This expression is valid whether or not taxation is optimal, although it does require that all pure profits are taxed (an assumption we retain here).

Recall that κ is a free parameter. When taxation is nonoptimal, no choice of κ will make the vector in square brackets $[\Lambda_t(\kappa)]$ identically zero; however, for any particular set of price change directions (δP), we could choose κ to make $\delta P[\Lambda_t(\kappa)]$ equal to zero. We want δP to be average in some appropriate sense. Unfortunately, there is no natural concept of "average" for this purpose. However, it is not unreasonable to choose δP proportional to the tax vector t; this is the price change we would get, for example, if all taxes were increased proportionally and tax incidence fell entirely on consumers. The practical advantage of this choice is that it leads to the same algebraic representation of the markup as before (10.21).

We return the focus in the following discussion to the shadow price of the project as a whole. The reader is invited to obtain parallel expressions for shadow-pricing government inputs or outputs separately. Further, we drop terms involving the private firms (implicitly assuming no collective-goods effects in production and competitive behavior); they can be added back in with no difficulty. The price change resulting from our α project $(\nabla_\alpha P)$ probably will not be exactly proportional to t, in which case the measures we have been developing will need to be corrected with a term that will depend on the difference: $\Delta P = \nabla_\alpha P - t$. Indeed, simple substitutions yield the following expression for the marginal value of the project:

$$\nabla_\alpha Z = \sum_h \beta^h \Omega^h \nabla_\alpha g - \mu Q \nabla_\alpha b + \mu t \nabla_g C \nabla_\alpha g + \Delta P[\Lambda_t(\mu)]. \tag{10.23}$$

For an average project, the last term in our new decomposition vanishes, and marginal cost $(Q\nabla_\alpha b)$ enters negatively with weight μ. All projects are marked up at this common rate, though particular ones may require further "cost corrections." The correction will be positive for projects that increase prices on relatively undertaxed goods [a k for which $\Lambda_{t_k}(\mu) > 0$] more than proportionally to the associated tax rate and vice versa.

Marginal benefits now are measured by welfare-weighted Samuelson prices with a correction for complementarities or substitutabilities between public goods and taxed goods. Since $\nabla_g C$ is computed with prices (and hence all private opportunity sets) fixed,[12] there is always some private good(s) that is complementary with a given g and at least one that is a substitute; only if the complementary ones tend to be taxed more heavily than the substitutes do we get a positive correction. Clearly, a project whose public-goods outputs were separable in demand from private goods would have no correction. It is noteworthy that any complementarity correction must be marked up in the same way as marginal cost.

Let us return briefly to the question of whether there is a bias for or against projects. Since we are thinking here of a general bias, the last term in (10.23) is irrelevant. Further, since a general project has no obvious net complementarity, the third term is also irrelevant. So, using superscript n to index a project that is "neutral" in this sense, we can decompose its net benefits into efficiency and equity terms as follows:

$$\nabla_\alpha Z^n = \sum_h \Omega^h \nabla_\alpha g^n - \gamma^n Q \nabla_\alpha b^n + \sum_h (\beta^h - 1)\left[\Omega^h \nabla_\alpha g^n - \gamma^n \frac{tc^h}{tC} Q \nabla_\alpha b^n\right],$$
$$\tag{10.24}$$

where $\gamma^n = tC/(tC + \langle t, \nabla_P C, t\rangle)$, and it measures the "distribution-free" markup factor. Note that in the new distributional term, marginal project

---

[12] We see here the importance of distinguishing between $C(\cdot)$ and $C^*(\cdot)$ since the latter would incorporate indirect effects through prices.

cost is allocated among consumers using weights (tc^h/tC). These weights represent the relative (statutory) tax payments.

Now, in both the distributional and the nondistributional terms, γ^n acts as a markup to marginal cost. Therefore, it seems reasonable to think of γ^n as the "marginal cost of government spending": Each unit of actual spending must be treated as if it were γ^n units in benefit–cost calculations.

We can get some feeling for the relative magnitude of γ^n in the case where a single good (say the first) is taxed. In this case, $\gamma^n = 1/(1+x)$, where

$$x = \frac{(t_1)^2}{t_1 C_1} \frac{\partial C_1}{\partial P_1} = -\frac{t_1}{P_1} \epsilon_1, \qquad (10.25)$$

where ϵ_1 is (as usual) the own-price elasticity of good 1. (Recall our sign convention, which makes elasticities negative in the normal case.)

The "perverse case" discussed earlier now occurs whenever the net demand function is positively sloped (or the net supply is backward bending); x will be positive and γ^n will be less than unity. However, in the normal case, γ^n may be quite a bit larger than unity. To see this, expand $1/(1+x)$ in a second-order Taylor series around $x = 0$:

$$\gamma^n \approx 1 - \frac{t_1}{P_1} \epsilon_1 + 2\left[\frac{t_1}{P_1} \epsilon_1\right]^2. \qquad (10.26)$$

Suppose the elasticity is -1 and the tax rate is 0.3. Then the marginal cost of government spending is approximately 1.43; a neutral project would need to show a benefit-to-cost markup at least this large in order to be desirable. Of course, higher (lower) elasticities would lead to a higher (lower) markup, but there seems to be a strong presumption that government projects should indeed be held to a higher standard than those in the private sector.[13]

Finally, we note that if taxation is sufficiently nonoptimal, γ^n might turn out to be much larger. Indeed, if the tax rate somehow approached 100 percent on a commodity having unitary demand elasticity, the preceding calculations would yield $\gamma^n = 4$ (although, admittedly, the second-order approximation would not be very accurate in this case). We will examine a situation that has some of this flavor in Chapter 12.

[13] These results need to be qualified somewhat since most projects will not be exactly "neutral" when a single good is taxed.

CHAPTER 11

Local public goods[1]

Will independent communities tend to oversupply or undersupply local public goods? Will they tend to overexpand or underexpand relative to first-best size? These questions have been debated in the literature extensively since they were first voiced by Tiebout (1956).[2] Arguments can be given on both sides of these issues. Consider the question of size. A typical argument for underexpansion would run as follows: Local communities will tend to discourage expansionary projects because such projects encourage in-migration and increase congestion to current residents. However, the increase in congestion in a single community is not a real social cost, since congestion levels in other communities will fall as a result of the migration. Hence, local communities will be too restrictive in their provision of local public services.

On the other hand, a contrasting argument for overexpansion can be given. Communities, in attracting residents, can bid tax revenue away from others; the extra tax revenue can be used to spread the costs of a given provision of public goods more thinly over the original population. Since the additional tax revenue is a pure transfer among communities, there is a private benefit to the expanding community but no corresponding social benefit. Hence, individual communities will attempt to overexpand (and will succeed to the extent that they can attract residents).

The question of over- or under-supply to a given population depends on a different set of considerations, as we shall see. We can sort out all the relevant considerations using the apparatus of first-order welfare measurement. To apply this apparatus, we must specify carefully what we mean by the status quo in local public-goods provision. We assume that the ideal design mechanisms of Chapter 5 either are inapplicable or cannot be implemented (naturally, we would not have a problem otherwise). Thus, we anticipate that communities will not be fully coordinated with one another and that planners will have imperfect information with regard to the preferences of (potential) constituents.

---

[1] Much of the analysis in this chapter is based on my two papers: Starrett (1980a, b). A related discussion is given by Wildasin (1985).
[2] Leading contributors to this debate include Oates (1972), Hamilton (1975, 1983), Zodrow and Meiszkowski (1983), and Meiszkowski–Toder (1983).

Many alternative assumptions are possible concerning the degree of sophistication exhibited in interactions. We will confine ourselves here to studying the consequences of a relatively low degree of sophistication. In particular, we assume that a particular community does not expect other communities to react systematically to its own policy decisions; consequently, each community takes as given the policies of its "competitors." Although particular policies typically will impinge in some way on others (e.g., by inducing in-migration), as long as there are a large number of competitors, the effect on any one of them will be small, and the assumption of "no reaction" seems reasonable. Of course, in the spatial model there may be situations where local proximity dictates a small number of competitors; in such cases Nash behavior is less plausible. However, analysis of more sophisticated reactions would take us into areas of game theory outside the scope of this book.

Further, we will suppose that clubs act in the interest of their own members only and do not search actively for configurations that would serve a different clientele. This is the type of behavior we would expect from U.S. political institutions where decision making is effectively carried out in a representative democratic forum. The idea of a "club entrepreneur" seems quite unrealistic in this context.

Although we consider the properties of Nash equilibria in what follows, we admit a much richer class of configurations as potential status quo. This class is similar in many respects to the class employed in Chapters 9 and 10 except that we allow different allocation choices in each club. Private-sector activity then involves not only the standard market choices but also a choice of club (multiple clubs with overlapping jurisdictions will not be considered). Equilibrium for a club requires that it be self-sufficient given the members it attracts. Of course, the assumption of Nash behavior out of Nash equilibrium typically involves a counterfactual – other actors do react (if only in small ways). Here, we will suppose that if forced to react, other communities will modify revenue collection so as to maintain provision levels; thus, if a particular community loses a tax base as residents leave, it raises taxes on remaining residents to compensate.

The principal real situation we have in mind for applications is spatial in nature: Clubs are local communities, and households choose clubs by choosing where to live. However, we can draw more closely on the previous notation while adding a little more generality if we develop the model first without explicit spatial structure.

11.1   Direct taxation

The answers to questions posed earlier depend crucially on the manner in which local public expenditure is financed. First, we will consider a

Tiebout-type tax, that is, one that varies from club to club but otherwise is independent of individual behavior. Later, we consider more general types of local taxation.

Since direct spillovers act just like nonexcludable externalities in the model of Chapters 4 and 9, we will leave them out of the formulation here (although we will discuss their implications). Thus, we assume that club members are fully excluded from the public-service (and congestion) levels of other clubs. Consequently, given a membership decision, the household choice problem will look very similar to our previous formulations. However, there is one exception. To accommodate the spatial interpretation, we need to distinguish private goods by the club (community) where they are consumed. And we will allow households to consume (or supply) *private* goods in other clubs, primarily to accommodate absentee ownership of land. Transportation would then appear naturally in the model as production activities for transforming goods in one club into the same goods in other clubs. Variables relevant to members of a particular club will be indicated by a superscript indexing that club.

To exploit the aforementioned similarities, we think of the household as making a two-stage decision: It decides what to do conditional on being in club k first and then picks among clubs. The familiar first-stage problem takes the form

$$\max_{c} U^h[g^k, G^k, c, k] \tag{11.1}$$

subject to

$$Pc = \pi_h - T^{kh},$$

where T^{kh} is the Tiebout tax in club k and other variables are as defined in Chapters 4 and 5. To accommodate locational differences, the vector c is given dimension equal to the number of clubs times the number of goods. If club k happens to be completely self-sufficient, meaning that it does not own any resources or make any market transactions in other clubs, aggregate net consumption by members of club k (C^k) will have zeros in all locations other than k. However, if members of club k make purchases (as tourists) in club j, C^k will have corresponding positive elements in the jth locations; and if they own land in j (as absentee landlords), there will be corresponding negative components.

When we want to focus on consumption of goods *located in* club k (as opposed to *by members of* club k), we will indicate the relevant aggregate subvector as $C(k)$. A similar notation also will be used on other variables such as production and prices. Thus, $P(k)$ is the vector of prices for goods located in club k. These vectors naturally have the dimension of the commodity space only. Note that, using these conventions, $P = [P(1), \ldots, P(K)]$, and similarly for other variables.

An element of $P(k)$ must be thought of as the FOB (freight-on-board) price. Therefore, to the extent that a household consumes goods in another club, it is performing the required transport activities, and our utility function is already "indirectly" subsuming these activities. Consequently, we will not expect the consumer to be indifferent as to where he consumes in this interpretation. Note that the model can be interpreted as non-spatial when neither the indirect utility function V^{kh} nor the price vector $P(k)$ depend explicitly on k.

We think of the variable h as indicating the *type* of an individual and assume for convenience that there are only a finite number of different types. Since differences in endowment will induce differences in preferences on *net* consumption, a distinct type should be associated with specific preferences and endowment.

The second-stage club choice problem for a household of type h is

$$\max_{k} V^{kh}[g^{k}, G^{k}, P, \pi_{h} - T^{kh}], \tag{11.2}$$

where $V^{kh}(\cdot)$ is the indirect utility function associated with problem (11.1). Club choice is inherently discrete, and this introduces some new complications into our analysis. In particular, since any project (no matter how small) may cause some households to relocate, there will be no such thing as a first-order project even in principle as long as we treat the household as an indivisible unit. Consequently, in order to proceed, we must treat households as a continuum much as we did in Chapters 4 and 5. More restrictive yet, we must treat households of a *given type* as a continuum. Thus, it is fair to say that the approximation necessary to formalize first-order analysis requires an extra layer of abstraction in this chapter.

Let n^{kh} be the number of people of type h who choose membership in club k and note the following important implication:

$$n^{kh} \neq 0 \rightarrow V^{kh} \equiv V^{h}, \quad \text{independent of } k. \tag{11.3}$$

Verbally, whenever type h individuals choose membership in more than one club, the utility level attained must be the same in all clubs joined. The formulation (11.2) and its implication (11.3) seem innocuous viewed from an ex ante perspective, but when applied in the context of a particular status quo, it implies that we are ignoring moving costs. In short-run contexts where such costs are important, the community may be relatively isolated from migration effects, and the following analysis will not apply.

There is nothing new to say about private firms here. In particular, we do not need to associate firms with clubs at all, although we will distinguish firm net outputs according to where they occur. We will assume, for convenience, that firms behave competitively, although second-best behavior could be incorporated just as in Chapter 9.

Local governments provide partially rivalrous collective goods to members in much the same way that the national government provided nonexcludable goods before. However, in budgeting for new programs, they must take account of possible resulting membership changes. Formally, the budget constraint in club k takes the form

$$Pb^k = \sum_h n^{kh} T^{kh}. \tag{11.4}$$

Note that our formulation allows local governments to engage in transportation.

A   *Welfare formulation*

We want to consider two perspectives now in evaluating project net benefits: (1) the point of view of society as a whole and (2) the point of view of the project-initiating club. Discrepancies in the corresponding measures naturally reflect whatever externalities club projects impose on others. Consequently, they will indicate the direction of biases in choices made by Nash clubs.

As before, we will separate distributional from nondistributional effects in these measures. Although the procedure looks much the same, there is an important difference in the interpretation of these terms. Indeed, even if a central authority has full power of lump-sum transfers, the resulting distribution still generally is nonoptimal in the present context. This phenomenon is closely related to the Mirrlees problem discussed in Chapter 5 and will arise in any situation where similar individuals face a discrete choice.

To see the issue in our current context, let us look at our general expression for first-order welfare change. Although not essential, we think it is reasonable to assume a minimal horizontal equity condition: Any two agents of the same type (as previously defined) must be treated symmetrically in the sense that interchanging them in the arguments of the welfare function does not change the social ordering. Since (under our assumption of free mobility) all agents of a given type must attain the same utility level, symmetry implies that $\partial W/\partial U^i$ must be the same for all agents of the same type in any initial status quo position. It is a corollary of this assumption that society does not have any preference over which clubs its members join, so that migration per se has no welfare implications.

Incorporating these assumptions, our measure may be expressed as

$$\nabla_\alpha Z = \sum_h \frac{\partial W}{\partial V^h} n^h \nabla_\alpha V^h = \sum_{h,k} \beta^{kh} n^{kh} \left[\frac{\nabla_\alpha V^{kh}}{\lambda^{kh}} \right], \qquad (11.5)$$

where β^{kh} is, as usual, the marginal welfare of a numeraire unit given to type h in club k. Now the Mirrlees problem derives from the fact that (generally) the λ's (and therefore the β's) are not independent of k; that is, households of the same type but residing in different clubs generally will have different marginal utilities of numeraire. For example, if club 1 has high taxes and high provision levels relative to club 2, the marginal value of private numeraire will be higher in club 1. When this situation occurs, a first-best planner would like to be able to transfer some numeraire from the individual with the lower marginal utility to the individual with the higher marginal utility; that is, he would like to enforce unequal treatment of equals. However, unequal treatment is not possible in a world of free mobility since the incidence of any tax imposed on residents in a particular club (location) will be shared equally by all agents of the same type. Consequently, distribution is inherently second best in these situations.[3]

We should note that there are some special situations where the Mirrlees problem does not arise. In particular, it disappears when clubs completely segregate types (so that no type occupies two different clubs). However, we are especially interested in situations where segregation is not complete so the problem is important to us.

How will the presence of second-best distribution affect our analysis? Ordinarily, when we confront an element of second best, we say that the planners need to take account of the way in which a particular project affects the degree of second best. However, in this case, there is nothing to take account of: All projects must have a neutral effect on the distribution of utilities within a type (leaving it flat) so they neither improve nor worsen the second-best position. Consequently, if utilities are distributed optimally among types (on average), first-order welfare change is measured in numeraire aggregates as before.

To see this formally, perform the decomposition

$$\nabla_\alpha Z = \sum_h \left[\sum_k \frac{n^{kh}}{\lambda^{kh}} \right] \nabla_\alpha V^h + \sum_h \sum_k \left[\beta^{kh} \frac{n^h}{\lambda^{kh}} - \frac{n^{kh}}{\lambda^{kh}} \right] \nabla_\alpha V^h. \quad (11.6)$$

The first term measures welfare in numeraire aggregates, whereas the second can be eliminated through a lump-sum redistribution policy among types. This policy involves computing the average welfare weight for each type and then equating these across types. Such a policy is analogous to

---

[3] The problem here is very similar to the difficulties faced by the planner in decentralizing optimal clubs; the reader may want to refer back to the relevant discussion in Chapter 5.

an optimal-redistribution policy in previous chapters, but we should keep in mind that it cannot achieve first best here. This fact will play an important role in the interpretation of later results.

B   *Fiscal externalities*

There is little new to say about the distribution term, so we will drop explicit reference to it for now. We flag our welfare measures with an asterisk to indicate this omission. Suppose that a particular community k contemplates a local public project involving a (partially) rivalrous collective good. This project is considered against the framework of a status quo defined by provision levels g^j, tax rates T^{jh}, and the associated private-sector equilibrium comprising location choices n^{jh}, public facility use levels η^{jh}, congestion levels $\sum_h n^{jh}\eta^{jh} \equiv G^j$ in community j, and market-clearing private goods prices P.

Due to the presence of migration, we must proceed somewhat differently in using market aggregation conditions to simplify welfare measures; in particular, it is no longer helpful to start from an opportunity cost representation. Let us go back to the basic first-order measure for a type h individual living in community k:

$$\frac{\nabla_\alpha V^{kh}}{\lambda^{kh}} = \Omega_g^{kh}\nabla_\alpha g^k + \Omega_G^{kh}\nabla_\alpha G^k - \nabla_\alpha Pc^{kh} - \nabla_\alpha T^{kh} + \nabla_\alpha \pi_h^k, \tag{11.7}$$

where Ω_g and Ω_G are the pseudoprice(s) for associated collective variables. We want to aggregate over members of club k; in order to get simple measures, we need a concept of the net supply (export) for region k. We know about net consumption of the club members (C^k), but what should we mean by the net production? Well, we need to think of these households as producing their "share" of net output for firms they own. So if a^{jkh} is the (ex ante) share of firm j, we define the *net supply* of type h in k (y^{kh}) by $y^{kh} = \sum_j a^{jkh}y^j$.

When we aggregate, we will get a concept of net export for the community. Defining aggregate net firm supply Y^k as $Y^k = \sum_h n^{kh}y^{kh}$, we have, for net export, $E^k = Y^k - b^k - C^k$. Now, we are ready to aggregate (11.7) making use of these new definitions. Multiplying by n^{kh}, summing over h, using duality relationships for competitive firms, and combining terms yields

$$\sum_h n^{kh}\frac{\nabla_\alpha V^{kh}}{\lambda^{kh}} = \Omega_g^k\nabla_\alpha g^k + \Omega_G^k\nabla_\alpha G^k + \nabla_\alpha PE^k - \sum_h n^{kh}\nabla_\alpha T^{kh} + \nabla_\alpha Pb^k. \tag{11.8}$$

The left side of the expression represents the welfare change to ex ante residents of community k (assuming there is no distribution term). Label it $\nabla_\alpha Z^{k*}$. Finally, we obtain a form most closely analogous to measures in Chapter 9 by substituting for the last two terms in (11.8) using the local government budget identity:

$$\nabla_\alpha Z^{k*} = \Omega_g^k \nabla_\alpha g^k - P\nabla_\alpha b^k + \Omega_G^k \nabla_\alpha G^k + \nabla_\alpha PE^k + \sum_h T^{kh} \nabla_\alpha n^{kh}. \quad (11.9)$$

In interpreting our new measure, it is useful to contrast it with similar expressions derived for nonexcludable goods in Chapter 9. First, of course, the presence of nonmarket rivalry introduces a term to reflect marginal congestion cost. But in addition, there are two other new terms. The first of these is a "terms-of-trade" effect (we label it TT_α). Such welfare terms have been noted in the theory of international trade as early as Meade (1955), so it should not be surprising to see them crop up in interregional trade. Indeed, the same sort of term would appear in the analysis of Chapter 9 if we opened the country model up to international trade. To the extent that a region (country) is a net exporter of some goods to the rest of the country (world), price rises for those goods benefit that region, and vice versa.

An interesting special case of the terms-of-trade effect arises when both households and local governments buy all their private goods at home. Then the only consequent welfare effect is through absentee ownership of firms and/or land. We can see this as follows: Since material balance conditions for goods located in region (club) k imply $\nabla_\alpha P(k)E(k)=0$,[4] we can decompose the terms-of-trade effect as follows:

$$TT_\alpha = [\nabla_\alpha PY^k - \nabla_\alpha P(k)Y(k)] - [\nabla_\alpha Pb^k - \nabla_\alpha P(k)b(k)]$$
$$- [\nabla_\alpha PC^k - \nabla_\alpha P(k)C(k)]. \quad (11.10)$$

The second term in square brackets is zero given that governments buy at home. Similarly, the third term will be zero unless there is absentee ownership of land or other resources (if all property in each community is owned by residents of that community, $C^k = \{0, \ldots, \{C(k)\}, \ldots, 0\}$).[5] The first term will be nonzero to the extent that firms owned by residents of community k do business in other communities.

There is good reason to believe that most terms-of-trade effects will be small in the present context where localities do not employ commodity taxes, even if there is substantial trade among regions. Projects are likely to have relatively minor effects on private-goods prices (particularly if

---

[4] Given our assumption of smooth demand and supply functions, if $E_j(k)$ is not zero (some j) at the status quo, it will be nonzero in a neighborhood. But then, $P_j(k)$ must be identically zero in that neighborhood by market clearing.

[5] The curly brackets appear in this representation because consumption has the natural orientation of a column vector.

the relevant markets are national in character) and even smaller *differential* effects on prices of goods in net supply (or demand) by any particular community. However, this presumption may not fit so well with respect to land values, which may be quite sensitive to project levels. Intuitively, project improvements will attract residents and force rents to rise. Indeed, land values may rise by the *full amount* of the net project benefit under some circumstances. We will explore formally the conditions for this "land value capitalization" in Chapter 13. Suppose, for the moment, that capitalization does occur and that all community land is owned by absentee landlords. Then, the terms-of-trade effect is not just important, it is everything: All project net benefits go to outsiders, and $\nabla_\alpha Z^{k*} = 0$.

The last term in (11.9) represents a "fiscal bonus." To the extent that community k is able to attract new residents and collect taxes from them, it can lower the cost (to ex ante residents) of the public services. This is a real welfare benefit to community k, although we would want to cancel any added congestion costs against it before evaluating the net benefit of a new resident (more on this later).[6]

Let us now ask about the welfare change to society as a whole. We make the "Cournot–Nash" assumption that communities other than k do not change their provision levels even though they may be forced (by migration) to change tax rates. Naturally, in summing utility change over *all* residents, the terms-of-trade effect disappears. We are left with

$$\nabla_\alpha Z^* = \Omega_g^k \nabla_\alpha g^k - P \nabla_\alpha b^k + \sum_i \Omega_G^i \nabla_\alpha G^i + \sum_{i,h} T^{ih} \nabla_\alpha n^{ih}. \quad (11.11)$$

The first three terms in our measure provide no surprises. However, the tax term seems strange in this context and requires some discussion. There are two different ways to understand the tax term. One is to explain the real economic benefit that lies behind it. The other is to interpret this term in light of the general theory of second best.

To illustrate the real economic benefit, let us look at the simplest case where a project in community k induces one individual of type h to move from community i to community k. In that case, it is easy to see that the tax term takes the simple form $T^{kh} - T^{ih}$. Thus, if the tax is higher in community k than in community i, there is a net positive contribution to social welfare, and vice versa. This is a real benefit; revenue in the recipient community can be used to reduce the tax burden of residents (a real benefit to residents) by more than the burden must be increased in community i. Of course, the move may worsen congestion in the aggregate, but this effect (if present) is captured in the third term of our welfare

---

6 This factor is identified and discussed in Buchanan–Goetz (1972) and Flatters–Henderson–Meiszkowski (1974).

measure. Furthermore, the individual who paid the higher tax cannot be worse off since he would not otherwise have moved. And any effects on the price system from the move must wash out (in the aggregate) for the usual reasons (cf. Chapter 9).

The other way to understand the tax term is by appealing to principles of second best developed in Chapter 9. The Tiebout-type taxes we are allowing are not truly lump sum from the point of view of an individual who is free to move since the tax he pays is a function of one of his own decision variables (his location). Consequently, any project that induces migration must have a second-best welfare impact as long as the tax rates differ from place to place. Carrying the analogy of Chapter 9 further, think of club membership as the Tiebout tax base. Then, the second-best tax term is measured by the sum of tax rates times the change in the tax base, as before.

It is tempting to interpret the tax term as reflecting economies of large-scale provision, since projects that induce people to move from low-provision (low-tax) areas to high-provision (high-tax) areas make a net positive welfare contribution. However, we should not interpret this to mean that more provision per se is a good thing. For one thing, if larger provision is associated with higher congestion, the congestion term may dominate. But even if the project had no net congestion effect, there is a scale benefit *only* if people *willingly* move to the higher-provision communities. Society is *not* necessarily better off if we *force* people to move to these areas against their will.

We obtain a measure of club-induced externality by looking at the difference between $\nabla_\alpha Z^*$ and $\nabla_\alpha Z^{k*}$ (call this difference $\nabla_\alpha Z^{\#*}$):

$$\nabla_\alpha Z^{\#*} = -\nabla_\alpha PE^k + \sum_{i \neq k} \Omega_G^i \nabla_\alpha G^i + \sum_{i \neq k} \sum_h T^{ih} \nabla_\alpha n^{ih}. \qquad (11.12)$$

Externalities are conveyed through terms of trade, congestion, and the tax base. The tax base term frequently is referred to as the "fiscal externality" in the literature on local public finance. Just as the extra tax base in the active community is a real benefit to that community, the lost tax base in a passive community is a real cost, and hence fiscal externality.

Naturally, all these externalities have implications for the Nash (or other) equilibrium configuration of clubs. In particular, they ought to imply something about the relative efficiency of club size and composition. We will explore these issues momentarily, but first it is useful to look at other types of local taxation.

11.2   Local commodity taxes

Let us now suppose that communities raise revenue through local commodity taxes. The two most natural candidates for applications are a local sales tax and a property tax, these being the most common sources of local finance. However, it is best for notational reasons to start with a general formulation and then specialize to the cases of interest. Concerning overall social welfare, the reader should realize that there is nothing new to say here. Indeed, it had better be the case that any measures we derive here agree with those in Chapter 9. Thus, primary interest focuses on the community-specific welfare change and associated externalities.[7]

Since households generally operate on both sides of the land market, we must adopt the model of Section 9.2 (which distinguishes between sales and purchases). However, to minimize notational complexity, we will not consider the most general case. In particular, we assume that there is no taxation of intermediate goods in production (so $Q^+ = Q^- = Q$). Of course, the Q vector (and all others of the same size) now have dimension equal to the number of private goods times the number of communities. With no direct taxation, household budgets take the form

$$P^- c^{h-} - P^+ c^{h+} = \pi_h. \tag{11.13}$$

Each community is limited to taxes on transactions taking place *in its community*. Thus, the subvectors $t^-(k) = P^-(k) - Q(k)$ and $t^+(k) = Q(k) - P^+(k)$ form the set of tax instruments for community k, and the local budget in that community now is written as

$$Qb^k = t^-(k) C^-(k) + t^+(k) C^+(k). \tag{11.14}$$

Note that transactions between households appear to be taxed twice, once on the buyer and once on the seller. However, this is an artifact of our formulation; the net effect is to tax such transactions at rate $P^- - P^+$.

The steps necessary to derive an expression for $\nabla_\alpha Z^{k*}$ are similar to those of the previous section, and the results are closely parallel, so we leave verification of the following representation to the reader:

$$\nabla_\alpha Z^{k*} = \Omega_g^k \nabla_\alpha g^k + \Omega_G^k \nabla_\alpha G^k - Q \nabla_\alpha b^k$$
$$+ t^-(k) \nabla_\alpha C^-(k) + t^+(k) \nabla_\alpha C^+(k) + TT_\alpha, \tag{11.15}$$

where

$$TT_\alpha = [\nabla_\alpha Q Y^k - \nabla_\alpha Q(k) Y(k)] - [\nabla_\alpha Q b^k - \nabla_\alpha Q(k) b(k)]$$
$$+ [\nabla_\alpha P^+ C^{k+} - \nabla_\alpha P^+(k) C^+(k)]$$
$$- [\nabla_\alpha P^- C^{k-} - \nabla_\alpha P^-(k) C^-(k)]. \tag{11.16}$$

The terms in representation (11.15) have the same interpretation as before except that sales and purchases now constitute the tax base and

[7] Our analysis here generalizes parts of Starrett (1980b), Goldstein–Pauly (1981), and Gordon (1983).

capital gains on trade imbalance now must be computed using the appropriate price for each transaction. As before, the fiscal bonus takes the form of tax rates times expansion in the tax base, but now there is good reason to believe that the fiscal bonus will be a "fiscal drag" instead. Before, expansionary projects attracted the tax base (people); now, increased tax rates may cause business in associated markets to move elsewhere.[8]

By contrast, the terms-of-trade effect now may be positive (and important). This will be true if the community taxes an exported good over which it has some monopoly power; in this case, increasing the tax (to raise more revenue) will likely increase the export price and generate a terms-of-trade benefit.[9]

Completing the calculations of the previous section, we have the following expression for social welfare change and externality:

$$\nabla_\alpha Z^* = \Omega_g^k \nabla_\alpha g^k - Q \nabla_\alpha b^k + \sum_i \Omega_G^i \nabla_\alpha G^i$$

$$+ \sum_i [t^-(i) \nabla_\alpha C^-(i) + t^+(i) \nabla_\alpha C^+(i)], \tag{11.17}$$

$$\nabla_\alpha Z^{\#*} = \sum_{i \neq k} [\Omega_G^i \nabla_\alpha G^i + t^-(i) \nabla_\alpha C^-(i) + t^+(i) \nabla_\alpha C^+(i)] - TT_\alpha. \tag{11.18}$$

Note that (11.17) has the same form as corresponding measures in Chapter 9 and indeed that terms-of-trade effects wash out from the point of view of society as a whole.

11.3   Biases in club choice

Let us review briefly the institutional framework that underlies measures of the previous sections. We started with a status quo that was arbitrary except that it had to be consistent with private-sector equilibrium; this meant that after households voted with their feet, clubs had to be self-financing with the packages offered. We then computed first-order welfare effects of a club project under the Cournot–Nash assumption that project levels in other clubs would remain unchanged.

A natural next step would be to examine properties of a Cournot–Nash equilibrium. Unfortunately, this is a formidable task here since we would need to be able to evaluate migration responses to project changes. However, merely by examining the composition of our externality terms, we

[8] This factor and its importance for local public finance is discussed and debated by Hamilton (1975, 1983b) and Zodrow–Meiszkowski (1983).
[9] This factor is identified and studied under the topic of tax exporting. See McLure (1967) and Meiszkowski–Toder (1983).

can get some feel for the likely direction of distortions in club choices. To the extent that an externality is positive, there is reason to believe that the corresponding activity will be undersupplied. Although there are known counterexamples to this principle (recall our discussion in Chapter 1), they involve dominating income effects and appear to be pathological.

Although many distortions are possible involving the composition of public goods within a club and/or the diversity of public goods across clubs, we will concentrate here on two particular distortions: (1) the average amount of public goods in a club and (2) the size (membership) of a club. To evaluate the first distortion, we look at the externality associated with a hypothetical project that increases g *holding membership fixed*, whereas to evaluate the second distortion, we look at a corresponding project that increases in-migration holding the *general level* of g fixed (although perhaps changing the composition). Of course, most real projects will involve mixtures of these, but the abstractions are useful for separating the two types of distortions.

We examine a general form for club externality [allowing for both Tiebout and commodity taxes and adding a term (DS_α) for the previously ignored direct spillovers]:

$$\nabla_\alpha Z^{\#*} = DS_\alpha + \sum_{i \neq k} \Omega_G^i \nabla_\alpha G^i - TT_\alpha$$

$$+ \sum_{i \neq k} \left[t^-(i) \nabla_\alpha C^-(i) + t^+(i) \nabla_\alpha C^+(i) + \sum_h T^{ih} \nabla_\alpha n^{ih} \right]. \quad (11.19)$$

The first two terms represent the standard externalities due to direct spillover and congestion; the third represents regional externalities due to terms-of-trade effects; and the other terms capture externalities transmitted through the tax system.

A   *Bias in provision levels*

Suppose we have a project that increases the "level" of g while having no migration effects. Which of the previous terms are likely to be significant and what signs will they have? In the absence of induced migration, there will be no fiscal externalities, and congestion effects are likely to be negligible as well. Thus, we can concentrate attention on direct spillovers, changes in the commodity tax base, and terms-of-trade effects.

Naturally, direct spillovers (if present) are going to generate a positive externality. The externality due to second-best commodity taxation is quite likely to be positive also. Increased levels of public-goods provision in club k generally require increased tax rates; to the extent that economic activity in k can and does go elsewhere, it enhances the tax base elsewhere and creates a positive externality. So, for example, if New York raises its revenue using a cigarette tax and an increased tax rate will cause people to take their tobacco purchases to New Jersey, some of the benefits of New York projects are exported to New Jersey. This factor will be quite important in the case of local sales taxes and probably explains why they generally play a minor role relative to the property tax in local public finance. However, the property tax also is shiftable to the extent that it falls on mobile capital. Although the degree of shift can be mitigated in principle through the use of zoning restrictions [requiring minimum capital improvements on the (unmovable!) land], it is not clear that this tactic is very effective in practice.[10]

One of the two potentially significant terms-of-trade effects is likely to be nonnegative as well – that associated with absentee ownership of land: Absentee landlords gain to the extent that local land values rise (of course, these values may not move much at all under the current circumstances). Only the "tax exporting" factor is negative (as outsiders pay part of the increased local taxes). Thus, externalities from provision levels are likely to be positive unless local revenue sources are dominated by taxation of a monopolized export. In particular, we expect a positive externality when local communities have negligible impacts on nonland private-goods prices. Under such circumstances, there is a presumption that Cournot–Nash communities will undersupply local public goods. Since it is hard to think of situations where local (or even state) constituencies have monopoly power in the goods markets, we think that some degree of undersupply is the likely outcome.[11]

The significance of any induced bias naturally will depend on the magnitude of the associated externalities, which in turn depends on the nature of ownership patterns and types of taxation. When communities involve substantial absentee ownership or rely heavily on a sales tax for revenue, the bias might be quite pronounced. Indeed, we argued before that if capitalization occurs, most (perhaps all) project benefits can be transferred to absentee owners. On the other hand, distortions will be of lesser significance to the extent that we observe home ownership, nationally determined prices, and unshiftable taxes (such as a tax on pure land rent).

B   Bias in club size

When discussing size, we need to worry about the "Mirrlees problem" discussed in Section 11.1A and the "Dreze nonconvexity" discussed in

---

[10] The effectiveness of these restrictions is subject to considerable debate. See White (1975), Hamilton (1983), and Zodrow–Meiszkowski (1983).

[11] Recalling the discussion in Chapter 7, we see here an argument for revenue sharing that matches local effort.

Chapter 5. Due to both these problems, we cannot expect Nash behavior to generate a first-best size distribution even if the preceding externalities are accounted for correctly; we need to take account of the further externality deriving from the fact that we treat equals equally, namely, the spatial separation costs imposed by land users in the interior of a community. Consequently, we must refer back to characterizations of optimality developed in Chapter 4.

Suppose we consider a prototype project that does not affect the general level of provision but induces (through, say, competition in composition) in-migration to the active club. What does the active club get for its effort? Well, there might be a terms-of-trade effect if monopoly power is present or absentee ownership is significant, but the major community benefit is likely to come from increases in its tax base, whereas the major cost will derive from increases in congestion levels. The net effect will depend on a number of factors.

When the local tax is a Tiebout tax, each new resident brings in the tax base associated with his type (and generates his type of specific level of congestion). Thus, a community would like to encourage entry of households with high "base-to-congestion" ratios and vice versa.[12] This incentive might lead to some biases in composition, but it is not yet clear whether it leads to a general tendency to over- or underexpansion. The community will see a general tendency to expand when the total increase in tax base benefits exceeds the total increase in congestion cost. Recalling the discussions of Chapter 4, this is the correct incentive for nonspatial clubs but *not* for spatial ones (where increases in transport cost need to be included in social costs). Thus, a spatial club will seek to expand even when the full marginal social cost exceeds the marginal benefit.

There is a good intuitive argument for why communities will ignore the increased transport costs in their calculations. Residents (who are the decision-making group) do not pay the market costs of expansion (only the congestion costs). Those who move in pay the market costs; either they pay the increased transport costs directly (if they live on the outskirts) or they pay them indirectly by moving into the center and paying a higher rent to a resident (owner) who moves out. Established owners make money on land and will encourage new residents even when it would be better from the point of view of society for a new community to form.

Now, suppose that local revenue is raised through a local sales or property tax. Clearly, the analysis will be unchanged as long as migrants bring their full tax base with them. However, there is likely to be some

---

12 Communities can attempt to exploit these opportunities by zoning to attract "desirable" members (frequently the rich) and discourage the undesirable (frequently poor) ones. See White (1975) and Beck (1983).

degree of crowding out that will cut into the new tax base.[13] For example, consider the extreme case of a land tax in communities with fixed land holdings (e.g., suburbs in a metropolitan area). Here, crowding out will be complete: The new entrant consumes some local land only to the extent that some old resident consumes less; the tax base is unchanged. Such communities will see only the congestion cost associated with new residents and have an incentive to underexpand relative to the first best. Thus, it is not surprising to find antidevelopment zoning restrictions in small suburbs of a large urban area.

Of course, to the extent that new residents induce new improvements on existing land or development of previously untaxed land, crowding out will be less important. Indeed, for metropolitan areas surrounded by unincorporated land, we would not expect much crowding out, and the conclusions will be as in the Tiebout tax case.

To summarize briefly, we have identified a general tendency for metropolitan areas to underprovide collective goods given their population size but to increase that size too much. However, these conclusions must be qualified in several ways. First, they can be reversed when specific factors such as monopoly power are sufficiently important. Further, they require that the communities can find policies that are effective in competing for residents and that outside constituencies do not retaliate in systematic ways.

[13] The importance of this factor was emphasized by Wheaton (1975) in a slightly different context.

CHAPTER 12

Intertemporal contexts with uncertainty

We now extend our discussion of first-order analysis to a model where time and uncertainty appear explicitly. As long as we can retain an assumption of complete markets, the apparatus of Chapters 9 and 10 carries over directly and leads to a criterion of discounted present value for evaluating projects. In this case, interest focuses on measuring shadow values of intertemporal prices (discount factors). However, once we take uncertainty seriously, we must drop the assumption of complete markets, and some corresponding modifications are required in our measures.

Extension of shadow-pricing principles to an intertemporal context enables us to define and quantify a *social rate of discount,* and we use this apparatus to discuss and evaluate some of the controversies as to its appropriate size. We find that the decomposition procedures of Chapter 9 are relatively more helpful in dealing with uncertainty and use them to identify and measure the *social risk premium.* Further, the fact of missing "uncertainty markets" leads to distributional second-best welfare measures in much the same way that failure to redistribute income leads to a second-best distributional term in the static model; the associated measure generalizes the concept of "pecuniary externality" that has been appearing in the literature on incomplete markets.

12.1 Temporal rate of discount

We begin with a discussion of issues involving time but not uncertainty. Later we will see how to incorporate the current discussion as a building block in general models involving time and uncertainty. The appropriate s-period social discount factor for numeraire units (dollars) should equal the project shadow price of an s-period government bond in an intertemporal version of the mixed economy. We evaluate this shadow price first in the optimal-commodity-tax setting (we will discuss what this means in an intertemporal context momentarily). Since we know that the relative valuation of private goods by the government should be equal to their relative producer's prices in this setting, the relevant price will be the s-period discount factor on bonds to producers. These discount factors then can be applied to spot market revenues and costs in computing the *discounted present value* of a project.

It is important to be clear on the context of the previous calculation. It is one where the government is engaged in private investment using market goods today and providing them s periods later (so that all transactions involve dollars inside the government budget). Suppose, instead (as will be the case with most public projects), that the government is using private goods today to produce *collective* (unmarketed) goods in the future. Then, two new factors must be considered in determining the present-value price of the collective good: (1) a pseudoprice must be used to measure collective-good valuation in terms of private dollars and (2) the "marginal cost of government spending" must be incorporated to convert dollars in the government budget (project cost) to (private) dollars. Consequently, the present-value price of the jth collective good s periods in the future will take the form

$$\frac{\Omega_s}{\mu \prod_{x=1}^{s} (1+r_x)}, \tag{12.1}$$

where μ is the conversion factor between the two types of dollars as in Chapters 8 and 10, and r refers now to producer rates of interest.

Assuming the normal case of $\mu > 1$, the government should discount the future at a higher rate (use a lower discount factor) than private firms. This prescription is another manifestation of the fact that the government should hold its projects to a higher standard when they must be financed out of indirect taxation. Note that the higher standard is imposed uniformly over time in that all discount factors are reduced by the same proportion; in particular, there would be no differential proscription against long-term versus short-term projects or vice versa. This conclusion rests on our maintained supposition that all agents have free access to the capital markets; we discuss the impact of restrictions momentarily.

Now, suppose we drop the assumption of optimal taxation. We know that the analysis must be altered in this case. Should we expect any dramatic differences in the magnitude of the social rate of discount? Although such differences were not evident in the static version, there are some strong reasons why they may indeed appear here. These reasons have to do with the taxation of savings in a general income tax. Given compounding effects over time, taxation of savings will imply (ceteris paribus) considerably higher effective rates of taxation on future consumption than on current consumption. To see this, suppose that producer interest rates and all spot prices are constant over time and that interest income is taxed at the constant rate τ. Assuming that the tax must be paid each period, the effective rate of return to consumer saving is $r(1-\tau)$. Consequently, the present value of a dollar s periods hence is different for consumers and producers (recall the discussion in Chapter 8). Labeling these rates ρ_s^h and ρ_s^f, respectively, we have

$$\rho_s^h = \frac{1}{[1+r(1-\tau)]^s}, \qquad \rho_s^f = \frac{1}{(1+r)^s}. \tag{12.2}$$

Interpreting discount rates as present-value prices of numeraire units, we see that the effective tax rate on dollars s periods hence is given by

$$\frac{\rho_s^h - \rho_s^f}{\rho_s^f} = \left[\frac{1+r}{1+r(1-\tau)}\right]^s - 1. \tag{12.3}$$

Notice that this tax rate goes up geometrically in s. It is very hard to believe that these tax rates could be optimal. Indeed, if we assume that things look pretty much the same in all periods (so that the relevant elasticities will be the same across periods), optimal tax rates should be constant over time.[1]

Given these observations, it is important to examine shadow-pricing formulations outside the optimal-tax framework. Let us return to the general formula (10.10). Although many factors potentially determine the shadow price, it seems reasonable that effects through distributive weights and noncompetitive firms will be dominated by the direct-cost and indirect tax terms. Therefore, let us consider the approximation

$$-\nabla_b Z \approx Q - t \nabla_b C^*, \tag{12.4}$$

where t must now be interpreted as the effective tax rates on dated consumption in situations where assets are taxed.[2]

The shadow prices will be quite sensitive to our assumptions about tax incidence. Suppose, first, that private-goods inputs translate directly into corresponding lost consumption. Then, $\nabla_b C^*$ will be minus the identity so it turns out that consumer prices $(Q+t)$ should be used as planning shadow prices. As applied to publicly provided private investment, this implies the discounting should be done at the consumer rates of interest that are *lower* than those used by private firms. The reason we get a different answer here than in the case of optimal taxation traces directly to the third-best distortion. Since this distortion implies too little private

---

[1] This type of argument has been used recently by advocates of a "flat" tax. See, e.g., Hall–Rabushka (1985).

[2] Taxes on assets will translate this way into taxes on consumption only if the tax rates are uniform; this requires, in particular, that interest payments are tax-deductible on all assets.

investment (due to the unwarranted taxation of savings), the government should be encouraged to substitute for the lost private activity. The same type of argument applies when there are quantity constraints (or other impediments) in the saving and/or investment market, so that the gap between consumer and producer prices is unwarranted.[3]

Of course, if we think about the more typical case where the government produces (nonmarketed) public goods, the analysis is different for reasons mentioned earlier. However, the presence of a savings tax will not have much effect on the measures of excess burden discussed in Chapter 10. Intuitively, at least, the extra excess-burden factor on the numeraire should equal 1 plus the effective tax rate [i.e., $(Q+t)/Q$, with $Q=1$]. This number will be quite small given plausible estimates for market parameters. For example, if $r = 10$ percent and $\tau = 50$ percent, this extra factor is only 1.05.

However, if we change our incidence assumptions, it is possible to get much higher effective discount rates. For example, suppose we assume public spending displaces private investment that would have paid off s periods in the future. To simplify, we think in terms of aggregates and restrict attention to the shadow price of "dollars today." If the displaced investment had been productive at the rate r, then $\nabla_b C^* = -(1+r)^s$, and [recalling (12.2)]

$$1 - t \, \nabla_b C^* = \left[\frac{1+r}{1+r\{1-\tau\}} \right]^s .$$ (12.5)

Clearly, the markup for government spending today would be very large (regardless of τ) if s were sufficiently far in the future.[4] Intuitively, consumption in the distant future is especially valuable at the margin due to the large tax penalty imposed on it; so opportunity cost is correspondingly high if it is paid out of such consumption. Indeed, this is a case where the incidence relationships that translate statutory costs into opportunity costs of the foregone alternative are extremely important in determining the true welfare cost of government spending.

Therefore, it is important to ask about the average length of time before opportunity costs are paid. Obviously, this is an empirical question concerning general equilibrium incidence, one we cannot fully answer here. However, we can see that the saving elasticity ought to be crucial and that if it is small, the opportunity cost of the project will not be much delayed. When the government increases the demand for private goods, concur-

---

[3] This sort of conclusion has appeared in the context of imperfect capital markets beginning with Arrow (1966).
[4] This type of reasoning has been used by Lind (1986) in arguing for high social rates of discount.

rent private spending must fall (assuming no unemployed resources). For investment to bear the full brunt of this decrease, saving must respond to market signals much more elastically than consumption. And for lost consumption to be transferred many years into the future requires a very high degree of savings sensitivity. Although claims have been made recently that savings elasticities are large, they are subject to a variety of criticisms; the jury still seems to be out on this issue.[5]

12.2 Uncertainty: bare-bones model[6]

We now discuss project analysis under uncertainty. As discussed in Chapter 6, a general model for the purposes at hand would involve an arbitrary number of trading dates and a "sequential" market structure for trading a limited set of risky assets at the various trading dates. Of course, if markets turn out to be complete (in the sense of Arrow–Debreu), we know that all trading effectively takes place at the outset, but this case is of limited interest to us here. Generally, we expect at the very least that recontracting on spot markets will occur at each date. Much of the analysis to follow can be carried out in the context of this general sequential market structure. However, for expositional and notational purposes, most of the discussion will focus on simpler special cases.

In particular, we will start with a two-period model in which the government is limited to the provision of private goods. These restrictions enable us to analyze risk premiums in the simplest possible setting. We consider a multiperiod model incorporating a full range of government activity in Section 12.4.

Our first model is of considerable historical interest since it is more or less identical to that used by Diamond (1967) and Dreze (1974) to study the stock market. In it, the spot markets are ignored (or at least suppressed) by assuming that consumption at each date is represented by a market aggregate. This framework nests itself naturally in a general formulation under the additional assumption that spot prices are unaffected by project levels (so that we can think in terms of a Hicksian aggregate).

Since there is nothing left to decide in the second (last) period, all decisions are made ex ante in the first period, when the household splits its resources between consumption now and a set of assets that allow for a limited degree of risk sharing across states of the world ex post in the second period. These assets may be offered through the market (in which

---

[5] See Kotlikoff (1984) and King (1985) for surveys of the relevant saving literature. The case for high elasticities was made by Summers (1981). For a critique and further references, see Starrett (1987).

[6] Much of this section is based on material in Starrett (1986).

case they are best thought of as equity or bonds in private or public firms) or directly by the government through tax and/or subsidy arrangements. Consumers choose portfolios to maximize expected (state-independent) utility. Given our present aggregation, there is no useful way to discuss indirect taxation, so we will assume for now that any taxes or subsidies are lump sum. To emphasize the connections between direct and market risk sharing, we will give ex post payments a positive (subsidy) orientation and label them S. Finally, we assume away any other sources of lump-sum income.

A typical market asset (j) pays off in a specific configuration of returns over states of the world $[d_j(\omega)]$ per unit held. This asset sells in the first period at a market-determined price v_j. As an example, it is useful to think of a safe government bond (if one exists, we will think of it as the "zeroth" asset). Then, $d_0(\omega)$ is a constant (we take it to be unity), and the price should be thought of as the safe discount factor (cost today of getting a sure dollar tomorrow); that is, $v_0 = \rho = 1/(1+r)$.

Our typical household now faces a portfolio problem of the form

$$\max E_\omega[U^h(c_1, d(\omega)a'^h + S^h(\omega))] \tag{12.6}$$

subject to

$$c_1 + va = -T_1^h,$$

where a is the vector of net trades and a' is that for gross holdings ex post (net trades plus initial holdings).[7] As usual, we will let $V^h(\cdot)$ be the associated indirect utility function. We impose no nonnegativity constraints on a' so there are no restrictions on short sales at present.

We exhibit, for future reference, the first-order optimality conditions[8]

$$E_\omega[\partial U^h(\omega)/\partial c_1] = \lambda^h, \tag{12.7}$$

and

$$E_\omega[[\partial U^h(\omega)/\partial c_2]\, d(\omega)] = \lambda^h v. \tag{12.8}$$

The scope of government projects is limited here to making changes in the d's or the T's and S's. When the d's are involved, we can think of the planners as either changing the return structure on their own bonds or regulating the behavior of private firms. For simplicity, we will assume (in this section) that the government has complete control over the ex ante distribution so that the ex ante welfare weights can be and are equalized

---

[7] Note that we treat asset returns as a row vector and holdings as a column vector.
[8] We continue our practice of suppressing arguments of functions when the meaning is clear. However, we attach (ω) where appropriate to indicate the presence of a random element.

(and we normalize so that the common value is unity). Then, proceeding as in previous chapters, the welfare change from a small project (α) may be written in the form[9]

$$\sum_h \frac{\nabla_\alpha V^h}{\lambda^h} = -\nabla_\alpha T_1 + \sum_h \left[\frac{E_\omega[[\partial U^h(\omega)/\partial c_2] \nabla_\alpha d(\omega)]}{\lambda^h} a'^h \right]$$

$$+ \sum_h \left[\frac{E_\omega[[\partial U^h(\omega)/\partial c_2] \nabla_\alpha S^h(\omega)]}{\lambda^h} \right]. \tag{12.9}$$

The rules associated with this expression are essentially those developed by Diamond and Dreze for the stock market. Let us focus on the valuation of asset returns (d). The pseudoprice to associate with changes in these returns has the same structure we associate with collective goods. To see this more clearly, it is helpful to introduce new variables:

$$\psi^h(\omega) = \frac{\partial U^h(\omega)/\partial c_2}{\lambda^h}. \tag{12.10}$$

The ψ's represent "personalized" pseudoprices on Arrow securities (hypothetical securities that pay off a dollar in a specific state of the world). They are personalized in that they will differ from household to household in the absence of actual Arrow securities. Should they somehow turn out to be equal for all households in each state of the world, it is as if markets were complete. Note for future reference that if there exists a safe asset paying rate of return r, (12.8) implies $E_\omega \psi^h(\omega) = 1/(1+r)$.

Now, firm j should evaluate a small change in its output program using the coefficients of $\nabla_\alpha d_j$ in (12.9). Labeling the associated pseudoprices $\Omega_d^j(\omega)$, we have

$$\Omega_d^j(\omega) = \sum_h \psi^h(\omega) a_j'^h. \tag{12.11}$$

Thus, the firm's valuation of returns in state ω is a weighted sum of those of its owners, weights deriving from ownership shares. There is an analogy here [emphasized by Dreze (1974)] with the theory of local public goods that yields important insights. All owners of a particular asset must share its common distribution of returns, so that distribution is "public" to shareholders. Of course, owners need not share equally, so components of the pseudoprice are weighted by ex post share holdings (share holdings play the same role as club participation in the local public-goods version). Note that the social objective of a firm issuing assets is well defined here

---

[9] In deriving this and later expressions, we have interchanged differentiation operators with expectations operators. When the underlying random variables take values on the continuum, this procedure requires justification. However, it can be shown to be valid under weak regularity conditions. See, e.g., Dunford–Schwartz (1968).

even though shareholders with differing ψ's will disagree concerning the desirable directions of movement.[10] Of course, this is a normal situation when we are dealing with public goods.

12.3   Risk premiums in the Diamond–Dreze model

Although the preceding discussion provides insight into the structure of incomplete uncertainty markets, it is not very useful when it comes to evaluating discount rates. For this purpose, it is helpful to use a decomposition procedure that isolates the contribution associated with risk (it is natural to think of this contribution as a *risk premium*). We define risk premiums in terms of differences between correct welfare measures and approximations based on simple expectations.

We generate our decomposition using the definition of *covariance* to substitute for expectations of products. For example,[11]

$$E[\psi^h(\omega)\,\nabla_\alpha S^h(\omega)] = E[\psi^h(\omega)]E[\nabla_\alpha S^h(\omega)]$$
$$+ \mathrm{COV}[\psi^h(\omega), \nabla_\alpha S^h(\omega)]. \qquad (12.12)$$

Performing the requisite series of substitutions decomposes (12.9) as

$$\sum_h \frac{\nabla_\alpha V^h}{\lambda^h} =$$

$$-\nabla_\alpha T_1 + \sum_h [E[\psi^h(\omega)]E[\nabla_\alpha d(\omega)]a'^h] + \sum_h E[\psi^h(\omega)]E[\nabla_\alpha S^h(\omega)]$$

$$+ \sum_h [\mathrm{COV}[\psi^h(\omega), \nabla_\alpha d(\omega)]a'^h] + \sum_h \mathrm{COV}[\psi^h(\omega), \nabla_\alpha S^h(\omega)]. \qquad (12.13)$$

We argue that the first line in our decomposition would represent the correct welfare measure in a "risk-neutral" world. The term $E[\psi^h(\omega)]$ represents a riskless (temporal) discount factor for household h (we label it ρ^h for future reference). In fact, if there exists a risk-free asset, we saw that this term must equal the discount factor on that riskless asset. Thus, the first line represents the expected present value of the marginal project with discounting carried out at the risk-free rate.

Consequently, the second line should be interpreted as a correction for risk, the first part associated with market assets and the second with direct government activity. These corrections are usefully interpreted in terms

---

[10] Actually, these disagreements are known to disappear when an appropriate "spanning" condition holds. See, e.g., Grossman–Stiglitz (1980).

[11] We suppress the random-variable index on expectations operators in the sequel when the meaning is clear.

of risk premiums the project must earn in its expected rate of return. To see this, assume we are looking at a marginal "direct" project with unit cost (so $\nabla_\alpha T_1 = 1$, $\nabla_\alpha d = 0$). This project is socially desirable if the corresponding right side of (12.13) is nonnegative, that is, if

$$\sum_h E[\psi^h(\omega)] E[\nabla_\alpha S^h(\omega)] - 1 + \sum_h \text{COV}[\psi^h(\omega), \nabla_\alpha S^h(\omega)] \geq 0. \qquad (12.14)$$

Substituting for personalized discount factors ρ^h and rearranging somewhat, the condition for acceptance becomes

$$\sum_h \rho^h E[\nabla_\alpha S^h(\omega)] - 1 \geq - \sum_h \text{COV}[\psi^h(\omega), \nabla_\alpha S^h(\omega)]. \qquad (12.15)$$

Thus, if we define the government risk premium for direct intervention (RP_g) as

$$\text{RP}_g = - \sum_h \text{COV}[\psi^h(\omega), \nabla_\alpha S^h(\omega)], \qquad (12.16)$$

the project should be accepted if its discounted expected return exceeds the risk premium. The corresponding analysis for market assets yields a risk premium (RP_m) of the form

$$\text{RP}_m = - \sum_h \text{COV}[\psi^h(\omega), \nabla_\alpha d(\omega) a'^h]. \qquad (12.17)$$

Examining these expressions, we can answer such questions as: (1) How do the social risk premiums relate to measures of individual risk aversion? (2) Should the government use a different discount factor for risk than the private sector?

A   Complete markets

It is useful in our discussion to reintroduce the case of "effectively complete markets" as a benchmark. Of course, we do not need the present analysis when markets are really complete, but the benchmark still is useful in identifying the risk premium to associate with "socially uninsurable" risk. The principal implication of complete markets here is that the personalized pseudoprices ψ^h must be equalized across individuals (obviously this must occur if Arrow security markets exist, and all complete market contexts are equivalent).

Notice that when the pseudoprices are equalized, all references to the individual disappear from the risk terms (and indeed from all terms in the welfare measure). Our risk premiums reduce to

$$\text{RP}_m = -\text{COV}[\psi(\omega), \nabla_\alpha d(\omega) \bar{a}] \qquad (12.18)$$

and

$$RP_g = -COV[\psi(\omega), \nabla_\alpha S(\omega)],\tag{12.19}$$

where $\bar{a}$ is the vector of total asset supplies.

Our analysis suggests immediately a precise definition of *fully insurable risk*. Namely, risk is fully insurable if ψ is independent of ω (i.e., if the marginal welfare of a dollar is state independent). When this independence condition holds, the risk premium terms disappear, and our welfare criteria reduces to discounted expected value. As is well known, completion of the markets could be achieved in this case by a full set of insurance markets.[12]

When some risks are socially uninsurable, the marginal welfare of a dollar will have to be higher in the "bad" states than it is in the "good" ones, and households must absorb this risk on balance. Our risk premiums then reflect the degree to which project net outputs correlate with the badness of the state. These correlations can be used to define *project betas* that correspond closely to asset betas in the capital asset-pricing (CAP) model.[13] Defining project beta to be the correlation coefficient between project return and goodness of state, the preceding covariances can be expressed as project betas multiplied by the product of the associated standard deviations. As in CAP, project betas can lie anywhere between -1 and $+1$. A project that provides more net benefits (on balance) in the bad states than it does in the good ones has a negative beta and will be more desirable in a risk-averse world than it would be in a risk-neutral one; for such a project, the risk premium will be negative since the project reduces aggregate uncertainty.

Presumably, the "typical" project tends to confer its benefits in the good states and incur its costs in the bad ones, leading to an associated positive risk premium. However, it is interesting to note that projects whose distribution of benefits is independent from the goodness of state generate *no* risk premium. The reader may well be surprised by this result since we generally expect the addition of independent uncertainty to increase risk. Fortunately, there is no paradox here. Remember that our analysis is *first order* and that projects do not change the risk structure to a first order. Only a larger project "adds independent risk."

Note that our discussion will apply equally well whether the project involves direct intervention or changes in private production. All that matters is the correlation of net returns with goodness of state. This observation may surprise readers who are familiar with the theorem of Arrow

[12] See Malinvaud (1973) for a demonstration.
[13] This model was introduced by Sharpe (1964) and Lintner (1965). For an exposition, see Mossin (1973) or Ross (1976).

and Lind (1970) on government discounting, since that theorem suggests conditions under which the government generally should discount less for risk than the private sector. But the theorem relies for its validity on differential capacities to provide risk sharing, so it does not apply in our present context of complete markets.

B   *Incomplete markets*

Let us return to the case of imperfect risk sharing, where the risk premiums are measured as

$$\mathrm{RP}_m = -\sum_h [\mathrm{COV}[\psi^h(\omega), \nabla_\alpha d(\omega)]a'^h] \tag{12.20}$$

and

$$\mathrm{RP}_g = -\sum_h \mathrm{COV}[\psi^h(\omega), \nabla_\alpha S^h(\omega)]. \tag{12.21}$$

We discuss first differences between these measures in the new context. Obviously, direct intervention involves more control. Whereas market assets constrain all holders to the same public return structure, the government is not necessarily so constrained. Direct intervention may have an advantage if the government is in a position to improve the degree of risk sharing (thereby giving more net benefits in state ω to those with especially high marginal valuations in that state and less to others).

However, there must be some limitations on the government's discretion in this regard. Otherwise, planners should provide full risk sharing (regardless of what else is done), and thereafter, we revert to the previous case in which public and private projects appear on equal footing. Moreover, the Arrow–Lind theorem *still* does not apply. To see this, let us look more closely at their proposition. The original context was one in which project costs were distributed *uniformly* across households, and it was asserted that as the number of households got larger, the risk premium would get smaller. This proposition fails here. Assuming (as seems appropriate) that we are comparing populations in which the ex ante degree of risk sharing is similar, our risk premium will be independent of the number of households: Spreading the costs means that each separate covariance term goes down at the rate $1/N$, but we sum N of these. Indeed, for any direct project in which the net return (tax) structure is *fixed* across individuals, the government risk premium looks just like that for the private sector. We need to be talking about *larger* projects before the Arrow–Lind theorem will "bite."[14]

---

[14] The capacity to spread risk through the tax system enables the government to reduce any fixed project to have first-order influence on each citizen given a large enough

To compute the relevant risk premiums (in the absence of directly comparable values for private projects), we need to relate our measures to estimated indices of risk aversion. Here, we indicate one possible approximation. We confine ourselves to a discussion of the direct-intervention term, although the reader should have no trouble supplying the (similar) analysis for market assets. To begin, observe the following identity:

$$\psi^h(\omega) \equiv \rho^h \left[\frac{\partial U^h(\omega)/\partial c_2}{E[\partial U^h(\omega)/\partial c_2]} \right]. \tag{12.22}$$

Then, define "certainty-equivalent second-period consumption" (c_{2*}^h) holding first-period consumption fixed by the condition

$$\frac{\partial U^h(c_1^h, c_{2*}^h)}{\partial c_2} = E \left[\frac{\partial U^h(c_1^h, c_2^h(\omega))}{\partial c_2} \right]. \tag{12.23}$$

Now, suppose that we expand the marginal utility of second-period consumption in a first-order Taylor series around the certainty equivalent. Naturally, this expansion is "exact" only if utility is quadratic; otherwise, the following expressions must be thought of as approximations. Utilizing the expansion, we can write

$$\frac{\partial U^h(\omega)}{\partial c_2} \approx E \left[\frac{\partial U^h(\omega)}{\partial c_2} \right] + \frac{\partial^2 U^h(c_1^h, c_{2*}^h)}{\partial (c_2)^2} [c_2^h(\omega) - c_{2*}^h], \tag{12.24}$$

and therefore,

$$\frac{\partial U^h(\omega)/\partial c_2}{E[\partial U^h(\omega)/\partial c_2]} \approx 1 - R_A^h(c_1^h, c_{2*}^h)[c_2^h(\omega) - c_{2*}^h], \tag{12.25}$$

where

$$R_A^h(\cdot) = - \frac{\partial^2 U^h(\cdot)/\partial (c_2)^2}{\partial U^h(\cdot)/\partial c_2} \tag{12.26}$$

is the generalized Arrow–Pratt[15] measure of absolute risk aversion for household h evaluated at the certainty equivalent consumption.

Finally, we assemble all these pieces to obtain the following expression for the risk premium:

Footnote 14 *(cont.)*
population. However, the private markets may not be as successful in this regard due to the Dreze nonconvexity (cf. Chapter 5). Spreading the risk associated with a large new project requires simultaneous changes in ownership and production plan that are not contemplated jointly by any agent in the private markets; this situation may lead to non-optimal risk diversification so that the private sector would require a higher risk premium than is socially necessary. I develop this point at length in Starrett (1986).

[15] These measures were introduced more or less simultaneously by Arrow (1965) and Pratt (1964).

$$RP_g \approx \sum_h \rho^h R_A^h(c_1^h, c_{2*}^h) \, \text{COV}[c_2^h(\omega), \nabla_\alpha S^h(\omega)]. \tag{12.27}$$

As before, the covariance terms could be expressed in terms of project betas and standard deviations to indicate the separate influences of correlation and variance. Now, the betas are household specific, representing the correlation of the project returns with the household status quo ante; hence, they reflect the degree of extra risk being borne by the associated household.[16]

Consequently, we can think of the risk premium as a weighted sum of absolute risk aversion measures, weights being temporal discount factors times covariances. Of course, when there exists a risk-free asset, all the ρ's will be equal, and the weights simplify accordingly. In practical applications, measures of individual risk aversion are common to all project evaluation (public and private) so evaluation of particular projects will focus on estimating the covariance terms. We will require information on variability of the project returns and a correlation coefficient with the underlying state. The estimation problems here are similar to those encountered in correcting for equity earlier (cf. Chapter 9).

12.4 Model with full sequential structure

We now generalize the model of previous sections to include many periods, many different types of commodities, and a full range of economic activity. We want to think of uncertainty as being resolved sequentially; that is, each period we learn something new (but not everything) about the true state of the world. The most natural formal modeling of this structure utilizes *event partitions* of the state space. Each period we enter one event out of a collection of possible realizations for that date. And for each possible event entered in date s there is a subpartition of possible events to enter in date $s+1$. This structure will be implicit in our formulation, although we suppress explicit reference to it for the sake of notational brevity.[17]

As discussed in Chapter 6, we expect decision making to be sequential in nature unless markets are effectively complete. It will be desirable to postpone choices (where possible) until after the relevant uncertainty is revealed. This fact introduces some new considerations into decision processes. Before good decisions are taken at any date, agents need to have some plan for how they will execute future decisions. Further, such

---

[16] Wilson (1982) obtains similar measures (though without the betas) under somewhat more stringent assumptions.
[17] See Radner (1982) for a full formalization of the model together with a discussion of equilibrium concepts and existence proofs for the associated market structures.

a plan requires that they form expectations about the nature of uncertainty faced. We follow the mainstream of economic thought by assuming that these expectations are rational in that they are the correct expectations conditional on all information currently available.[18]

Let E_s be the expectations operator conditioning on information available at date s. Since we are not dealing with differential information here, this operator is the same for all agents. Strictly speaking, we should associate this operator not with the date but with the particular event entered at that date. However, we hope the meaning will be clear without introducing extra notation.

When market structure is inherently incomplete, the set of markets that are "active" ought to be endogenous to the model. That is, we need some economic explanation as to why some markets come into existence while others do not. Although there is an extensive literature on these questions, most of it relates to the presence of differential information.[19] Rather than model these factors explicitly, we assume that the set of active markets is given. This set always includes spot markets for each date together with a limited set of assets for trading across dates and events.

Our primary interest in this section is to see how the presence of such a sequential, incomplete market structure in the private economy affects first-order project analysis for the mixed economy. Thus, we reintroduce public goods and indirect taxation, assume the existence of a Radner (1979) equilibrium conditional on fixed public decisions, and ask how to evaluate the welfare of small projects. We will pursue the decomposition approach of Chapter 9 and show that the impact of incomplete markets can be fully captured by an additive "third-best" term.

We add one (admittedly strong) assumption to those of Radner (1979), namely, that utility is additively separable over time. This is done partly so that we can simplify decision-making formulations using the dynamic programming approach. Furthermore, this assumption greatly facilitates the recovery of utility from demand information, as we will see in Chapter 16; thus, it is useful to develop the formulation here. Most of what we say in this chapter can be generalized, but at the cost of extra notational complexity.

As before, P_s represents spot prices at date s and v_s represents the vector of prices for assets traded at that date. For simplicity, we suppose

---

[18] It is well known that the assumption of rational expectations is very demanding on the information-processing capabilities of agents. However, there is no useful weakening of this assumption that we know of. See Grossman (1981) for an exposition and defense of this assumption.

[19] For example, Akerlof (1970) argued that certain kinds of markets will disappear when quality is unobserved by some of the participants. See also Leland (1979).

that assets pay all their dividends in numeraire units. Specifically, asset j pays d_{js} dollars per unit in period s. Ex ante, dividends constitute a random variable, paying off different amounts in the various possible events that might be entered at that date. For example, if uncertainty involves a binary "boom" or "bust," dividends will be a corresponding binary random variable. Of course, prices must be thought of as random variables in the same sense, and expectations will be formed on the basis of these random variables.

The correct procedure for sequential dynamic optimization involves deciding what will be best to do in the future conditional on realizations and earlier decisions and then "backing up" to make the best current decisions given these consequences.[20] With an additive separable objective, this procedure can be summarized by a simple recursive optimization. Let $U_s(g_s, c_s)$ be the contribution to consumer utility from consumption at date s (sometimes this contribution is referred to as *felicity*). Since felicity in the future is assumed not to depend on consumption of the past, we can utilize a concept of indirect utility from date s forward. Namely, let $V_s(\cdot)$ be the best aggregate felicity that can be achieved from date s forward by taking optimal decisions. The arguments of this function will include all parameters faced by our consumer in the future together with *state* variables determined from past behavior.

We choose to model the asset payoff structure so that there will be a single state variable (accumulated wealth). Toward this end, we employ the fiction that each agent sells all his assets at the end of a period and makes new gross purchases (a') at the beginning of the next period; asset dividends are paid out at the end of the period just before (fictional) sales. Now, our consumer's sequential problem can be summarized in the following formulation:

$$\max_{c_s, a'_s} [U_s(g_s, c_s) + \rho_{s+1} E_s V_{s+1}(g_{s+1}, P_{s+1}, v_{s+1}, m_{s+1}, \dots)] \tag{12.28}$$

subject to

$$P_s c_s + v_s a'_s = m_s,$$

where

$$m_{s+1} = (d_{s+1} + v_{s+1}) a'_s - T_{s+1}.$$

Note that we allow for the possibility of lump-sum taxes and private ownership of firms whose equity is included in the set of available assets.

Bellman's principle of optimality tells us that the indirect utility function for (12.28) is precisely $V_s(g_s, P_s, v_s, m_s, \dots)$: If one chooses today's

---

[20] This principle of dynamic optimization was developed extensively by Bellman (1957). It was adapted to an uncertainty context by Howard (1960).

variables to maximize today's felicity plus the discounted best future utility, one achieves the best possible current utility.

To carry out the analysis of Chapter 9 for projects initiated in date s, we need to evaluate the derivatives of $V_s(\cdot)$. These are evaluated recursively starting with the contemporaneous variables (λ_s now is marginal utility of the contemporaneous state variable):

$$\nabla_{g_s} V_s = \nabla_{g_s} U_s, \qquad \nabla_{P_s} V_s = -\lambda_s c_s,$$

$$\nabla_{v_s} V_s = -\lambda_s a_s', \qquad \nabla_{m_s} V_s = \lambda_s. \tag{12.29}$$

We evaluate derivatives with respect to prices one period hence by first using the envelope theorem and then substituting recursively from (12.29) with s replaced by $s+1$[21]:

$$\nabla_{P_{s+1}} V_s = \rho_{s+1} E_s \nabla_{P_{s+1}} V_{s+1} = -\rho_{s+1} E_s(\lambda_{s+1} c_{s+1}). \tag{12.30}$$

We get analogous expressions for the other variables, although things are slightly more complicated when analyzing future dividends since these affect current welfare through impact on the future state variable. The reader should see how the procedure can be iterated to obtain derivatives for variables two periods in the future, three periods in the future, and so on.

A   *Discounting opportunity cost*

We have seen in previous chapters that an opportunity cost form of welfare measure is robust against a variety of potential second-best distortions. Will this robustness extend to include the presence of incomplete markets? The answer is yes, but our demonstration is somewhat complicated by the fact that the sequence of consumer budget constraints does not collapse to a single expected wealth constraint.

Let us separate out effects on consumer welfare from contemporaneous variables, variables one period forward in time, and so on, and label these $MU(s)$, $MU(s+1)$, and so forth. In evaluating each of these, we substitute using the budget constraint appropriate to the associated period, yielding

$$\frac{MU(s)}{\lambda_s} = \Omega_s \nabla_\alpha g_s - \nabla_\alpha P_s c_s - \nabla_\alpha v_s a_s' + \nabla_\alpha m_s$$

$$= \Omega_s \nabla_\alpha g_s + P_s \nabla_\alpha c_s + v_s \nabla_\alpha a_s'. \tag{12.31}$$

---

[21] At this point we are differentiating with respect to a random variable. This procedure is justified under the same conditions that enable us to interchange differentiation and integration operators. See footnote 9.

$$\frac{MU(s+1)}{\lambda_s} = E_s[\psi_{s+1}[\Omega_{s+1}\nabla_\alpha g_{s+1} - \nabla_\alpha P_{s+1}c_{s+1} + \nabla_\alpha v_{s+1}a'_{s+1}$$

$$+ \nabla_\alpha (d_{s+1}+v_{s+1})a'_s - \nabla_\alpha T_{s+1}]]$$

$$= E_s[\psi_{s+1}[\Omega_{s+1}\nabla_\alpha g_{s+1} + P_{s+1}\nabla_\alpha c_{s+1}$$

$$+ v_{s+1}\nabla_\alpha a'_{s+1} - (d_{s+1}+v_{s+1})\nabla_\alpha a'_s]], \qquad (12.32)$$

where

$$\psi_{s+1} = \rho_{s+1}\frac{\lambda_{s+1}}{\lambda_s}. \qquad (12.33)$$

It should be clear that ψ_{s+1} represents (ex ante) the pseudovalue of an Arrow security paying off in the various events one period hence. Therefore, the notation chosen here is consistent with that used in the previous section. At this point, changes in asset holdings still appear in the welfare measures. However, even with incomplete markets, the induced changes in asset holdings do not have any first-order welfare impacts. To see this, examine the first-order conditions for consumer asset choice:

$$\lambda_s v_s = \rho_{s+1}E_s[\lambda_{s+1}(d_{s+1}+v_{s+1})]. \qquad (12.34)$$

This optimization condition implies that the last terms in (12.31) and (12.32) cancel each other. Further, recursive iteration will show that the next to the last term in (12.32) must cancel against a corresponding term involving variables two periods into the future, and so forth.

Thus, we see that first-order project benefits again can be measured as the difference between marginal direct benefits and marginal opportunity cost, where each should be discounted for risk using principles developed in the previous section. The preceding iterative procedure determines appropriate multiperiod discount factors; for example, the two-period discount term takes the form

$$\psi_{s+2} = \rho_{s+1}\rho_{s+2}\frac{\lambda_{s+2}}{\lambda_s}. \qquad (12.35)$$

Iterating further, we can find the multiperiod generalization of one-period risk discount factors.

B   *Behavior toward risk*

It appears, therefore, that the principles of risk discounting are similar to those elaborated in previous sections. However, sequential structure does introduce a qualitatively new type of risk, namely, that associated with uncertainty that is revealed before relevant decisions must be made.[22] For example, the consumer will be uncertain today about tomorrow's prices, but he can wait until tomorrow (when prices will be revealed) before deciding how much to consume. Obviously, the ability to defer decisions makes the underlying uncertainty less costly. In fact, consumers may actually have a preference for this type of uncertainty *even* when they are risk averse by the usual definition.

To identify the possible effects of "timeless" risk, we decompose the measure of opportunity cost of good i one period hence as in Section 12.3:

$$E_s[\psi_{s+1}P_{s+1,i}\nabla_\alpha c_{s+1,i}] = E_s[\psi_{s+1}]E_s[P_{s+1,i}\nabla_\alpha c_{s+1,i}]$$

$$+ \text{COV}[\psi_{s+1}, P_{s+1,i}\nabla_\alpha c_{s+1,i}]. \tag{12.36}$$

Considerations determining the covariance term are much the same as before. If the individual exhibits aversion to temporal risk, ψ will vary inversely with the goodness of state, and a risk premium will be required to the extent that opportunity cost varies in the same way. But now, the consumer has some new "control" since he can vary consumption in response to the price realization. He can buy a lot when the price is low and less when the price is high. If he is not too risk averse to take advantage of this "arbitrage" opportunity, he can lower the expected opportunity cost over what it would be if the price were nonstochastic. This consideration will be decisive if he is risk neutral (so that the covariance term disappears) and may still dominate even if he is risk averse.

These considerations are important in certain kinds of contexts. For example, options prices tend to depend positively on the variance of the underlying spot price (holders get a higher expected return as the variability goes up since they "exercise" only at the high prices). Also, it explains why employment recruiters generally like to see lots of variability in the applicant pool (they only plan to hire those in the upper tail). However, this aspect of timeless uncertainty does not seem to be very important in determining risk discount factors for public projects for reasons that will become apparent shortly.

C   *Decomposition of opportunity cost*

We now seek to decompose opportunity cost into more easily observable terms. It turns out that incomplete markets make a difference here; even if the ex ante income distribution is optimal, future opportunity costs

---

[22] Such risk was referred to as *timeless* by Dreze–Modigliani (1972), who were among the first to study it systematically.

will not aggregate across individuals as long as these individuals have differential valuations on dollars in the various possible events. Indeed, policy effects that are purely distributional ex post will have welfare effects ex ante if they improve at the margin the second-best nature of risk sharing. Viewed from the point of view of second-best decompositions, there must be a new welfare term associated with nonoptimal risk sharing (in the status quo).

Although the associated decomposition is not so useful from the point of view of practical measurement, it does provide some theoretical insight. Let us concentrate on contributions to opportunity cost j periods (call this term OP_{s+j}). After aggregating across individuals, we can factor this term into ex ante and ex post distribution terms plus a residual as follows:

$$OP_{s+j} = DA_{s+j} + DP_{s+j} + E_s[\bar{\psi}_{s+j} P_{s+j} \nabla_\alpha C_{s+j}], \tag{12.37}$$

where

$$DA_{s+j} = \sum_h (\beta^h - 1) E_s[\psi^h_{s+j} P_{s+j} \nabla_\alpha c^h_{s+j}], \tag{12.38}$$

and

$$DP_{s+j} = \sum_h E_s[(\psi^h_{s+j} - \bar{\psi}_{s+1}) P_{s+j} \nabla_\alpha c^h_{s+j}], \tag{12.39}$$

where $\bar{\psi}$ is the population average over ψ^h's.

Note that the D terms are distributional in the usual sense; DA will be zero when the ex ante distribution is optimal, and the DP terms will be zero when the future distribution is optimized across states (naturally, this latter condition is satisfied when markets are complete). Now, the residual term in (12.37) decomposes just as in Chapter 9:

$$E_s[\bar{\psi}_{s+j} P_{s+j} \nabla_\alpha C_{s+j}] = -E_s[\bar{\psi}_{s+j} Q_{s+j} \nabla_\alpha b_{s+j}] + E_s[\bar{\psi}_{s+j} Q_{s+j} \nabla_\alpha Y_{s+j}]$$
$$+ E_s[\bar{\psi}_{s+j} t_{s+j} \nabla_\alpha C_{s+j}]. \tag{12.40}$$

Consequently, the gap between opportunity cost and market cost does indeed look the same as before except for a new term measuring marginal improvement in risk sharing. As in the previous section, we can express the risk correction (for each cost element) in terms of a risk premium to be used in discounting the associated expected values.

Two further points are worthy of note. First, it seems quite unlikely that project managers can take advantage of timeless risk. Assuming that the project, once started, will be built, there is not much flexibility on input demand across random events. Second, there is no presumption that competitive behavior by firms will serve to eliminate the private production term in (12.40). Unless some sort of spanning condition holds, the firm always retains some monopoly power in a subset of potential risk-sharing markets; only under very severe assumptions about what constitutes "competitive" behavior will private firms be induced to take first-best actions.[23]

12.5   Project analysis with uncertainty and incomplete markets

Earlier, we developed extensive practical rules for project analysis in an atemporal, certainty context. How do these need to be modified in a general intertemporal context with incomplete markets? First, we will have to incorporate appropriate risk discount factors using relevant social risk premiums and project betas. Then we evaluate project outputs and opportunity cost using a criteria of risk adjusted expected value.

However, new complications arise if we want to do the accounting in terms of *actual* project cost. The presence of missing markets introduces a new externality into the second-best calculus. Each project has a potential impact on the degree of risk sharing, and this impact should be counted as a contribution to welfare. This externality sometimes is referred to as "pecuniary," presumably because it can arise from pure price effects; a project whose sole effect on the economy is to change prices (and that would therefore make no contribution to economic efficiency in the context of Chapter 9) may now improve efficiency merely by transferring income among individuals across states of the world. Unfortunately, it will be quite difficult, if not impossible, to measure this effect in practical applications.

Further, we must evaluate second-best terms attributable to private firms and indirect taxation; these evaluations are complicated by the fact that we do not have a very satisfactory theory of the firm in sequence economies; and even if we did, we need information on how the private economy would react in unobserved random events, information that will be difficult and costly to collect.

Although these new difficulties may be a serious impediment to welfare measurement in some circumstances, there is a line of thought in the literature that suggests they are generally unimportant. This view would have it that all actions that can be taken by the government or private firms lie in a limited subspace of risk-sharing possibilities so that there is no "danger" of changing the degree of risk sharing through new projects. However, it remains to be seen whether some such spanning condition really holds empirically.

---

[23] The theory of the firm in sequence economies has been the subject of considerable debate. See Dreze (1974), Hart (1979), Grossman–Hart (1979), and Makowski (1983).

The presence of incomplete markets can lead to some striking welfare conclusions, although they fit naturally in the context of our second-best calculus. For example, suppose incompleteness constitutes the *only* element of market failure (in particular, there is no indirect taxation and the ex ante distribution is optimal). Then, projects that satisfy all the usual first-best optimality conditions generally still will be Pareto inefficient. Geanakoplos and Polemarchakis (1986) give an example of this in which they show that the equity markets generally will be Pareto inefficient even within the class of outcomes they could potentially generate. Whether or not such considerations are important also remains to be seen.

CHAPTER 13

Identifying shadow values: hedonic methods and capitalization

Much of our purpose in the past four chapters has revolved around reformulating and decomposing social decision problems so as to simplify analysis and interpretation; but at the same time we have been trying to reduce information-gathering requirements by constructing welfare measures from observable information (such as tax revenue, market demand, and the like). We have succeeded reasonably well in developing utility (and welfare) indicators from demand-and-supply information, but the associated methods are practical only when the relevant supply-and-demand functions can be observed without error. Even when transactions data exist (as for market goods), the necessary observations are rarely complete, and the econometrician is left with difficult obstacles; however, these difficulties seem minor compared to corresponding problems associated with collective goods for which the corresponding markets do not exist. Here, we will explore ways of identifying the demand for collective goods from sufficiently rich information on actual market transactions. Later, in Chapter 16, we will address the underlying econometric problems briefly.

How are we going to estimate the necessary "demand prices" for collective goods? We saw in Chapter 5 that attempts to elicit this information directly run into serious incentive compatibility problems. Although there is some hope for designing mechanisms that will avoid these problems, we are still a long way from having practical methods with general applicability.

However, perhaps we can identify demand for collective goods from observable behavior on markets for private goods. The intuitive idea is best seen through some examples. Suppose that we want to know a household's valuation of clean air and can observe its purchases of air conditioning. Surely, we can infer something about the strength of its preference from the amount of air conditioning bought. Similarly, we ought to be able to infer something about the value of water recreation and lake view from the rent premium on lake front property. Or, suppose we observe wages for a variety of jobs that differ only in their risk of disability. Should we not be able to infer something from this information about the "utility" cost of disability?

If we have available information about behavior "far" away from the status quo equilibrium or are willing to make global functional form assumptions, some very powerful methods are available for identifying demand for nonmarketed goods based on the aforementioned intuition. We discuss these methods later in the context of large-project analysis (see Chapter 16). Here, we focus on a method that identifies shadow values using only local information. This method is best known in the context of hedonic price models, but we will develop it in a more general form first and treat such models as a special case later.[1]

13.1   Identification based on spanning

The rigorous methods can be introduced through examples based on the preceding intuition. We begin with one based on the air conditioning case. Let g be ambient air quality and a expenditures on air conditioning (in terms of a composite numeraire good). We suppose that resultant air quality can be represented by a function $\eta(g, a)$ in such a way that utility depends only on η and net consumption of the numeraire. It seems reasonable to assume that we know the function η (e.g., from engineering studies).

A typical household now divides its private goods between direct consumption and air conditioning so as to

$$\max_{a} U^{h}(\eta(g, a), m^{h} - a), \tag{13.1}$$

where m^{h} is (as usual) exogenous income. This choice serves to identify the shadow price of air quality as follows: First-order conditions imply

$$\frac{\partial U/\partial \eta}{\lambda} = \frac{1}{\partial \eta/\partial a}. \tag{13.2}$$

If the demand for private inputs (a) is observable without error, the right side of (13.2) is observable, so the left side is identified. It follows that the shadow price ($[(\partial U/\partial \eta)/\lambda][\partial \eta/\partial g]$) is also identified.

As a second way of identifying the value of clean air (or equivalently the marginal damage of pollution), consider the following example, which utilizes rent gradients.[2] We suppose that our representative individual chooses location(s) within a community. This choice involves a trade-off between air quality, rents, and transport costs. Conditional on the choice, our individual faces a standard problem:

[1] The methods discussed here were introduced in the hedonic literature by Rosen (1974). They appeared in the urban economics literature with Ridker–Henning (1967) followed by Anderson–Crocker (1971, 1972).
[2] Lind (1973) was among the first to suggest a mechanism of this sort. The example here is adapted from Polinski–Shavell (1975).

$$\max_{c, \ell} U(\eta[s], c, \ell) \tag{13.3}$$

subject to

$$c + r[s]\ell + \phi[s] = m,$$

where $\eta[s]$ represents air quality at location s, ℓ is net consumption of land, $r[s]$ is the rental rate at location s, and $\phi[s]$ represents transport or commuting costs associated with location s.

Thus, our household's overall problem involves maximizing (13.3) over choices of c, ℓ, *and s*. Here, first-order conditions for choice of s serve to identify the shadow price of air quality:

$$\frac{\partial U/\partial \eta}{\lambda} = \left[\frac{d\phi}{ds} + \ell[s] \frac{dr}{ds} \right] \Big/ \frac{d\eta}{ds}. \tag{13.4}$$

Presumably, we can observe residential density ($\ell[s]$) and the rent gradient (dr/ds) from market data. Thus, assuming the other functions can be identified from engineering and environmental studies, the shadow price is identified. Here, the household aversion to pollution is balanced against transport and rent costs in an observable way.

Note that neither of the two examples requires that households share identical (or even similar) characteristics, although both require some data disaggregated by household characteristics (e.g., air-conditioning purchases).

A   *General activity analysis framework*

What general features of these examples make them work? Well, the dimensionality of things we need to infer needs to be no bigger than the dimensionality of choice variables; effectively, this gives us enough equations (from first-order conditions) to identify all the unknowns. We will not expect this "dimensionality" condition to hold generally. For example, it will never hold if all choice variables enter independently in the utility function. Thus, the method can work *only* when some variables act as intermediate goods in consumer choice. (Location plays this role in the second example; note that if this variable should enter utility directly, the procedure breaks down.)

Therefore, we take an "activity" approach to the household problem. We let $\eta(g, a)$ represent a (column) vector function of activity outputs as functions of collective-goods levels g and private decision variables a. The important restrictions for us here concern dimensionality: Utility depends *only* on activity levels, and the number of activities is no larger than the number of private decision variables. Let $\Gamma(a)$ be the cost of a.

Note that even in our partial equilibrium framework, we do not want to assume that Γ is linear in a; indeed, in the second example, $a = (c, \ell, s)$ and $\Gamma(a) = c + r[s]\ell + \phi[s]$.

Household optimization now takes the form

$$\max_{a} U[\eta(g, a)] \tag{13.5}$$

subject to

$$\Gamma(a) = m.$$

First-order conditions for choice of a may be written as

$$\frac{\nabla_\eta U \nabla_a \eta}{\lambda} = \nabla_a \Gamma. \tag{13.6}$$

Now as long as the matrix $\nabla_a \eta$ has an inverse (or a generalized inverse if it is not square), we can solve for $\nabla_\eta U / \lambda$ and write the shadow price vector for g as

$$\frac{\nabla_\eta U \nabla_g \eta}{\lambda} = \nabla_a \Gamma [\nabla_a \eta]^{-1} \nabla_g \eta. \tag{13.7}$$

Clearly, for this procedure to work, the functions $\eta(g, a)$ and $\nabla_a \Gamma(a)$ must be known, and the gradient matrix of η with respect to a must have full row rank (i.e., rank equal to the dimension of the η vector). The rank condition cannot possibly hold unless the a vector is at least as large as the η vector, a restriction we were expecting to face. But there is a further "spanning" requirement associated with the rank condition: it must be possible to move the η vector in any direction by an appropriate change in the a vector; otherwise, we will be unable to learn the entire shadow price vector by observing small variations in a only.

It is easy to give examples where the spanning condition fails. Suppose that there is at least one collective good that enters the utility function separately from all other arguments. Then, one of the rows in our matrix will be zero so it cannot have full-row rank. Obviously, we should not expect to learn anything about the valuation of this collective good using the current method.

B   *Relationship to hedonic price methods*

Much literature exists on inferring the demand for characteristics from market prices.[3] The procedure typically is described as follows: A commodity such as land (or autos) is imbued with a collection of characteristics

---

[3] See Rosen (1974), Brown-Rosen (1982), and Kanemoto-Nakamura (1984).

such as view or air quality (or speed, comfort). By observing market data, we estimate price as a function of these characteristics. Then, we infer the marginal value of each characteristic from the associated partial derivative of this function.

The "hedonic" method can be viewed as a special case of our spanning procedure in which the public variables (g) are identified directly with characteristics η. Imposing the restrictions $\eta(g, a) = g(a)$, shadow prices can be inferred from (13.6):

$$\frac{\nabla_g U}{\lambda} = \nabla_a \Gamma [\nabla_a g]^{-1}. \tag{13.8}$$

Now, whenever there exists a well-defined function relating market cost to underlying characteristics [label this function $\hat{\Gamma}(g)$], we see from the implicit-function theorem that the right side of (13.8) may be written as $\nabla_g \hat{\Gamma}$; thus, we have justified the hedonic procedure. Note that in this special case, *all* we need to observe is market relationships (we do not need information about the form of household activities or production technologies).

However, it should be clear from our discussion that the hedonic method has buried in it the same kind of spanning conditions we encountered earlier; without them, the hedonic price function cannot fully reveal underlying preferences (we will see why momentarily). This is an important point, since it is not always made clear in discussions of hedonic procedures.[4] Indeed, the real art to learning something about indirect demands is in figuring out how to isolate the relevant effect (i.e., guarantee the necessary spanning condition).

13.2   Identification with similar agents

Since the spanning conditions are rather severe, it would be nice if we could relax them. In particular, we would like to reduce the dimensionality requirements on choice variables. It would be particularly desirable if we could treat some of these as discrete (zero dimensional); most of the hedonic price examples involve discrete choices: The set of available automobiles (or types of air conditioners) is finite, and the set of potential locations probably is best thought of as finite as well.

We now examine hedonic procedures in this type of situation. Let s index the set of available products (locations). Conditional on s an agent of type i has an indirect utility function of the form $V^i(g[s], \Gamma[s], m^i, s)$.

---

[4] There is a considerable literature on econometric identification problems that arise in estimating hedonic price functions. See Brown–Rosen (1982) and Kanemoto–Nakamura (1984).

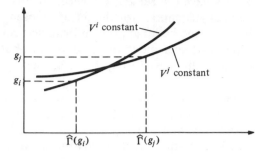

Figure 13.1

First, suppose (as in the preceding) that we can do analysis on the variable s. Optimal choice then entails the necessary conditions

$$\nabla_g V^i \nabla_s g + \nabla_\Gamma V^i \nabla_s \Gamma + \nabla_s V = 0. \tag{13.9}$$

If we expect to identify the marginal valuation on characteristics, the spanning requirements are clear: s must not affect utility directly ($\nabla_s V = 0$), and we must be able to invert the matrix $\nabla_s g$; in particular, s must have at least the dimension of g.

Suppose we can satisfy the first requirement (people care about s only for the characteristics embodied), but s is an inherently discrete variable. Obviously, we can still observe some points on a hedonic price function $\hat{\Gamma}(g)$; do they tell us anything about preferences? Well, revealed preference does imply the following inequalities:

$$V^i(g^i, \hat{\Gamma}(g^i), m^i) \geq V^i(g^j, \hat{\Gamma}(g^j), m^i), \quad \text{all } j, \tag{13.10}$$

where g^i is the level chosen by type i. However, if people systematically sort themselves out over the product space by preference type (so that all of the preceding inequalities are strict), use of hedonic price functions to infer willingness to pay will tend to overstate the value of incremental public characteristics. To see this, suppose that g is one dimensional and g^j exceeds g^i. Then, if we use $\hat{\Gamma}(g^j) - \hat{\Gamma}(g^i)$ as a measure of how much it would be worth to type i to have g^j rather than g^i, we overstate his true willingness to pay (since he is actually worse off with $[g^j, \hat{\Gamma}(g^j)]$ than with $[g^i, \hat{\Gamma}(g^i)]$ (see Figure 13.1). Similarly, if g^j is less than g^i, then $\hat{\Gamma}(g^i) - \hat{\Gamma}(g^j)$ will understate the true cost of lost public characteristics.

Although it is possible in some circumstances to make inferences concerning the magnitude of these errors, we will not develop approximations of this sort here.[5] Rather, we return to the possibility of exact measures

[5] See Scotchmer (1985a) for further discussion.

in situations where all agents have the same preferences [so that all inequalities in (13.10) are actually equalities for the set of "chosen" products or locations]. In this case, the hedonic price information reveals a discrete set of points on the consumer indifference curve and thus gives exact information about the willingness to pay for a particular set of changes.

Such information may be quite valuable to us when we turn to large-project analysis in the last part of this book. However, suppose we are still interested only in measures of first-order benefit. Can we infer these from the available hedonic information? Not exactly unless we interpolate correctly between the known points. If these points are relatively isolated, there will necessarily be some range of uncertainty concerning appropriate shadow prices.

13.3   Relationships between hedonic methods and capitalization

The ideas discussed in the preceding are closely related to the issue of capitalization in local public finance.[6] Capitalization occurs when net benefits from changes in local public goods and/or local taxes induce corresponding changes in local land values. Clearly, there are conceptual similarities between land rent as a hedonic price and land value capitalization; however, they are not exactly the same phenomena. The first situation is one in which differences in land rent at different locations correctly reflect the relative value of amenities at these locations. Land value capitalization makes similar claims concerning (hypothetical) changes at the *same* locations. Nevertheless, it should not be surprising to find that capitalization rests on structural assumptions that are very similar to those underlying hedonic prices.

Whether "full" capitalization occurs depends on the structure of local public-goods equilibrium. Although we want to emphasize positive results here, we will discuss what happens when key assumptions are relaxed. Further, differences in structural assumptions can generate identifiable differences in the correct measures of benefits. We will point out these differences and draw some of their implications for the questions most frequently posed in the capitalization literature.

Capitalization generally seems to rely on there being similarities among agents at various locations. Some capitalization effects are generated by competitive forces linking communities. Suppose that a project is built in one community designed to make people better off there. Now, if people in all communities have similar tastes and are free to move among the

---

[6] Our discussion of this topic is based largely on Starrett (1981, 1983). References to the earlier literature are given in those papers.

communities, outsiders will be attracted to the project-building community. And they will continue to move until the welfare incentive disappears. The only factor that can stop this movement is a differential location cost, that is, an increase in land rents in the active community. We will refer to the resulting capitalization as *external* capitalization.

Naturally, when we drop the assumption of free mobility between communities or the assumption of similar tastes across communities, the intuition for external capitalization is weaker. Indeed, some have argued that we should not expect land value capitalization in specialized (Tiebout) communities that are immune to migration forces due to differences in tastes [see, e.g., Hamilton (1975)].

However, a different force for capitalization may come into play when similar households live in the same community. Suppose that community collective goods are "local" in character because proximity matters. For example, the user has to make trips in order to appreciate such public goods as parks, museums, civic centers, sports complexes, and even roads and highways. Now, if there is a positive correlation between the amounts of public goods and the differential desirability of locations, some degree of capitalization will occur as rents adjust. This type of argument has been used in the literature to justify the use of rent gradients for measuring the externality cost of pollution near a source (such as airport or factory).[7] We refer to capitalization based on these forces as *internal* capitalization and study it first.

The analysis to follow is couched in the framework of Chapter 11. There is an active community that institutes a change in provision levels, and we explore the relationship between benefits and community land values, assuming that other constituencies play a passive role. We restrict the generality a little by assuming that local revenue is derived from some combination of a property tax and a Tiebout tax (thus, local sales taxation is not considered). We further restrict ourselves to the case of competitive behavior by firms.

13.4   Internal capitalization

We assume in this section that communities are fully insulated against migration to or from the outside. Thus, in particular, the population and composition of a community is invariant to project choice. We still can think of communities as linked in other ways (as through absentee ownership).

---

[7] See Ridker–Henning (1967), Polinsky–Shavell (1975, 1976) and Freeman (1979). Empirical estimates based on these ideas can be found in the St. Louis air pollution study reported in Mullet (1974).

To proceed, we look at an explicitly spatial version of a constituency in which land variables are split off from the rest of the private-goods vector. Since we want to keep track of the total value of land resources, we treat the consumption of land (ℓ) as *gross* consumption and incorporate the resource value of land in the income term m. For convenience, we suppose that a household consumes land only in its place of residence. We let s be this location choice within a community and use r for land prices (P continues to be the vector of other consumption prices). Conditional on location choice, the indirect utility functions of Chapter 11 will be functions of collective-goods levels, private-goods prices, resource income (from land and equity) minus direct taxes, and location. The "last-stage" problem may be stated as

$$\max_s V^h(g, G, P, r_s, m^h - T^h, s). \tag{13.11}$$

(Note that we have dropped explicit reference to the community for now.) Observe that this formulation allows location to affect preference directly (e.g., due to such things as view); thus, we do not require a spanning condition.

Due to our special treatment of land, the definition of household type is slightly different from that employed in Chapter 11. Here, two individuals will be considered of the same type if they have the same resource incomes (though endowments might differ) and indirect preference functions. Note that this definition implies that two households of the same type ex ante will be of different types ex post if their property incomes are affected differently by the project.

The first important assumption behind full internal capitalization is that households do not systematically sort themselves out by type within the community. Of course, if everyone in the community is identical, this is a triviality; but if there are diverse preferences (or even diverse income levels) represented in the community, we require that households of *each type* be indifferent as to where they live. Thus, for example, if households differ by income levels only, we require that preferences be separable in income levels. We comment later on this assumption and the consequences of relaxing it.

Given "no sorting," achieved utility levels will be independent of location, and we can measure each household's utility as it would accrue at *any* particular place within the community. It will be convenient for us to choose the boundary (σ) for this purpose. The reason is as follows: If people live at the boundary, they get smaller direct benefits from the project than others (assuming that proximity does matter). Since they do just as well as others overall, they must be getting their benefits some other way, namely, through increases in the value of their property.

When all residents of the community are identical (and the number of residents is fixed), it is natural to measure community welfare by that of a representative resident. However, when there are type differences, we naturally need to worry about distributional concerns. Since land rent changes are measured in numeraire aggregates, we cannot expect rents to capitalize welfare unless the latter is measured in similar aggregates, that is, unless ex ante distribution is optimal. Consequently, capitalization measures apply to the nondistributional component of a welfare decomposition. Therefore, we concentrate on that component for the time being and "flag" that fact by appending an asterisk to our welfare measures (as in Chapter 11). Using V_s^h for the indirect utility function of a type h agent living at s, our "no-sorting" condition implies that we could measure marginal project benefit as

$$\nabla_\alpha Z^* = \sum_h n^h \frac{\nabla_\alpha V^h}{\lambda_\sigma^h}. \tag{13.12}$$

Now let us think about the strongest form capitalization could take. Suppose that all *direct* project benefits are *intramarginal* in that boundary residents are marginally unaffected. This does not require that they get no benefits from local public goods and services, only that they get no *additional* benefits from the *marginal* project. For example, if the local public good is a museum or park, boundary residents may make so few trips that (at their current level of activity) they could make no better use of a larger facility. Suppose further that nonland transactions prices to residents are unaffected by the project. This will be true if, for example, the associated markets are national in scope and the community is a small part of the nation.

Then, *all* benefits to boundary residents derive from changes in land values and components of other income. Formally, carrying out the differentiation of indirect utility and dropping terms assumed to be zero yields

$$\nabla_\alpha Z^* = -N\ell_\sigma \nabla_\alpha r_\sigma + \nabla_\alpha \Pi + \nabla_\alpha \hat{R} - \nabla_\alpha \hat{T}, \tag{13.13}$$

where N is the total population of the community, Π is profit income, $\hat{R}$ is land value after any property tax is paid, and $\hat{T}$ is direct tax liability, all aggregated over community residents.

When direct taxation is used to pay for the marginal project, the tax term in (13.13) captures those costs, and the remaining terms must measure marginal *gross* benefit. On the other hand, if there is no direct taxation (so the project is paid for out of property tax revenue), the remaining terms measure marginal *net* benefit. In either case, the exact form and interpretation of capitalization depends on additional assumptions concerning the property markets.

A   *Home ownership*

Suppose that all property (land and firms) is locally owned. Referring back to the discussion in Chapter 11, this assumption, in conjunction with others we have made, implies that there are no externalities among communities. In particular, our measure of welfare change to the community also serves to measure welfare for the society as a whole.

Profits (Π) now represent profits generated in the community of interest. Assuming that local firms behave competitively, we know that $\nabla_\alpha \Pi$ takes the form $\nabla_\alpha PY$. But the only prices that change are land prices, so we have

$$\nabla_\alpha \Pi = \nabla_\alpha PY = -\nabla_\alpha R_f, \tag{13.14}$$

where R_f is the *gross of tax* value of *industrial* land in the community.

Combining the last two equations and adding the property taxes (if any) to both owners' property values and their other (direct) tax liability yields

$$\nabla_\alpha Z^* = -N\ell_\sigma \nabla_\alpha r_\sigma + \nabla_\alpha R_r - \nabla_\alpha T, \tag{13.15}$$

where R_r is the gross of tax value of residential land and T is total tax revenue in the community.

We see that capitalization relates to *residential* land value here. However, it should be noted that there is an alternatiave view of the firm that is inconsistent with our formulation and would alter this result. Our entire method of analysis is predicated on the assumption that small changes in prices lead to small changes in decision variables. This assumption fails if, for example, all firms exhibit constant returns to scale and are always in long-run equilibrium. In that case, a small rise in rents (ceteris paribus) would cause all firms to leave instantly; all land becomes residential land, and the distinction between residential and industrial land loses its significance. However, we feel that the long run is too long to be relevant here. Firms are not free to leave when rents rise, and the increasing rent payments by firms should be counted against profits; residential land seems the appropriate base for capitalization.

Note that irrespective of the type of taxation, the consumer (gross of tax) value of residential land serves to capitalize gross project benefits. However, the relationship is exact only to the extent that boundary rents do not change. We can infer from (13.15) that when the boundary rent rises, the change in residential land value overstates gross benefits and vice versa. Since the local land market is assumed isolated from outside demand, the effects on boundary rent will derive from internal pressures on the spatial size (area) of the community.

It is easiest to see this in the case where the community is isolated in a "sea" of farmland. Then, the value of farmland serves to fix boundary rents so the rental value at σ cannot change unless the boundary moves from σ. It seems likely that the rental change at σ will be small, if not negligible, in most situations. There will be pressures to push out the boundary only if land is more complementary in demand with the public goods produced by the project than with the private goods foregone due to extra taxation.

B   *Absentee ownership*

Suppose we now allow more general ownership patterns. The first modification we must make is to distinguish between welfare change to society and that to the community of action. Let us label this community k and rewrite our basic capitalization result as

$$\nabla_\alpha Z^{*k} = -N^k \ell_\sigma^k \nabla_\alpha r_\sigma^k + \nabla_\alpha \Pi^k + \nabla_\alpha \hat{R}^k - \nabla_\alpha \hat{T}^k, \tag{13.16}$$

where the property values now refer to property owned by residents of community k. Now, we can think about how to measure welfare change to society by recalling how we measured externalities in Chapter 11.

Given our current assumptions, the only externality terms will be those representing absentee ownership. Increases in local property values owned by "foreigners" measure an external benefit, whereas any changes in foreign property values owned by residents of k generate a similar externality. Thus, adding in the externality measured by foreign ownership of local resources and subtracting out the term for reverse ownership, we find[8]

$$\nabla_\alpha Z^* = -N^k \ell_\sigma^k \nabla_\alpha r_\sigma^k + \nabla_\alpha \Pi(k) + \nabla_\alpha \hat{R}(k) - \nabla_\alpha \hat{T}^k$$
$$= -N^k \ell_\sigma^k \nabla_\alpha r_\sigma^k + \nabla_\alpha \Pi(k) + \nabla_\alpha R(k) - \nabla_\alpha T^k, \tag{13.17}$$

where the second equality is obtained by incorporating property taxes in both local property values and tax revenue, as before. But we already know from previous discussion that the resulting property value terms collapse to the change in residential land value. Thus, we have, finally,

$$\nabla_\alpha Z^* = -N^k \ell_\sigma^k \nabla_\alpha r_\sigma^k + \nabla_\alpha R_r(k) - \nabla_\alpha T^k. \tag{13.18}$$

As before, residential property values in the active community capitalize gross benefits to society as a whole. However, these will not accurately measure gross benefits *to the active community* when there is

[8] Recall from Chapter 11 that $\Pi(k)$ and $R(k)$ represent profit and rental values generated *in community k.*

absentee ownership. Interestingly, it may turn out that the correct measure for the community is *all* land value. This will be true when local residents own local land whereas local firms are owned on a national basis, largely by outsiders (so that increases in industrial land value constitute an externality).

C   Relaxing assumptions

The two key assumptions made were "no direct effect at boundary" and "no sorting within the community." Relaxing either of these will mitigate the capitalization force. Clearly, if boundary residents get some of their benefits directly, they get less of their benefits from property values. Indeed, in the extreme case where proximity is irrelevant, projects will not affect the rent gradient, and capitalization will occur only to the extent that boundary rents increase. Since we have argued that these changes are likely to be small and since there is no systematic way in which they will be linked to the desirability of the project, capitalization will be unimportant in that case. Thus, we do not expect to see internal capitalization in (spatially) small communities.

When households sort themselves out within the community, those choosing the boundary generally will not get as much from the project as those living closer in. The reason is that households choosing interior locations do so precisely because they care relatively more about the local public goods. These intramarginal groups then appropriate some of the benefit in a way that does not get reflected in the rent gradient.[9] Consequently, capitalization will be incomplete, and unfortunately, it will be difficult to measure the degree of capitalization unless we know something about the nature of preference differences. The situation here is very similar to the failure of hedonic price functions to correctly measure willingness to pay when consumers sort themselves out in characteristics space.

However, once there is enough preference diversity within the community to break up the internal capitalization forces, it seems likely that there will be preference similarities across communities so that migration forces will come into play.[10] We turn now to the "external" model in which these forces are primary.

[9] See Starrett (1981) for examples and further discussion.
[10] It is possible to construct models in which the preference space becomes partitioned into nonoverlapping segments, each of which constitutes a community (Ellickson, 1973; Westhoff, 1977). However, with many communities, such a model will imply considerable similarity within community so the internal model ought to apply approximately.

13.5   External capitalization

We now drop the two fundamental assumptions of the "internal" model. As just noted, unless there are some competitive forces linking communities, we do not expect to observe systematic capitalization in this case. However, if tastes are similar *across* communities, intercommunity competition will induce capitalizing effects on land values. Let us consider the case in which this competition is strongest, namely, when the composition of agents inside and outside the active community are essentially identical. Recall that this is the sort of pattern we would expect to see when there are substantial complementarities among types so that Tiebout sorting is inefficient.

Thus, we suppose that the active community (k) has the same composition by type ex ante as the world at large. Formally, we write this as

$$\frac{n^{kh}}{N^k} = \frac{n^h}{N},$$

(13.19)

where N^k is the ex ante population of community k and N for the exogenous total population. In addition, we assume that income effects associated with the project in k do not serve to sort households out by location. That is, if we look at two households of the same ex ante type (same preferences and ex ante resource incomes), there is at least one location somewhere that they would both still be willing to choose, ex post (even though their incomes may have been affected differently). Although this assumption seems a little strange here, we have shown elsewhere (Starrett, 1981) that differential income effects can actually insulate communities from the forces of external capitalization.

When measuring project benefits, the important implication of these assumptions is that any differences experienced by two households of the same ex ante type must be captured by differences in their resource income increments. (We could measure each of their utility changes at a common residence location where all other variables would be the same for both.) Except in this dimension, it is impossible for the active community to improve things for its residents relative to others since these "others" will move in to take advantage of any other differential. Property values will change so as to neutralize the moving incentives, and benefits must accrue to the associated owners. Given that the composition by type is the same (ex ante) in community k as in the rest of the country, it follows that differences in the average (first-order) welfare change between k and the rest of the country (indexed by # as in Chapter 11) will be measured by the corresponding differences in property value increments; that is,

$$\frac{\nabla_\alpha Z^{*k}}{N^k} - \frac{\nabla_\alpha Z^{*\#}}{N^\#} = \frac{1}{N^k} \nabla_\alpha(\hat{R}^k + \Pi^k) - \frac{1}{N^\#} \nabla_\alpha(\hat{R}^\# + \Pi^\#), \qquad (13.20)$$

where population sizes are measured ex ante. Consequently, we can solve for welfare change in the active community as

$$\nabla_\alpha Z^{*k} = \frac{N^k}{N^\#} \nabla_\alpha Z^{*\#} + \nabla_\alpha(\hat{R}^k + \Pi^k) - \frac{N^k}{N^\#} \nabla_\alpha(\hat{R}^\# + \Pi^\#). \qquad (13.21)$$

Since total welfare change is simply the sum of changes in k and elsewhere, we can write

$$\nabla_\alpha Z^* = \frac{N}{N^\#} \nabla_\alpha Z^{*\#} + \nabla_\alpha(\hat{R}^k + \Pi^k) - \frac{N^k}{N^\#} \nabla_\alpha(\hat{R}^\# + \Pi^\#). \qquad (13.22)$$

These two equations constitute a root form for external capitalization in that they relate welfare changes to corresponding property value changes. More specific forms can be obtained under various assumptions on the pattern of ex ante ownership. We consider only one of these patterns in detail (the one that seems most natural) and leave other cases to the reader.

Suppose that all local land is owned (ex ante) by local residents, whereas each community owns its share of national profits. Then, the profit income terms cancel in the preceding expressions, whereas the land income terms may be interpreted as rent *generated* in the associated regions. Consequently,

$$\nabla_\alpha Z^{*k} = \frac{N^k}{N^\#} \nabla_\alpha Z^{*\#} + \nabla_\alpha \hat{R}(k) - \frac{N^k}{N^\#} \nabla_\alpha \hat{R}(\#), \qquad (13.23)$$

$$\nabla_\alpha Z^* = \frac{N}{N^\#} \nabla_\alpha Z^{*\#} + \nabla_\alpha \hat{R}(k) - \frac{N^k}{N^\#} \nabla_\alpha \hat{R}(\#). \qquad (13.24)$$

Here, capitalization takes a particularly simple form when the active community is "small" enough compared to the nation so that terms involving the outside world are negligible in (13.23). Smallness here requires that $N^k/N^\#$ be sufficiently close to zero and the external influences be diffused sufficiently to be relatively small as well. Then change in (net of tax) local land rent will approximately capitalize *net* project benefits from the perspective of the active community; however, net *social* benefits will be misrepresented by these rent increases to the extent that externalities are generated [$N/N^\#$ will be approximately unity in (13.24)]; that is,

$$\nabla_\alpha Z^{*k} \approx \nabla_\alpha \hat{R}(k), \qquad (13.25)$$

and

$$\nabla_\alpha Z^* \approx \nabla_\alpha Z^{*\#} + \nabla_\alpha \hat{R}(k). \qquad (13.26)$$

When the local tax is of the Tiebout type, capitalization appears "weaker" than in the corresponding internal model – consumer land values capitalize net rather than gross project benefits. However, when the local tax is a property tax, the results here are very similar to those found in the internal model. Net of tax rental values measure net project benefits from the point of view of the active community, whereas gross of tax rental values measure gross project benefits; both measures misrepresent the corresponding social benefit to the extent that there are externalities.[11]

Some of the considerations determining externality are the same as in the internal model. In particular, absentee ownership considerations are similar. Since we are assuming here that local firms are largely owned by outsiders, the increased local cost of industrial land is largely paid by the rest of the country so, as before, only residential land value is relevant from the point of view of net social benefit, although all land value enters from the narrower point of view of the active community. Of course, if firms were locally owned, residential land value would be relevant from both points of view.

But now, with migration forces in effect, the externality term also contains potential fiscal effects. Since we argued in Chapter 11 that the externalities associated with migration effects are very likely to be negative in the present spatial context, land value increases generally will overstate true social benefit even if we restrict the base to residential land. This is another way of saying that reliance on land values as a guide will lead to overexpansion of the associated communities.

13.6   Comparison and perspective on capitalization measures

As we have seen, the extent and exact form of capitalization depend on a myriad of factors. However, some general principles are worth noting.

Capitalization can involve either welfare *net* of costs or *gross* of costs. When the local tax is exclusively a property tax and capitalization forces work perfectly, gross benefits are capitalized by gross of tax land values and net benefits by net of tax values. In these cases, we can think of the property tax as being capitalized into (consumer) land values[12]; it is

---

[11] Naturally, there will be no externalities in "utility-taking" models where the active community is assumed not to affect outside welfare. For examples of full capitalization in such a context, see Polinsky–Rubenfeld (1978) and Hochman (1981).

[12] This interpretation of capitalization is emphasized by Pauly (1976). For a discussion of evidence on this score, see Oates (1969) and Bloom–Ladd–Yinger (1983).

"passed on" to consumers rather than absorbed by owners as in previously accepted models of land. However, there is no paradox here. Consumers pay the tax only to the extent that they get something in return; if net benefits are negative, land values to owners will fall correspondingly.

When the local tax is of the Tiebout variety, land values tend to capitalize net benefits in the external model and gross benefits in the internal model. That is, gross capitalization occurs when the demand for improved land comes from households that will pay the tax no matter what they do, whereas net capitalization arises when new demanders choose whether to pay the tax.

There is a general presumption that from the point of view of social welfare, residential land value is the relevant base for capitalization measures (rather than total land value), at least in the "intermediate run" where firm locations are fixed so that industrial land has clear meaning. The intuitive reason for excluding industrial land is that rent increases on such land involve increased costs (and thus lower profits) for owners of the firms.

Exact measures depend on two sets of strong (though complementary) assumptions concerning community structure. At one extreme we assumed a Tiebout structure in which agents are similar within but different between communities. At the other extreme we analyzed a structure in which there is heterogeneity within communities but homogeneity across communities. Since these compositions do represent opposite extremes, there is a presumption that reality could not get too far away from one of them without beginning to approach the other. Consequently, it seems likely that some (imperfect) capitalization will occur at least in relatively homogeneous societies. This conclusion is most compelling in urban societies where communities have a lot of spatial structure and mobility is the established norm. We would not expect to see much capitalization in a rural society where communities are small (so that the internal model has no force) and people are tied to their homes so that migration forces are weak as well.

We close the chapter with some comment on the use of land rent as an indicator of performance or a community objective. Let us suppose that we can predict in advance the effect of proposed projects on community land rents. Then we would be in a position to use rent changes as a measure of benefits and select projects so as to maximize aggregate net of tax residential rent.[13] To the extent that this procedure is operational and leads to correct decisions, capitalization solves our problems of first-order measurement.

[13] For examples of models with this feature, see Brueckner (1983) or Sonstelie–Portney (1978).

Suppose we contemplate a model in which there are no fiscal externalities or nonland terms-of-trade effects, and capitalization forces work perfectly. Then we know that net social benefit will be reflected in net of tax residential land values, which therefore provide a correct objective for the community. When a property tax is the source of local revenue, use of this objective effectively converts that tax to a benefits tax.

There are several potential objections to "rent maximization." First, the implied welfare measure is sure to be imperfect unless capitalization is exact. Second, we know incentives will be distorted to the extent that fiscal externalities and/or terms-of-trade effects are important. In particular, land rent tends to overstate the benefits of expansionary projects. Third, we may object on equity grounds. To the extent that capitalization occurs, benefits tend to accrue to landlords at the expense of renters. If renters are considered more deserving, the presence of capitalization clearly will worsen the distribution of benefits within society, and changes in rent alone will again overstate true social benefit.

Evaluating large projects

CHAPTER 14

Search for exact measures

Up to now, our project analysis has been conducted in a first-order framework without much discussion of limitations of the approach. Part IV of this book addresses these limitations and develops more general procedures for project analysis when first order is inadequate. Unfortunately, as we shall see, the new methods are much more difficult to implement from a practical point of view. For this reason it is desirable to make the most use we can of the first-order approach.

Assuming that there are no significant indivisibilities, it is always possible to construct general decision-making procedures on the basis of the first-order approach. Each large project (or combination of large projects) can be constructed from a sequence of small projects, and these can be evaluated iteratively using the methods of Part III. To make this procedure operational, we need a rule for deciding the sequence by which projects are introduced. Many rules are possible, but for now let us suppose that they are introduced in order of their "efficiency"; that is, we implement the project with the highest $dW/d\alpha$ first, recompute a status quo, look for the next best project, and iterate.[1] Of course, we stop when there are no more projects that generate a positive increment in welfare.

Iterative planning methods of this type have a long history in the literature.[2] They are known to generate overall optimal performance as long as the economic environment is *convex*. But they work badly when there are significant elements of increasing returns to scale or other nonconvexities. This is unfortunate for us because we know from our discussion in Chapter 4 that most collective-goods allocation problems involve some element of scale economy. It follows that we must worry about our use of first-order analysis unless the optimal provision of a collective good is

[1] To make this concept of efficiency precise, we would need a natural unit for α. Further, we would either need to collect hypothetical information about positions far from the status quo or wait after each iteration for the new equilibrium to be established before proceeding. We ignore such issues here since we are not going to pursue iterative methods in detail. For more discussion of the issues involved, see Arrow (1966) and Bradford (1975).
[2] Proofs that such procedures work are based on the *gradient method* of concave programming. See Wagner (1969) for a mathematical discussion. Economic applications usually are couched in a framework of "artificial" time; see, e.g., Malinvaud (1967) and Dreze-de la Vallé Poussin (1971).

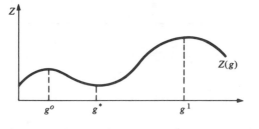

Figure 14.1

still small enough so that we can think of its *total* provision as a first-order increment (the nonconvexity is inessential in that case).

14.1   Marginal analysis in presence of nonconvexity

Several problems arise when we apply first-order analysis to projects involving significant nonconvexities. The first to look at derives from the fact that necessary conditions for optimality are not sufficient in the presence of nonconvexity.[3] Suppose that welfare as a function of project levels has the shape depicted in Figure 14.1. Marginal analysis initiated from any status quo in the region $(0, g^*)$ leads to a final allocation of g^o, which clearly is inferior to the global first best g^1; indeed, a start slightly to the left of g^* results in movement away from the first best. In fact, when there are strongly increasing returns to scale, marginal analysis will almost certainly turn out to be inadequate. The first few units of such a project will always be undesirable if (as seems reasonable) no benefits are enjoyed until the project reaches a certain minimum size. Unfortunately, this characterization is all too typical of many public projects such as roads, power projects, space programs, and the like. We require more powerful methods to measure welfare benefits of these types of projects.

Before turning to a discussion of these methods, we point out a second pitfall of project analysis in the presence of essential nonconvexities. Suppose that we have learned how to measure the benefits of large projects and have a menu of such projects in front of us. Suppose further that each one looks desirable in isolation. Should we do them all? If not, which ones?

[3] By imposing *additional* conditions on the degree of nonconvexity in technology relative to the convexity of preferences, it is sometimes possible to rescue marginal analysis. However, these conditions are quite difficult to check in practice. See Aoki (1970) and Brown–Heal (1980).

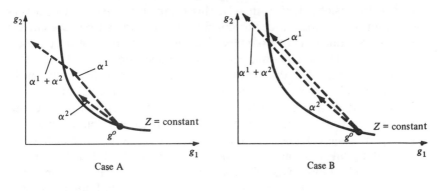

Figure 14.2

There is no simple answer to these questions, as the following examples illustrate (see Figure 14.2). In both cases depicted, there is a status quo g^o and a social indifference curve ($Z = $ const.) through it. Projects (α) are represented by vectors away from the status quo, and we assume that each project is indivisible in that it must be done "all or nothing." Clearly, in case A, each project is desirable in isolation yet they are not desirable in combination. The difficulty derives from the fact that instituting project 1 changes marginal valuations at the status quo and therefore changes the worth of project 2; the *only* case in which projects can be evaluated independently is when the menu of projects is still small enough so that their collective (or partial) implementation does not change marginal valuations. In that case, the relevant portion of the social indifference curve is a straight line, and each project (or collection of projects) is desirable if and only if it leads to a position above that line.[4]

Case B shows that the order in which projects are considered can be quite important. Whichever project is considered first will "pass," after which the other project will be rejected. Under these circumstances, obviously, we want to consider project 2 first. But how can we know to do this? Marginal analysis is no help since it will appear that project 1 is the more efficient of the two (if we focused on hypothetical small increments). Clearly, we must look at the whole menu of projects simultaneously in order to avoid mistakes like choosing project 1 before considering project 2. Indeed, the concept of independent projects is useless. The correct definition of "project" now involves a selection of which component projects to do (and how much of each to do if there is some choice

[4] Even in this situation, the order of consideration matters if planners are somehow restricted from doing all desirable projects. See Bradford (1975) for further discussion.

on that dimension). Unfortunately, this means that there will be a very large number of possibilities to consider before we can be sure correct decisions are made. (For example, given 100 component projects, there are 2^{100} possible combinations for the social decision.)

The reader will recall that we came up against this dimensionality problem long ago in Chapter 2 when we discussed political decision making. The previous examples show that the methods of decentralization developed in intervening chapters may not be so helpful when dealing with many projects involving large nonconvexities. However, we also know that making all decisions simultaneously is definitely infeasible so that some type of compromises will be needed. We will say what we can about these in the next chapter. For now we turn to the more limited question of how to measure the benefits of a large project in isolation.

14.2   Compensating variation in a market context

Let us begin with quite limited objectives. We suppose that there is only one individual whose welfare is influenced only through changes in price and income (no public goods). We can think of a project here as involving government operation of a natural monopoly; planners can set price and (possibly) collect lump-sum taxes to cover any shortfall of revenue to cost. Our objective is to measure social welfare (individual utility, here) associated with possible price–net income combinations. Stated another way, we are asking for a way of recovering the indirect utility function from observable data.

The literature on "theory of choice" spends a great deal of time on the question of when preference functions are recoverable from choices among sets of alternatives.[5] Here, we focus on the special case in which choice sets are identified with budget sets (so that choice functions are demand functions). A constructive procedure is available for this case. The intuition behind this method is that of "consumer surplus": Utility is measured by the integral under the demand curve – each consumption unit should be valued at the marginal willingness to pay for it, and total benefit is the sum (or integral) of these incremental benefits. Unfortunately, the correct measure is not so simple as naive consumer surplus and is very demanding on the available market data, as we shall see. It is so demanding, in fact, that we will want to consider some shortcuts and approximations in the next chapter.

Suppose we try to implement the idea of adding up incremental values. We can start with the first-order measures already developed. Specializing

[5] See Sen (1970) for a discussion of results and further references.

the analysis of Chapter 9 to the case where indirect utility is a function of price and income only, we find

$$\nabla_\alpha V = \lambda(P, m)[\nabla_\alpha m - c(P, m)\, \nabla_\alpha P] \tag{14.1}$$

or

$$\nabla_\alpha V = \lambda(P, m)[P\, \nabla_\alpha c], \tag{14.2}$$

the difference depending on whether we substitute from the consumer budget constraint (which is an identity in α). Since α parameterizes the project size, we think of P and m (and thereby, c) as functions of α, and we evaluate any particular project $P(\alpha), m(\alpha)$ by integrating the preceding expression from zero to α. Now the naive view of consumer surplus results from assuming that λ (the marginal utility of income) is constant. In that case, using the second form (14.2), integration would yield

$$V(\alpha) - V(0) = \lambda \int_{x=0}^\alpha P(x)\, \nabla_\alpha c(P(x), m(x))\, dx. \tag{14.3}$$

We see that change in utility would indeed be the area under the "inverse" demand function. If we preferred to express our measure in terms of direct demand functions, we could work with (14.1) instead, yielding

$$V(\alpha) - V(0) = \left[m(\alpha) - m(0) - \int_{x=0}^\alpha c(P(x), m(x))\, \nabla_\alpha P(x)\, dx \right]. \tag{14.4}$$

The first of these forms accords most closely to the intuitive view that each unit is to be valued at a marginal willingness to pay. However, the second form turns out to be more useful in applications.

Here and later it is useful to change variables and integrate with respect to prices and incomes instead of the artificial scale parameter. And in doing so, we can make use of the fact that path integrals of an exact differential must be independent of the path chosen.[6] This means that in evaluating $V(P(\alpha), m(\alpha))$ we can choose any path in (P, m) space connected to the status quo (in particular, it is not required that intermediate points correspond to feasible projects). Of course, when we want to compare projects using a single integral, it will be important that intermediate points correspond to real projects; but for now, we seek simplicity and choose a path that moves prices first and incomes second, yielding

$$V^1 - V^o = \lambda \left[-\int_{x=P^o}^{P^1} \sum_i c_i(x, m^o)\, dx_i + m^1 - m^o \right]. \tag{14.5}$$

Note that we have not explicitly indicated the path for price integration. Again we would be free to choose, and standard practice would

[6] For a demonstration of this and related facts about integration, see Taylor (1955), chapter 13.

generate a path that lowered (or raised) prices one at a time; in that case our measure would integrate under demand curves market by market. However, there is a caveat here. Since the path chosen must be *connected*, one could not legitimately integrate under each demand function holding all other prices at the status quo levels. Once an order of introduction is chosen and the first price lowered, it must appear at the new (project) level as an argument in other market demands as they are integrated. Thus, at least when there are cross-price effects between markets, even the naive approach previously outlined requires fairly rich demand information for implementation.

But what about our assumption concerning the constancy of the marginal utility of income? Unfortunately, it is not just restrictive but is actually inconsistent. We can see why by invoking again the principle of path independence. According to that principle, we could have performed the previous integration by moving incomes first and prices second, in which case m^α would be the appropriate argument in the consumption function. Since the integral must be the same, consumption must be independent of income level (all income elasticities must be zero). This is not just unreasonable but is actually impossible since extra income always will be spent on something.[7] We will explore later the possibility of salvaging naive surplus measures as approximations in certain contexts, but for now we drop the idea and resume our search for exact measures.

Let us proceed by "solving" the defining equation for an indifference curve in price–income space (i.e., a level curve of the indirect utility function).[8] The solution is called the *income compensation function* $I(P \mid P^o, m^0)$. This function indicates the amount of income that would be required at prices P to make our consumer indifferent to the status quo combination (P^o, m^o).[9] (See Figure 14.3 for an illustration.) It is implicitly defined mathematically by the identity

$$V(P, I(P \mid P^o, m^o)) \equiv V(P^o, m^o). \tag{14.6}$$

Next we recover $I(\cdot)$ from market data by integrating its differential. Differentiating the defining identity and using duality relationships yields

$$\nabla_P I(P \mid P^o, m^o) = -\nabla_P V(\cdot)/[\nabla_m V(\cdot)] = c(P, I(P \mid P^o, m^o)) \equiv \hat{c}(P). \tag{14.7}$$

We now have a system of first-order partial differential equations for $I(P)$. Although we will not be able to solve for $I(\cdot)$ in closed form, these

---

[7] This point is emphasized by Samuelson (1947) in his early critique of consumer surplus.

[8] Our derivations here follow most closely those of Hurwicz–Uzawa (1971), although the basic ideas go back to Hicks (1941).

[9] All of the constructions to follow can be carried out equally well using an *expenditure function* defined on the direct utility function. See Diamond–McFadden (1974).

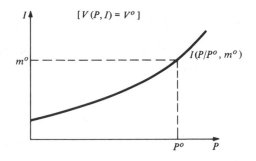

Figure 14.3

equations can be numerically integrated given sufficiently rich demand data. Computations are done as follows: (1) Choose a small increment δP, (2) use (14.7) to compute $\delta I = \nabla_p I \, \delta P$, (3) update to a new status quo $(P = P^o + \delta P, \; I = I^o + \delta I)$ and evaluate demand at this new price income combination, and (4) iterate until P^1 is reached. By choosing the increment sufficiently small, we can approximate the income compensation function as closely as we like. We may write this integral informally as

$$I(P^1) - I(P^o) = \int_{x=P^o}^{P^1} \sum_i \hat{c}_i(x) \, dx_i. \tag{14.8}$$

(Note that we have suppressed reference to the status quo for convenience.)

The functions $\hat{c}(P)$ (which we construct in the preceding procedure) are referred to as the *compensated* demand functions, the term "compensated" referring to the fact that as prices change, the consumer is compensated with income in such a way as to keep him on the same indifference curve. The price derivatives of these functions therefore represent the pure Slutsky substitution effects. (As an exercise, the reader should derive the famous Slutsky equations and prove Slutsky symmetry using the constructions we have developed; we will use these equations in the next chapter.)

Let us see how the income compensation function might be used to do project analysis. We consider a "natural monopoly" project that will lower prices from P^o to P^1. Suppose for now that we know how to measure the costs of this project, and they are $\Gamma(P^1)$ in numeraire units. Then, after initiation of the project, the consumer would be left with status quo income less this amount. Therefore, the project is desirable if and only if $I(P^o) - \Gamma(P^1) \geq I(P^1)$. After rearranging and substitution, the test for acceptance becomes

$$\theta(P^1) \equiv \int_{x=P^1}^{P^o} \sum_i \hat{c}_i(x)\, dx_i - \Gamma(P^1) \geq 0. \tag{14.9}$$

It is conceptually useful to think of implementing the project by collecting the compensating variation $[I(P^o) - I(P^1)]$ and then returning the surplus $\theta(P)$ (compensating variation minus cost). As long as this surplus is nonnegative, the consumer is at least as well off, and the project is desirable.

The procedure just outlined extends naturally to the case of many consumers if we are willing to use the compensation principle as a decision-making criterion. The project should be undertaken if lump-sum taxes (T^h) can be assigned in such a way that each individual ends up with a nonnegative surplus,

$$I^h(P^o) - T^h(P^1) \geq I^h(P^1), \quad \text{all } h, \tag{14.10}$$

and total tax collection pays for the project,

$$\sum_h T^h(P^1) = \Gamma(P^1). \tag{14.11}$$

As long as the planners are completely free in how they assign the taxes (possibly paying subsidies if there are any "losers"), these conditions can be satisfied if and only if the total surplus is nonnegative,[10] that is, if

$$\sum_h \theta^h(P^1) = \int_{x=P^1}^{P^o} \sum_{h,i} c_i^h[x, I^h(x)]\, dx_i - \Gamma(P^1) \geq 0. \tag{14.12}$$

The planner is to accept the project if (14.12) is satisfied and reject it otherwise.[11] Although this criteria is stated in terms of aggregates, the necessary taxes and subsidies cannot be known without full disaggregated information. Of course, we could apply the test without bothering to make transfers, in which case we would be using a "compensation test without compensation." At the very least, such a procedure involves interpersonal comparisons, and in some circumstances it is invalid no matter what assumptions are made.[12] We will return to issues of compensation and the welfare criteria momentarily.

Even if we do not make compensation, we still cannot recover the necessary information from aggregate data. This is because such data cannot possibly incorporate the necessary income compensations individual by

---

10 The argument here is similar to that used in showing that when individuals are completely free to choose net saving levels, the sequence of period-by-period budget constraints collapses to a single present-value constraint. Refer back to Chapter 6 for further discussion.

11 Even if the correct tax/subsidies are used, we might still object to the criterion since it is an application of the Pareto rule in the context of a status quo (recall our critique of such applications in Chapter 2). We comment further on welfare implications in what follows.

12 See Kaldor (1939), Hicks (1939a), and Scitovsky (1941) for a discussion of pitfalls in using compensation tests without compensation.

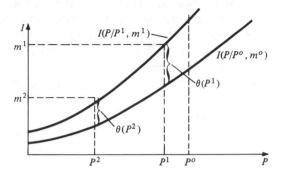

Figure 14.4

individual. We can only recover the income compensation functions if we start with *individual* demand functions.

Although the considerations just mentioned raise questions concerning the usefulness of the test, a more fundamental objection emerges when we try to use our criterion to compare *alternative* projects (we know from discussions at the outset of this chapter that such comparisons are important). We may as well return our discussion to the case of a single individual, since the difficulty already emerges there. Suppose that we compare projects by the size of the surplus they generate. That is, project 1 is preferred to project 2 if $\theta(P^1) \geq \theta(P^2)$. But is returned surplus a good measure of utility improvement? Not unless extra money generates the same amount of extra utility regardless of the reference point. When this condition fails, our test is invalid, as is best seen with the help of Figure 14.4.

As drawn, indifference curves become steeper in price–income space the better off is the individual; this reflects the reasonable stipulation that our individual consumes more of the good on the horizontal axis as he gets better off (recall 14.7). Clearly, project 1 may generate a higher surplus $[\theta(P^1) \geq \theta(P^2)]$ yet be inferior to project 2; the compensation test tends to discriminate against the larger project in this situation. Only if the indifference curves are vertical parallel shifts will the compensation test be a valid criterion for comparisons.

Unfortunately, we have come full circle. Indifference curves are parallel shifts only if the derivatives of the income compensation function are independent of income level (for fixed price). But since the gradient of the income compensation function is the consumption function, we are safe only if consumption is independent of income, a condition that we rejected earlier as inconsistent as well as unreasonable.[13]

---

[13] The discussion here is based largely on arguments made by Chipman–Moore (1977, 1980).

Back to the drawing boards! However, it turns out that our efforts have not been wasted entirely. The constructions we developed can be modified slightly to get a "true" measure of utility. Referring back to the previous diagram, it looks as though $I(P^o | P, m)$ is such a utility indicator [since it measures the vertical intercept at P^o of the indifference curve associated with the price–income pair (P, m)]. Let us justify this observation more formally.

All we are going to get here is an ordinal representation of utility. Thus, we are claiming that there exists a *monotone increasing* function $F(\cdot)$ such that

$$I(P^o | P, m) = F[V(P, m)]. \tag{14.13}$$

When P equals P^o it is clear by construction that we want to use m as our utility measure. Thus, we define F implicitly on the range of V by the equation $F[V(P^o, m)] = m$. The reader should check that F so defined is strictly monotone increasing as long as extra income is always desirable at the margin. Note from this definition that our transformation serves to measure utility in numeraire units (the same units for all). This fact will prove helpful when we turn later to issues of interpersonal comparisons.

Now, consider F evaluated at some arbitrary pair P^*, m^* (call its value there F^*). By construction, $F[V(P^o, F^*)] = F^*$, so using the fact that F is strictly monotone increasing, we know

$$V(P^o, F^*) = F^{-1}(F^*) = V(P^*, m^*). \tag{14.14}$$

But then, from the definition of the income compensation function, $F^* = I(P^o | P^*, m^*)$, so

$$F[V(P^*, m^*)] = F^* = I(P^o | P^*, m^*), \tag{14.15}$$

as was to be shown. Since we want to retain the convention that variables after the vertical bar are parameters of the associated function, it is useful to represent the income compensation function as $V(P^*, m^* | P^o)$ when it is used in the present context. (Note that P^o is a legitimate parameter of this function.)

Measuring utility from market data can now be done by reducing to the previous case as follows:

$$V(P, m | P^o) \equiv m + I(P^o | P, m) - I(P | P, m)$$

$$= m + \int_{x=P}^{P^o} \sum_i c_i[x, I(x | P, m)]\, dx_i. \tag{14.16}$$

We are back to a measure using market data (indeed, one that uses the same compensated demand functions as before). That is good, but we better take stock of some practical difficulties we will have to face in order to use it. First, there is the problem mentioned earlier involving aggregation: Even if we could justify adding utilities, we could not obtain the necessary measures from aggregate demand data.

Second, although our new measure can be used to compare projects, a separate integration must be performed for each different project level considered. For each such project, the demand functions to be integrated must be compensated at the associated (final) project levels.

14.3   Measures for a mixed economy

Our method for obtaining a utility indicator by integrating a differential generalizes in principle to incorporate collective goods. We sketch the relevant procedure leaving the details to the reader. First, define an income compensation function $I(g, P \mid g^o, P^o, m^o)$ by the equation

$$V(g, P, I(g, P \mid g^o, P^o, m^o)) = V(g^o, P^o, m^o). \tag{14.17}$$

Then, as before, we can show that $I(g^o, P^o \mid g, P, m)$ is a legitimate utility indicator for any fixed choice of g^o and P^o. To remind ourselves of this fact, we relabel this function $V(g, P, m \mid g^o, P^o)$.

After differentiating and using duality relationships, we "reintegrate" along some path that may be taken to be a continuous sequence of potential projects. The result is

$$V(g(\alpha), P(\alpha), m(\alpha) \mid g^o, P^o)$$

$$= \int_{g^o}^{g(\alpha)} \sum_i \Omega_i(g, P, I(g, P \mid g(\alpha), P(\alpha), m(\alpha))) \, dg_i$$

$$+ \int_{P(\alpha)}^{P^o} \sum_i c_i(g, P, I(g, P \mid g(\alpha), P(\alpha), m(\alpha))) \, dP_i + m(\alpha), \tag{14.18}$$

where

$$\Omega(g, P, I(g, P \mid x(\alpha))) = \frac{\nabla_g U(g, c(g, P, I(g, P \mid x(\alpha))))}{\lambda(g, P, I(g, P \mid x(\alpha)))}. \tag{14.19}$$

[We have used the shorthand notation $x(\cdot)$ to represent the collection of functions to the right of the vertical bar in this expression.]

Note the element of symmetry in the treatment of market and nonmarket goods. For market goods, we integrate compensated demand functions with respect to price, as before. For collective goods, we integrate compensated *inverse* demand functions with respect to quantity.

Although this theoretical symmetry is worth noting, we will face much more serious impediments when we attempt to compute welfare measures in the mixed economy. When real markets actually exist, we could at least get aggregated (and possibly disaggregated) market demand data. Obviously, we have nothing similar to work with for collective goods and must find other ways to obtain the information. As the reader might guess, it is hard enough to get the information that would correspond to simple demand data, much less something as sophisticated as compensated demand.

Further measurement problems arise from the fact that market demands being integrated typically no longer involve direct outputs of the project but rather opportunity cost foregone. When dealing with first-order measures, we were able to break such terms up into direct project cost and other measurable items. However, such a decomposition is not possible here without additional assumptions. We discuss these and other measurement problems in the next two chapters.

We return briefly to the issue of welfare aggregation assuming that we are able to measure individual utility. Recall that our representations use income to measure utility at status quo prices and public-goods levels. What we need now is a welfare function $W(\cdot)$ defined on these utility levels. Since utilities are expressed in a common numeraire unit, a classical utilitarian would simply sum individual utilities. Note that use of this welfare function is similar to applying the compensation principle without compensation. Aside from possible objections on equity grounds, there is nothing inherently wrong with this procedure here. Inconsistencies arise only if we try to sum indicators [such as $\theta(P)$] that do not correctly measure utility. Of course, if we do want to build some egalitarianism into our welfare function, we must introduce further nonlinearities into corresponding measures; all hope of using aggregate data will be lost. Thus, practical considerations will lead us to construct "utilitarian" measures against which we can weigh equity considerations, much in the same spirit as our formal decompositions in Chapter 9.

14.4   Uncertainty and expected surplus

Before leaving the world of exact measures, we should indicate how they can accommodate time and uncertainty. Let us apply procedures of previous sections to the general sequential choice model of Section 12.4. First, we define the income compensation function $I_s(\cdot \mid \cdot)$ from the identity

$$V_s[x_s, I(x_s, x_{s+1}, \ldots \mid x_s^o, m_s^o, x_{s+1}^o, \ldots), x_{s+1}, \ldots] = V_s(x^o), \qquad (14.20)$$

where x_s represents all price and public-goods variables dated s and all vectors dated in the future are to be interpreted as random variables. As before, we attempt to recover $I(\cdot \mid \cdot)$ by identifying its partial derivatives from economic observation and then integrating.

Let us focus on partial derivatives with respect to consumption goods prices. Utilizing the analysis from Chapter 12, it is straightforward to derive

$$\nabla_{p_s} I_s(\cdot) = \hat{c}_s(\cdot) \qquad\qquad (14.21)$$

$$\nabla_{p_{s+1}} I_s(\cdot) = \rho_{s+1}(\cdot) E_s[\psi_{s+1}(\cdot)\hat{c}_{s+1}(\cdot)], \qquad (14.22)$$

where $\hat{c}(\cdot)$ is the compensated demand function, as before. Hence, we will evaluate changes in contemporaneous prices by integrating compensated demands as in the static case; however, we should note that today's consumption depends in principle on all of the parameters of the future.

When consumers are risk neutral (so that ψ_{s+1} is independent of event), (14.22) will integrate as expected compensated surplus (discounted at the safe rate of interest). Otherwise, it is clear that a risk correction is necessary, and since the ψ's can be expected to change as the price distribution changes, we see that the integration problem will become quite complicated. We could, of course, separate out the risk premium term as in Chapter 12, but it is hard to see how we could use integration to improve on the first-order risk measures derived there. The situation here shares some of the complicating features encountered in dealing properly with equity in large-project analysis.

The "bottom line" from our discussions here is rather negative. Although there are ways in principle of constructing welfare measures from information on demand, the data requirements are daunting if we want to evaluate large projects. We need a lot of detailed hypothetical information at a very disaggregated level. We will discuss briefly methods of estimating the required measures from limited sources of information in Chapter 16. First, however, we consider some theoretical approximations that are less demanding on the data.

CHAPTER 15

Surplus approximations

We explored methods of measuring welfare change for large projects in the preceding chapter. Although we found it possible in principle to recover the necessary measures from sufficiently rich demand information, we were forced to conclude that the required information would almost never be available in practice. Indeed, most benefit–cost studies either restrict themselves to first-order analysis or use "naive" measures of "surplus" based on parametric estimates of aggregate demand functions.

Here, we investigate ways in which the state of the art might be improved somewhat. We search for measures that are closer to exact than those just mentioned yet are still accessible from data we might reasonably be able to collect. The first method examined will be "second-order approximations," the natural generalization of first-order analysis to include one more term in the Taylor expansion. Measures based on second order or any order for that matter) have the advantage that they require only local information for implementation. Essentially, the method gives up on collecting hypothetical information concerning demand conditions in unobserved parts of the economic environment and instead extrapolates to those areas using curvatures at the status quo. Naturally, the method will be good only to the extent that there is some stability to the curvatures.

Quite apart from pragmatic issues, second-order approximation allows us to study the properties of second best when the status quo happens to be first best (first-order analysis simply generates first-best measures in this case). In particular, we will be able to quantify the concept of deadweight loss.

An alternative method of approximation makes use of upper and lower bounds. Suppose that, although we do not have precise global information, we can put a priori bounds on what things are like "out there." We can use these restrictions to generate upper and lower bounds on welfare measures. The best developed example of this approach is that of Willig (1976), who utilized bounds on income elasticities. We will discuss his method and some generalizations in Section 15.4.

Finally, there remains the possibility of using naive surplus as an approximation. It will be clear from the discussion in the first two sections

246

that we generally can do better than naive surplus; but there are cases where we cannot do much better and may not want to try. We take up this issue in Section 15.5.

Most of our discussion will take place in the context of a certainty world. However, results of Sections 15.4 and 15.5 will have natural generalizations to the simple uncertainty contexts discussed in the preceding chapter. We will point these out as we go along. Unfortunately, we are unable to find any simple generalizations for the second-order approximations.

15.1   Second-order approximations of individual utility

As in the preceding chapter, we begin with the case in which all goods are marketed. We show first how to measure individual utility to a second order and discuss aggregation later. We use $I(P^o|, P, m)$ to represent utility and relabel this function $V(P, m | P^o)$ to emphasize the fact that we work with an indirect utility function that is parameterized by the price vector P^o. Referring back to the previous chapter, we recall the exact formula:

$$V(P, m | P^o) = \int_{x=P}^{P^o} \sum_i c_i(x, I(x | P, m)) \, dx_i + m, \qquad (15.1)$$

where we keep in mind that the variable x varies over a particular (though arbitrary) closed path connecting P and P^o. In performing our Taylor expansions, we choose (P^o, m) as the status quo. Thus, we are choosing utility units in such a way that the marginal utility of a unit of numeraire is unity at the status quo. This choice will be important to keep in mind when we discuss interpersonal comparisons later.

Thinking (as before) of project size as being parameterized by a scalar α, we seek the best second-order approximation to utility change as a function of α. Using the formula (15.1), we compute[1]

$$\frac{dV(P(\alpha), m(\alpha) | P^o)}{d\alpha}$$

$$= \frac{dm(\alpha)}{d\alpha} - \nabla_\alpha P(\alpha) c(P(\alpha), m(\alpha))$$

$$+ \int_{x=P(\alpha)}^{P^o} \left[\sum_i \frac{\partial c_i(x, V(P(\alpha), m(\alpha) | x))}{\partial m} \frac{dV(P(\alpha), m(\alpha) | x)}{d\alpha} \right] dx_i$$

---

[1] In computing derivatives here and later, we appeal to a multivariate form of the fundamental theorem of the calculus when differentiating with respect to limits of integration. See Widder (1961), chapter 7, for details.

$$= P(\alpha)\, \nabla_\alpha c(P(\alpha), m(\alpha))$$

$$+ \int_{x=P(\alpha)}^{P^o} \left[\sum_i \frac{\partial c_i(x, V(P(\alpha), m(\alpha)\,|\,x))}{\partial m}\, \frac{dV(P(\alpha), m(\alpha)\,|\,x)}{d\alpha} \right] dx_i,$$

$$(15.2)$$

where we made use of the consumer budget constraint as before to obtain the second equality. Also, here and later we make liberal use of the identities

$$V(P, m\,|\,P) \equiv m, \qquad \nabla_m V(P, m\,|\,P) \equiv 1, \qquad \nabla_p V(P, m\,|\,P) \equiv c(P, m).$$

$$(15.3)$$

This formula does not look very helpful as it stands since derivatives of V appear on both sides. However, we can evaluate first (and higher order) derivatives *at the status quo* using this apparatus. Substituting status quo values in (15.2) naturally gives us back the first-order measures we have seen before. To compute the required second derivative, we differentiate (15.2) and evaluate at $\alpha = 0$. (Thus, all derivative terms inside the integral sign disappear, eliminating the circular feature of the general formula.) We further simplify our notation by using a superscript o to index functions evaluated at the status quo. Consequently, we find[2]

$$\left. \frac{d^2 V}{d\alpha^2} \right|_{\alpha=0} = P^o\, \nabla_{\alpha\alpha}^2 c^o + \langle \nabla_\alpha P^o, \nabla_P c^o, \nabla_\alpha P^o \rangle + \nabla_\alpha P^o\, \nabla_m c^o\, \frac{dm^o}{d\alpha}$$

$$- [\nabla_\alpha P^o\, \nabla_m c^o] \left[\frac{dm^o}{d\alpha} - \nabla_\alpha P^o c^o \right], \qquad (15.4)$$

where the last term in square brackets is obtained by substituting from (15.2) evaluated at $\alpha = 0$. Note that terms involving $dm^o/d\alpha$ cancel in this expression. Also, the last two remaining terms can be combined using the formula relating uncompensated and compensated (Slutsky) derivatives,[3] yielding

$$\left. \frac{d^2 V}{d\alpha^2} \right|_{\alpha=0} = P^o\, \nabla_{\alpha\alpha}^2 c^o + \langle \nabla_\alpha P^o, \nabla_P \hat{c}^o, \nabla_\alpha P^o \rangle. \qquad (15.5)$$

[2] See the preface on notation to refresh your memory on our use of bilinear forms.
[3] Since $\hat{c}(P) = c(P, I(P\,|\,P^o \cdot m^o))$,

$$\frac{\partial \hat{c}_i}{\partial P_j} = \frac{\partial c_i}{\partial P_j} + \frac{\partial c_i}{\partial m}\, \hat{c}_j,$$

which can be written in our vector notation as

$$\nabla_P \hat{c} = \nabla_P c + \hat{c}\{\nabla_m c\}.$$

Also, using transpose and quadratic form conventions, we can write

$$[\nabla_\alpha P^o\, \nabla_m c^o][\nabla_\alpha P^o c^o] = [\nabla_\alpha P^o c^o][\{\nabla_m c^o\}\{\nabla_\alpha P^o\}] = \langle \nabla_\alpha P^o, c^o\{\nabla_m c^o\}, \nabla_\alpha P^o \rangle.$$

Now we can combine (15.2) (evaluated at $\alpha = 0$) and (15.5) to obtain a second-order measure for utility change. In so doing, we employ the notation $\delta^i x$ to represent the ith order approximation (in α) to the *change* in a function x:

$$\delta^2 V = P^o \delta^2 c + \tfrac{1}{2}\langle \delta^1 P, \nabla_P \hat{c}^o, \delta^1 P \rangle. \tag{15.6}$$

Our formula has a nice, intuitive interpretation. If we ignored the second term, utility would be measured by hyperplanes whose normal is the consumer price vector; thus, the second term can be thought of as correcting for curvature of the indifference surface. Of course, this term is always nonpositive since the Slutsky substitution matrix is negative semidefinite under our assumptions. Geometrically, we are saying that since indifference surfaces lie "above" tangent hyperplanes, utility levels must fall (or at least not rise) as we move along the hyperplane away from the status quo.

Before discussing aggregation, it is useful to contrast (15.6) to what we would have obtained had we used the "compensation test" as a measure of welfare change. Thereby we can identify (to a second order) the error involved in using compensating variation to measure welfare. Recall that a compensation test measures individual welfare change as

$$\theta(\alpha) \equiv m(\alpha) - I(P(\alpha) \mid P^o, m^o). \tag{15.7}$$

Performing the same analysis with the same substitutions as before yields

$$\delta^2 \theta = P^o \delta^2 c + \tfrac{1}{2}\langle \delta^1 P, \nabla_P \hat{c}^o, \delta^1 P \rangle + (\delta^1 V)(\delta^1 P) \nabla_m c. \tag{15.8}$$

Comparing with (15.6), we see that the error from using compensating variation is measured by the last term in (15.8).

Note the likely direction of bias. Assuming that the project is going to improve welfare (by lowering prices) and the absence of any "Giffen" goods, the error term will be negative. Thus, if α parameterizes the amount of some price reduction, we would understate the true second-order value of the project using a compensation test. Furthermore, optimizing on θ would result in a smaller-than-optimal choice of α. We confirm, therefore, the geometric argument for bias given in the previous chapter.

15.2   Aggregation of second-order measures

When we turn to measures of welfare, we ought to take nonlinearities in the welfare function into account in constructing the best second-order approximation. However, this approach does not turn out to be useful in generating tractable measures. Consequently, we restrict attention to the utilitarian view outlined earlier. Looking back at (15.6), we see that utility is measured there (to a second order) in numeraire units so simple summation yields

$$\delta^2 Z^* = P^o \, \delta^2 C + \frac{1}{2} \left\langle \delta^1 P, \sum_h \nabla_P \hat{c}^{ho}, \delta^1 P \right\rangle, \tag{15.9}$$

where, as usual, the asterisk means that equity considerations are ignored. Now, second-order opportunity cost can be decomposed just as in Chapter 9 since the relevant material balance conditions are identities in underlying parameters. Consequently,

$$\delta^2 Z^* = -Q^o \, \delta^2 b + t^o \, \delta^2 C + Q^o \, \delta^2 Y + \frac{1}{2} \left\langle \delta^1 P, \sum_h \nabla_P \hat{c}^{ho}, \delta^1 P \right\rangle. \tag{15.10}$$

Before interpreting (15.10), it is important to recall the institutional setting to which it applies. Since household indirect utility depends at present only on *market* parameters, any publicly provided goods must be regarded as exogenously fixed. Thus, government projects are restricted to the class of "natural monopolies"; net input to these monopolies is represented by the vector b (some of whose components presumably will be negative), and taxes may be used to make up for any losses to the public enterprise.

A   *Competitive firms*

When firms behave competitively, there is a very natural and useful interpretation of curvature corrections in terms of competitive demand-and-supply functions. We recall that $Q(\alpha) \, \nabla_\alpha Y(\alpha) = 0$ identically in α under those conditions. Differentiating the identity and making use of profit function duality yields

$$Q(\alpha) \, \nabla^2_{\alpha\alpha} Y(\alpha) = -\nabla_\alpha Q(\alpha) \, \nabla_\alpha Y(\alpha)$$
$$= -\langle \nabla_\alpha Q(\alpha), \nabla^2_{QQ} \Pi(\alpha), \nabla_\alpha Q(\alpha) \rangle, \tag{15.11}$$

and substituting for the production term in (15.10), we obtain

$$\delta^2 Z^* = -Q^o \, \delta^2 b + t^o \, \delta^2 C$$
$$- \frac{1}{2} \langle \delta^1 Q, \nabla^2_{QQ} \Pi^o, \delta^1 Q \rangle + \frac{1}{2} \left\langle \delta^1 P, \sum_h \nabla_P \hat{c}^{ho}, \delta^1 P \right\rangle. \tag{15.12}$$

Since the profit function is known to be convex, *both* terms in the second line make *negative* contributions to welfare. At present, we should think of these as corrections for curvature needed when we pass from first- to second-order measurement. We can relate these terms to demand-and-supply functions. Since

$$\delta^1 Y = \delta^1 Q \, \nabla_{QQ}^2 \Pi, \qquad \delta^1 \hat{c}^h = \delta^1 P \, \nabla_P \hat{c}^h, \tag{15.13}$$

the bilinear forms may be rewritten as

$$-\frac{1}{2} \langle \delta^1 Q, \nabla_{QQ}^2 \Pi^o, \delta^1 Q \rangle + \frac{1}{2} \left\langle \delta^1 P, \sum_h \nabla_P \hat{c}^{ho}, \delta^1 P \right\rangle$$

$$= \frac{1}{2} (\delta^1 P) \left(\sum_h \delta^1 \hat{c}^h \right) - \frac{1}{2} (\delta^1 Q)(\delta^1 Y). \tag{15.14}$$

Components of these terms are now measured as one-half change in price times change in quantity, the latter taken from the relevant supply or compensated demand function. Geometrically, they represent areas between the demand (or supply) functions and the price line, where we use the best linear approximation to these functions. Obviously, evaluation will require only local demand-and-supply information, although we need to know about income effects in order to compute compensated demand derivatives.

Of course, we could replace compensated demands with market demands if we were willing to add back a correction term for income effects. The resulting second-order measure is

$$\delta^2 Z^* = -Q^o \, \delta^2 b + t^o \, \delta^2 C - \frac{1}{2} \delta^1 P \sum_h \frac{\partial c^{ho}}{\partial m} \delta^1 V^h$$

$$+ \frac{1}{2} (\delta^1 P)(\delta^1 C) - \frac{1}{2} (\delta^1 Q)(\delta^1 Y). \tag{15.15}$$

Unfortunately, however, this formulation contains a circular element since utility changes appear on the right side.

We are now in a position to draw some implications of second-order analysis for the public administration of natural monopolies. Suppose, for the moment, that taxation is direct and distribution optimal so that we can ignore the tax and distributional considerations. Then, we find that second-order welfare is measured by "net profitability" (naturally, some components of the b vector will be negative here) minus the net surplus terms.

At first blush, this result looks paradoxical. Presumably, government wants to be involved in running private firms only when they involve substantial increasing returns to scale (economies of large size). But, of course, in that case marginal-cost pricing leads to negative profits, suggesting that all projects are undesirable (since the curvature terms are definitely negative)! However, the paradox disappears when we recognize that "profits" are being evaluated at *initial* prices whereas marginal-cost pricing involves *final* prices. We may conclude correctly that the project must make sufficient hypothetical profit at status quo prices to overcome the negative-curvature terms in order to be desirable. We will examine marginal-cost pricing rules for large projects more closely in Chapter 17.

Returning to (15.12), we see that as long as standard convexity assumptions hold in the private markets, use of first-order measures when the project is at least second order in size will lead to an overstatement in the net benefits. First-order analysis always fails to account properly for elements of "diminishing marginal benefit" and "increasing marginal cost."

B   *Deadweight loss*

Our curvature terms are closely related to the concept of deadweight loss, on which there is an extensive literature.[4] To see how, let us use our measures to evaluate the second-order cost of indirect taxation. To this end, we interpret the government project as constituting a substitution of indirect for direct taxation. Here, $\nabla_\alpha b \equiv 0$ and $t^o = 0$, so (aside from the distribution term) second-order welfare change is measured exactly by those curvature terms. Since we know they are negative, the efficiency component of welfare must fall and hence the term "deadweight loss." Labeling this loss DL, we have the two alternative expressions [derived from (15.12) and (15.15), respectively]

$$\mathrm{DL} = -\frac{1}{2} \langle \delta^1 Q, \nabla^2_{QQ} \Pi^o, \delta^1 Q \rangle + \frac{1}{2} \left\langle \delta^1 P, \sum_h \nabla_P \hat{c}^{ho}, \delta^1 P \right\rangle$$

$$= \frac{1}{2} (\delta^1 t)(\delta^1 Y) - \frac{1}{2} \delta^1 P \sum_h \frac{\partial c^{ho}}{\partial m} \delta^1 V^h. \tag{15.16}$$

The first of these forms corresponds to the Boiteux measure of welfare loss, and the second corresponds to that of Hotelling.[5] Of course, the Hotelling version contains a circular element, as already mentioned. However, this circularity can be made to disappear under one additional assumption (made implicitly by Hotelling and others). We know that the introduction of commodity taxes has no first-order *welfare* effect. If it is done in such a way as to have no first-order *utility* effect, the last term in (15.16) disappears and $\mathrm{DL} = \frac{1}{2}(\delta^1 t)(\delta^1 Y)$. Then, deadweight loss can be measured by summing areas of triangles formed between (linear ap-

[4] Early formulations of this concept were given by Boiteux (1951), Debreu (1951), and Hotelling (1932).
[5] Diewert (1981) derives these measures using a slightly different framework. See his paper also for more discussion of the earlier literature.

proximations to) market supply and demand functions when indirect taxes (t) are instituted.[6]

Returning to the more general case of Section 15.2A, we should note that increased indirect taxation at the expense of lump-sum taxation *need not* reduce welfare when the status quo already involved some indirect taxation. The status quo second best may be improved (positive $t^o \, \delta^2 C$) by enough to overcome the negative-curvature terms. Thus, we see another illustration of this "general principle of second best."

15.3 Second-order measures for a mixed economy

To develop analogous measures for the mixed economy, we must begin by expanding (14.18) rather than (14.16). Since these expressions for utility are quite similar in form, it should not surprise the reader to find that the expansions are similar as well. However, the analysis is not quite a trivial modification since demand for public goods is an inverse demand and does not appear in the budget constraint. Consequently, we will spell out the necessary steps in some detail.

We can exploit the similarities with previous sections best by treating market demand cum public goods inverse demand as a single grand demand vector and similarly thinking of the associated dual variables (private-goods prices and public-goods levels) as an aggregated vector. Unfortunately, doing this involves use of "transpose" notation since we are mixing prices (with natural orientation as row vectors) and quantities (with natural orientation as column vectors). Resigning ourselves to this, we define

$$\tilde{c} = \begin{bmatrix} \{-\Omega\} \\ c \end{bmatrix}, \qquad \tilde{P} = [\{g\}, P]. \tag{15.17}$$

Note that we are going to treat $\tilde{c}$ as a column vector and $\tilde{P}$ as a row vector.

Using this notation, we can write (14.18) in the form

$$V(\tilde{P}, m \mid \tilde{P}^o) = \int_{x=\tilde{P}}^{\tilde{P}^o} \sum_i \tilde{c}_i(x, I(x \mid \tilde{P}, m)) \, dx_i + m. \tag{15.18}$$

Comparing (15.18) with (15.1), we see that they are isomorphic (with appropriate changes of variables). Consequently, the expression for the first derivative of V takes the same form as it did before (15.2) with the corresponding change of variables. As before, we substitute the individual budget constraint. Since this constraint does not involve the nonmarket goods, they turn up separately in the new expression, and we find

---

[6] Such triangle measures were popularized by Harberger (1971).

$$\frac{dV(\tilde{P}(\alpha), m(\alpha) \mid \tilde{P}^o)}{d\alpha}$$

$$= \Omega(\alpha) \, \nabla_\alpha g(\alpha) + P(\alpha) \, \nabla_\alpha c(\alpha)$$

$$+ \int_{x=\tilde{P}(\alpha)}^{\tilde{P}^o} \left[\sum_i \frac{\partial \tilde{c}_i(x, V(\tilde{P}(\alpha), m(\alpha) \mid x))}{\partial m} \, \frac{dV(\tilde{P}(\alpha), m(\alpha) \mid x)}{d\alpha} \right] dx_i.$$

$$(15.19)$$

Fortunately, this new term creates no new difficulties. When we take a second derivative (and evaluate at $\alpha = 0$), we obtain

$$\left. \frac{d^2 V}{d\alpha^2} \right|_{\alpha=0} = P^o \, \nabla_{\alpha\alpha}^2 c^o + \Omega^o \, \nabla_{\alpha\alpha}^2 g^o + \langle \nabla_\alpha \tilde{P}^o, \nabla_{\tilde{P}} \tilde{c}^o, \nabla_\alpha \tilde{P}^o \rangle$$

$$+ \nabla_\alpha \tilde{P}^o \, \nabla_m \tilde{c}^o \, \frac{dm^o}{d\alpha} - [\nabla_\alpha \tilde{P}^o \, \nabla_m \tilde{c}^o] \left[\frac{dm^o}{d\alpha} - \nabla_\alpha \tilde{P}^o \tilde{c} \right].$$

$$(15.20)$$

Since our isomorphism now carries over directly, we immediately have

$$\left. \frac{d^2 V}{d\alpha^2} \right|_{\alpha=0} = \Omega^o \, \nabla_{\alpha\alpha}^2 g^o + P^o \, \nabla_{\alpha\alpha}^2 c^o + \langle \nabla_\alpha \tilde{P}^o, \nabla_{\tilde{P}} \hat{\tilde{c}}^o, \nabla_\alpha \tilde{P}^o \rangle \qquad (15.21)$$

and

$$\delta^2 V = \Omega^o \, \delta^2 g + P^o \, \delta^2 c + \tfrac{1}{2} \langle \delta^1 \tilde{P}, \nabla_{\tilde{P}} \hat{\tilde{c}}^o, \delta^1 \tilde{P} \rangle. \qquad (15.22)$$

Clearly, now we are to evaluate *all* second-order consumption changes (both public and private) at status quo prices and correct for curvature with a quadratic form in the *grand* compensated demand function. Note further that, upon aggregation, the term $P^o \, \delta^2 C$ can be decomposed into market cost plus second-best terms, so all the apparatus of Chapter 9 still is available to us by way of evaluating opportunity cost. Thus, to implement second-order measures, we need all the information needed for first order together with a full set of compensated demand derivatives.

15.4   Upper and lower bounds

Suppose that we do not want to rely on constant curvatures (linear supply and demand functions) but do feel quite confident that we can put bounds on the variation of these curvatures. Should it not be possible to translate such bounds into corresponding "confidence intervals" for utility (or welfare) change? The answer is yes, using a procedure first worked out by Robert Willig. Since the error in using naive surplus to measure utility involves only income effects, we need bounds on curvatures only in the income dimensions, namely, income elasticities.

Unfortunately, to work with elasticities in a reasonable way, we must change our notation somewhat. The consumption base used in defining an elasticity ought to be *gross* rather than *net* consumption. Call this gross consumption c'; recalling that z has been used in the past to represent exogenous resources, gross income is measured as $m' = m + Pz$, and we write the gross consumption function as $c'(P, m') = c(P, m' - Pz) + z$. Further, it is useful to define a corresponding translation of the income compensation function: $I'(P \mid P(\alpha), m'(\alpha)) = I(P \mid P(\alpha), m'(\alpha) - P(\alpha)z) + Pz$.

A   *Market variables*

As in previous sections, we start with a single individual and restrict attention to variables that affect him through the market. Assume that we can impose the following uniform bounds on income elasticities:

$$\underline{\epsilon} \le \frac{\partial c_i'(P, m')}{\partial m} \frac{m'}{c_i'(P, m')} \le \bar{\epsilon}, \quad \text{all } i. \tag{15.23}$$

Note that the bounds must be uniform in that they do not depend on the good in question (i) or price and income levels. These inequalities can be used to put bounds on the amount that consumption can vary as the income level changes. Simple integration yields[7]

$$\left[\frac{m_2'}{m_1'}\right]^{\underline{\epsilon}} \le \frac{c_i'(P, m_2')}{c_i'(P, m_1')} \le \left[\frac{m_2'}{m_1'}\right]^{\bar{\epsilon}}. \tag{15.24}$$

The particular error of concern to us occurs when we are using "market-determined" income whereas we should be using "compensated" income. Suppose we substitute $I'(P \mid P(\alpha), m'(\alpha))$ for m_2' in (15.24) while leaving m_1' as a free variable. Then, in light of the duality relationships between the income compensation function and compensated demands, we obtain two partial differential "inequalities" for $I'(\cdot)$ in terms of uncompensated demands evaluated at the free income level. Since both are handled in the same way, we focus on the first:

$$\frac{\partial I'(P \mid P(\alpha), m'(\alpha))}{\partial P_i} \ge [I'(P \mid P(\alpha), m'(\alpha))]^{\underline{\epsilon}} \left[\frac{c_i'(P, m')}{(m')^{\underline{\epsilon}}}\right]. \tag{15.25}$$

We now integrate this system of inequalities (one for each good) over any contiguous price path connecting P^o and $P(\alpha)$ to obtain an inequality

---

[7] Integration techniques used in this section are exposited in Taylor (1955).

for $V'(P(\alpha), m'(\alpha) \mid P^o) = I'(P^o \mid P(\alpha), m'(\alpha))$.[8] (Note that V' is the scalar translation of V that measures utility of the status quo by m' rather than m.) The usefulness of this procedure derives from the fact that a closed-form solution can be obtained [recall that we were already in a position to calculate $V(\cdot)$ through numerical integration]. Using the principle of separation, we find

$$\frac{[I'(P^o \mid \cdot)]^{1-\underline{\varepsilon}}}{1-\underline{\varepsilon}} - \frac{[I'(P(\alpha) \mid \cdot)]^{1-\underline{\varepsilon}}}{1-\underline{\varepsilon}} \geq (m')^{-\underline{\varepsilon}} \int_{x=P(\alpha)}^{P^o} \sum_i c_i'(x, m') \, dx_i.$$

(15.26)

Notice that the integral in this expression represents naive consumer surplus (but computed using gross demand functions and holding gross income fixed). To simplify notation, let us label this integral $\Theta(m', \alpha)$. Although it seems natural to think of the associated fixed income level as being the status quo (m'^o), we leave it as a free choice here for reasons that will become apparent shortly. Since the functional form $F(x) = x^\gamma/\gamma$ is strictly monotone increasing for all γ, we can "solve" (15.26) for $I'(\cdot)$ using the boundary condition $I'(P(\alpha) \mid P(\alpha), m'(\alpha)) = m'(\alpha)$:

$$V'(P(\alpha), m'(\alpha) \mid P^o) \geq \left[(1-\underline{\varepsilon}) \frac{\Theta(m', \alpha)}{(m')^{\underline{\varepsilon}}} + [m'(\alpha)]^{1-\underline{\varepsilon}} \right]^{[1/(1-\underline{\varepsilon})]}. \quad (15.27)$$

The reader should check that we can derive the opposite inequality with $\bar{\varepsilon}$ substituted for $\underline{\varepsilon}$.

B   Public goods

We can extend the previous analysis to encompass both public and private goods by exploiting the isomorphism between utility measures (15.1) and (15.18). However, to do so, we will need to make "bounding" assumptions on income elasticities of *inverse* public-goods demands. Indeed, the assumption isomorphic to (15.23) would be[9]

$$\underline{\varepsilon} \leq \frac{\partial \Omega_i(\tilde{P}, m')}{\partial m} \frac{m'}{\Omega_i(\tilde{P}, m')} \leq \bar{\varepsilon}, \quad \text{all } i. \quad (15.28)$$

Consequently, our formula (15.27) applies equally well for measuring utility in the mixed economy if we insert consumer surplus defined by

---

[8] Willig (1976) discusses mostly a situation in which a single price changes, in which case we need not worry about the path of integration.

[9] Actually, the isomorphism does not look quite right here since Ω has a negative orientation in the $\tilde{c}$ vector. However, the reader can check that all signs come out right using (15.24).

$$\tilde{\Theta}(m', \alpha) = \int_{x = \tilde{P}(\alpha)}^{\tilde{P}^o} \sum_i \tilde{c}_i'(x, m') \, dx_i. \tag{15.29}$$

As always, consumer surplus is computed by integrating along any contiguous path connecting the status quo with the project. Clearly, a single integral can be formulated to "run through" a range of projects as the endpoint is varied, although the path then becomes fixed. Naturally, we will have to know the relevant facts concerning complementarities between public and private goods before we can evaluate the integral along such a path.

C   Welfare in a mixed economy

There are several ways in which inequalities such as (15.27) can be used in applications, assuming that naive surplus can be estimated. First, if we are content with confidence intervals, we can use such inequalities as is. Alternatively, we could make a "best guess" as to the average income elasticity (call it ϵ^*) and approximate $V(\cdot)$ by

$$V'(\tilde{P}(\alpha), m'(\alpha) \mid \tilde{P}^o) \approx \left[(1 - \epsilon^*) \frac{\tilde{\Theta}(m', \alpha)}{(m')^{\epsilon^*}} + [m'(\alpha)]^{1 - \epsilon^*} \right]^{[1/(1 - \epsilon^*)]}.$$
$$\tag{15.30}$$

This measure has the advantage that only one integration need be performed, the limits of integration being determined by the particular project being evaluated; the demand functions being integrated are simple market demand functions, and we are free to set gross income (m') at status quo levels.

Unfortunately, however, market data still need to be available at the individual level. Even if we are "utilitarian" enough to believe that the sum of utilities has some welfare significance, such a sum cannot be estimated using aggregate surplus due to the nonlinearity in (15.30). And naturally, we need to have some degree of confidence in our predictions of income elasticities in outlying regions before either the bounds or the estimate will be very informative.

D   Uncertainty

We identified situations in the previous chapter where ex ante utility could be measured as "expected compensated surplus." Clearly, in these cases we can approximate compensated surplus using the measures just developed and then take expectations. But, again, the nonlinearities complicate matters, as we will not find measures in terms of "expected naive surplus." Thus, even in the simplest situations involving risk, our measures will be cumbersome to say the least.

15.5   Direct use of naive surplus

Under certain further conditions, we can find good approximate measures that are linear in naive surplus. The following discussion concentrates on approximations derived from assuming some average income elasticity, though we could equally well make corresponding statements involving upper and lower bounds. The extra conditions required here are roughly that willingness to pay for the project be a small fraction of gross income. (Note that the required "smallness" here is considerably weaker than that required to justify first-order analysis; we can imagine many projects that are large enough to have nonnegligible effects on prices yet still constitute a relatively small item in the "package" of goods consumed by each household.) When this condition holds, we can approximate using a Taylor series expansion in the variable $\chi = \Theta/m'$. Expanding (15.30) to two terms in this way yields

$$V'(\tilde{P}(\alpha), m'(\alpha) \mid \tilde{P}^o) \approx m'(\alpha) + m' \left[\frac{m'(\alpha)}{m'} \right]^{\epsilon^*} \chi + \frac{m'}{2} \left[\frac{m'(x)}{m'} \right]^{2\epsilon^*-1} \epsilon^* \chi^2$$

$$+ \text{higher-order terms in } \chi, \text{ for some } x \in [0, \alpha]. \quad (15.31)$$

Now if the quadratic term is sufficiently small, we can "chop off" the expansion after the first term and obtain a measure linear in surplus. Clearly, it is sufficient for this purpose that ϵ^* be small. This should hardly surprise the reader since we saw long ago that naive surplus measures welfare in the absence of income effects. However, we also found a logical inconsistency in assuming no income effects, and it naturally reappears here: The weighted sum of income elasticities for consumption goods (weights taken to be consumption shares) must equal 1. Therefore, it is hard to see how ϵ^* will be close to zero unless we happen to be restricting attention to a particular subset of consumption goods for which income elasticities are low.

But regardless of the size of e^*, the quadratic term will be negligible when χ is small enough (e.g., when willingness to pay constitutes 5 percent of income, $\chi^2 = 0.0025$). When we do ignore second- and higher-order terms, it seems convenient to set m' (which was arbitrary before) equal to $m'(\alpha)$ so as to generate the approximation:

$$V'(\tilde{P}(\alpha), m'(\alpha) \mid \tilde{P}^o) \approx m'(\alpha) + \tilde{\Theta}(m'(\alpha), \alpha). \quad (15.32)$$

Now, the size of income elasticities is irrelevant so (in particular) formulas for upper and lower bounds will be "close" to one another. Consequently, utility will be closely approximated by naive surplus as long as higher-order terms are indeed small.[10]

Since the new approximation is linear in surplus terms, it will aggregate nicely if we take the utilitarian point of view; indeed, welfare can be measured by integrating aggregate demand. However, there is one somewhat nonstandard feature in the naive surplus measures we use for this purpose. Namely, the income level (though not a function of the variable of integration) is that of the "α project" rather than the status quo. When gross income levels are affected by the project, this means that we have lost one nice feature discussed earlier: We cannot evaluate a spectrum of projects using a single integral (with projects as alternative endpoints). Demands for each project must be evaluated using gross income levels appropriate to *that project*. Furthermore, these income levels must be represented in *available* market data or else the measure will not be practical anyway.[11]

Given these difficulties, we would like to use status quo income levels in the surplus measures. To this end, we could approximate individual utility as

$$V'^h(\tilde{P}(\alpha), m'(\alpha) \mid \tilde{P}^o) \approx m'^h(\alpha) + \left[\frac{m'^h(\alpha)}{m'^{oh}}\right]^{\epsilon^{*h}} \tilde{\Theta}^h(m'^{oh}, \alpha), \qquad (15.33)$$

where ϵ^* is the appropriate average elasticity. This formulation uses surplus based on status quo income but marks it up by a factor representing the average income effect. A single integral (with variable endpoint) can be used to compute individual surplus as a function of project level; but unfortunately, we now lose simple aggregation unless these markup factors happen to be the same for all households.

What should we do under these circumstances? If we are going to try to be sophisticated, it seems we may as well go back to using such expressions as (15.27) and (15.30) (for which we need detailed cross-sectional data). Otherwise, we may as well use aggregate surplus with some average markup to capture (albeit crudely) income effects. In the following chapter we discuss practical ways of measuring surplus and appropriate rules for combining these measures to generate a benefit–cost calculus.

---

[10] Since the second-order term is sure to be positive whenever the income elasticity is positive, our first-order approximation will not be an unbiased estimate of utility; we might want to make some small correction to account for the second-order term in some cirsumstances.

[11] This difficulty does not arise when welfare is measured by the "compensation test" and therefore has not received much attention in the literature. However, use of such a test for comparing projects cannot be justified, as we argued earlier.

CHAPTER 16

Practical methods for large-project evaluation

In the previous two chapters, we discussed ways of integrating first-order information to get exact or approximate measures of utility (and welfare) for large changes. When the associated variables are traded in markets, we can recover the associated measures from sufficiently rich demand data. However, it is highly implausible that we can collect demand information detailed enough to perform the required numerical integrations. Moreover, since we are primarily concerned with allocating *collective* (hence, *un*marketed) goods, market demand information alone (no matter how detailed) will not be sufficient unless we can generalize the spanning procedures of Chapter 13. This chapter discusses ways of recovering (or in most cases estimating) required information from observable data and using resulting measures to evaluate and compare alternative large projects.

We first look at methods for recovering surplus or willingness to pay for collective goods from sufficiently rich information on market demand. However, since "full information" is virtually never available, we need to look at ways of estimating or otherwise learning about utility. A standard estimating procedure involves imposing parametric restrictions on the form of utility (or demand) functions and estimating the parameters econometrically. We explain and evaluate this method in Section 16.2. Alternatively, we might try to learn about utility by designing a planning mechanism that induces agents to reveal their true surplus. Of course, we know from our discussions in Chapter 5 that the potential for solving broad classes of economic problems with a single planning mechanism is quite limited. But suppose we are willing to assume that naive surplus is good enough and simply want to estimate it for some particular collective good. In that case, a relatively practical method (known as the Groves–Clarke mechanism) is available. This method is discussed in Section 16.3.

We close the chapter with some rules and pitfalls associated with using surplus measures to do benefit–cost analysis. In particular, we discuss efficient procedures for choosing appropriate subsets from a group of competing large projects.

260

16.1 Recovering willingness to pay for collective goods

Suppose that an appropriate spanning condition holds so that we are able to obtain information on shadow values using the methods of Section 13.1. Could we "integrate" this information into a measure of utility change? We can, if we can get enough sample points for each type of individual. To see how, let us expand on our discussion of the general activity analysis framework. In order to make close comparisons to the developments of Chapter 14, we add some "market parameters" to this model; specifically, we write the cost function as $\Gamma(p, a)$, where p is this new set of parameters. (These parameters might represent prices of transportation or land in the location choice example of Chapter 13.) Recall the problem (13.5) with this modification:

$$\max_a U(\eta(g, a)) \tag{16.1}$$

subject to

$$\Gamma(p, a) = m.$$

This problem defines an indirect utility function $V(g, p, m)$ with marginal rates of substitution

$$\frac{\nabla_g V}{\lambda} = \frac{\nabla_\eta U \nabla_g \eta}{\lambda}, \tag{16.2}$$

$$\frac{\nabla_p V}{\lambda} = -\nabla_p \Gamma. \tag{16.3}$$

We saw in Chapter 13 that when appropriate spanning conditions hold, the right side of (16.2) is observable as a function of g, p, and m. Also, given that the choices of a can be observed as functions of these parameters, the right side of (16.3) is similarly identified. We refer to these functions as $F^g(g, p, m)$ and $F^p(g, p, m)$, respectively.

Consequently (recalling procedures of Chapter 14), the income compensation function could be recovered in principle from the following system of partial differential equations[1]:

$$\nabla_g I(g, P) = -F^g(g, p, I), \tag{16.4}$$

$$\nabla_p I(g, p) = -F^p(g, p, I). \tag{16.5}$$

To perform the required integration, we need to find a collection of similar individuals ("similar" meaning they have the same utility function

---

[1] We suppress the reference point in income compensation functions here for notational convenience.

and endowment) facing a rich spectrum of parameters. But unfortunately, this condition is difficult to satisfy in situations where the spanning model is likely to apply. Individuals typically get to choose among attributes at some point in these situations (they choose type of car, package of local public services, and the like). Consequently, we expect that individuals with similar tastes will choose similar attributes (so that we will not observe much cross-sectional variation among similar agents). Thus, the class of situations where we can expect to observe both "spanning" and "sufficient similarity" is likely to be limited at best.

Even if we can observe the necessary variation, we will need compensated demand functions for each "type" of agent affected by the public variables in order to get a measure of aggregate benefits. All these requirements taken together seem prohibitively difficult to meet. However, it turns out that once we are willing to assume that hypothetical demand information can be obtained, the other (spanning) requirements can be dropped. To see this, let us return to a standard version of the consumer problem[2]:

$$\max_{c} U(g, c) \tag{16.6}$$

subject to

$$Pc = m.$$

We want to recover the income compensation function (and therefore the utility function) from information on consumption demand only. Of course, the demand for private goods c reveals part of this function through our standard duality relationships:

$$\nabla_P I(g, P) = c(g, P, I). \tag{16.7}$$

Suppose we are willing to assume that private goods are indispensable to the enjoyment of collective goods. Then, intuitively at least, the consumer surplus from consuming private goods ought to capture nonmarket benefits derived from the presence of collective goods. We make this intuition precise as follows. If a certain collection of private goods is indispensable, when consumption levels of these goods are set to zero, the marginal value of the collective goods should be zero. Thus, if we set the prices of these goods sufficiently high (infinity will do), changes in collective-goods levels should have no effect on indirect utility. Partitioning

---

[2] I am indebted to Suzanne Scotchmer for calling this method to my attention and suggesting the following general method of proof. Early references utilizing this procedure include Maler (1971) and Bradford–Hildenbrandt (1977).

the private-goods vector as (c_1, c_2), where c_1 is indispensable, we formalize our assumption as

$$\nabla_g I(g, \infty, P_2) = 0, \quad \text{all } g, P_2. \tag{16.8}$$

(Note that we implicitly assume that the numeraire is not in the indispensable set.)

Now, we use the fundamental theorem of the calculus to write $\nabla_g I$ as the (line) integral of its derivative with respect to prices of indispensable goods. Using (16.8) to determine the constant of integration, we have

$$\nabla_g I(g, P) = -\int_{x_1 = P_1}^{\infty} \nabla^2_{g P_1} I(g, x_1, P_2) \, dx_1. \tag{16.9}$$

Finally, drawing on the symmetry of cross-partials and the duality relationships (16.7) yields

$$\nabla_g I(g, P) = -\int_{x_1 = P_1}^{\infty} \nabla_g c_1(g, x_1, P_2, I(\cdot)) \, dx_1. \tag{16.10}$$

Thus, the marginal willingness to pay for public goods is measured as the incremental change in (compensated) consumer surplus of indispensable goods, as suggested. Note that path independence implies that we can pick any collection of indispensable goods for these calculations, so naturally, we want to pick the smallest possible such set. For example, if we could argue that radios were essential to the enjoyment of public programming, willingness to pay for these programs could be recovered from looking only at the demand function for radios.

Comparing the accomplishment here with the corresponding analysis in Chapter 13, we see that we have obtained shadow prices of public goods without the spanning assumptions employed there. Since the assumption embodied in (16.10) seems quite weak, the only "cost" paid for this achievement is that we now require hypothetical demand information to carry out the computations (whereas before we used only local information obtainable from the status quo equilibrium).

Of course, once we have sufficiently rich hypothetical demand information, we can integrate (16.10) to obtain measures of the benefit from large changes in g:

$$I(g^1, P) - I(g^o, P) = -\int_{x_1 = P_1}^{\infty} [c_1(g^1, x_1, P_2, I(\cdot)) \\ - c_1(g^o, x_1, P_2, I(\cdot))] \, dx_1. \tag{16.11}$$

Thus, we see that under fairly weak assumptions we could measure the net benefits from public projects if we could observe market demands as a function of a sufficiently rich collection of parameter values. We turn our attention now to problems involving identification of these functions.

Exact observation would require that we encounter situations in which indispensable goods are unaffordable; these situations are implausible at best and will actually be impossible when the relevant goods are indispensable, not just for enjoying public goods but for life on any terms. Therefore, some sort of extrapolation is likely to be required. Unfortunately, the approximations discussed in Chapter 15 are not so useful in the present context. Since computations in (16.11) [or (16.10) for that matter] require information "far away" from the status quo, second-order approximations are unlikely to be very accurate. Furthermore, our arguments for naive surplus (computed from uncompensated demands) as a good approximation fall apart when we are talking about the entire surplus in several markets; there is no reason why *that much* surplus need be a small fraction of gross income and, consequently, no reason why the second-order terms in (15.31) should be small.

In this connection we should point out that the method just discussed may be of more practical use on the production side of the economy. Suppose we want to measure the value of public inputs to a collection of competitive firms. Write the aggregate "indirect" profit function of these firms as $\Pi(g, P)$. As we know, the derivatives of Π with respect to P are simply aggregate input demands (the issue of compensation is moot). Therefore, the increase in profits due to increased public inputs will be measured just as in (16.11) except we use standard input demand functions.

16.2   Parametric econometric identification

All the welfare measurement methods developed to this point are operational only to the extent that the appropriate elements of market demand are fully observable without error. Unfortunately, such ideal conditions virtually never prevail, even with respect to status quo demand levels, much less individual compensated demand functions. Although detailed discussion of estimation procedures in the presence of limited information, measurement error, and the like are beyond the scope of this book, we discuss briefly some procedures that are most frequently used in public economics.

When demand functions are not fully observable, we cannot recover the entire utility function from observable market data unless we can somehow restrict the class of possible utility functions a priori. On the other hand, if we are willing to assume that we know the utility *functional form* (defined over a sufficiently broad consumption space and characterized by a finite number of parameters), we ought to be able to determine those parameters from a limited set of observations. And having discovered the parameters, naturally we would be able to measure the utility contribution of any particular project.[3]

The questions of whether a particular parameter set is identified and if so how best to estimate it belong in the realm of econometrics and will not concern us much here. However, we will outline the basic considerations and give an example to illustrate the strengths and weaknesses of the approach. Suppose we believe that all households in some specified group have a utility function characterized by a vector of parameters, γ. That is, knowledge of γ completely determines this function, and it is the same for all members of the group. Formally, we are saying that utility is a *known* function $F(\gamma, g, c)$.

Now suppose that we are able to obtain data on market behavior for these households. (We drop reference to consumer "activities" and return to the standard framework.) That is, we observe them choosing c when faced with some range of values for g, P, and m. We can think of the first-order conditions as a system of equations linking these variables with γ. Formally, we could obtain a system for estimation by eliminating the multiplier λ from the first-order system:

$$\nabla_c F(\gamma, g, c) = \lambda P, \tag{16.12}$$

$$Pc = m. \tag{16.13}$$

Now, if the situation were really as just described, it would be a simple matter to determine γ from a small number of observations. But, unfortunately, we never know the specification precisely, so we are always going to be left with an estimation problem. Some practitioners append error terms to the system (16.12) and (16.13) in rather ad hoc ways and proceed with an econometric estimation. However, it is hard to see how to justify such a procedure or interpret its results unless we can tell a consistent story about where the errors come from and why they enter in any particular way. While recognizing that consistent specification is quite difficult, we really ought to insist on it.

To illustrate the requirements of this technique, let us look at one example where it can be used, namely, where we observe "Tiebout segregation" in a spatial club. In this case, we expect all the households in the community to have identical preferences yet there is a natural diversity

---

[3] This approach has a long history; it has been used in various forms by McFadden (1978), Jorgenson–Lau (1974), and Lau (1969). See Hausman (1981) for a discussion of econometric problems and techniques used in implementation.

in the market variables (such as rent) and collective variables (such as air quality) that they face. Of course, we still must assume a particular functional form for utility. To illustrate, we pick

$$U(g, s, c, \ell) = g^{\gamma 1} s^{\gamma 2} \ell^{\gamma 3} c^{(1-\gamma 3)}, \tag{16.14}$$

where all variables have the same meaning as in the previous spatial examples. Note that, in contrast to those examples, we allow preferences to depend on location here (spanning does not hold).[4] Now, we suppose that all our households are maximizing this function subject to the budget constraint:

$$c + r[s]\ell + \phi[s] = m. \tag{16.15}$$

It turns out that a log-linear system can be obtained for estimation in this example. First we solve for the indirect utility function conditional on a given location s in closed form:

$$V(g, s, r, \phi, m) = \kappa g^{\gamma 1} s^{\gamma 2} r^{-\gamma 3} [m - \phi], \tag{16.16}$$

where κ is an irrelevant constant. Now, locational indifference implies that for all locations occupied in equilibrium the same utility levels are generated.[5] Consequently,

$$V = \kappa g[s]^{\gamma 1} s^{\gamma 2} r[s]^{-\gamma 3} [m - \phi[s]], \tag{16.17}$$

where V is the common level. All data points should satisfy this equation if there are no observation or measurement errors. If we believe that the only error enters in the form of an unobserved collective input that does not correlate with other variables (admittedly an heroic assumption), the corresponding error term will enter multiplicatively in (16.17), and we would want to estimate the log-linear equation:

$$\log r[s] = \kappa_1 + \frac{\gamma^1}{\gamma^3} \log g[s] + \frac{\gamma^2}{\gamma^3} \log s + \frac{1}{\gamma^3} \log[m - \phi[s]] + \epsilon, \tag{16.18}$$

where κ_1 is a new constant that will depend on the level of V. Note that all structural parameters are just identified in this equation (at least under the assumption of linear error structure).

As we have just seen, the Tiebout model is ideal for the purpose at hand; it is a natural context for finding identical individuals facing a spectrum of choices. Will there be other similar contexts? Some people argue that we can reasonably suppose *all* preferences to be identical as long as we are careful to specify a rich enough set of arguments to these functions

---

[4] The following example is adapted quite closely from Polinsky–Shavell (1976).
[5] Arguments justifying this equilibrium condition were exposited in Chapter 5.

(examples of such arguments might be state of health, characteristics of parents, gender, and the like). Assuming that these variables can be measured *and* that there are enough degrees of freedom left over, the preceding methods could be applied to any cross section of households. We simply think of individual characteristics as represented by a new set of (observable) parameters in the function $F(\cdot)$. Of course, if people differ in too many ways or ways that are unobservable, cross-sectional information will be inadequate for recovering preferences.

Alternatively, we may be able to achieve identification using time series data. Recalling the sequential model of Chapter 12, the ideal case for this purpose is one where current demand is fully separable over time (depending only on contemporaneous variables) and independent of the random event entered. In this case, time and the random event will generate the necessary price variation to estimate the invariant contemporaneous demand function. Unfortunately, this situation never can apply exactly due to the presence of the active saving decision. To see this, refer back to the problem (12.18). Even under the assumption of additively separable utility, the choice of c_s will depend on the marginal utility of future income (shadow price of m_{s+1}) (some practitioners finesse this complication by assuming a constant marginal utility of income, but the reader should be skeptical of such procedures after our discussions in Chapter 14). This link must be identified and compensated for econometrically even when utility is separable and independent of event.

When utility is "event dependent," time series identification suffers for exactly the same reasons preference differences interfere with cross-sectional identification. If *every aspect* of the state of the world affects the form of individual utility, there is no hope: Only one state is ever revealed, and there is no way of knowing what individual utility looks like in other states. However, if uncertainty involves "individual risk" in that only a small "personal" subspace of the grand state space matters to any individual and if similar individuals face a spectrum of these personal states in the grand realization, the resulting demand functions will be rich enough to reveal state-dependent utility.

Assuming that enough restrictions can be imposed to achieve identification, it is still not obvious how they should be imposed. That is, there is no natural way to choose a functional form for estimation. Of course, we can use the goodness of fit in an estimating equation such as (16.18) as a check. However, as long as there is any unexplained variance, we know that we are wrong at least to some degree, and it is not at all clear how we could measure the cost of this error in the space of possible utility functions.

Even if the available data fit *perfectly*, there are still potential problems with this procedure. We can only hope to be sure of identifying the correct utility form *over ranges of observed variables*. This is quite unfortunate since we may end up using the results to evaluate projects that take us outside that range. The nature of this pitfall can be illustrated in the preceding example. The data on which it is based involve *no* wealth variations (indeed, all we are observing is points on an indifference curve). Consequently, these data cannot be used to identify wealth effects despite the fact that our functional form appears to do so. *Any other* utility function having the same indifference curve as the one estimated would fit the data just as well.

Of course, we can think of ways to circumvent this particular difficulty. We find communities with similar utilities but different income levels and fit the combined data. However, the general shortcoming always remains. Any functional form implies an extrapolation outside the range of data on which it is estimated, and it is hard to see how we can justify the use of these extrapolations.

Unfortunately, the problem here is quite fundamental and certainly not a special feature of the econometric procedure under discussion. *Every* extrapolation implies a corresponding functional form; for example, we saw that the extrapolation based on second-order approximation "implies" quadratic utility. And similar statements can be made about interpolations. Thus, when the data are inadequate to fully recover utility functions from choice functions, we must resort to some type of functional form restriction or rely on an "upper- and lower-bound" approach. The best that one can hope for is an approach that allows for a reasonable range of individual differences, consistent specification of the residual error structure, and "flexibility" of functional form over the ranges that matter. Even this much hope may be rather forlorn since these criteria seem to conflict with one another in practice.

Viewed in this light, we might reiterate the case for first- and second-order project analysis. The information required to get first- and second-order measures is considerably less demanding on the data than are constructions of individual utility. Thus, whenever the "range that matters" can be justified as small, these methods are quite compelling.

16.3   Groves–Clarke mechanism

We return now, briefly, to a discussion of mechanisms that simultaneously elicit preferences and make decisions. Although we gave up on them as generic planning procedures in Chapter 5, they are worth a second look once we restrict our objectives to the evaluation of a single project. However, the negative results of that chapter should alert us to the fact that mechanisms to be discussed are intrinsically linked to some of the special structural assumptions we make.[6]

Groves–Clarke mechanisms can be formulated to handle more general problems than we will discuss here. But given our current emphasis on *practical* methods, we restrict attention to cases where the procedure would be reasonably simple to implement, namely, partial equilibrium situations in which only naive surplus matters (both to individuals and to the planner). Consequently, we assume that individual utility takes the form

$$U^h = \Theta^h(g) + m^h, \tag{16.19}$$

where g is the vector of collective goods under consideration. Recall from our discussions in the previous chapter that this form will result if private-goods prices are unaffected by the choice of g and the level of g does not generate income effects. This restriction on the preference domain is sufficient to admit the possibility of a dominant-strategy mechanism.

Let $\Gamma(g)$ represent the planner's cost function computed at the fixed private-goods prices. The general structure of a Groves–Clarke procedure is as follows: (1) Agents report surplus (willingness-to-pay) functions to the center; (2) the center assigns a net tax schedule that may depend on the reported surpluses to each agent; and (3) the center determines levels of g on the basis of reported surpluses and known costs. Agents are assumed to know the entire mechanism structure when they report their surpluses.

An optimal design is one in which the tax functions and decision rule are constructed so that (a) agents have incentives to report their true surpluses and (b) the decision(s) taken are welfare optimal. We might also ask that taxes collected exactly cover the costs of the project, but this turns out to be impossible. We comment on this difficulty and its importance later.

The welfare function utilized here is "classical utilitarian" sum of individual utilities. This may seem restrictive but actually is not given the assumptions already made. Since the allowed tax schedules generally include lump-sum components, we are assuming lump-sum transfers are possible. But then, if welfare weights were anything but equal, the center would find it desirable to transfer money from those with low weights to those with high weights ad infinitum (given the constancy of the marginal

---

[6] The procedures discussed here were discovered independently by Groves (1973) and Clarke (1971), although special cases are attributable to Vickrey (1961). See Groves–Ledyard (1977) and Green–Laffont (1979) for a complete discussion of the topic. A useful graphical discussion is given by Tideman–Tullock (1976).

utility of income). Consequently, we may as well restrict to constant-and-equal welfare weights right from the start.

Given this welfare function and the fact that we look for a "truthful" mechanism, decision rule 3 is determined. When agents report surplus functions $\hat{\Theta}^h$, the planner must choose

$$g^* = \arg \max \left[\sum_h \hat{\Theta}^h(g) - \Gamma(g) \right]. \tag{16.20}$$

Our problem reduces to finding tax functions that induce truth telling in light of this decision rule.

Suppose we were to simply assign shares of Γ for taxes. We know from Chapter 5 that if these shares *happen* to be the Lindahl shares, everyone will indeed report the truth. But unfortunately, Lindahl shares are *unknown* to the center so the assignment would have to be somewhat arbitrary; and any agent who is assigned too large a share has an incentive to underreport his preference since increasing his report confers external benefits on the rest of society (which must be paying less on average than its Lindahl share). The Groves–Clarke mechanism corrects for this externality by subsidizing each agent at the rate of this reported external benefit.

To this end, consider the tax schedules

$$T^h(g) = \chi_h \Gamma(g) - \left[\sum_{i \neq h} \hat{\Theta}^i(g) - \left(\sum_{i \neq h} \chi_i \right) \Gamma(g) \right], \tag{16.21}$$

where the χ's are arbitrary cost shares that add to 1. These schedules complete the description of the Groves–Clarke mechanism for the current economic environment. And we can show that it is a dominant-strategy mechanism with "truth-telling" as the dominant strategy for each agent. As an immediate consequence, the decision rule that emerges must be socially optimal.[7]

To demonstrate dominance, look at the objective of agent h given his tax assignment (when others report $\hat{\Theta}$):

$$V^h = \Theta^h(g) - T^h(g) = \Theta^h(g) + \sum_{i \neq h} \hat{\Theta}^j(g) - \Gamma(g). \tag{16.22}$$

Clearly, by correcting for externality, we have given agent h the social objective. Now if h reports the truth, the center will choose g to maximize (16.22), the best outcome h could *possibly* get given the tax function he faces. Any other report he could make will lead to another choice of g that *cannot* be better for him and very likely will be worse. Since

---

[7] Actually, it is shown by Green–Laffont (1979) that the *only* incentive-compatible mechanisms are essentially of the same form.

this statement is true *regardless* of what others have reported, truth is a dominant strategy as asserted.

Thus, we have discovered a dominant-strategy mechanism for allocating collective goods under some special structural assumptions. However, when it comes to actual implementation, we still face some practical problems. First, there is the budget issue alluded to earlier. As formulated, the preceding procedure is almost certain to run a deficit. To see this, look at the difference between costs and aggregate taxes collected:

$$\Gamma(g) - \sum_h T^h(g) = (N-1)\left[\sum_h \Theta^h(g) - \Gamma(g)\right]. \tag{16.23}$$

Assuming that the project generates a positive surplus, the mechanism loses money (and perhaps lots of it!).

Of course, we can correct for this problem by adding a lump-sum component to the tax. Indeed, suppose we add to h's tax a component of the form $\max_g \sum_{i \neq h}[\hat{\Theta}^i(g) - \chi^i\Gamma(g)]$. (Note that this component is lump sum as far as household h is concerned.) Then it is easy to see (we leave verification to the reader) that the project always makes a "profit" when the corresponding mechanism is used.

However, as mentioned earlier, it is not possible to design tax rules that always *balance* the project budget *regardless* of the preferences revealed.[8] One implication of this fact is that we are not going to be able to use Groves–Clarke mechanisms to solve all our social problems simultaneously. But this should hardly surprise us given the aforementioned negative results. Could we still use such mechanisms to allocate a limited subset of collective goods? Well, maybe, but the informational requirements still look formidable. Although we do not have to run the "personalized" markets of the Lindahl method, we still need to collect information from each affected person.

Perhaps such information collection is not entirely absurd in our world with its compulsory tax returns and the like, but we would like to reduce the information requirements if possible. And we can if we are willing to make some regularity assumptions about statistical samples. Indeed, if we could assure ourselves that a 2 percent sample is representative of individual preferences, the mechanism can be run using such a sample. Of course, we could not expect the sample to cover project costs, but we already gave up on that idea anyway.

---

[8] This is proved for the formulation at hand in Green–Laffont (1979). However, there are other formulations in which it is possible to achieve budget balance. These involve situations in which the distribution of preferences is known and we are trying to elicit tastes in a particular realization. See D'Asprement–Gerard-Varet (1979).

The Groves–Clarke mechanism with representative sampling has some real practical potential. Its biggest limiting drawback is that it could only be applied to projects with simple (one-dimensional) descriptions. Once project description gets moderately complex, it is hard to imagine people reporting complete willingness-to-pay functions as required.

16.4   Commonly used framework

Except in cases where a Groves–Clarke mechanism can be used, we need a workable framework for doing large-project analysis. From earlier discussions we know that such a framework will involve unpleasant compromises involving approximations to reality on the one hand and tractability on the other. Here we will outline the most commonly used framework and indicate clearly the assumptions and compromises inherent in it.

Let us start from the exact general representation of utility (14.18):

$$V(g(\alpha), P(\alpha), m(\alpha) \mid g^o, P^o)$$

$$= \int_{g^o}^{g(\alpha)} \sum_i \Omega_i(g, P, I(g, P \mid g(\alpha), P(\alpha), m(\alpha))) \, dg_i$$

$$+ \int_{P(\alpha)}^{P^o} \sum_i c_i(g, P, I(g, P \mid g(\alpha), P(\alpha), m(\alpha))) \, dP_i + m(\alpha).$$

$$(16.24)$$

We seek a compromise that makes use of aggregate data only. Thus, at the very least, we must ignore distributional considerations and measure welfare as the sum of utilities. Further, we want to minimize the required volume of general equilibrium information. To this end, we assume that the particular class of projects under consideration will have negligible effects on "most" prices. Here, let us suppose that we are looking at the provision of collective goods, and these projects will have no effect on private-goods prices (only on collective-goods pseudoprices). Then, surplus terms involving private goods disappear, and after substitution from the aggregate budget constraint, we have[9]

$$Z^*(g(\alpha), m(\alpha) \mid g^o, P^o)$$

$$\approx \int_{g^o}^{g(\alpha)} \sum_h \Omega^h(g, P^o, I^h(g, P^o \mid g(\alpha), P^o, m(\alpha))) \, dg$$

$$- P^o b(\alpha) + P^o Y(\alpha).$$

$$(16.25)$$

---

[9] More generally, we could allow for price changes on a limited collection of private goods. Details are left to the reader, though we will incorporate this generalization in our subsequent study of the peak-load problem (Chapter 17).

It is common to simplify the remaining surplus term further by replacing compensated by uncompensated demands, usually without any correction for income effect. However, we would argue for some sort of markup or markdown here (recall our analysis in the previous chapter). It is inconsistent to suppose that the project changes *neither* consumer prices *nor* exogenous income levels (how could project costs be paid?). Project costs are paid either out of unshiftable taxes or from commodity taxes that fall on firms, and the corresponding lost income is likely to affect willingness to pay for collective goods. Consequently, we recommend an uncompensated approximation of the form

$$Z^*(g(\alpha), m(\alpha) \mid g^o, P^o)$$

$$\approx \kappa(\alpha) \int_{g^o}^{g(\alpha)} \sum_h \Omega^h(g, P^o m^o) \, dg - P^o b(\alpha) + P^o Y(\alpha), \qquad (16.26)$$

where κ represents the appropriate markdown.

When there is no commodity taxation, the last term in (16.26) is aggregate private profit. Otherwise, it can be further broken down into private profit plus tax revenue. Most studies ignore these terms and compare potential projects on the basis of surplus minus cost. To the extent that uncertainty is dealt with at all, it is handled by working with expected surplus and expected cost. Of course, this treatment is valid only in a risk-neutral world.

16.5   Project interactions and concept of alternative cost

Let us suppose that we are willing to live with naive surplus as our measure of collective-goods benefits. Then, the Groves–Clarke mechanism or the framework just developed can be applied to evaluate projects considered in isolation. However, we argued in Chapter 14 that it is quite dangerous to consider projects in isolation when the relevant projects are necessarily large. We return to these issues now and discuss them in the context of benefit–cost analysis using surplus measures. Although the presence of alternatives does indeed complicate matters in some respects, it actually facilitates shortcuts that reduce the required information about surplus in some instances.

We introduce these considerations with a stylized example patterned roughly on the choice of water projects in southern California. Three projects are available that can be employed separately or in combination:

1.   Water can be piped from the Colorado River at a cost of $30 per acre-foot. However, due to limited water rights, a maximum of g^c acre-feet is available from this source.

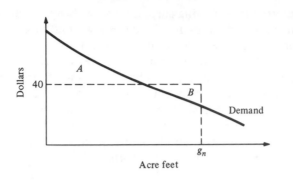

Figure 16.1

2.   Desalination plants can be built that will produce water at $100 per acre-foot. The minimum plant size is g_s.
3.   Dams can be built and water pumped from northern California at a cost of $40 per acre-foot. The minimum feasible capacity is g_n.

Note that the presence of minimum feasible sizes implies that projects have to be large so that marginal analysis is inadequate. Suppose we were to consider project 3 in isolation and that the demand for water were as depicted in Figure 16.1. Clearly, as drawn, we would not want to exceed the minimum feasible scale; we compare the area labeled A with that labeled B and accept the project if A exceeds B (as it does here).

But clearly this cannot be the optimal decision in all circumstances. Indeed, if it should happen that $g^c > g_n$, we *know* it would be better to take all our water from the Colorado. And that may still be the best choice even when $g^c < g_n$. Obviously, we need to compare the best outcomes from each project (or combination) and maximize over these. One way to do that here is to value the water at its cost from the best alternative project. We refer to this cost as the *alternative cost*.

Thus, in considering project 3, we value "early" units at the *minimum* of the demand price and the cost saved by *not* using the next best alternative project (Colorado River water). This procedure leads to the benefit–cost diagram of Figure 16.2. Now, we compare area E with B and C, accepting only if $E > B + C$.

As drawn, the northern California project is not desirable. It would be better to get by (at least for a while) using the allotment of Colorado River water. We can further illustrate the use of alternative cost by looking at the hypothetical situation a few years later when demand has grown (see Figure 16.3).

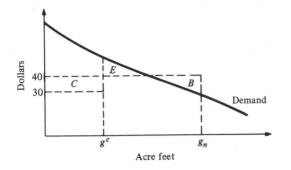

Figure 16.2

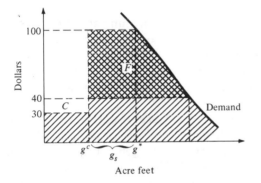

Figure 16.3

Suppose for the moment that $g^* - g^c > g_s$. Then, we value the first g^c units of water at its best alternative cost ($30). More water than this can be had only at the alternative desalination price of $100. Given that we know that demand will justify producing the minimal g_s units, it is appropriate to evaluate the next $g^* - g^c$ units of water at $100. Consequently, the potential benefits from northern California water are represented by the shaded area in Figure 16.3.

Hence, the project is desirable as long as area C is less than (crosshatched) area F. Of course, we can actually do even better here by combining Colorado water with some from northern California; indeed, the appropriate optimization problem involves choosing $\hat{g}$ (the Colorado allotment) to maximize G minus H minus I in Figure 16.4 (overleaf).

So far, the use of alternative cost has been neat and clean. Notice how it has reduced the required surplus information; from what has been said

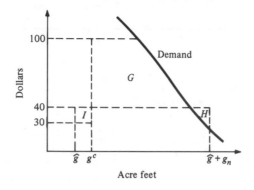

Figure 16.4

so far, it seems that we never need to know anything about the demand function to the left of g^*. As long as we know the amount of water at which the demand price reaches $100, we needed no further information about the demand for smaller amounts (the information was irrelevant since we knew that we would want to provide at least g^* one way or another).

However, there are some caveats to our use of alternative cost. It is always a legitimate procedure when the fall back projects satisfy standard convexity assumptions. However, in more general cases, the correct alternative may not be easy to identify. To illustrate possible difficulties, let us return to the previous example but suppose that $g_s > g^* - g^c$. In this case, we can no longer be sure from the outset that desalination is desirable in the absence of northern California water. And once the alternative is uncertain, the concept of alternative cost is not well defined. Clearly, a correct procedure will require that we back up one step to analyze the desirability of desalination. Without going into more detail (the reader is invited to try his hand), suffice it to say that some of the simplicity is lost and more information about surplus is required.

Fortunately, project interactions will not be so significant in all circumstances. They are important only when members of a group of projects all affect the marginal valuation of a common good (or goods). Whenever it is safe to assume that some particular project affects the pseudoprice of its own (project-specific) output only, interactions will be irrelevant.

CHAPTER 17

Peak-load problem[1]

We end the book with analysis of a problem that has a long and important tradition in the theory of public policy. This topic is particularly appropriate for discussion here because it draws on and illustrates many tools of analysis developed earlier. In particular, the "peak-load" problem involves an important element of user nonrivalry, is inherently intertemporal in nature, incorporates several different levels of decentralization, and requires the use of surplus measures in a fairly sophisticated way.

We discuss a version of the peak-load problem having the following specific features. Some type of public service is produced using capital (referred to as *capacity*) and variable inputs. We will think of both capacity and services as one dimensional, although this is done for simplicity rather than because of any inherent difficulties in the generalization. Construction of capacity involves economies of scale. We implicitly assume that these are important enough so that efficient construction sizes are likely to affect the demand price for services; consequently, we will need some measures of surplus to evaluate welfare changes. Examples of projects that fit this mold reasonably well include bridges, highways, and power projects. Despite the fact that uncertainty about future demand is undeniably an important feature of such projects, we will not deal with it here.

Several features of this description should be familiar from earlier chapters. For example, capacity plays the role of common property discussed in Chapter 5, and the presence of an increasing returns element fits the framework of the Ramsey pricing model in Chapter 8. Rather than reiterate the previous analyses, we concentrate on new issues raised by the intertemporal nature of the problem. Consequently, we assume that services are provided by a single public agency (so that common property externalities are internalized) and that lump-sum taxes are possible (so that second-best Ramsey pricing is unnecessary).[2]

Most capacity problems of this type are recursive in nature. Either capacity falls over time due to depreciation, or demand grows, or both.

---

[1] Some of the material in this chapter is drawn from Starrett (1978).
[2] See Mohring (1970) and Boiteux (1971) for a discussion of peak-load pricing in the presence of a second-best revenue constraint.

When this feature is present, the timing of new constructions becomes an important element in the problem and the general framework becomes similar in some respects to the optimal-club problem (where the repetition is over space). We will expand on this relationship later.

Our analysis of the peak-load problem will break down into two parts. The first deals primarily with the nonrepetitive elements of the problem and constitutes a relatively general analysis of the allocation of a partially nonrivalrous good. The discussion will be couched in discrete time, and relevant decentralizations will take place in a general equilibrium context. When we turn to the repetitive element, we find it useful (indeed almost necessary) to employ a continuous-time framework and add extra assumptions enabling us to work with cost functions and consumer surplus.

17.1   General welfare problem

Let K_s represent capacity in place at time s. This capacity may be made up of various vintages in our version where construction is repetitive. If k_i units are constructed at date i, we assume that $k_i \zeta(s, i)$ effective units will still be available in date s. We do not allow for more general sorts of depreciation since we want to treat capacity as a single variable. However, no further assumptions are made on the form of the depreciation function here, although additional specialization will be required later. Hence, the amount of capacity available at time s may be written as

$$K_s = \sum_{i \leq s} k_i \zeta(s, i). \tag{17.1}$$

Theoretically, construction could take place at each date. Results stated in what follows will be valid even for this case, although some of the approximations may not be reasonable. However, we have in mind a situation in which the diseconomies of small-scale construction are large enough and the time interval small enough so that it is never optimal to build new capacity each period. We could axiomatize this outcome but will not do so here.[3]

The production of capacity is specified as follows. Let b^{kj} be the vector of inputs devoted to producing capacity in place at date j. The associated vector index generally will run over both goods and dates (before j) so that a typical vector will represent a profile of investment inputs over time. We represent the production function for capacity at date s as

$$k_s = f^{ks}(b^{ks}). \tag{17.2}$$

---

[3] The reader might refer to Dixit–Mirrlees–Stern (1975) for a similar axiomatization involving saving decisions.

Let η be services produced from capacity and assume a production function (for date s) of the form

$$\eta_s = f^{\eta s}(b_s^\eta, K_s), \tag{17.3}$$

where b_s^η represents a vector of variable inputs. Since it seems reasonable that most important economies of scale involve the production of capacity rather than services from capacity, we will assume that the f^η functions are concave and exhibit constant returns to scale.

Beyond this, we make no further assumptions concerning the shape of production relationships. Note, in particular, that we do not assume stationarity; the technologies may be changing in arbitrary ways for now. Later, we will explore the implications of stationarity for the allocation rules to be developed.

Production relationships among other commodities will not be considered explicitly. Rather, we will treat the total availability of these goods as exogenous to the model. Let Y_s be this exogenous vector. There is no difficulty in incorporating a production technology for Y_s, but none of the results that follow change qualitatively, and the added complexity would be cumbersome. Letting C_s be the aggregate consumption vector of other goods at date s, we have the (vector of) material balance constraints:

$$C + b^\eta + \sum_i b^{ki} = Y. \tag{17.4}$$

To avoid the appearance of prejudging decentralization issues, we return initially to the "command economy" framework of Chapter 3. Consequently, we study the welfare problem

$$\max W[U^1(\eta^1, c^1), \dots, U^N(\eta^N, c^N)] \tag{17.5}$$

subject to

$$\sum_h c^h + b^\eta + \sum_i b^{ki} = Y,$$

$$\sum_h \eta_s^h = \eta_s, \quad \text{each } s,$$

$$\eta_s = f^{\eta s}\left[b_s^\eta, \sum_{i \leq s} k_i \zeta(s, i)\right], \quad \text{all } s,$$

$$k_i = f^{ki}(b^{ki}), \quad \text{all } i,$$

together with nonnegativity constraints. Note that our formulation is general enough to encompass either the overlapping-generations or the dynasty view of the family (household life-spans are implicitly specified by the collection of dated arguments that "matter" in the utility function). Indeed, none of the results to be discussed turn on this distinction.

However, in connection with this last remark, it will be important to consider nonnegativity constraints since they are expected to be binding for some variables of our problem (e.g., households will not consume outside their lifetimes). Although we will not write these into the problem each time, we will incorporate them in stating necessary conditions for optimality.

17.2   Peak-load phase

It is useful for a variety of reasons to break our welfare problem down into two stages. In the first stage, capacity choices are thought of as fixed and all flow variables are chosen optimally as functions of capacity. In the second stage, capacity is chosen optimally. We think of the first-stage problem as the peak-load phase since it involves allocating the use of fixed capacity over periods of potential "peak" and "off-peak" demand.

The first-stage problem is exactly the same in form as (17.5) except that we think of the capacity variables k as temporarily fixed. This conditional optimization then defines welfare as a function of the vector k. We represent this function by $Z(k)$.

Our main reason for introducing this two-stage procedure is that the peak-load subproblem isolates the convex part of our overall problem. Therefore, the Lagrangian necessary conditions are also sufficient for an optimum, conditional on capacity levels. Thus, optimal planning at this stage can be characterized by a decentralization in terms of pseudoprices and cost functions.[4] The reader is reminded that pseudoprices represent present value (as of some fixed initial date) here. We will convert to a corresponding current-value form later.

Retaining continuity with past practice, we use a vector P for multipliers on material balance constraints and Ω for the multiplier on public services. We think of solving our planning problem by maximizing a Lagrangian function subject to production constraints and adjusting the P's and Ω's to achieve material balance in goods and services. At this point (with capacity levels fixed), our problem is fully convex so this procedure is guaranteed to converge to the optimum allocation.

As in Chapter 3, the maximization problem breaks down into a series of independent subproblems. Let us look first at subproblems involving choices of inputs. Since pseudocosts enter negatively in the Lagrangian, these take the form of cost minimization. For the case of services, date s, the planner seeks to

---

[4] Much of the early work on these rules was done by french economists at Electricite de France. See Dreze (1964) or Nelson (1964).

$$\min_{b_s} P_s b_s \tag{17.6}$$

subject to

$$\eta_s = f^{\eta s}[b_s, K_s],$$

where K_s is aggregate capacity available at s. Naturally, we derive from this the pseudocompetitive rule that factors should be hired until pseudo-price equals pseudovalue of marginal product. Also, the solution defines an indirect cost function: $\Gamma^{\eta s}(\eta_s, K_s, P_s)$.

Capacity production generates an exactly analogous cost minimization problem leading to indirect cost functions that we label $\Gamma^{ki}(k_i, P)$. Now (with multipliers still thought of as fixed), the residual choice problem may be stated as[5]

$$\max_{c, \eta} W[U^1(\eta^1, c^1), \ldots, U^N(\eta^N, c^N)] - P \sum_h c^h - \Omega \sum_h \eta^h$$

$$+ \Omega\eta - \sum_s \Gamma^{\eta s}(\eta_s, K_s, P_s) - \sum_i \Gamma^{ki}(k_i, P) \tag{17.7}$$

subject only to nonnegativity constraints.

Choice of private consumption levels generates the pseudodecentralization conditions

$$\frac{\partial W}{\partial U^h} \nabla_\eta U^h \le \Omega, \qquad \left[\frac{\partial W}{\partial U^h} \nabla_\eta U^h\right]\eta^h = \Omega\eta^h, \quad \text{all } h, \tag{17.8}$$

$$\frac{\partial W}{\partial U^h} \nabla_c U^h \le P, \qquad \left[\frac{\partial W}{\partial U^h} \nabla_c U^h\right]c'^h = Pc'^h, \quad \text{all } h, \tag{17.9}$$

whereas choice of overall service level leads to the prescription of marginal-cost pseudopricing[6]:

$$\Omega_s = \frac{\partial \Gamma^{\eta s}(\eta_s, K_s, P_s)}{\partial \eta}. \tag{17.10}$$

Now, drawing on arguments from Chapters 4 and 5, we claim that optimal allocation in the peak-load phase can be generated through an actual market decentralization assuming that competitive behavior can be assured. The situation here is exactly analogous to the pollution tickets scheme discussed in Chapter 4 (where the aggregate pollution level played the role of the fixed component); given that capacity levels are chosen

---

[5] We use the fact here that optimization can be performed in any desired sequence when problems are fully convex.

[6] The principle of marginal-cost pricing in planned economies goes back at least as far as Lange (1936) and Lerner (1944). The model presented here is closest in spirit to that of Panzar–Willig (1976).

independently, optimal allocation of other variables can be left to the market. Pseudoprices become market prices, and the Lagrangian adjustment process is handled by market-clearing price adjustments.

In our decentralization, households buy goods and public services on competitive markets. The public enterprise sells services to consumers, buys variable inputs from the market, and (for given capacity levels) maximizes profits on the production of services. In addition, it is always instructed to minimize the cost of whatever capacity levels are chosen. Lump-sum redistributions may be required to optimize on the income distribution and (possibly) finance a public enterprise deficit. Naturally, many of the incentive problems that we took up earlier in the book are relevant here as well, but we will not address them further. Analysis of the peak-load problem shifts to the following questions: (1) What are the operational interpretations and implications of marginal cost pricing? (2) Can equilibrium prices and associated revenues be used as guides to determine optimal-capacity levels?

We can begin to answer both these questions by decomposing the service charges into two parts, one covering operating costs and the remainder serving as a capital (or depreciation) fund. The decomposition is accomplished using Euler's theorem.[7] Since we assumed that services were produced under conditions of constant returns to scale, the associated cost function is homogeneous of degree 1[8] so Euler's theorem implies

$$\Gamma^{\eta s} = \eta^s \frac{\partial \Gamma^{\eta s}}{\partial \eta} + K_s \frac{\partial \Gamma^{\eta s}}{\partial K}. \tag{17.11}$$

Consequently, we can write revenues as

$$\Omega_s \eta_s = \eta_s \frac{\partial \Gamma^{\eta s}}{\partial \eta} = \Gamma^{\eta s} - K_s \frac{\partial \Gamma^{\eta s}}{\partial K}. \tag{17.12}$$

We see that revenue from service charges at each date covers variable cost of services provided at that date *plus* a term related to the marginal contribution of capacity (naturally, we expect $\partial \Gamma / \partial k$ to be negative). This term constitutes our *capital fund,* and we label it $\Psi_s(K)$. Sometimes it will be convenient to break the fund down into components attributable to separate investment projects. For project j,

$$\Psi_s(\zeta(j,s)k_j) = \zeta(j,s)k_j \frac{\partial \Gamma^{\eta s}}{\partial K}. \tag{17.13}$$

---

[7] See Intriligator (1971) for a derivation and interpretation of this theorem. Also, refer to Section 5.2 for a related discussion.

[8] See Diewert (1979) for a justification of this statement. Note that were we to assume nonconstant returns to scale in the production of services, the decomposition would lead only to an inequality.

We will see momentarily the sense in which our capital fund signals the desirability of extra investment.

The most significant operational feature of the peak-load price is its variability over time while capacity is fixed. Only if marginal cost is independent of service level (or if demand is perfectly elastic) would we expect to see a constant price. But examining (17.11), we see that marginal cost is constant only if capacity contributes nothing at the margin; otherwise, marginal cost must be above average cost and, hence, rising.

The early literature focused on a special case where marginal operating costs were constant up until the point where "capacity" is reached, at which point they become infinite. Then peak-load pricing takes the simple form: Charge the constant marginal operating cost as long as the consequent demand remains below capacity; otherwise, charge whatever price is necessary to bring demand down to capacity. Note that as long as demand remains below capacity, price is constant, and only operating costs are covered by revenues. During such periods, capacity is being treated as if it were perfectly nonrivalrous (recall the treatment of uncrowded commons). However, this situation surely should not prevail in all periods; if it did, we could (and should) lower capacity without losing anything in production. Viewed this way, we see that the correct capacity level should be related to the amount of money collected in our capital funds.

Even when capacity is not so rigidly constraining, optimal pricing will have the effect of holding down service levels during periods of highest demand and spreading the load toward periods of lower demand (using price differential as an incentive).

17.3   Optimal capacity for single project

We now think of the planners as choosing capacity levels in the context of the mixed economy where everything else is decentralized. Thus, we can make use of the marginal welfare measures developed in Chapter 9. Here, the role of project level α is played by capacity built at a particular date. The relevant measure (9.12) simplifies greatly since we are making all the assumptions of first best: There will be no terms associated with distribution, indirect taxation, or noncompetitive behavior. Further, all consumption goods are sold on private markets so there is no collective consumption good (g). Consequently, all that is left are terms for marginal project cost, and we have

$$\frac{\partial Z}{\partial k_j} = -\sum_{s>j} \frac{\partial \Gamma^{\eta s}}{\partial K} \zeta(j,s) - \frac{\partial \Gamma^{kj}}{\partial k}. \tag{17.14}$$

Now, a necessary condition for optimal-capacity choice requires that the right side of (17.14) be zero (unless k_j is itself zero). Of course, our new problem is not concave so necessary conditions are inadequate to characterize the optimum. Nonetheless, we begin by examining these conditions, leaving discussions of sufficiency until later. Multiplying this necessary condition by k_j and substituting from (17.13) yields

$$\sum_{s>j} \Psi_s(\zeta(j,s)k_j) = \frac{\partial \Gamma^{kj}}{\partial k} k_j. \tag{17.15}$$

Thus, we see that the capital fund generated by a particular project over its lifetime should just equal the size of the project times its marginal construction cost. So the capital funds do indeed signal the desirability of investment; if we build too little capacity, the capital funds will become too large, indicating that added capacity would have been valued in excess of its marginal construction cost. Notice that this rule (and indeed virtually everything we have said so far) applies whether or not there is a recursive structure. In particular, it applies to the case of a single project. For that case, at least, it takes us about as far as we can go without collecting information on consumer willingness to pay.

Unfortunately, this rule is not very powerful when it comes to practical decision making. For one thing, the "price signals" come at the wrong time (after the project is built), requiring forecasts into the distant future for implementation. Furthermore, even assuming that we know how to estimate service prices and demands in the indefinite future, (17.15) cannot even tell us for sure whether the project should be constructed at all. The only case in which we could be sure would be one in which our decentralization could be extended to a *full* competitive equilibrium. This would require that the public enterprise cover *all* costs. Examining (17.15) closely, we see that this condition is unlikely to be met under current assumptions. If the construction project exhibits increasing returns to scale in the range of potential demand, we find that marginal construction cost is below average cost; consequently, the capital fund fails to cover all capital costs, and our decentralization must make up the difference through the use of lump-sum taxes.

Such an essential nonconvexity generates indeterminacies that cannot be resolved through marginal analysis, as we have seen at various points in previous chapters. Just to remind the reader of the nature of this problem, we sketch a stylized version of its nature here. Figure 17.1 depicts three possible profiles of welfare as a function of project size. Our investment rule picks out *any* point on these graphs where the function is locally flat. Comparing the first two cases, we see that the project may or

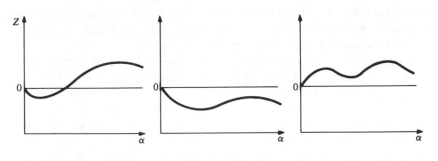

Figure 17.1

may not be desirable; we could only tell by using a surplus measure to compare the welfare of the best project with that of the status quo. Further, looking at the third case, we see that there may be indeterminacy *even* when we can be sure that some version of the project should be constructed. To effectively evaluate a single project, we would have to examine full consumer surplus as a function of project size.[9]

17.4   Optimal timing of recursive investments

When investments are repetitive in nature, we may be able to resolve some of the indeterminacy noted. Further, we may be able to collect some of the necessary surplus information as we go along. Of course, in saying that investments are repetitive, we are implying that one project is more than desirable. It must be that demand is known to eventually exceed the scale of a single project. Once this is known, the timing of the next investment becomes a new decision variable. Furthermore, the presence of this future investment date generates an element of reversibility into the process that enables us to isolate decision rules from information about the indefinite future.

To explore these ideas, we want to do some analysis on the timing of investment. Since the relevant analysis is quite cumbersome in discrete time, we pass to a continuous-time formulation. Unfortunately, this choice necessitates a number of simplifying assumptions in order to achieve a tractable analysis. Moreover, the full power of recursive analysis is not exploited unless further assumptions are made concerning the relative stationarity of demand over time. Here, we present the "cleanest" possible analysis based on these somewhat severe assumptions. We have shown

[9] The issue here is nicely exposited in Malinvaud (1972).

elsewhere (Starrett, 1979a) that results reported in what follows have approximate analogs when the assumptions are relaxed, but the arguments are convoluted and will not be repeated here.

When a construction date is postponed, capacity at that date changes by a discrete amount. Consequently, we can no longer think of project changes as strictly first order and must pass to a general surplus representation of welfare. We adopt the framework of Section 16.4 and assume further that projects under consideration have no differential effect on private profits (so that corresponding terms can be ignored). Now we switch to a continuous-time formulation; sums become integrals and prices become functions on the time dimension. Since we cannot deal effectively with functions as arguments, we make one further separability assumption on the structure of demand; namely, service demand depends only on current service price.

We also take this opportunity to change from a present-value to a current-value representation; that is, we think of all prices, incomes, and cost functions as measured in current values and discount appropriately to get present values. Our representation takes the form[10]

$$Z(K) = \int_s \left[\int_{\Omega_s(K)}^{\Omega^o} \eta_s(x)\, dx + \Omega_s(K)\, \eta_s(\Omega(K)) - \Gamma^{\eta s}(\eta_s(\Omega(K)), K_s) \right]$$

$$\times \exp\left(-\int^s r_x\, dx \right) ds - \sum_i \Gamma^{ki}(k_i) \exp\left(-\int^i r_x\, dx \right). \qquad (17.16)$$

Our separability assumptions have the following important consequence: the bracketed term in (17.16) depends on project levels only through capacity at date s. To see this, observe that the marginal-cost pricing rule together with the demand relation $\eta_s = \eta_s(\Omega_s)$ determine both η_s and Ω_s as functions of s and K_s only. We label the terms in square brackets $V(s, K_s)$ and note that $\partial V / \partial K_s = -\partial \Gamma^{\eta s} / \partial K_s$ (all other terms in this derivative cancel when we make use of first-order conditions and the fundamental theorem of the calculus). The function $V(\cdot)$ can be thought of as representing the indirect welfare derived from having capacity K in place at date s.

How can we take best advantage of the recursive structure in determining an optimal investment plan? Intuitively, we would like to use information gained between construction dates to determine the date and size of the next construction. Toward this end, let us consider some variations in the capacity program that affect only capacity levels between a pair of

---

[10] Since project services are sold on the market, net cost now includes a term representing this revenue $[\Omega_s(K)\eta_s(K)]$. Note also that we do not include any correction for income effect on service demand.

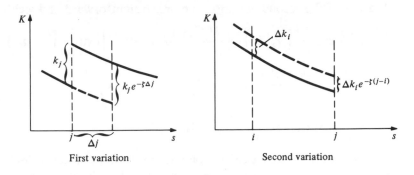

Figure 17.2

construction dates (we label the first construction date i and its successor j). In the absence of depreciation, we can easily construct such variations. We either postpone a construction date slightly (without changing construction size) or we build a little less at date i and correspondingly more at date j.

Due to vintage effects, such variations are generally not possible in the presence of depreciation unless the rate of depreciation is independent of vintage, that is, unless depreciation is exponential. Under that assumption, we can exactly compensate for a later construction date by building a little less (so that capacity from then on will be unchanged). Required capacity changes for the two variations above are (where ζ is the constant rate of depreciation):

First variation: $dk_j/dj = -\zeta k_j$;
Second variation: $dk_j/dk_i = -e^{-\zeta(j-i)}$.

Both variations now affect the economy only during the period between construction dates (we call this time interval an *investment cycle*). It is helpful to visualize these variations with the help of Figure 17.2.

Since neither of these variations can improve welfare given an optimal plan, each will contribute a necessary condition for optimality; and these conditions will involve economic information taken only within the corresponding investment cycle. We have to be a little careful in evaluating the first of these, since capacity changes discretely at date j. However, the derivative of Z turns out to be continuous nonetheless,[11] and we derive the necessary condition:

$$V(j, K_j) - V(j, K_j - k_j) = r_j \Gamma^{kj}(k_j) + \zeta k_j \frac{d\Gamma^{kj}}{dk}(k_j). \qquad (17.17)$$

---

[11] See Starrett (1978) for a rigorous demonstration.

Analysis of the second variation is more straightforward and yields

$$
\frac{d\Gamma^{ki}(k_i)}{dk}\exp\left(-\int_i r_x\,dx\right)-\left[\frac{d\Gamma^{kj}(k_j)}{dk}K_ie^{-\zeta(j-i)}\right]\exp\left(-\int^j r_x\,dx\right)
$$

$$
=\int_{s=i}^{j}\left[\frac{\partial V(s,K_s)}{\partial K}K_ie^{-\zeta(s-i)}\right]\exp\left(-\int^s r_x\,dx\right)ds
$$

$$
\equiv\int_{s=i}^{j}\Psi_s(K_s)\exp\left(-\int^s r_x\,dx\right)ds.
\tag{17.18}
$$

What sort of guidance can the planner get from these new rules? Well, assuming that i and k_i were chosen correctly, they should serve to determine j and k_j. Further, the second rule involves information that is completely observable from our decentralization since the right side represents additions to the capital fund over the entire investment cycle. This fund reflects the benefits of added capacity in the interval and should be balanced against marginal construction costs in an optimal plan.[12]

Generally, this rule cannot determine either k_j or j but rather specifies a relationship between them. Delaying j generates larger and larger capital funds, but according to the second rule, this might be justified by a large difference in marginal costs. Since marginal construction cost falls in capacity built (increasing returns to scale), later construction dates might be associated with larger construction projects. We need further information to pin things down, but presumably we can get it from the first rule.

The first rule is not so clearly "operational" since it involves a surplus term associated with adding lumpy capacity at date j. However, we may be able to estimate this term from information revealed by demand for services over the investment cycle. We can do this to the extent that (a) effective capacity during the cycle covered the interval (K_j-k_j, K_j) and (b) demand exhibits some regularity properties over the interval so that demand revealed during the interval can be used to infer surplus at the end of the interval.

Here, we look at one special case where an exact correspondence can be found, namely, where demand functions and cost functions are time stationary so that $V(s,K)$ is independent of s. In that case, our surplus term can be related to the accumulated capital fund as follows. First, write surplus as the integral of its differential:

$$
V(K_j)-V(K_j-k_j)=\int_{K_j-k_j}^{K_j}\frac{dV(K)}{dK}\,dk.
\tag{17.19}
$$

---

[12] Our second rule actually is valid whether or not we make the special assumptions of this section, as long as we know that there are two separate dates at which some positive investment will be desirable. See Starrett (1979a) for details.

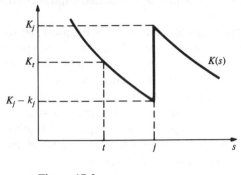

Figure 17.3

Now, $dV(K)/dK$ can be inferred from market information if we can find some period in the past when K was the available capacity. Thus, for every K in the interval $(K_j - k_j, K_j)$, search for a date t when $K_t = K$ (see Figure 17.3). Given exponential depreciation and a sufficiently long period since the last investment, this date can be found by solving the equation

$$K = K_i e^{-\zeta(t-i)}. \tag{17.20}$$

We use this equation to implicitly define $t = t(K)$; note that $t(K_j - k_j) = j$ and

$$\frac{dK}{dt} = -\zeta K_i e^{-\zeta(t-i)}. \tag{17.21}$$

Making this change of variable enables us to write the surplus term as

$$V(K_j) - V(K_j - k_j) = \zeta \int_{t(K_j)}^{j} \frac{dV(K_s)}{dK} K_i e^{-\zeta(s-i)}\, ds$$

$$= \zeta \int_{t(K_j)}^{j} \Psi_s(K_s)\, ds. \tag{17.22}$$

Thus, when the investment cycle is sufficiently long, the surplus lost by postponing our construction date a little can be computed from demand information revealed over the previous cycle, and in fact, the first rule (17.17) gives us an independent relationship between the capital funds and construction costs:

$$\int_{t(K_j)}^{j} \Psi_s(K_s)\, ds = \frac{r_j}{\zeta} \Gamma^{kj}(k_j) + k_j \frac{d\Gamma^{kj}}{dk}(k_j). \tag{17.23}$$

Notice that the relevant capital fund here involves no interest accumulation. That is, at date j it represents the sum (integral) of all revenues received over the preceding cycle. If such monies are deposited in an interest-bearing account (as they should be), the actual capital fund will be correspondingly larger.

The first rule has some surprising implications. For example, let us see what it tells us about the time profile of the capital policy. Suppose we conjecture that the optimal policy is stationary, meaning that effective capacity is constant across adjacent investment dates. But then, $t(K_j) = i$, and the time interval in (17.23) is exactly the previous investment cycle. We conclude that the capital fund accumulated over our cycle would more than cover the valuation of the next project at marginal cost *plus* r/δ times its *total* cost. Clearly, if $r > \delta$, excess revenues cover both measures of cost, and r/δ would have to be quite small before the excess revenues would fail to cover at least total cost. We are forced to conclude that even though no individual project covers all its capital costs (17.15), excess revenues collected over each cycle more than cover the cost of the next construction.

Of course, this conclusion fails if optimal capacity is growing over time (so that $K_j > K_i$); then, $t(K_j) < i$, and money we were counting on collecting in the interval $[t(K_j), i]$ is not available in the actual capital fund. Thus, the actual capital fund may not cover all costs. Furthermore, demand over this interval is not revealed by the market and will have to be estimated by other means.

There is at least one other economic context in which the first rule can be made operational, namely, when demand grows at a constant rate (with or without geometric depreciation of capacity). In this case, if we measure *effective capacity* as capacity per "unit" of demand, effective capacity will vary over the investment cycle, and the demand function thus revealed will identify appropriate surplus at the new construction date. The resulting construction rules are similar to what we have already seen, although the growth rate does play a role. For details, see Starrett (1978).

Even if we could observe necessary demands, these rules still would be insufficient to completely determine optimal policy. *If* we knew the correct initial capacity, they would enable us to solve recursively forward for all future investments. But it is not clear how we should get started. Unfortunately, there is no way around this difficulty without contemplating information about the indefinite future. The problem here is analogous to that encountered with the myopic rule in capital theory with reversible investment.[13] The direction of investment is effectively reversible at the next construction date in our recursive model, so a modified myopic rule stipulates that we can make correct decisions using information from the investment cycle only. However, as in the classical case, there

---

[13] See Arrow–Kurz (1970) for background discussion of this topic.

will be an indeterminacy in the boundary conditions. Ultimately, the general profile of investments in this project must depend on social time preference as well as on future demands for the project's outputs relative to other things.

Epilog

The reader will note that I do not reach any final conclusion or provide a neat summary in this book. This choice is deliberate and is based on my belief that the subject cannot be summed up in any useful way. On the one hand, I find myself at this point somewhat overwhelmed by the sheer volume of material in the theory of public economics. Indeed, I am a little embarrassed when I realize how many subjects have been ignored or at best treated in a cursory manner in this book. On the other hand, I am somewhat discouraged at the prospect of doing the sort of good applied project analysis that I have tried to espouse. The kind of information necessary to evaluate demands for collective goods, correctly incorporate equity considerations, measure unemployment benefits, or compute risk discount factors is very difficult to come by even in the world of small projects much less the general framework of Part IV. To the extent that I set out to provide practical methods, I have promised more than I can deliver.

Although it seems unreasonable to expect operational cookbook recipes for project analysis anytime soon, there are important practical lessons to be learned from the modern theory surveyed here. In particular, this theory can help us identify faulty methods and decisions; partly for this reason, I spent a lot of time explaining what *not* to do and identifying biases that will result from incorrect procedures. It is very important to reject the view that since welfare measurement is still quite imprecise, we may as well leave public decision making to the politicians. To do so invites mistakes that are costly on a scale that dwarfs any possible measurement error.

References

Akerlof, G. (1970): "The Market for 'Lemons': Qualitative Uncertainty and the Market Mechanism," *QJE,* 84; 488–500.

Aoki, M. (1970): "A Note on Marshallian Process Under Increasing Returns," *QJE,* 84; 100–12.

Anderson, R. Jr. and T. Crocker (1971): "Air Pollution and Residential Property Values," *Urban Studies,* 8; 171–80.

(1972): "Air Pollution and Property Values: A Reply," *ReSTAT,* 54; 470–3.

Arnott, R. (1979): "Optimal City Size in a Spatial Economy," *JUE,* 6; 65–89.

Arnott, R. and J. Stiglitz (1979): "Aggregate Land Rents, Expenditure on Public Goods, and Optimal City Size," *QJE,* 93; 471–500.

Arrow, K. (1950): *Social Choice and Individual Values,* New York: Wiley.

(1951): "An Extension of the Classical Theorems of Welfare Economics," in *Proceedings of the Second Berkeley Symposium on Mathematical Statistics and Probability,* Berkeley: University of California Press.

(1953): "Le Role des Valeurs Boursieres pour la Repartition la Meilleure des Risques," *Econometrica,* 11; 41–7.

(1965): *Aspects of the Theory of Risk Bearing,* Helsinki: Yrjo Jahnssonin Saatio.

(1966): "Discounting and Public Investment Criteria," in *Water Research* (A. Kneese and S. Smith, eds.), Baltimore: Johns Hopkins, 13–32.

(1970a): *Essays in the Theory of Risk-Bearing,* Amsterdam: North-Holland.

(1970b): "The Organization of Economic Activity: Issues Pertinent to the Choice of Market versus Non-Market Allocation," in *Public Expenditure and Policy Analysis* (R. Haveman and J. Margolis, eds.), Chicago: Markham, 59–73.

Arrow, K. and A. Enthoven (1961): "Quasi-Concave Programming," *Econometrica,* 29; 779–800.

Arrow, K. and F. Hahn (1970): *General Competitive Analysis,* San Francisco: Holden Day.

Arrow, K. and M. Kurz (1970): *Public Investment, the Rate of Return and Optimal Fiscal Policy,* Baltimore: Johns Hopkins.

Arrow, K. and R. Lind (1970): "Uncertainty and the Evaluation of Public Investment Decisions," *AER,* 60; 364–78.

Atkinson, A. and N. Stern (1974): "Pigou, Taxation and Public Goods," *ReSTUD,* 41; 119–28.

Atkinson, A. and J. Stiglitz (1972): "The Structure of Indirect Taxation and Economic Efficiency," *JPubE,* 1; 97–119.

(1980): *Lectures on Public Economics,* New York: McGraw-Hill.

Auerbach, A. (1982): "The Theory of Excess Burden and Optimal Taxation," NBER Working Paper No. 1025, Cambridge, MA.

Auerbach, A. and M. King (1983): "Taxation, Portfolio Choice and Debt–Equity Ratios, A General Equilibrium Model," *QJE,* 98; 587–610.

Aumann, R. (1966): "Existence of Competitive Equilibria in Markets with a Continuum of Traders," *Econometrica,* 34; 1–17.

Balasko, Y. (1978): "Economic Equilibrium and Catastrophe Theory: An Introduction," *Econometrica,* 46; 557–69.

Barro, R. (1974): "Are Government Bonds Net Wealth?" *JPE,* 82; 1095–1118.

Barro, R. and H. Grossman (1976): *Money, Employment and Inflation,* London: Cambridge University Press.

Bator, F. (1958): "Anatomy of Market Failure," *QJE,* 72; 351–79.

Baumol, W. (1967): *Business Behavior,* New York: Harcourt, Brace & World.

(1968): "On the Social Rate of Discount," *AER,* 58; 788–802.

Baumol, W. and D. Bradford (1970): "Optimal Departures from Marginal Cost Pricing," *AER,* 60; 265–83.

Baumol, W. and W. Oates (1975): *The Theory of Environmental Policy,* Englewood Cliffs, NJ: Prentice-Hall.

Beck, J. (1983): "Tax Competition, Uniform Assessment, and the Benefit Principle," *JUE,* 13; 127–46.

Beckmann, M. (1969): "On the Distribution of Urban Rent and Residential Density," *JET,* 1; 60–7.

Bellman, R. (1957): *Dynamic Programming,* Princeton: Princeton University Press.

Benassy, J. (1977): "On Quantity Signals and the Foundations of Effective Demand Theory," *Scand. JEcon,* 79; 147–68.

Berge, C. (1963): *Topological Spaces,* London: Oliver and Boyd.

Berglas, E. (1976): "Distribution of Tastes and Skills and the Provision of Local Public Goods," *JPubE,* 6; 409–23.

(1982): "User Charges, Local Public Services, and Taxation of Land Rents," *Public Finance,* 37; 178–88.

Berglas, E. and D. Pines (1981): "Clubs, Local Public Goods, and Transportation Models: A Synthesis," *JPubE,* 15; 141–62.

Bergstrom, T. and R. Goodman (1973): "Private Demands for Public Goods," *AER,* 63; 280–96.

Bergstrom, T., L. Blume, and H. Varian (1986): "On the Private Provision of Public Goods," *JPubE,* 29; 25–9.

Berliant, M. (1985): "Equilibrium Models with Land: A Criticism and an Alternative," *Regional Science and Urban Economics,* 15; 325–40.

Bernheim, D. and K. Bagwell (1986): "Is Everything Neutral?" NBER Discussion Paper No. 2086, Stanford University.

Bewley, T. (1981): "A Critique of Tiebout's Theory of Local Public Expenditures," *Econometrica,* 49; 713–40.

Black, D. (1958): *The Theory of Committees and Elections,* Cambridge: Cambridge University Press.

Bloom, H., H. Ladd, and J. Yinger (1983): "Are Property Taxes Capitalized into House Values?" in *Local Provision of Public Services: The Tiebout Model after Twenty-Five Years* (G. Zodrow, ed.), New York: Academic, 145–63.

Boiteux, M. (1951): "Le Revenue Distruable et les Pertes Economique," *Econometrica,* 19; 112–33.

(1971): "On the Management of Public Monopolies Subject to Budgetary Constraints," *JET,* 3; 219–40.

Bowen, H. (1943): "The Interpretation of Voting in the Allocation of Economic Resources," *QJE,* 58; 27–48.

Bradford, D. (1975): "Constraints on Government Investment Opportunities and the Choice of the Discount Rate," *AER,* 65; 887–99.

Bradford, D. and G. Hildenbrandt (1977): "Observable Preferences for Public Goods," *JPubE,* 8; 111–31.

Bradford, D. and W. Oates (1971): "The Analysis of Revenue Sharing in a New Approach to Collective Fiscal Decisions," *QJE,* 85; 416–39.

Brown, D. and G. Heal (1980): "Two Part Tariffs, Marginal Cost Pricing and Increasing Returns in a General Equilibrium Model," *JPubE,* 13; 25–49.

Brown, J. and H. Rosen (1982): "On the Estimation of Structural Hedonic Price Models," *Econometrica,* 50; 765–8.

Brueckner, J. (1983): "Property Value Maximization and Public Sector Efficiency," *JUE,* 14; 1–16.

Buchanan, J. (1965): "An Economic Theory of Clubs," *Economica,* 33; 1–14.

(1977): *Freedom in Constitutional Contract,* College Station: Texas A&M Press.

Buchanan, J. and C. Goetz (1972): "Efficiency Limits of Fiscal Mobility: An Assessment of the Tiebout Model," *JPubE,* 1; 25–43.

Burbridge, J. (1983): "Government Debt in an Overlapping Generations Model with Bequests and Gifts," *AER,* 73; 222–7.

Cass, D. (1972): "On Capital Overaccumulation in the Aggregative Neoclassical Model of Economic Growth," *JET,* 4; 200–23.

Chenery, H. and P. Clark (1959): *Interindustry Economics,* New York: Wiley.

Chipman, J. and J. Moore (1977): "The Scope of Consumer's Surplus Arguments," in *Evolution, Welfare and Time in Economics* (A. Tang, F. Westfield, and J. Worley, eds.), Lexington, MA: Lexington Books.

(1980): "Compensating Variation, Consumer's Surplus, and Welfare," *AER,* 70; 933–49.

Clarke, E. (1971): "Multipart Pricing of Public Goods," *Public Choice,* 11; 17–33.

Coase, R. (1960): "On the Problem of Social Cost," *Journal of Law and Economics,* 3; 1–44.

Courant, P., E. Gramlich, and D. Rubenfeld (1979): "The Stimulative Effects of Intergovernmental Grants: Or Why Money Sticks Where It Hits," in *Fiscal Federalism and Grants-in-Aid* (P. Mieszkowski and W. Oakland, eds.), Washington DC: Urban Institute, 5–21.

Dasgupta, P. and J. Stiglitz (1972): "On Optimal Taxation and Public Production," *ReSTUD,* 39; 87–103.

(1974): "Benefit–Cost Analysis and Trade Policies," *JPE,* 82; 1–33.

Dasgupta, P., P. Hammond, and E. Maskin (1979): "The Implementation of Social Choice Rules," *ReSTUD,* 46; 185–216.

Dasgupta, P., S. Marglin, and A. Sen (1972): *Guidelines for Project Evaluation,* New York: United Nations.

d'Asprement, C. and L. Gerard-Varet (1979): "Incentives and Incomplete Information," *JPubE,* 11; 25–45.

Davis, O. and A. Whinston (1962): "Externalities, Welfare, and the Theory of Games, *JPE,* 70; 241–62.

Davis, O., M. de Groot, and M. Hinich (1972): "Social Preference Orderings and Majority Rule," *Econometrica,* 40; 147–57.

Deaton, A. (1981): "Optimal Taxes and the Structure of Preferences," *Econometrica,* 49; 1245–60.

Debreu, G. (1951): "The Coefficient of Resource Utilization," *Econometrica,* 19; 273–92.

(1954): "Valuation Equilibrium and Pareto Optimum," *Proceedings of the National Academy of Sciences,* 40; 588–92.

(1976): "Regular Differentiable Economics," *AER,* 66; 280–7.

de Meza, D. and J. Gould (1985): "Free Access vs. Private Ownership: A Comparison," *JET,* 36; 387–91.

Diamond, P. (1965): "National Debt in a Neoclassical Growth Model," *AER,* 55; 1125–50.

(1967): "The Role of the Stock Market in a General Equilibrium Model with Technological Uncertainty," *AER,* 57; 759–73.

(1975): "A Many-Person Ramsey Tax Rule," *JPubE,* 4; 335–42.

Diamond, P. and D. McFadden (1974): "Some Uses of the Expenditure Function in Public Finance," *JPubE,* 3; 3–21.

Diamond, P. and J. Mirrlees (1971): "Optimal Taxation and Public Production I: Production Efficiency and II: Tax Rules," *AER,* 61; 8–27, 261–78.

(1973): "Aggregate Production with Consumption Externalities," *QJE,* 87; 1–24.

Dierker, E. (1982): "Regular Economies," in *Handbook of Mathematical Economics,* Vol. II (K. Arrow and M. Intriligator, eds.), Amsterdam: North-Holland, 795–830.

Diewert, E. (1979): "Duality Approaches to Microeconomic Theory," in *Handbook of Mathematical Economics* (K. Arrow and M. Intriligator, eds.), Amsterdam: North-Holland, 535–600.

(1981): "The Measurement of Deadweight Loss Revisited," *Econometrica,* 49; 1225–44.

Dixit, A. (1970): "On the Optimum Structure of Commodity Taxes," *AER,* 60; 295–301.

(1976): "Public Finance in a Keynesian Temporary Equilibrium," *JET,* 12; 242–58.

Dixit, A., J. Mirrlees, and N. Stern (1975): "Optimal Saving with Economies of Scale," *ReSTUD,* 42; 303–26.

Dorfman, R., P. Samuelson, and R. Solow (1958): *Linear Programming and Economic Analysis,* New York: McGraw-Hill.

Dreze, J. (1964): "Some Postwar Contributions of French Economists to Theory and Public Policy," *AER,* 54 (Supplement).

   (1974): "Investment under Private Ownership: Optimality, Equilibrium and Stability," in *Allocation under Uncertainty: Equilibrium and Optimality,* New York: Macmillan, chapter 9.

Dreze, J. and D. de la Vallé Poussin (1971): "A Tatonnement Process for Public Goods," *ReSTUD,* 38; 133–50.

Dreze, J. and F. Modigliani (1972): "Consumption Decisions Under Uncertainty," *JET,* 5; 308–35.

Duffie, D. and W. Shafer (1986): "Equilibrium in Incomplete Markets: II Generic Existence in Stochastic Economies," *Journal of Mathematical Economics,* 15; 199–216.

Dunford, N. and J. Schwartz (1968): *Linear Operators, Part I,* New York: Wiley.

Ellickson, B. (1973): "A Generalization of the Pure Theory of Public Goods," *AER,* 63; 417–32.

Epple, D., R. Filimon, and T. Romer (1983): "Housing, Voting, and Moving: Equilibrium in a Model of Local Public Goods with Multiple Jurisdictions," *Research in Urban Economics,* 3; 59–90.

Feldstein, M. (1972): "Distributional Equity and the Optimal Structure of Public Prices," *AER,* 62; 32–6.

   (1975): "Wealth Neutrality and Local Choice in Public Education," *AER,* 65; 75–89.

Ferguson, J. (1964): *Public Debt and Future Generations.* Chapel Hill: University of North Carolina Press.

Fishburn, P. (1970): *Utility Theory for Decision Making,* New York: Wiley.

Flatters, F., V. Henderson, and P. Meiszkowski (1974): "Public Goods, Efficiency and Regional Fiscal Equalization," *JPubE,* 3; 99–112.

Foley, D. (1967): "Resource Allocation and the Public Sector," *Yale Economic Essays,* 7; 43–98.

Foster, E. and H. Sonnenschein (1970): "Price Distortion and Economic Welfare," *Econometrica,* 38; 66–72.

Freeman, A. (1979): *The Benefits of Environmental Improvement,* Baltimore: Johns Hopkins Press.

Friedman, M. (1962): *Capitalism and Freedom,* Chicago: University of Chicago Press.

Galbraith, J. (1967): *The New Industrial State,* New York: Houghton Mifflin.

Geanakoplos, J. and H. Polemarchakis (1986): "Existence, Regularity and Constrained Suboptimality of Competitive Allocations when the Asset Market Is Incomplete," in *Essays in Honor of Kenneth J. Arrow,* Vol. III (W. Heller, R. Starr, and D. Starrett, eds.), London: Cambridge University Press, 65–96.

George, H. (1955): *Progress and Poverty,* New York: Robert Schalkenbach Foundation.

Gibbard, A. (1973): "Manipulation of Voting Schemes: A General Result," *Econometrica,* 41; 587–601.

Goldstein, G. and M. Pauly (1981): "Tiebout Bias on the Demand for Local Goods," *JPubE,* 16; 131–44.

Goode, R. (1976): *The Individual Income Tax,* Washington, DC: Brookings.

Gordon, R. (1983): "An Optimal Taxation Approach to Fiscal Federalism," *QJE,* 98; 567–86.

Green, J. and W. Heller (1982): "Mathematical Analysis and Convexity with Applications to Economics," in *Handbook of Mathematical Economics,* Vol. I (K. Arrow and M. Intriligator, eds.), Amsterdam: North-Holland.

Green, J. and J. Laffont (1979): *Individual Incentive in Public Decision-Making,* Amsterdam: North-Holland.

Greenberg, J. (1983): "Local Public Goods with Mobility: Existence and Optimality of a General Equilibrium," *JET,* 30; 17–33.

Grossman, S. (1981): "An Introduction to the Theory of Rational Expectations Under Asymmetric Information," *ReSTUD,* 48; 541–60.

Grossman, S. and O. Hart (1979): "A Theory of Competitive Equilibrium in Stock Market Economies," *Econometrica,* 47; 293–329.

Grossman, S. and J. Stiglitz (1980): "Stockholder Unanimity in Making Production and Financial Decisions," *QJE,* 94; 543–66.

Groves, T. (1973): "Incentives in Teams," *Econometrica,* 41; 617–31.

Groves, T. and J. Ledyard (1977): "Optimal Allocation of Public Goods: A Solution to the 'Free-Rider' Problem," *Econometrica,* 45; 783–809.

Hall, R. and A. Rabushka (1985): *The Flat Tax,* Stanford: Hoover Institute Press.

Hamilton, B. (1975): "Zoning and Property Taxation in a System of Local Governments," *Urban Studies,* 12; 205–11.

(1983a): "The Flypaper Effect and Other Anomolies," *JPubE,* 22; 347–62.

(1983b): "A Review: Is the Property Tax a Benefit Tax?" in *Local Provision of Public Services: The Tiebout Model after Twenty-Five Years* (G. Zodrow, ed.), New York: Academic, 85–108.

Harberger, A. (1971): "Three Postulates for Applied Welfare Analysis," *JEL,* 9; 785–97.

(1978): "On the Use of Distributional Weights in Social Cost Benefit Analysis," *JPE,* 86; S87–S120.

Harsanyi, J. (1955): "Cardinal Welfare, Individual Ethics, and Interpersonal Comparability of Utility," *JPE,* 61; 309–21.

Hart, O. (1975): "On the Optimality of Equilibrium when the Market Structure Is Incomplete," *JET,* 11; 418–43.

(1979): "On Stockholder Unanimity in Large Stock Market Economies," *Econometrica,* 47; 1058–84.

Hartwick, J. (1980): "The Henry George Rule, Optimal Population, and Interregional Equity," *Canadian Journal of Economics,* 13; 695–700.

Hausman, J. (1981): "Exact Consumer's Surplus and Deadweight Loss," *AER,* 71; 662–76.

Head, J. (1962): "Public Goods and Public Policy," *Public Finance,* 17; 197–219.

Helpman, E. and E. Sadka (1982): "Consumption versus Wage Taxation," *QJE,* 97; 363–72.

Henderson, V. (1985): "The Tiebout Model: Bring Back the Entrepreneurs," *JPE*, 93; 248–64.

Hicks, J. (1939a): "Foundations of Welfare Economics," *Economic Journal*, 49; 696–712.

(1939b): *Value and Capital*, London: Oxford University Press.

(1941): "The Rehabilitation of Consumer's Surplus," *ReSTUD*, 8; 108–16.

Hochman, O. (1981): "Land Rents, Optimal Taxation and Local Fiscal Independence in an Economy with Local Public Goods," *JPubE*, 15; 59–85.

(1982): "Congestable Local Public Goods in an Urban Setting," *JUE*, 11; 290–310.

Hotelling, H. (1932): "Edgeworth's Taxation Paradox and the Nature of Demand and Supply Functions," *JPE*, 40; 577–616.

Howard, R. (1960): *Dynamic Programming and Markov Processes*, Cambridge, MA: MIT Press.

Hurwicz, L. (1972): "On Informationally Decentralized Systems," in *Decision and Organization* (R. Radner and B. McGuire, eds.), Amsterdam: North-Holland.

Hurwicz, L. and H. Uzawa (1971): "On the Integrability of Demand Functions," in *Preferences, Utility and Demand* (J. Chipman, L. Hurwicz, M. Richter, and H. Sonnenschein, eds.), New York: Harcourt Brace Jovanovich, 114–48.

Intriligator, M. (1971): *Mathematical Optimization and Economic Theory*, Englewood Cliffs, NJ: Prentice-Hall.

Jorgenson, D. and L. Lau (1974): "The Duality of Technology and Economic Behavior," *ReSTUD*, 41; 181–200.

Kahneman, D. and A. Tversky (1979): "Prospect Theory; An Analysis of Decision under Risk," *Econometrica*, 47; 263–92.

Kaldor, N. (1939): "Welfare Propositions of Economics and Interpersonal Comparisons of Utility," *Economic Journal*, 49; 549–52.

Kanemoto, Y. (1980): *Theories of Urban Externalities*, New York: North-Holland.

Kanemoto, Y. and R. Nakamura (1984): "A New Approach to the Estimation of Structural Equations in Hedonic Models," Discussion Paper No. 223, Institute of Socio-economic Planning, University of Tsukuba, Sakura, Japan.

Karlin, S. (1959): *Mathematical Methods and Theory in Games, Programming and Economics*, Reading, MA: Addison-Wesley.

King, M. (1977): *Public Policy and the Corporation*, London: Chapman and Hall.

(1985): "The Economics of Saving: A Survey of Recent Contributions," in *Frontiers of Economics* (K. Arrow and S. Honkapohja, eds.), Oxford: Basil Blackwell, 227–94.

Koopmans, T. (1957): *Three Essays on the State of Economic Science*, New York: McGraw-Hill.

Kornai, J. (1967): "Mathematical Programming of Long-Term Plans in Hungary," in *Activity Analysis in the Theory of Growth and Planning* (E. Malinvaud and M. Bacharach, eds.), New York: St. Martin's, 211–31.

(1971): *Anti-Equilibrium*, Amsterdam: North-Holland.

Kotlikoff, L. (1984): "Taxation and Savings: A Neoclassical Perspective," *Journal of Economic Literature,* 22; 1576–1629.

Kramer, G. (1973): "On a Class of Equilibrium Conditions for Majority Rule," *Econometrica,* 41; 285–97.

Kreps, D. (1977): "A Note on Fulfilled Expectations Equilibrium," *JET,* 14; 32–43.

Lange, O. (1936): "On the Economic Theory of Socialism," *ReSTUD,* 4; 53–71, 123–42.

Lau, L. (1969): "Duality and the Structure of Utility Functions," *JET,* 1; 374–96.

Leland, H. (1979): "Quacks, Lemons and Licensing: A Theory of Minimum Quality Standards," *JPE,* 87; 1328–46.

Leontief, W. (1951): *The Structure of the American Economy, 1919–1939,* New York: Oxford University Press.

Lerner, A. (1944): *The Economics of Control,* New York: Macmillan.

Lesourne, J. (1975): *Cost–Benefit Analysis and Economic Theory,* Amsterdam: North-Holland.

Lind, R. (1973): "Spatial Equilibrium, the Theory of Rents and the Measurement of Benefits from Public Programs," *QJE,* 87; 188–207.

   (1986): "The Shadow Price of Capital: Implications for the Opportunity Cost of Public Programs, the Burden of the Debt, and Tax Reform," in *Essays in Honor of Kenneth J. Arrow,* Vol. I (W. Heller, R. Starr, and D. Starrett, eds.), London: Cambridge University Press, 189–212.

Lindahl, E. (1967): "Just Taxation: A Positive Solution," in *Classics in the Theory of Public Finance* (R. Musgrave and A. Peacock, eds.), New York: St. Martin's, 168–76.

Lintner, J. (1965): "The Valuation of Risky Assets and the Selection of Risky Investments in Stock Portfolios and Capital Budgets," *ReSTAT,* 47; 13–37.

Lipsey, R. and K. Lancaster (1957): "The General Theory of Second Best," *ReSTUD,* 24; 11–32.

Little, I. and J. Mirrlees (1974): *Project Appraisal and Planning for Developing Countries,* London: Heinemann.

McFadden, D. (1978): "Cost, Revenue and Profit Functions," in *Production Economies, A Dual Approach to Theory and Applications,* Amsterdam: North-Holland.

McGuire, M. (1974): "Group Segregation and Optimal Jurisdictions," *JPE,* 82; 112–32.

Machina, M. (1983): "The Economic Theory of Individual Behavior toward Risk: Theory, Evidence and New Directions," IMSSS Technical Report No. 433, Stanford, CA.

McLure, C. (1967): "The Interstate Exporting of State and Local Taxes: Estimates for 1962," *National Tax Journal,* 20; 49–77.

   (1971): "Revenue Sharing – Alternatives to Rational Fiscal Federalism," *Public Policy,* 82; 112–32.

Makowski, L. (1983): "Competitive Stock Markets," *ReSTUD,* 50; 305–30.

Maler, K. (1971): "A Method of Estimating Social Benefits from Pollution Control," in *The Economics of the Environment* (P. Bohm and A. Kneese, eds.), New York: MacMillan.

302   **References**

Malinvaud, E. (1967): "Decentralized Procedures for Planning," in *Activity Analysis in the Theory of Growth and Planning* (E. Malinvaud and M. Bacharach, eds.), New York: St. Martin's, 170–207.

(1972): *Lectures on Microeconomic Theory,* Amsterdam: North-Holland.

(1973): "Markets for an Exchange Economy with Individual Risk," *Econometrica,* 41; 383–410.

(1977): *The Theory of Unemployment Reconsidered,* Oxford: Basil Blackwell.

March, J. and H. Simon (1963): *Organizations,* New York: Wiley.

Maskin, E. (1979): "Implementation and Strong Nash Equilibrium," in *Aggregation and Revelation of Preferences* (J. Laffont, ed.), Amsterdam: North-Holland.

(1983): "The Theory of Implementation in Nash Equilibrium," MIT Working Paper No. 333, Cambridge, MA.

Meade, J. (1955): *Trade and Welfare,* Oxford: Oxford University Press.

Meiszkowski, P. and E. Toder (1983): "Taxation of Energy Resource," in *Fiscal Federalism and the Taxation of Natural Resources* (C. McLure and P. Meiszkowski, eds.), Lexington: Heath, 65–92.

Mirrlees, J. (1972a): "On Producer Taxation," *ReSTUD,* 39; 105–11.

(1972b): "The Optimum Town," *Swedish Journal of Economics,* 74; 114–35.

(1987): "The Theory of Optimal Taxation," in *Handbook of Mathematical Economics,* Vol. III (K. Arrow and M. Intriligator, eds.), Amsterdam: North-Holland.

Mitra, T. (1979): "Identifying Inefficiency in Smooth Aggregative Models of Economic Growth: A Unifying Criterion," *Journal of Mathematical Economics,* 6; 85–111.

Mohring, H. (1970): "The Peak Load Problem with Increasing Returns and Pricing Constraints," *American Economic Review,* 60; 693–705.

Mossin, J. (1973): *Theory of Financial Markets,* Englewood Cliffs, NJ: Prentice-Hall.

Mueller, D. (1976): "Public Choice: A Survey," *JEL,* 14; 395–433.

Mullet, G. (1974): "A Comment on Air Pollution and Property Values: A Study of the St. Louis Area," *Journal of Regional Science,* 14; 137–8.

Musgrave, R. (1959): *The Theory of Public Finance,* New York: McGraw-Hill.

Nash, J. (1950): "Equilibrium Points in *n*-Person Games," *Proceedings of the National Academy of Sciences,* 36; 48–50.

Negishi, T. (1972): *General Equilibrium Theory and International Trade,* Amsterdam: North-Holland.

Nelson, J., ed. (1964): *Marginal Cost Pricing in Practice,* Englewood Cliffs, NJ: Prentice-Hall.

Nozick, R. (1974): *Anarchy, State and Utopia,* New York: Basic Books.

Oates, W. (1969): "The Effects of Property Taxes and Local Spending on Property Values: An Empirical Study of Tax Capitalization and the Tiebout Hypothesis," *JPE,* 77; 957–71.

(1972): *Fiscal Federalism,* New York: Harcourt Brace Jovanovich.

Otani, Y. and J. Sicilian (1977): "Externalities and Problems of Nonconvexity and Overhead Costs in Welfare Economics," *JET,* 14; 239–51.

Panzar, J. and R. Willig (1976): "A Neoclassical Approach to Peak-Load Pricing," *Bell Journal,* Autumn.

Pauly, M. (1970): "Optimality, 'Public' Goods and Local Governments: A General Theoretical Analysis," *JPE,* 78; 572–84.

(1976): "A Model of Local Government Expenditure and Tax Capitalization," *JPubE,* 6; 231–42.

Pencavel, J. (1987): "Labor Supply – A Survey," in *Handbook of Labor Economics,* Amsterdam: North-Holland.

Pigou, A. (1947): *A Study in Public Finance,* London: Macmillan.

Polinsky, A. and D. Rubenfeld (1978): "The Long-Run Effects of a Residential Property Tax and Local Public Services," *JUE,* 5; 241–62.

Polinsky, A. and S. Shavell (1975): "The Air Pollution and Property Value Debate," *ReSTAT,* 57; 100–4.

(1976): "Amenities and Property Values in a Model of an Urban Area," *JPubE,* 5; 119–29.

Pratt, J. (1964): "Risk Aversion in the Small and in the Large," *Econometrica,* 32; 122–36.

Radner, R. (1979): "Rational Expectations Equilibrium: Generic Existence and the Information Revealed by Prices," *Econometrica,* 47; 655–78.

(1982): "Equilibrium under Uncertainty," in *Handbook of Mathematical Economics,* Vol. II (K. Arrow and M. Intriligator, eds.), Amsterdam: North-Holland.

Raiffa, H. and R. Schlaifer (1961): *Applied Statistical Decision Theory,* Boston: Harvard Business School.

Ramsey, F. (1927): "A Contributon to the Theory of Taxation," *Economic Journal,* 37; 47–61.

Rawls, J. (1971): *A Theory of Justice,* Cambridge, MA: Harvard University Press.

Richter, D. (1978): "Existence and Computation of a Tiebout General Equilibrium," *Econometrica,* 46; 779–805.

Ridker, R. and J. Henning (1967): "The Determinants of Residential Property Values with Special Reference to Air Pollution," *ReSTAT,* 49; 246–57.

Roberts, D. and H. Sonnenschein (1977): "On the Foundations of the Theory of Monopolistic Competition," *Econometrica,* 45; 101–13.

Roberts, K. (1979): "The Characterization of Implementable Choice Rules," in *Aggregation and Revelation of Preferences* (J. Laffont, ed.), Amsterdam: North-Holland.

Romer, T. and H. Rosenthal (1983): "Voting and Spending: Some Empirical Relationships in the Political Economy of Local Public Finance," in *Local Provision of Public Services: The Tiebout Model after Twenty-Five Years* (G. Zodrow, ed.), New York, Academic, 165–83.

Rosen, S. (1974): "Hedonic Prices and Implicit Markets: Product Differentiation in Pure Competition," *JPE,* 82; 34–55.

Ross, S. (1976): "The Arbitrage Theory of Capital Asset Pricing," *JET,* 13; 341–60.

Sadka, E. (1977): "A Theorem on Uniform Taxation," *JPubE,* 7; 387–91.

Samuelson, P. (1947): *Foundations of Economic Analysis,* Cambridge, MA: Harvard University Press.

304   **References**

(1954): "The Pure Theory of Public Expenditure," *ReSTAT,* 36; 387–9.

Sandler, T. and J. Tschirhart (1980): "The Economic Theory of Clubs: An Evaluative Survey," *JEL,* 18; 1481–1521.

Sandmo, A. (1974): "A Note on the Structure of Indirect Taxation," *AER,* 64; 701–6.

Savage, L. (1954): *The Foundations of Statistics,* New York: Wiley.

Scitovsky, T. (1941): "A Note on Welfare Propositions in Economics," *ReSTUD,* 9; 77–88.

Scotchmer, S. (1985a): "Hedonic Prices and Cost/Benefit Analysis," *JET,* 37; 55–75.

(1985b): "Profit Maximizing Clubs," *JPubE,* 27; 25–45.

Scotchmer, S. and M. Wooders (1986): "Optimal and Equilibrium Organizations," Working Paper, HIER, Harvard University.

Sen, A. (1970): *Collective Choice and Social Welfare,* San Francisco: Holden-Day.

Sharpe, W. (1964): "Capital Asset Prices: A Theory of Market Equilibrium under Conditions of Risk," *Journal of Finance,* 19; 425–42.

Shoven, J. (1974): "A Proof of the Existence of a General Equilibrium with ad Valorem Commodity Taxes," *JET,* 8; 1–25.

Sonstelie, J. and P. Portney (1978): "Profit Maximizing Communities and the Theory of Local Public Expenditure," *JUE,* 5; 263–77.

Starett, D. (1970): "The Efficiency of Competitive Programs," *Econometrica,* 38; 704–11.

(1972): "Fundamental Non-Convexities in the Theory of Externalities," *JET,* 4; 180–99.

(1974): "Principles of Optimal Location in a Large Homogeneous Area," *JET,* 9; 418–48.

(1977): "Measuring Returns to Scale in the Aggregate, and the Scale Effect of Public Goods," *Econometrica,* 45; 1439–55.

(1978): "Marginal Cost Pricing of Recursive Lumpy Investments," *ReSTUD,* 45; 215–27.

(1979a): "Decentralization with Nonconvexity, Rules for a General Capital Investment Problem," *The Journal of Economics,* 5; 12–20.

(1979b): "Second Best Welfare Economics in the Mixed Economy," *JPubE,* 12; 329–49.

(1980a): "Measuring Externalities and Second Best Distortions in the Theory of Local Public Goods," *Econometrica,* 48; 627–42.

(1980b): "On the Method of Taxation and the Provision of Local Public Goods," *AER,* 70; 380–92.

(1981): "Land Value Capitalization in Local Public Finance," *JPE,* 89; 306–27.

(1983): "Welfare Measures Based on Capitalization, A Unified General Treatment," in *Research in Urban Economics,* Vol. 3 (V. Henderson, ed.), London: JAI, 117–36.

(1986): "On the Social Risk Premium," in *Essays in Honor of Kenneth J. Arrow,* Vol. I (W. Heller, R. Starr, and D. Starrett, eds.), London: Cambridge University Press, 159–76.

(1988): "Taxation and Savings," in *Uneasy Compromise: Problems with a Hybrid Tax System,* Washington, DC: Brookings Institution.

Stiglitz, J. (1983): "The Theory of Local Public Goods Twenty-Five Years after Tiebout: A Perspective," in *Local Provision of Public Services: The Tiebout Model after Twenty-Five Years* (G. Zodrow, ed.), New York: Academic, 17–54.

Stiglitz, J. and P. Dasgupta (1971): "Differential Taxation, Public Goods, and Economic Efficiency," *ReSTUD,* 38; 151–74.

Summers, L. (1981): "Capital Taxation and Capital Accumulation in a Life Cycle Model," *AER,* 71; 533–44.

Taylor, A. (1955): *Advanced Calculus,* Waltham, MA: Blaisdell.

Tideman, N. and G. Tullock (1976): "A New and Superior Process for Making Social Choices," *JPE,* 84; 1145–60.

Tiebout, C. (1956): "A Pure Theory of Local Expenditures," *JPE,* 64; 416–24.

Tirole, J. (1985): "Asset Bubbles and Overlapping Generations," *Econometrica,* 53; 1071–1100.

Tresch, R. (1981): *Public Finance: A Normative Theory,* Plano, TX: Business Publications.

Varian, H. (1978): *Microeconomic Analysis,* New York: Norton.

Vickrey, W. (1961): "Counterspeculation, Auctions, and Competitive Sealed Tenders," *Journal of Finance,* 16; 8–37.

Wagner, H. (1969): *Principles of Operations Research,* Englewood Cliffs, NJ: Prentice-Hall.

Warr, P. (1977): "On the Shadow Pricing of Traded Commodities," *JPE,* 85; 865–72.

Weitzman, M. (1974): "Free Access vs. Private Ownership as Alternative Systems for Managing Common Property," *JET,* 8; 225–34.

Westhoff, F. (1977): "Existence of Equilibria in Economies with a Local Public Good," *JET,* 14; 84–112.

Wheaton, W. (1975): "Consumer Mobility and Community Tax Bases: The Financing of Local Public Goods," *JPubE,* 4; 377–84.

White, M. (1975): "Firm Location in a Zoned Metropolitan Area," in *Fiscal Zoning and Land Use Controls* (E. Mills and W. Oates, eds.), Lexington, MA: Lexington Books.

Widder, D. (1961): *Advanced Calculus,* Englewood Cliffs, NJ: Prentice-Hall.

Wildasin, D. (1985): "Urban Public Finance," University of Indiana, Bloomington.

(1986): "Theoretical Analysis of Local Public Economics," University of Indiana, Bloomington.

Wildavsky, A. (1979): *The Politics of the Budgetary Process,* New York: Little, Brown.

Wilde, J. (1971): "Grants in Aid: An Analysis of Design and Response," *National Tax Journal,* 24; 143–56.

Willig, R. (1976): "Consumer's Surplus without Apology," *AER,* 66; 589–97.

Wilson, J. (1986): "Trade in a Tiebout Economy," University of Indiana, Bloomington.

Wilson, R. (1982): "Risk Measurement of Public Projets," in *Discounting for Time and Risk in Energy Policy,* Washington, DC: Resources for the Future.

Wooders, M. (1978): "Equilibria, the Core, and Jurisdiction Structures in Economies with a Local Public Good," *JET,* 18; 328–48.

(1980): "The Tiebout Hypothesis: Near Optimality in Local Public Goods Economies," *Econometrica,* 48; 1467–86.

Zodrow, G. and P. Meiszkowski (1982): "The Incidence of the Property Tax: The Benefit View versus the New View," in *Local Provision of Public Services: The Tiebout Model after Twenty-five Years* (G. Zodrow, ed.), New York, Academic, 109–30.

Author index

Subject index